Adobe

Illustrator CC
2014 release

Adobe

CLASSROOM IN A BOOK®
The official training workbook from Adobe

Brian Wood

WHERE ARE THE LESSON FILES?

Purchasing this Classroom in a Book gives you access to the lesson files you'll need to complete the exercises in the book.

You'll find the files you need on your **Account** page at peachpit.com on the **Lesson & Update Files** tab.

For complete instructions, see "Accessing the Classroom in a Book files" in the Getting Started section of this book.

The example below shows how the files appear on your **Account** page (the exact list for your book may look a little different). The files are packaged as ZIP archives, which you will need to expand after downloading. You can download the lessons individually or as a single large ZIP file if your network connection is fast enough.

CONTENTS

7 ADDING TYPE TO A POSTER   210

GETTING STARTED

Adobe® Illustrator® CC is the industry-standard illustration application for print, multimedia, and online graphics. Whether you are a designer or a technical illustrator producing artwork for print publishing, an artist producing multimedia graphics, or a creator of web pages or online content, Adobe Illustrator offers you the tools you need to get professional-quality results.

About Classroom in a Book

Adobe Illustrator CC Classroom in a Book® (2014 release) is part of the official training series for Adobe graphics and publishing software developed with the support of Adobe product experts.

The lessons are designed so that you can learn at your own pace. If you're new to Adobe Illustrator, you'll learn the fundamentals you need to master to put the application to work. If you are an experienced user, you'll find that *Classroom in a Book* teaches many advanced features, including tips and techniques for using the latest version of Adobe Illustrator.

Although each lesson provides step-by-step instructions for creating a specific project, there's room for exploration and experimentation. You can follow the book from start to finish, or do only the lessons that correspond to your interests and needs. Each lesson concludes with a review section summarizing what you've covered.

Prerequisites

Before beginning to use *Adobe Illustrator CC Classroom in a Book (2014 release)*, you should have working knowledge of your computer and its operating system. Make sure that you know how to use the mouse and standard menus and commands, and also how to open, save, and close files. If you need to review these techniques, see the printed or online documentation for your Windows or Mac OS.

● **Note:** When instructions differ by platform, Mac OS commands appear first, and then the Windows commands, with the platform noted in parentheses. For example, "press the Option (Mac OS) or Alt (Windows) key and click away from the artwork."

Installing the program

Before you begin using *Adobe Illustrator CC Classroom in a Book (2014 release)*, make sure that your system is set up correctly and that you've installed the required software and hardware.

You must purchase the Adobe Illustrator CC software separately. For complete instructions on installing the software, visit helpx.adobe.com/illustrator.html. You must install Illustrator from Adobe Creative Cloud onto your hard disk. Follow the onscreen instructions.

Fonts used in this book

The Classroom in a Book lesson files use fonts that are a part of the Typekit Portfolio plan included with your Creative Cloud subscription, and trial Creative Cloud members have access to a selection of fonts from Typekit for web and desktop use.

For more information about fonts and installation, see the Adobe Illustrator CC Read Me file on the web at helpx.adobe.com/illustrator.html.

Accessing the Classroom in a Book files

In order to work through the projects in this book, you will need to download the lesson files from peachpit.com. You can download the files for individual lessons, or download them all in a single file. Although each lesson stands alone, some lessons use files from other lessons, so you'll need to keep the entire collection of lesson assets on your computer as you work through the book.

To access the Classroom in a Book files:

1   On a Mac or PC, go to www.peachpit.com/redeem and enter the code found at the back of your book.

2   If you do not have a Peachpit.com account, you will be prompted to create one.

3   The downloadable files will be listed under Lesson & Update Files tab on your Account page.

4   Click the lesson file links to download them to your computer. The files are compressed into Zip archives to speed up download time and to protect the contents from damage during transfer. You must uncompress (or "unzip") the files to restore them to their original size and format before you use them with the book. Modern Mac and Windows systems are set up to open Zip archives by simply double-clicking.

5   On your hard drive, create a new folder in a convenient location and give it the name "Lessons," following the standard procedure for your operating system:

   • If you're running Windows, right-click and choose New > Folder. Then enter the new name for your folder.

   • If you're using Mac OS, in the Finder, choose File > New Folder. Type the new name and drag the folder to the location you want to use.

6   Drag the unzipped Lessons folder (which contains folders named Lesson01, Lesson02, and so on) that you downloaded onto your hard drive to your new folder named "Lessons." When you begin each lesson, navigate to the folder with that lesson number to access all the assets you need to complete the lesson.

Restoring default preferences

The preferences file controls how command settings appear on your screen when you open the Adobe Illustrator program. Each time you quit Adobe Illustrator, the position of the panels and certain command settings are recorded in different preference files. If you want to restore the tools and settings to their original default settings, you can delete the current Adobe Illustrator CC preferences file. Adobe Illustrator creates a new preferences file, if one doesn't already exist, the next time you start the program and save a file.

You must restore the default preferences for Illustrator before you begin each lesson. This ensures that the tools and panels function as described in this book. When you have finished the book, you can restore your saved settings, if you like.

To delete or save the current Illustrator preferences file

1   Exit Adobe Illustrator CC.

2   Locate the **Adobe Illustrator Prefs** file as follows:

   • (Mac OS 10.7 and later**) The Adobe Illustrator Prefs file is located in the folder [startup drive]/Users/[username]/Library/Preferences/Adobe Illustrator 18 Settings/en_US*.

   • (Windows 7 [Service Pack 1], or Windows 8) The Adobe Illustrator Prefs file is located in the folder [startup drive]\Users\[username]\AppData\Roaming\Adobe\Adobe Illustrator 18 Settings\en_US*\x86 or x64.

*Folder name may be different depending on the language version you have installed.
On Mac OS 10.7 (Lion) and later, the Library folder is hidden by default. To access this folder, in Finder, choose Go > Go To Folder. Type **~/Library in the Go To The Folder dialog box and then click Go.

● **Note:** If you cannot locate the preferences file, try using your operating system's Find command, and search for "Adobe Illustrator Prefs."

● **Note:** In Windows 7 or later, the AppData folder is hidden by default. To make it visible, open Folder Options in Control Panel and click the View tab. In the Advanced Settings pane, find Hidden Files and folders and select Show Hidden Files and Folders or Show hidden files, folders, or drives.

If you can't find the file, you either haven't started Adobe Illustrator CC yet or you have moved the preferences file. The preferences file is created after you quit the program the first time and is updated thereafter.

▶ **Tip:** To quickly locate and delete the Adobe Illustrator preferences file each time you begin a new lesson, create a shortcut (Windows) or an alias (Mac OS) to the Adobe Illustrator 18 Settings folder.

3   Copy the file and save it to another folder on your hard disk (if you wish to restore those preferences) or Delete it.

4   Start Adobe Illustrator CC. You most likely will see a dialog box that asks if you would like to use the settings from the cloud. Click Disable Sync Settings.

To restore saved preferences after completing the lessons

1   Exit Adobe Illustrator CC.

2   Delete the current preferences file. Find the original preferences file that you saved and move it to the Adobe Illustrator 18 Settings folder.

● **Note:** You can move the original preferences file rather than renaming it.

Additional resources

Adobe Illustrator CC Classroom in a Book (2014 release) is not meant to replace documentation that comes with the program or to be a comprehensive reference for every feature. Only the commands and options used in the lessons are explained in this book. For comprehensive information about program features and tutorials, please refer to these resources:

Adobe Illustrator Help and Support: helpx.adobe.com/illustrator.html is where you can find and browse Help and Support content on adobe.com. Adobe Illustrator Help and Adobe Illustrator Support Center are accessible from the Help menu in Illustrator CC 2014 (2014 release) or by pressing F1.

Adobe Creative Cloud Learning: for inspiration, key techniques, cross-product workflows, and updates on new features go to the Creative Cloud Learn page helpx.adobe.com/creative-cloud/learn/tutorials.html. Available to all.

Adobe Forums: forums.adobe.com lets you tap into peer-to-peer discussions, questions and answers on Adobe products.

Adobe TV: tv.adobe.com is an online video resource for expert instruction and inspiration about Adobe products, including a How To channel to get you started with your product.

Adobe Inspire: www.adobe.com/inspire.html offers thoughtful articles on design and design issues, a gallery showcasing the work of top-notch designers, tutorials, and more.

Resources for educators: www.adobe.com/education and edex.adobe.com offer a treasure trove of information for instructors who teach classes on Adobe software. Find solutions for education at all levels, including free curricula that use an integrated approach to teaching Adobe software and can be used to prepare for the Adobe Certified Associate exams.

Also check out these useful links:

Adobe Illustrator CC product home page: www.adobe.com/products/illustrator

Adobe Add-ons: creative.adobe.com/addons is a central resource for finding tools, services, extensions, code samples, and more to supplement and extend your Adobe products.

Adobe Authorized Training Centers

Adobe Authorized Training Centers offer instructor-led courses and training on Adobe products. A directory of AATCs is available at partners.adobe.com.

Sync settings using Adobe Creative Cloud

When you work on multiple machines, managing and syncing preferences, presets, and libraries among the machines can be time-consuming, complex, and prone to error. The Sync Settings feature enables individual users to sync their preferences, presets, and libraries to the Creative Cloud. This means that if you use two machines, say one at home and the other at work, the Sync Settings feature makes it easy for you to keep those settings synchronized across two machines. Also, if you have replaced your old machine with a new one and have re-installed Illustrator, this feature will let you bring back all those settings on the new machine.

For more information about syncing, visit helpx.adobe.com/illustrator/using/sync-settings.html

WHAT'S NEW IN ADOBE ILLUSTRATOR CC (2014 RELEASE)

Adobe® Illustrator® CC (2014 release) is packed with new and innovative features to help you produce artwork more efficiently for print, Web, and digital video publication. In this section, you'll learn about many of these new features—how they function and how you can use them in your work.

Creative Cloud Libraries

With Creative Cloud Libraries, you can organize creative assets, such as colors, type styles, brushes and graphics, and automatically sync them to Creative Cloud, allowing you to access them whenever and wherever you need them from a single, convenient panel within Illustrator. Libraries make it easy to maintain design consistency across projects, and not have to dig around in files and folders to find the assets you need.

Curvature tool

With the new Curvature tool (), you can draw and edit paths quickly and visually to create paths with smooth refined curves and straight lines. Click once to place points and see the drawing curve "flex" around the points dynamically. Double-click to create corner points for straight lines.

Edit paths while drawing or after the path is complete using the same tool; no need to hassle with anchor points and handles. Just by clicking or double-clicking on the curvature points creates smooth points or corner points at any time. But if you need the fine control you're used to with traditional anchor points and handles, just edit your drawing with any of the Illustrator path editing tools.

Touch workspace

The Touch workspace lets you create on the go what you could once only accomplish sitting at your desk: it's Illustrator you can take with you. Designed for Windows 8 tablets, the Touch workspace surfaces the essential tools and controls for drawing and editing with a pressure-sensitive pen and multi-touch gestures. You can create logos, icons, explore custom lettering and typography, create UI wireframes, and more.

The Touch workspace brings traditional drawing templates and French curves to the Illustrator workspace. These templates and curves project a scalable, movable outline that can be traced against to quickly create refined curves. At any time, you can immediately switch between the Touch and traditional workspaces to access the full range of Illustrator tools and controls.

Area type Autosizing

With area type Autosizing, you can automatically resize the height of area type frames when you add, delete, or edit text. As the text is edited and re-edited, the frame shrinks and grows to accommodate the changing amount of copy, and eliminates overset text without manually sizing and resizing frames. You can easily toggle Autosizing on or off, so it's there when it's needed and off when it's not, e.g., when main text flows, or threads, across layout elements like columns or artboards.

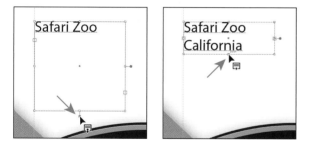

Live Shapes

All rectangles and rounded rectangles have modifiable corners. While each corner can have an independent radius value, all attributes are retained even when you scale or rotate the rectangle. Rectangles and rounded rectangles now remember all modifications made, be it width, height, rotation, corner treatment. This capability means you can always return to the original shape of the object.

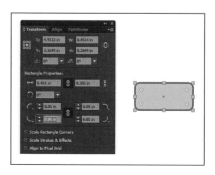

Typekit integration

When you open an Illustrator artwork file, and find fonts missing, the online Typekit desktop font library is automatically searched for the missing font (you must have an Internet connection for this function). If the missing font is available online, you have the option of syncing it to your current computer. If you choose not to fix the missing fonts when the file is opened in Illustrator, text elements using unavailable fonts are highlighted in pink and rendered using a default font.

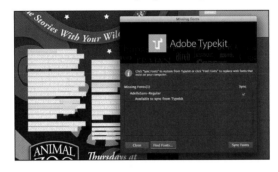

Pen tool preview and drawing-related enhancements

The Pen tool displays a preview of what will be drawn on your artboard before you click and drop the next point. This helps you visualize the next curve before you commit to the next point and saves you the time spent in drawing, reviewing, and then redrawing paths that need to be redone.

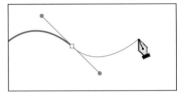

Pencil tool enhancements

The Pencil tool has been updated with an additional Fidelity setting for finer control over the paths you draw. This additional level has been extended to the Paintbrush and Blob Brush tools as well.

Path segment reshaping

Drag path segments into the shape you desire. New path reshaping technology, available in the Anchor Point and Direct Selection tools and accessible from the Pen tool, provides a more direct and intuitive way to edit path segments.

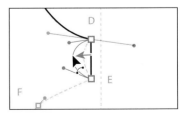

Join tool

Use the Join tool (✗) to intelligently join paths that cross, overlap, or have open ends without affecting the original paths. Using the same tool, you can simultaneously join paths and trim unwanted segments using intuitive scrubbing gestures.

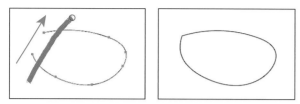

Other enhancements

- **Windows GPU acceleration**—New GPU acceleration for Windows lets you work faster on Windows 7 or 8 computers. This feature requires an Adobe-certified NVIDIA graphics card with at least 1GB of VRAM.

- **SVG enhancements**—In the SVG Save Options dialog, the "Use <textPath>..." check box is selected by default. This reduces generated markup, resulting in smaller SVG output files. Markup for generated preview HTML has also been cleaned up.

- **Anchor point enhancements**—Fine adjustment of curves is now easier. New anchor point controls allow unequal or different-direction handles to be dragged as you draw to control the smoothness of each segment. You can even change a corner point to smooth without ruining your shape.

- **Custom Tools panels**—Create specialized Tools panels by dragging and dropping just the tools you need—like drawing, editing, or selection tools—into a custom panel. The full Tools panel can then be hidden, allowing for a clean, efficient workspace.

- **Settings import and export**—Share your Illustrator settings across multiple computers. Simply export them to a folder where they can then be imported by other users. While Sync Settings lets you standardize settings on your own computers, now you can also share them across your organization.

Although this list touches on just a few of the new and enhanced features of Illustrator CC (2014 release), it exemplifies Adobe's commitment to providing the best tools possible for your publishing needs. We hope you enjoy working with Illustrator CC (2014 release) as much as we do.

—The Adobe Illustrator CC (2014 release) Classroom in a Book Team

A QUICK TOUR OF ADOBE® ILLUSTRATOR® CC (2014 RELEASE)

Lesson overview

In this interactive demonstration of Adobe Illustrator CC (2014 release), you'll get an overview of the main features of the application.

 This lesson takes approximately 60 minutes to complete.

Download the project files for this lesson from the Lesson & Update Files tab on your Account page at www.peachpit.com and store them on your computer in a convenient location, as described in the Getting Started section of this book.

Your Account page is also where you'll find any updates to the chapters or to the lesson files. Look on the Lesson & Update Files tab to access the most current content.

In this demonstration of Adobe Illustrator CC, you will be introduced to some key fundamentals for working in the application.

Getting started

For the first lesson of this book, you will get a quick tour of the tools and features in Adobe Illustrator CC, offering a sense of the many possibilities. Along the way, you will create artwork for an amusement park.

1 To ensure that the tools and panels function exactly as described in this lesson, delete or deactivate (by renaming) the Adobe Illustrator CC preferences file. See "Restoring default preferences" in the Getting Started section at the beginning of the book.

● **Note:** If you have not already downloaded the project files for this lesson to your computer from your Account page, make sure to do so now. See "Getting Started" at the beginning of the book.

2 Start Adobe Illustrator CC.

Creating a new document

● **Note:** Learn more about creating and editing artboards in Lesson 4, "Transforming Artwork."

An Illustrator document can contain up to 100 artboards (*artboards* are similar to *pages* in a program like Adobe InDesign®). Next, you will create a document with only one artboard.

1 Choose Window > Workspace > Reset Essentials.

● **Note:** If you don't see "Reset Essentials" in the Workspace menu, choose Window > Workspace > Essentials before choosing Window > Workspace > Reset Essentials.

2 Choose File > New.

3 In the New Document dialog box, change only the following options (leaving the rest at their default settings):

- Name: **AmusementWorld**
- Units: **Inches**
- Width: **16 in**
- Height: **14 in**

4 Click OK. A new blank document appears.

Sync settings using Adobe Creative Cloud™

● **Note:** For more information on syncing with the Creative Cloud, see "Sync settings using Adobe Creative Cloud" in the Getting Started section of this book.

When you launch Adobe Illustrator CC for the first time, with no previous sync information available, you will see a prompt asking whether you want to start a sync with Adobe Creative Cloud.

- Click Disable Sync Settings (if the dialog box appears).

1   Choose File > Save As. In the Save As dialog box, leave the name as
    AmusementWorld.ai and navigate to the Lessons > Lesson00 folder. Leave the
    Format option set to Adobe Illustrator (ai) (Mac OS) or Save As Type option
    set to Adobe Illustrator (*.AI) (Windows), and click Save. In the Illustrator
    Options dialog box, leave the Illustrator options at their default settings, and then
    click OK.

2   Choose View > Rulers > Show Rulers to show rulers in the Document window.

3   Choose View > Fit Artboard In Window, and then choose View > Zoom Out.
    The white area is the artboard, and where your printable artwork will go.

Drawing shapes

Drawing shapes is the cornerstone of Illustrator, and you will create many of them in
the coming lessons. Next, you will create several shapes.

● **Note:** Learn more
about creating and
editing shapes in
Lesson 3, "Using Shapes
to Create Artwork for
a Postcard."

1   Select the Rectangle tool (▨) in the Tools panel on the left.

2   Position the pointer in the upper-left
    corner of the artboard (see the red X in
    the figure). When the word "intersect"
    appears next to the pointer, click and
    drag down and to the right edge of
    the white artboard. When the gray
    measurement label shows a width of
    16 in and a height of 14 in, release the
    mouse button.

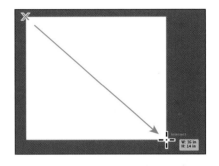

● **Note:** If the Transform panel opens, click the "x" in the corner of the Transform panel group to
close it.

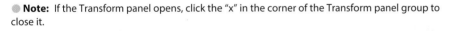

3   Click and hold down on the Rectangle tool in the
    Tools panel. Click to select the Ellipse tool (⬭).

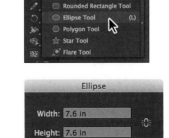

4   Click roughly in the center of the artboard to
    open the Ellipse dialog box. Change the Width
    to **7.6 in** and the Height value to **7.6 in** by typing
    in the values. Click OK to create a circle that will
    become the world. Leave the circle selected.

▶ **Tip:** You can also
click the Constrain
Width And Height
Proportions button (▨)
to change both
values together.

Applying color

● **Note:** Learn more about creating and applying color in Lesson 6, "Using Color and Patterns to Enhance Signage."

Applying colors to artwork is a common Illustrator task. Experimenting and applying color is easy using the Color panel, Swatches panel, Color Guide panel, and Edit Colors/Recolor Artwork dialog box.

1　Select the Selection tool (▶) in the Tools panel on the left. With the circle still selected, click the Fill color in the Control panel (circled in the figure) to reveal the Swatches panel. Position the pointer over a blue swatch (in the second row of colors). When the tool tip appears that shows "C=85, M=50, Y=0, K=0," click to apply the blue swatch to the fill.

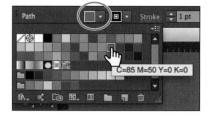

2　Press the Escape key to hide the Swatches panel.

3　Click the Stroke color in the Control panel (circled in the figure). Click the None color (▱) to remove the stroke (border) of the circle. Press the Escape key to hide the Swatches panel.

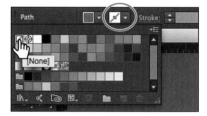

4　Choose Select > Deselect, and then choose File > Save.

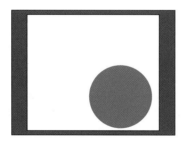

Working with layers

● **Note:** Learn more about working with layers and the Layers panel in Lesson 8, "Organizing Your Artwork with Layers."

Layers allow you to organize and more easily select artwork. Next, using the Layers panel, you will organize your artwork.

1　Choose Window > Layers to show the Layers panel in the workspace.

2　Double-click directly on the text "Layer 1" (the layer name) in the Layers panel. Type **Background**, and press Enter or Return to change the layer name.

Naming layers can be helpful when organizing content. Currently, all artwork is on this layer.

3 Click the Create New Layer button () at the bottom of the Layers panel. Double-click "Layer 2" (the new layer name), and type **Content**. Press Enter or Return.

4 With the Selection tool (▶) selected, click to select the blue circle. Choose Edit > Cut.

5 Choose View > Fit Artboard In Window.

6 Click once on the layer named Content to select it in the Layers panel. New artwork is added to the selected layer.

7 Choose Edit > Paste to paste the circle on the selected layer (Content), in the center of the artboard.

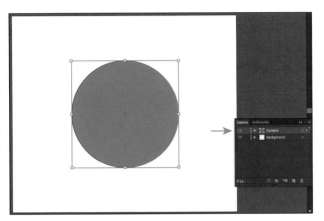

8 Choose Select > Deselect.

Drawing with the Pencil tool

The Pencil tool (✏) lets you draw free-form open and closed paths that contain curves and straight lines. As you draw with the Pencil tool, anchor points are created on the path where necessary and according to the Pencil tool options you set.

1 Double-click the Pencil tool (✏) in the Tools panel on the left to open the Pencil Tool Options dialog box. Drag the Fidelity slider all the way to the right (to Smooth). Click OK.

Changing the Fidelity will help to smooth out the path as you draw.

2 Press the letter D to set the default fill (White) and stroke (Black) for the artwork you are about to create.

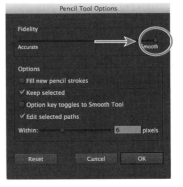

● **Note:** Learn more about working with the Pencil tool and other drawing tools in Lesson 5, "Creating an Illustration with the Drawing Tools."

3   Choose Window > Swatches to show
    the Swatches panel. Click the Fill box
    (circled in the figure) and select the
    None (□) swatch to remove the fill.
    Leave the Swatches panel open.

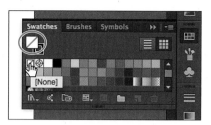

Next, you'll create a figure similar to the
one shown below. The path you draw won't
match exactly as shown, and that's okay.

4   On the artboard, starting where you
    see the red X in the figure, click and
    drag to create a path around the blue
    circle. Draw all the way around the
    blue circle and come back *close* to
    where you started drawing. Make sure
    that you don't see a circle (✎₀) next to
    the Pencil tool, indicating that the path
    will be closed. *If you see the circle next
    to the Pencil, release the mouse button,
    press Delete and try the path again.*
    Release the mouse button to stop
    drawing the path.

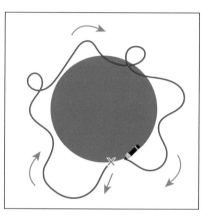

5   Leave the path selected.

Editing strokes

● **Note:** Learn more
about working with
strokes in Lesson 3,
"Using Shapes to Create
Artwork for a Postcard."

In addition to changing the color of strokes, you can also format them in many other
ways. That's what you'll do next with the path you just drew.

1   With the path still selected, click the word
    "Stroke" in the Control panel above the
    document to open the Stroke panel. Change
    the following options:

    • Stroke Weight: **60 pt**

    • Dashed Line: **Selected**

    • Dash: **28 pt**

    • Gap: **3 pt**

2   Press the Escape key to hide the Stroke panel.

3   In the Swatches panel, click the Stroke box, and then select the "CMYK Red"
    swatch in the first row of colors. Leave the shape selected.

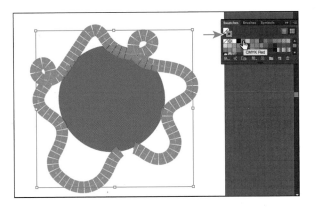

Working with the Width tool

The Width tool (🐛) allows you to create a variable width stroke and to save the width as a profile that can be applied to other objects. Next, you'll change the width of the red path.

● **Note:** Learn more about the Width tool in Lesson 3, "Using Shapes to Create Artwork for a Postcard."

1 Select the Width tool (🐛) in the Tools panel. Position the pointer over the left side of the red path (see the figure). When the pointer shows a plus sign (+) next to it, drag toward the center of the path. When the gray measurement label next to the pointer shows a Width of approximately 0.2 in, release the mouse button.

● **Note:** A width point is created on the path where you dragged. This allows you to edit that width at any time.

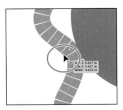 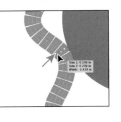 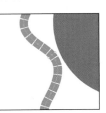

2 Position the pointer at the bottom of the path on the curve (see the figure below). When the pointer shows a plus sign (+) next to it, drag away from the red path. When the gray measurement label shows a Width of approximately 0.5 in, release the mouse button.

3 Move to the right side of the path and drag away from the path to make the stroke wider (see the second part of the following figure).

4 Move to the top loop and drag toward the path to make the width narrower (see the third part of the following figure).

▶ **Tip:** You can always choose Edit > Undo Width Point Change to remove the last point and try again.

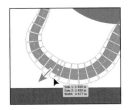 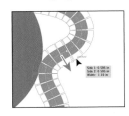 

5 Try editing other parts of the path and see how it is affected. Use the next figure as a reference for how we adjusted the rest of the path. If you edit a part of the path and don't like the edit, you can choose Edit > Undo Width Point Change and try it again.

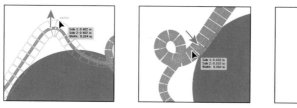

6 With the path still selected, choose Object > Arrange > Send To Back to send it behind the blue circle.

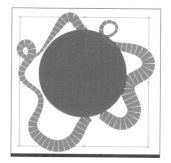

Creating shapes using the Shape Builder tool

● **Note:** Learn more about working with the Shape Builder tool in Lesson 3, "Using Shapes to Create Artwork for a Postcard."

The Shape Builder tool ( ) is an interactive tool for creating complex shapes by merging and erasing simpler shapes. Next, you will finish a castle tower using the Shape Builder tool.

1 Choose File > Open, and open the Pieces.ai file in the Lessons > Lesson00 folder on your hard disk.

The Pieces.ai file contains a series of individual shapes (rectangles) that make up a tower and a group of shapes that make a flag. You'll finish the tower by combining the shapes using the Shape Builder tool.

2 Choose Select > All On Active Artboard to select the tower shapes. The flag shapes are locked, which means they can't be selected without unlocking them.

3 Select the Shape Builder tool ( ) in the Tools panel on the left. Position the pointer to the left and above all of the selected shapes (see the red X in the figure). Press the Shift key and drag to the right and down. Make sure you don't drag across the green rectangle, otherwise it will be added to the other shapes (see the figure). Release the mouse button and then the Shift key to combine the shapes.

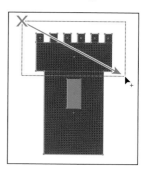

4   Position the pointer over the green rectangle. Holding down the Option (Mac OS) or Alt (Windows) key, when you see a mesh pattern appear in the fill of the object, click to subtract the highlighted green shape from the larger tower shape.

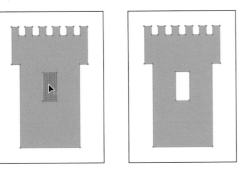

5   Select the Selection tool (⬆) in the Tools panel on the left, and in the Swatches panel, click the Fill box (if needed) and choose the purple/blue color with the yellow tool tip that shows as "C=100, M=100, Y=25, K=25."

Copying content

In Illustrator, there are a lot of ways to copy content. In this section, you will use several methods for copying content between documents and in a single document.

1   Choose Object > Unlock All to unlock the flag.

2   Choose Select > All On Active Artboard to select all of the shapes.

3   Choose Edit > Copy.

4   Choose File > Close to close the file without saving.

5   With the AmusementWorld.ai file showing, choose Edit Paste to paste the artwork into the center of the Document window.

6   Choose Select > Deselect.

7   With the Selection tool (⬆) selected in the Tools panel, click and drag the tower shape to position it like you see in the figure. Leave it selected.

As you drag, you will see green alignment guides and a gray measurement label. These are a part of the Smart Guides feature you will learn about in a later lesson.

8   With the tower artwork still selected, Option-drag (Mac OS) or Alt-drag (Windows) a copy of the tower to the right and position it like you see in the figure. Release the mouse button and then the key.

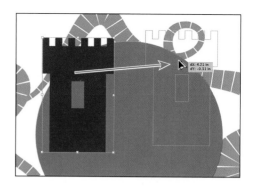

9   Choose Edit > Copy, and then choose Edit > Paste to paste a copy in the center of the Document window.

10 Drag the tower up like in the next figure.

11 In the Swatches panel (Window > Swatches), click the Fill box and select the White swatch.

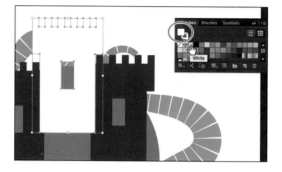

12 Choose Object > Arrange > Send To Back to send the white tower behind the other artwork.

Working with symbols

● **Note:** Learn more about working with symbols in Lesson 13, "Using Symbols to Create a Map."

A *symbol* is a reusable art object stored in the Symbols panel. You will now create a symbol from artwork.

1   Click the flag artwork you pasted previously.

2   Choose Window > Symbols to open the Symbols panel. Click the New Symbol button (⬛) at the bottom of the Symbols panel.

3   In the Symbol Options dialog box that appears, name the symbol **Flag**, and click OK.

The artwork now appears as a saved symbol in the Symbols panel, and the flag artwork on the artboard you used to create the symbol is now a symbol instance.

4 Choose View > Outline to see the artwork without fills. Drag the flag by the stroke (border), up to the top of the white tower.

You'll need to select the flag by the stroke (border) since there is no fill to click on in Outline mode.

5 Choose Object > Arrange > Send To Back.

6 Choose View > Preview.

7 From the Symbols panel, drag the Flag symbol thumbnail onto the artboard like you see in the figure. Drag one more Flag symbol from the Symbols panel onto the artboard and position it like you see in the figure. Leave the last symbol instance on the artboard selected.

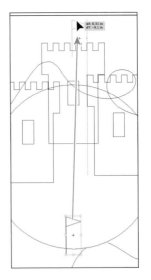

● **Note:** Your Flag symbol instances may be in different locations than those in the figure. That's okay.

8 With one of the flags selected, click the Edit Symbol button in the Control panel above the artwork. This allows you to edit the symbol artwork in Isolation mode without affecting the other artwork.

9 In the dialog box that appears, click OK.

10 Click the gray flag shape on the artboard. Click the Fill color in the Control panel and select the yellow swatch with the tool tip that shows "C=0, M=10, Y=95, K=0" to change the fill color of the flag. Press the Escape key to close the Swatches panel.

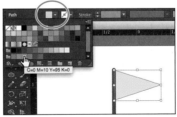

11 Press the Escape key to exit the editing (Isolation) mode and notice that the other flags have changed.

▶ **Tip:** You can also double-click away from the selected artwork to exit Isolation mode.

12 Click one of the blue towers, and then Shift-click the other blue tower to select both. Choose Object > Arrange > Bring To Front to arrange the towers on top of the flags.

13 Click the blue circle, and choose Object > Arrange > Bring To Front to place the circle on the towers. Drag it into position like you see in the figure.

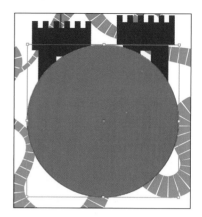

Placing images in Illustrator

● **Note:** Learn more about placing images in Lesson 14, "Using Illustrator CC with Other Adobe Applications."

In Illustrator, you can place raster images, like JPEG (jpg, jpeg, jpe) and Adobe Photoshop® (psd, pdd) files, and either link to them or embed them. Next, you will place an image of a map.

1 Choose File > Place. In the Place dialog box, navigate to the Lesson00 folder in the Lessons folder and select the Map.psd file. Make sure that the Link option in the dialog box is selected, and click Place.

2 Click to place the map on the artboard. Drag the map over the blue circle so it is positioned roughly like you see in the figure.

3 Choose File > Save.

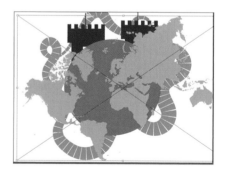

Using Image Trace

● **Note:** Learn more about Image Trace in Lesson 3, "Using Shapes to Create Artwork for a Postcard."

You can use Image Trace to convert photographs (raster images) into vector artwork. Next, you will trace the Photoshop file.

1 Choose Window > Image Trace to open the Image Trace panel.

2 In the Image Trace panel, choose "3 Colors" from the Preset menu.

The image is converted to vector paths, but it is not yet editable.

3 In the Image Trace panel, click the toggle arrow to the left of Advanced. Select Ignore White near the bottom of the panel. Close the Image Trace panel by clicking the small "x" in the corner.

4 With the map still selected, click the Expand button in the Control panel to make the object editable artwork.

The map image is now a series of vector shapes that are grouped together.

5 Choose Object > Arrange > Send Backward to put the map behind the blue circle.

6 Choose Window > Workspace > Reset Essentials.

Creating a clipping mask

A *clipping mask* is an object that masks other artwork so that only areas that lie within its shape are visible—in effect, clipping the artwork to the shape of the mask. Next, you will copy the blue circle and use the copy to mask the map.

1 With the Selection tool ( ) selected, click the blue circle.

2 Choose Edit > Copy, and then choose Edit > Paste In Front to paste a copy of the circle directly on top of the original circle.

3 With the circle still selected, press the Shift key, and click the map artwork to select it as well.

4 Choose Object > Clipping Mask > Make.

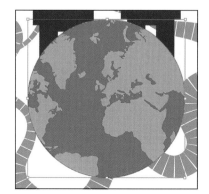

● **Note:** Learn more about working with clipping masks in Lesson 14, "Using Illustrator CC with Other Adobe Applications."

Creating and editing gradients

● **Note:** Learn more about working with gradients in Lesson 9, "Blending Colors and Shapes."

Gradients are color blends of two or more colors that you can apply to the fill or stroke of artwork. Next, you will apply a gradient to the background shape.

1 Click the white rectangle in the background to select it.

2 Choose Window > Gradient to show the Gradient panel on the right side of the workspace. In the Gradient panel, change the following options:

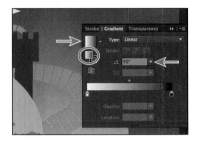

- Click the white Fill box (circled in the figure), if it's not already selected, so that you can apply the gradient to the fill of the rectangle shape.

- Click the Gradient menu button () to the left of the word "Type," and choose "White, Black" from the menu.

- Choose **90** from the Angle menu.

3 Drag the white color stop in the Gradient panel (see the figure below) to the right until the Location value below it shows roughly **50%**.

4 Double-click the black color stop on the right side of the gradient slider in the Gradient panel (circled in the figure below). In the panel that appears, click the Color button () (if it's not already selected), and change the color values to C=**75**, M=**0**, Y=**15**, K=**0**. Press the Escape key to hide the Color panel.

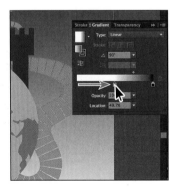
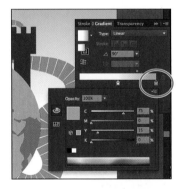

5 Click the Stroke color in the Control panel (circled in the figure). Click the None color (⬚) to remove the stroke (border) of the rectangle (if necessary). Press the Escape key to hide the Swatches panel.

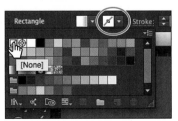

Next, you'll create a circle and apply a transparent gradient on the world.

6 Click within the green of the map artwork, and choose Object > Lock > Selection.

7 Click again on the map, and you will select the blue circle behind it since the map artwork is locked and can't be selected.

8 Choose Edit > Copy, and then Edit > Paste In Place to paste it on top of all other artwork.

9 In the Gradient panel, change the following options:

- Click the Fill box (circled in the figure), if it's not already selected, so that you can apply the gradient to the fill of the rectangle shape.

- Click the Gradient menu button (■) to the left of the word "Type," and choose "White, Black" from the menu.

- Choose Radial from the Type menu.

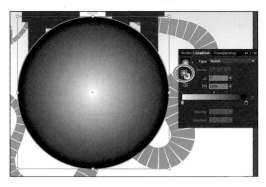

10 Double-click the black color stop on the right side of the gradient slider in the Gradient panel (circled in the figure). In the panel that appears, click the Swatches button (■), and select the white swatch. Change the Opacity to **0**. Press Enter or Return to hide the Color panel.

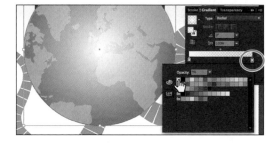

11 Select the Gradient tool (■) in the Tools panel on the left. Click and drag across the circle, starting at the red X in the figure, to reposition and resize the gradient.

12 Choose Object > Lock > Selection to lock the gradient circle.

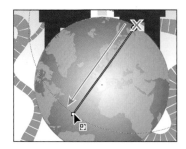

Working with type

● **Note:** Learn more about working with type in Lesson 7, "Adding Type to a Poster."

Next, you will add some text to the project and apply formatting. You will choose a Typekit font that requires an Internet connection. If you don't have an Internet connection, you can choose another font.

1 Select the Type tool (**T**) in the Tools panel on the left, and click in a blank area of the artboard. Type **Amusement Park**.

2 With the cursor still in the text, choose Select > All to select it.

3 In the Control panel above the artwork, type **73 pt** in the Font Size field (to the right of the Font Family), and press the Enter or Return key.

▶ **Tip:** If you don't see the character options like font size in the Control panel, click the word "Character" to see the Character panel.

4 Click the Fill color in the Control panel above the artwork and choose the purple/blue color with the yellow tool tip that shows as "C=100, M=100, Y=25, K=25."

Next, you will apply a Typekit font. You will need an Internet connection. *If you don't have an Internet connection or access to the Typekit fonts, you can choose any other font from the font menu.*

5 Click the arrow to the right of the Font field. Click the Add Fonts From Typekit button to sync a font from Typekit. This opens a browser, launches the Typekit.com website, and signs you in to the site.

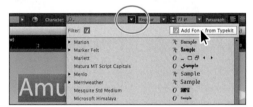

● **Note:** If you are taken to the Typekit.com home page, you can simply click the Browse Fonts button. It may also ask you to login with your Adobe ID.

6 In the browser, click the Sans Serif button to sort the listing of fonts and make sure that the Desktop Use button is selected. Choose Name from the Sort By field to sort the fonts alphabetically.

7 Find Azo Sans Uber in the list (or another font, if you don't see that one). Hover over it and click +Use Fonts.

8 Click Sync Selected Fonts in the window that appears.

9 After it is synced, click the Launch The Creative Cloud Application button to open the Creative Cloud Desktop application.

In the Creative Cloud desktop application, you will be able to see any messages indicating that font syncing is turned off (turn it on in that case) or any other issues.

10 Return to Illustrator. With the text still selected, in the Font field in the Control panel, begin typing **Azo**.

11 Click Azo Sans Uber Regular in the menu that appears to apply the font.

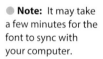

● **Note:** It may take a few minutes for the font to sync with your computer.

12 Select the Selection tool (▶), and drag the text roughly into position over the world, like you see in the figure and leave it selected.

Warping text

● **Note:** Learn more about working with a warp in Lesson 7, "Adding Type to a Poster."

Next, you will see how you can warp text into different shapes using a preset envelope warp.

1   With the text object still selected, choose Object > Envelope Distort > Make With Warp.

2   In the Warp Options dialog box, make sure that Arc is chosen from the Style menu. Change the Bend to **36%** and select Preview. Click OK.

Working with brushes

● **Note:** Learn more about working with brushes in Lesson 10, "Using Brushes to Create a Poster."

Brushes let you stylize the appearance of paths. You can apply brush strokes to existing paths, or you can use the Paintbrush tool (✐) to draw a path and apply a brush stroke simultaneously.

1   Select the Line Segment tool (╱) in the Tools panel on the left. Pressing the Shift key, click and drag from the left side of the artboard (see the red X in the figure) to the right. When the gray measurement label shows a width of roughly 15.3 in, release the mouse button and then the key.

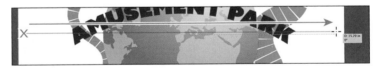

2   Choose Window > Brush Libraries > Decorative > Decorative_Banners And Seals to open the brush library as a panel.

3   Click the Banner 1 brush in the panel to apply it to the path. Click the "x" in the corner of the Decorative_Banners And Seals panel to close it.

4 Change the Stroke weight to **5 pt** in the Control panel above the artwork.

The brush is an art brush, which means that it stretches the banner artwork (in this case) along the path.

5 Choose Object > Arrange > Send Backward to arrange the banner behind the text.

6 Select the Selection tool (➤) and drag both into position like you see in the figure.

Working with effects

Effects alter the appearance of an object without changing the base object. Next, you will apply the Drop Shadow effect to the world artwork.

● **Note:** Learn more about effects in Lesson 11, "Exploring Creative Uses of Effects and Graphic Styles."

1 With the Selection tool (➤), click the blue circle.

2 Choose Effect > Stylize > Drop Shadow. In the Drop Shadow dialog box, set the following options (if necessary):

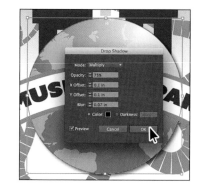

- Mode: **Multiply** (the default setting)
- Opacity: **75%** (the default setting)
- X Offset and Y Offset: **0.1 in** (the default setting)
- Blur: **0.07 in** (the default setting)

3 Select Preview, and then click OK.

4 Choose File > Save, and then choose File > Close.

1 GETTING TO KNOW THE WORK AREA

Lesson overview

In this lesson, you'll explore the workspace and learn how to do the following:

- Open an Adobe Illustrator CC file.
- Adjust the user interface brightness.
- Work with the Tools panel.
- Work with panels.
- Reset and save your workspace.
- Use viewing options to change the display magnification.
- Navigate multiple artboards and documents.
- Explore document groups.
- Find resources for using Illustrator.

This lesson takes approximately 45 minutes to complete.

Download the project files for this lesson from the Lesson & Update Files tab on your Account page at www.peachpit.com and store them on your computer in a convenient location, as described in the Getting Started section of this book.

Your Account page is also where you'll find any updates to the chapters or to the lesson files. Look on the Lesson & Update Files tab to access the most current content.

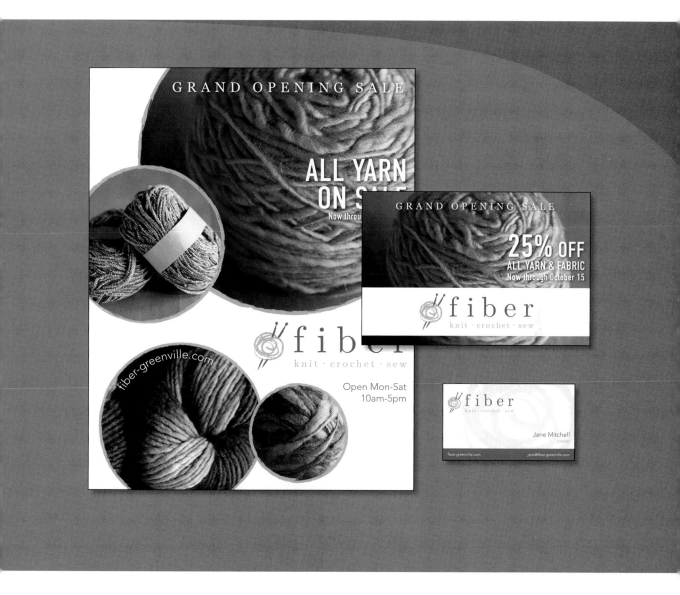

To make the best use of the extensive drawing, painting, and editing capabilities of Adobe Illustrator CC, it's important to learn how to navigate the workspace. The workspace consists of the Application bar, menus, Tools panel, Control panel, Document window, and the default set of panels.

Introducing Adobe Illustrator

► **Tip:** To learn more about bitmap graphics, search for "Importing bitmap images" in Illustrator Help (Help > Illustrator Help).

In Illustrator, you primarily create and work with vector graphics (sometimes called vector shapes or vector objects). *Vector graphics* are made up of lines and curves defined by mathematical objects called vectors. You can freely move or modify vector graphics without losing detail or clarity because they are resolution-independent. In other words, vector graphics maintain crisp edges when resized, printed to a PostScript printer, saved in a PDF file, or imported into a vector-based graphics application. As a result, vector graphics are the best choice for artwork, such as logos, that will be used at various sizes and in various output media.

Illustrator also allows you to incorporate *bitmap images*—technically called *raster images*—that use a rectangular grid of picture elements (pixels) to represent the visual. Each pixel is assigned a specific location and color value. Raster images can be created in a program like Adobe Photoshop.

This logo is drawn as vector art.

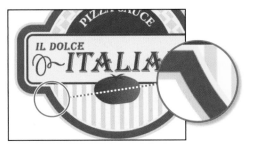

This logo is raster artwork.

Starting Illustrator and opening a file

You'll be working with multiple art files during this lesson, but before you begin, you'll restore the default preferences for Adobe Illustrator CC. Resetting the preferences is not something that you'll need to do when working on your own projects, but it ensures that what you see onscreen matches the descriptions in the lessons.

● **Note:** If you have not already downloaded the project files for this lesson to your computer from your Account page, make sure to do so now. See the "Getting Started" section at the beginning of the book.

1 To ensure that the tools and panels function exactly as described in this lesson, delete or deactivate (by renaming) the Adobe Illustrator CC preferences file. See "Restoring default preferences" in the Getting Started section at the beginning of the book.

2 Double-click the Adobe Illustrator CC icon to start Adobe Illustrator.

3 Choose Window > Workspace > Reset Essentials to ensure that the workspace is set to the default settings.

4 Choose File > Open, to open the L1_start1.ai file. In the Lesson01 folder in the Lessons folder on your hard disk, select the L1_start1.ai file and click Open.

This lesson contains a fictitious business name, address, and website address made up for the purposes of the project.

5 Click Disable Sync Settings if the sync dialog box appears.

● **Note:** For more information on syncing with Adobe Creative Cloud, see the sidebar "Syncing with the Adobe Creative Cloud" at the end of this lesson.

6 Choose View > Fit Artboard In Window.

This fits the active artboard into the Document window so that you can see the entire artboard. As you'll soon learn, an artboard is the area that contains your printable artwork and is similar to a page in Adobe InDesign.

7 Click the word "Libraries" in the panel tab on the right to collapse it, if the Libraries panel is showing (see the following figure).

● **Note:** As of the writing of this book, the Libraries panel appears in the default workspace.

● **Note:** If you don't see "Reset Essentials" in the Workspace menu, choose Window > Workspace > Essentials before choosing Window > Workspace > Reset Essentials.

● **Note:** On Windows, going forward, if you see a message about compatible GPU, click OK.

When the file is open and Illustrator is fully launched, the Application bar, menus, Tools panel, Control panel, and panel groups appear on the screen. Docked on the right side of the screen, you will see that default panels appear as icons. Illustrator also consolidates many of your most frequently accessed options in the Control panel below the menu bar. This lets you work with fewer visible panels and gives you a larger area in which to work.

You will use the L1_start1.ai file to practice navigating, zooming, and investigating an Illustrator document and the workspace.

8 Choose File > Save As. In the Save As dialog box, name the file
businesscard.ai and save it in the Lesson01 folder. Leave the Format option
set to Adobe Illustrator (ai) (Mac OS) or Save As Type option set to Adobe
Illustrator (*.AI) (Windows). Click Save. If a warning dialog box appears
referencing spot colors and transparency, click Continue. In the Illustrator
Options dialog box, leave the options at their default settings and click OK.

The Illustrator Options dialog box contains options that can control how the file
is saved, allow you to save to a previous version of Illustrator, and more.

Understanding the workspace

You create and manipulate your documents and files using various elements,
such as panels, bars, and windows. Any arrangement of these elements is called a
workspace. When you first start Illustrator, you see the default workspace, which
you can customize for the tasks you perform. You can create and save multiple
workspaces—one for editing and another for viewing, for example—and switch
among them as you work.

● **Note:** The figures in this lesson are taken using the Windows operating system and may look
slightly different from what you see, especially if you are using the Mac OS.

Below, the areas of the default workspace are described:

A. Application bar

B. Control panel

C. Panels

D. Tools panel

E. Document window

F. Status bar

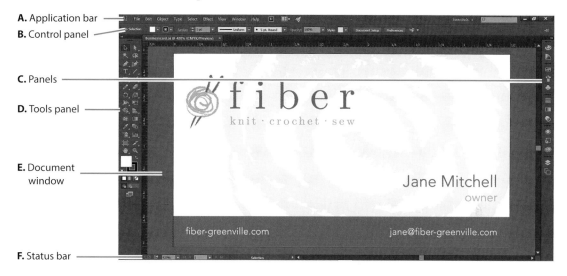

A. The **Application bar** across the top contains a workspace switcher, a menu bar (Windows only, depending on screen resolution), and application controls.

⬤ **Note:** For the Mac OS, the menu items appear above the Application bar (see below).

B. The **Control panel** displays options for the currently selected object.

C. **Panels** help you monitor and modify your work. Certain panels are displayed by default, and you can display any panel by choosing it from the Window menu. Many panels have menus with panel-specific options. Panels can be grouped, stacked, docked, or free-floating.

D. The **Tools panel** contains tools for creating and editing images, artwork, page elements, and more. Related tools are grouped together.

E. The **Document window** displays the file you're working on.

F. The **Status bar** appears at the lower-left edge of the Document window. It displays information, zooming, and navigation controls.

⬤ **Note:** The GPU Performance icon (▨) currently only shows on Windows. The GPU Performance feature introduces a preview mode (GPU Preview) which enables rendering of Illustrator artwork on the graphics processor (Windows only).

Adjusting the user-interface brightness

Similar to Adobe InDesign or Adobe Photoshop, Illustrator supports a brightness adjustment for the application user interface. This is a program preference setting that allows you to choose a brightness setting from four preset levels or to specify a custom value.

In this section, you will change the setting to see its effect, and then you will change it back to the program default.

1   Choose Illustrator > Preferences > User Interface (Mac OS) or Edit > Preferences > User Interface (Windows).

2   Choose Light from the Brightness menu of the User Interface options.

Notice that the interface has become lighter overall. This can be useful if the default interface is too dark, for instance.

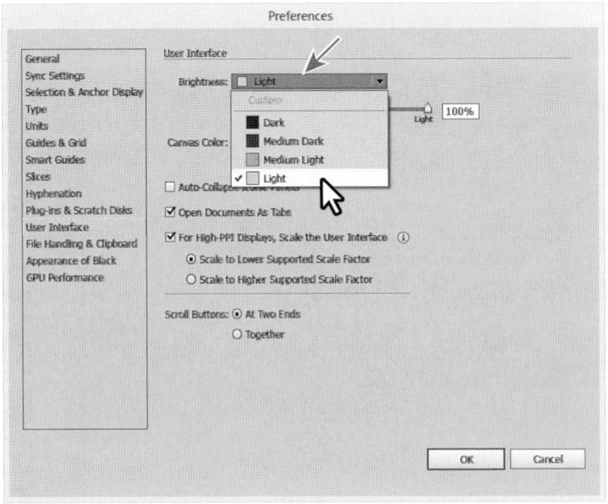

● **Note:** On Mac OS, you won't see some of the options you see in the figure (Windows), and that's okay.

3   Drag the Brightness slider to the left until you see a value of 50%.

You can drag the Brightness slider beneath the Brightness menu to the left or to the right to adjust the overall brightness using a custom value.

4   Choose Medium Dark from the Brightness menu.

5   Select White for the Canvas Color option beneath the Brightness slider.

The *canvas* is the area outside of the artboards in your document.

6   Click Cancel so you don't save the preference settings.

If you decide to change the interface brightness, what you see may differ in appearance from the figures in this book. We left the brightness at the default.

Working with the Tools panel

The Tools panel contains selection tools, drawing and painting tools, editing tools, viewing tools, the Fill and Stroke boxes, drawing modes, and screen modes. As you work through the lessons, you'll learn about the specific function of each tool.

● **Note:** The Tools panel shown here and throughout this lesson has two columns. You may see a one-column Tools panel, depending on your screen resolution and workspace.

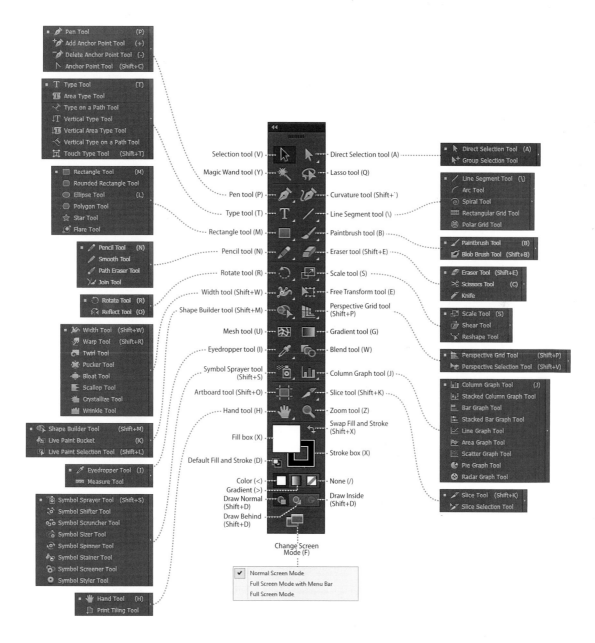

► Tip: You can modify the default keyboard shortcuts that Illustrator comes with. To do this, choose Edit > Keyboard Shortcuts. For more information, see "Keyboard Shortcuts," in Illustrator Help.

1   Position the pointer over the Selection tool (****) in the Tools panel. Notice that the name (Selection tool) and keyboard shortcut (V) are displayed.

► Tip: You can turn the tool tips on or off by choosing Illustrator > Preferences > General (Mac OS) or Edit > Preferences > General (Windows) and deselecting Show Tool Tips.

2   Position the pointer over the Direct Selection tool (****), and click and hold down the mouse button. You'll see additional selection tools appear in a menu. Click the Group Selection tool to select it.

Any tool in the Tools panel that displays a small triangle contains additional tools that can be selected in this way.

► Tip: You can also select hidden tools by pressing the Option key (Mac OS) or Alt key (Windows) and clicking the tool in the Tools panel. Each click selects the next hidden tool in the hidden tool sequence.

3   Click and hold down the mouse button on the Rectangle tool (**■**) to reveal more tools. Click the arrow at the right edge of the hidden tools panel to separate the tools from the Tools panel so that you can access them at all times.

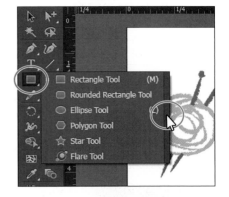

► Tip: You can also collapse the floating tool panels or dock them to the workspace or each other.

4   Click the Close button (X) in the upper-left corner (Mac OS) or upper-right corner (Windows) on the floating tool panel's title bar to close it. The tools return to the Tools panel.

Next, you'll learn how to resize and float the Tools panel. In the figures in this lesson, the Tools panel is a double column by default. You may see a single-column Tools panel to start with, depending on your screen resolution and workspace, and that's okay.

5 Click the double arrow in the upper-left corner of the Tools panel to either expand the one column into two columns or collapse the two columns into one (depending on your screen resolution). Click the double arrow again to expand or collapse the Tools panel.

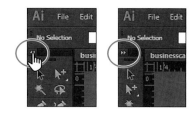

6 Click the dark-gray title bar at the top of the Tools panel or the dashed line beneath the title bar, and drag the panel into the workspace. The Tools panel is now floating in the workspace.

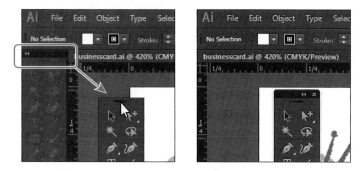

▶ **Tip:** You can click the double arrow at the top of the Tools panel or double-click the title bar at the top of the Tools panel to switch between two columns and one column. Just be careful not to click the X.

7 To dock the Tools panel again, drag its title bar or the dashed line below it to the left side of the screen (Mac OS) or Application window (Windows). When the pointer reaches the left edge, a translucent blue border, called the *drop zone*, appears. Release the mouse button to dock the Tools panel neatly into the side of the workspace.

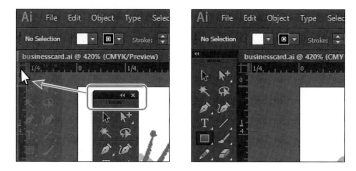

Custom Tools panels

You may find yourself using a specific set of tools most of the time. In Illustrator, you can create custom tools panels that contain the tools you use most often.

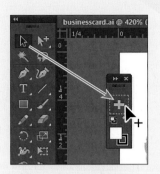

By choosing Window > Tools > New Tools Panel, you can create a custom tools panel. They are saved with Illustrator and can be closed and opened, regardless of which document is open. They are free-floating, and can also be docked and saved in a custom workspace you create. Each new custom tools panel has stroke and fill controls at the bottom, and a plus sign (+) where you can drag copies of tools from the main Tools panel onto the custom panel you are creating.

Note: *Dragging tools from the default Tools panel copies them to the custom tools panel, rather than moves them.*

Exploring the Control panel

The Control panel is the panel that's docked at the top of the workspace, just above the docked Tools panel. It offers quick access to options, commands, and other panels relevant to the currently selected content. You can click text like "Stroke" or "Opacity" to display a related panel. For example, clicking the word "Stroke" will display the Stroke panel.

1   Select the Selection tool (▶) in the Tools panel, and click the letter "f" in the word "fiber" in the artwork on the artboard.

Notice that options for that object appear in the Control panel, including the word "Group," color options, Stroke, and more.

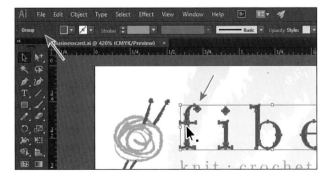

2   With any tool, drag the gripper bar (the dashed line along the left edge) of the
    Control panel into the workspace.

    Once the Control panel is free-floating, you can drag the dark-gray gripper bar
    that appears on the left edge of the Control panel to move it to the top or bottom
    of the workspace.

Tip: You can also dock the Control panel by choosing Dock To Top or Dock To Bottom from the Control panel menu (▣) on the right side of the Control panel.

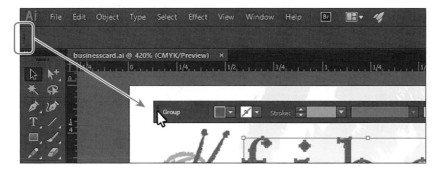

Tip: The Control panel can be dragged by the dark-gray gripper bar on the left edge to the bottom of the screen (Mac OS) or Application window (Windows). When the pointer (not the panel) reaches the bottom of the screen (Mac OS) or Application window (Windows), a blue line appears, indicating the drop zone in which it will be docked. You can then release the mouse button to dock it.

3   Drag the Control panel by the gripper bar on the left edge of the panel. When
    the pointer reaches the bottom of the Application bar, to the right of the Tools
    panel, a blue line appears indicating the drop zone. When you release the mouse
    button, the panel is docked.

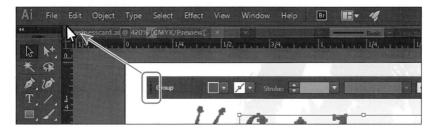

4   Choose Select > Deselect so that the content on the artboard is no
    longer selected.

Working with panels

Panels, which are listed alphabetically in the Window menu, give you quick access to many tools that make modifying artwork easier. By default, some panels are docked and appear as icons on the right side of the workspace.

Next, you'll experiment with hiding, closing, and opening panels.

▶ **Tip:** You can also choose Window > Workspace > Reset Essentials to reset the panels.

1 First, choose Reset Essentials from the workspace switcher in the upper-right corner of the Application bar to reset the panels to their original location.

2 Click the Swatches panel icon (▦) on the right side of the workspace to expand the panel, or choose Window > Swatches.

Notice that the Swatches panel appears with two other panels—the Brushes panel and the Symbols panel. They are all part of the same panel group.

3 Click the Symbols panel tab to view the Symbols panel.

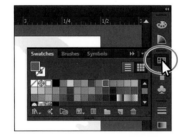

4 Now click the Color panel icon (🎨) in the dock. Notice that a new panel group appears and that the panel group that contained the Swatches panel collapses.

● **Note:** The Color panel you see may look different and that's okay.

5 Click and drag the gripper bar at the bottom of the Color panel down to resize the panel, showing more of the color spectrum.

▶ **Tip:** To collapse a panel back to an icon, you can click its tab, its icon, or the double arrow in the panel title bar.

6 Click the Color panel icon to collapse the panel group.

▶ **Tip:** To find a hidden panel, choose the panel name from the Window menu. A check mark to the left of the panel name indicates that the panel is already open and in front of other panels in its panel group. If you choose a panel name that is already selected in the Window menu, the panel and its group collapse.

7 Click the double arrow at the top of the dock to expand the panels. Click the double arrow again to collapse the panels. Use this method to show more than one panel group at a time. Your panels may look different when expanded, and that's okay.

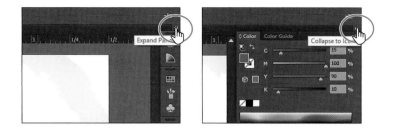

▶ **Tip:** To expand or collapse the panel dock, you can also double-click the panel dock title bar at the top.

8 To increase the width of all the panels in the dock, drag the left edge of the docked panels to the left until text appears. To decrease the width, click and drag the left edge of the docked panels to the right until the text disappears.

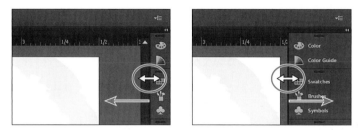

9 Choose Window > Workspace > Reset Essentials to reset the workspace.

10 Drag the Swatches panel icon (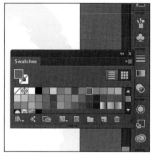) away from the dock to remove the panel from the dock and make it a free-floating panel. Notice that the panel stays collapsed as an icon when it is free-floating.

11 Click the double arrow in the Swatches panel title bar to expand the panel so you can see its contents.

Drag the Swatches panel.   Expand the panel.   The result.

You can also move panels from one panel group to another. In this way, you can create custom panel groups that contain the panels you use most often.

▶ **Tip:** To close a panel, drag the panel away from the dock and click the X in the panel title bar. You can also right-click a docked panel tab or panel icon and choose Close from the menu.

12 Drag the Swatches panel by the panel tab, the panel title bar, or the area behind the panel tab onto the Brushes (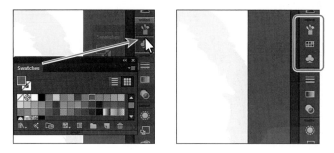) and Symbols (⬤) panel icons. Release the mouse button when you see a blue line between the panel icons and an outline around the Brushes panel group.

Next, you'll organize the panels to create more room in your workspace.

Tip: Press Tab to hide all panels. Press Tab again to show them all again. You can hide or show all panels except for the Tools and Control panels by pressing Shift+Tab to toggle between hide and show.

13 Choose Reset Essentials from the workspace switcher in the Application bar to make sure that the panels are reset to their default state.

14 Click the double arrow at the top of the dock to expand the panels.

15 Click the Color Guide panel tab to make sure it's selected. Double-click the panel tab to reduce the size of the panel. Double-click the tab again to minimize the panel. This can also be done when a panel is free-floating (not docked).

Double-click the panel tab.

Double-click again.

The panel is collapsed.

● **Note:** Many panels only require that you double-click the panel tab twice to return to the full-size view of the panel. If you double-click one more time, the panel fully expands.

▶ **Tip:** To reduce and expand the panel size, instead of double-clicking the panel tab, you can click the small arrow icon to the left of the panel name in the panel tab, if present.

Editing panel groups

Panel groups can be docked, undocked, and arranged in either collapsed or expanded modes. Next, you will resize and reorganize panel groups, which can make it easier to see more important panels.

1 Click the Symbols panel tab if not already selected. Drag the dividing line between the Symbols panel group and the Stroke panel group below it, up to resize the group.

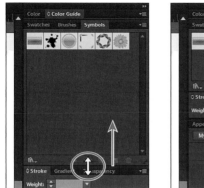 

● **Note:** You may not be able to drag the divider very far, depending on your screen size, screen resolution, and number of panels expanded.

● **Note:** If you drag a group into the dock and drop it into an existing group, the two groups merge. Reset the workspace and open the panel group to try again.

2 Choose Reset Essentials from the workspace switcher on the far right side of the Application bar above the Control panel.

3 Choose Window > Align to open the Align panel group. Drag the title bar of the Align panel group (the bar above the tabs) to the docked panels on the right side of the workspace. Position the pointer below the group that the Symbols panel icon (●) is in until a single blue line appears below the group. Release the mouse button to create a new group in the dock.

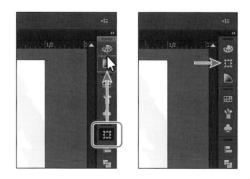

Next, you will drag a panel from one group to another in the docked panels.

4 Drag the Transform panel icon (▦) up so that the pointer is just below the Color panel icon (●). A blue line appears between the Color panel icon and the Color Guide panel icon (▣), outlining the Color panel group in blue. Release the mouse button.

Arranging the panels in groups can help you work faster.

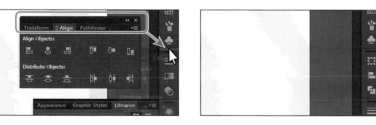

▶ **Tip:** You can also reorder entire panel groups in the dock by dragging the double gray line at the top of each panel group up or down.

Resetting and saving your workspace

You can reset your Tools panel and other panels to their default positions, which you've been doing throughout this lesson. You can also save the position of panels so that you can easily access them at any time by creating a workspace. Next, you will create a workspace to access a group of commonly used panels.

▶ **Tip:** Docking panels next to each other on the right side of the workspace is a great way to conserve space. A docked panel can also be collapsed and resized to conserve even more space.

1 Choose Reset Essentials from the workspace switcher in the Application bar.

2 Click the Libraries panel tab to hide the panel group, if necessary.

3 Choose Window > Pathfinder to open the Pathfinder panel group. Click and drag the Pathfinder panel tab to the right side of the workspace. When the pointer approaches the left edge of the docked panels, a blue line appears. Release the mouse button to dock the panel.

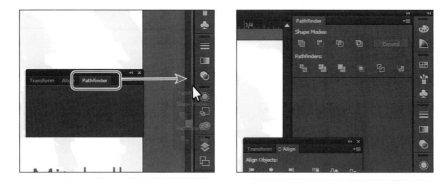

4 Click the Close button (X) in the upper-left corner (Mac OS) or upper-right corner (Windows) to close the remaining panel group, which contains the Align and Transform panels.

● **Note:** To delete saved workspaces, choose Window > Workspace > Manage Workspaces. Select the workspace name, and click the Delete Workspace button.

5 Choose Window > Workspace > New Workspace. Change the Name to **Navigation** in the New Workspace dialog box, and click OK (the name could be anything). The workspace named Navigation is now saved with Illustrator until you remove it.

6 Choose Window > Workspace > Essentials, and then choose Window > Workspace > Reset Essentials. Notice that the panels return to their default positions. Choose Window > Workspace > Navigation. Toggle between the two workspaces using the Window > Workspace command, and return to the Essentials workspace before starting the next exercise.

▶ **Tip:** To change a saved workspace, reset the panels as you'd like them to appear, and then choose Window > Workspace > New Workspace. In the New Workspace dialog box, name the workspace with the original name. A message appears in the dialog box warning that you will overwrite an existing workspace with the same name if you go ahead and click OK.

Using panel menus

Most panels have more options that are available in a panel menu. Clicking the panel menu icon (![panel menu icon]) in the upper-right corner gives you access to additional options for the selected panel, including changing the panel display in some cases.

Next, you will change the display of the Symbols panel using its panel menu.

1   Click the Symbols panel icon (![icon]) on the right side of the workspace. You can also choose Window > Symbols to display this panel.

2   Click the panel menu icon (![icon]) in the upper-right corner of the Symbols panel.

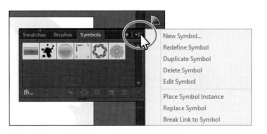

3   Choose Small List View from the panel menu.

This displays the symbol names, together with thumbnails. Because the options in the panel menu apply only to the active panel, only the Symbols panel view is affected.

4   Click the Symbols panel menu icon (![icon]) and choose Thumbnail View to return the symbols to their original view. Click the Symbols panel tab to hide the panel again.

In addition to the panel menus, context-sensitive menus display commands relevant to the active tool, selection, or panel. Usually the commands in a context menu are available in another part of the workspace, but using a context menu can save you time.

5   Position the pointer over the Document window or the contents of a panel. Then, right-click to show a context menu with specific options.

The context-sensitive menu shown here is displayed when you right-click the artboard with nothing selected.

● **Note:** If you position the pointer over the tab or title bar for a panel, and right-click, you can close a panel or a panel group in the context menu that appears.

Changing the view of artwork

When working in files, it's likely that you'll need to change the magnification level and navigate among artboards. The magnification level, which can range from 3.13% to 6400%, is displayed in the title bar (or document tab) next to the file name and in the lower-left corner of the Document window. Using any of the viewing tools and commands affects only the display of the artwork, not the actual size of the artwork.

Using view commands

To enlarge or reduce the view of artwork using the View menu, do one of the following:

- Choose View > Zoom In to enlarge the display of the businesscard.ai artwork.

- Choose View > Zoom Out to reduce the view of the businesscard.ai artwork.

▶ **Tip:** You can also zoom in using the keyboard shortcut Command++ (Mac OS) or Ctrl++ (Windows). That's Command *and* + (Mac OS) or Ctrl *and* + (Windows). You can also zoom out using the keyboard shortcut Command+– (Mac OS) or Ctrl+– (Windows). That's Command *and* – (Mac OS) or Ctrl *and* – (Windows).

Each time you choose a Zoom option, the view of the artwork is resized to the closest preset zoom level. The preset zoom levels appear in a menu in the lower-left corner of the Document window, identified by a down arrow next to a percentage.

You can also use the View menu to fit the artwork for the active artboard to your screen to fit all artboards into the view area, or to view artwork at actual size.

▶ **Tip:** You can also double-click the Hand tool (✋) in the Tools panel to fit the active artboard in the Document window.

1 Choose View > Fit Artboard In Window.

● **Note:** Because the canvas (the area outside the artboards) extends to 227", you can easily lose sight of your illustration. By choosing View > Fit Artboard In Window or by using the keyboard shortcuts Command+0 (Mac OS) or Ctrl+0 (Windows), artwork is centered in the viewing area.

▶ **Tip:** You can also double-click the Zoom tool (🔍) in the Tools panel to display artwork at 100%.

2 Choose View > Actual Size to display the artwork at actual size.

The artwork is displayed at 100%. The actual size of your artwork determines how much of it can be viewed onscreen at 100%.

3 Choose View > Fit Artboard In Window before continuing to the next section.

Using the Zoom tool

In addition to the View menu options, you can use the Zoom tool (🔍) to magnify and reduce the view of artwork to predefined magnification levels.

1 Select the Zoom tool (🔍) in the Tools panel, and then move the pointer into the Document window.

Notice that a plus sign (+) appears at the center of the Zoom tool pointer.

2   Position the Zoom tool over the
    text "Jane Mitchell," and click once.
    The artwork is displayed at a
    higher magnification.

    Notice that where you clicked
    is now in the center of the
    Document window.

3   Click two more times on the "Jane Mitchell" text. The view is increased again,
    and you'll notice that the area you clicked is magnified.

4   With the Zoom tool still selected, position the pointer over the text "Jane
    Mitchell" and hold down the Option (Mac OS) or Alt (Windows) key. A minus
    sign (−) appears at the center of the Zoom tool pointer. With the Option or Alt
    key pressed, click the artwork twice to reduce the view of the artwork.

    For a more controlled zoom, you can drag a marquee around a specific area of
    your artwork. This magnifies only the selected area.

5   Choose View > Fit Artboard In Window.

6   With the Zoom tool still selected, click and drag a marquee around the fiber
    logo in the upper-left corner of the artboard. When you see the marquee around
    the area you are dragging, release the mouse button. The marqueed area is now
    enlarged to fit the size of the Document window (as best it can).

7   Double-click the Hand tool (✋) in the Tools panel to fit the artboard in the
    Document window.

The Zoom tool is used frequently during the editing process to enlarge and reduce
the view of artwork. Because of this, Illustrator allows you to select it using the
keyboard at any time without first deselecting any other tool you may be using.

8   Select any other tool in the Tools panel, and move the pointer into the
    Document window.

9   Press Command+spacebar (Mac OS) or Ctrl+spacebar (Windows) to use the
    Zoom tool. Click or drag to zoom in on any area of the artwork, and then release
    the keys.

● **Note:** The percent
of the magnification
is determined by the
size of the marquee
you draw with the
Zoom tool (🔍)—the
smaller the marquee,
the higher the level of
magnification.

● **Note:** In certain
versions of Mac OS, the
keyboard shortcuts for
the Zoom tool (🔍) open
Spotlight or Finder. If
you decide to use these
shortcuts in Illustrator,
you may want to turn
off or change those
keyboard shortcuts
in the Mac OS System
Preferences.

10 To zoom out using the keyboard, hold down Command+Option+spacebar (Mac OS) or Ctrl+Alt+spacebar (Windows). Click the desired area to reduce the view of the artwork, and then release the keys.

11 Double-click the Hand tool in the Tools panel to fit the artboard in the Document window.

Touch workspace

In Adobe Illustrator CC (2014 release), the Touch workspace is designed for Windows 8 tablets. The Touch workspace surfaces the essential tools and controls for drawing and editing with a pressure sensitive pen and multi-touch gestures.

You can create logos, icons, explore custom lettering and typography, create UI wireframes, and more. The Touch workspace brings traditional drawing templates, French curves, to the Illustrator workspace. These shapes project a scalable, movable outline that can be traced against to quickly create refined curves.

At any time (on a supported device), you can immediately switch between the Touch and traditional workspaces to access the full range of Illustrator tools and controls. For more information on working with touch devices and Illustrator visit Help (Help > Illustrator Help).

On touch devices (a Direct touch device [a touchscreen device], or an Indirect touch device [the Trackpad on a Mac computer], touchpads, or the Wacom Intuos5 device), you can also use standard touch gestures (pinch and swipe) for:

- Pinch in or out, using two fingers (like the thumb and forefinger) to zoom.
- Place two fingers on the document, and move the fingers together to pan within the document.
- Swipe or flick to navigate artboards.
- In artboard editing mode, use two fingers to rotate the artboard by 90°.

Scrolling through a document

● **Note:** The spacebar shortcut for the Hand tool (✋) does not work when the Type tool (**T**) is active and the cursor is in text. To access the Hand tool when the cursor is in text, press the Option (Mac OS) or Alt (Windows) key.

You can use the Hand tool (✋) to pan to different areas of a document. Using the Hand tool allows you to push the document around much like you would a piece of paper on your desk.

1 With the Hand tool (✋) selected in the Tools panel, drag down in the Document window. As you drag, the artwork moves with the hand.

As with the Zoom tool (🔍), you can select the Hand tool with a keyboard shortcut without first deselecting the active tool.

2 Click any other tool except the Type tool (**T**) in the Tools panel, and move the pointer into the Document window.

3 Hold down the spacebar on the keyboard to temporarily select the Hand tool, and then drag to bring the artwork back into the center of your view.

4   Double-click the Hand tool to fit the active artboard in the Document window.

Viewing artwork

To save time when working with large or complex documents, you can create your own custom views within a document so that you can quickly jump to specific areas and zoom levels. Set up the view that you want to save, and then choose View > New View. Name the view, and click OK. The view is saved with the document.

1   Choose View > Email (at the very bottom of the View menu), to zoom in to a saved zoom view of the image. This custom view was saved with the document by the author.

2   Choose View > Fit Artboard In Window.

When you open a file, it is automatically displayed in Preview mode, which shows how the artwork will print. When you're working with large or complex illustrations, you may want to view only the outlines, or *wireframes*, of objects in your artwork so that the screen doesn't have to redraw the artwork each time you make a change. This is called Outline mode. Outline mode can be helpful when selecting objects, as you will see in Lesson 2, "Techniques for Selecting Artwork."

3   Choose View > Outline.

Only the outlines of the objects are displayed. Use this view to find objects that might not be visible in Preview mode.

4   Choose View > Preview to see all the attributes of the artwork.

5   Choose View > Overprint Preview to view any lines or shapes that are set to overprint.

This view is helpful for those in the print industry who need to see how inks interact when set to overprint. You may not actually see much of a change in the content when you change to this mode.

6   Choose View > Pixel Preview to see how the artwork will look when it is rasterized and viewed onscreen in a Web browser. Choose View > Pixel Preview to deselect pixel preview.

● **Note:** Depending on the resolution of your screen, the bottom of the View menu and the menu options may be cut off. You may need to click the black arrow at the bottom of the View menu several times to see more options.

▶ **Tip:** Press Command+Y (Mac OS) or Ctrl+Y (Windows) to toggle between Preview and Outline modes.

● **Note:** When switching between viewing modes, visual changes may not be readily apparent. Zooming in and out (View > Zoom In and View > Zoom Out) may help you see the differences more easily.

Preview mode.

Outline mode.

Overprint mode.

Pixel Preview mode.

7   Choose View > Fit Artboard In Window to view the entire active artboard.

Navigating multiple artboards

Illustrator allows for multiple artboards within a single file. This is a great way to create a document so that you can have collateral pieces, like a brochure, a postcard, and a business card, in the same document. You can easily share content among designs, create multi-page PDFs, and print multiple pages by creating more than one artboard. For more information on artboards, check out the sidebar titled "Artboard overview" at the end of this section.

Multiple artboards can be added when you initially create an Illustrator document by choosing File > New. You can also add or remove artboards after the document is created by using the Artboard tool in the Tools panel.

Next, you will learn how to efficiently navigate a document that contains multiple artboards.

1 Choose File > Open and, in the Lesson01 folder, select the L1_start2.ai file located in the Lessons folder on your hard disk. Click Open to open the file.

2 Choose View > Fit All In Window to fit all artboards in the Document window. Notice that there are two artboards in the document.

The artboards in a document can be arranged in any order, orientation, or artboard size—they can even overlap. Suppose that you want to create a four-page brochure. You can create different artboards for every page of the brochure, all with the same size and orientation. They can be arranged horizontally or vertically or in whatever way you like.

The L1_start2.ai document has two artboards that contain the designs for the front of a postcard and a business flyer.

3 Press Command+– (Mac OS) or Ctrl+– (Windows) until you can see the logo in the upper-left corner of the canvas, which is outside the artboards.

4 Choose View > Fit Artboard In Window.

This command fits the currently active artboard in the window. The active artboard is identified in the Artboard Navigation menu in the lower-left corner of the Document window.

● **Note:** Learn how to work more with artboards in Lesson 4, "Transforming Artwork."

5 Choose 2 Artboard 2 from the Artboard Navigation menu in the lower-left corner. The postcard appears in the Document window.

6 Choose View > Zoom Out. Notice that zooming occurs on the currently active artboard.

Notice the arrows to the right and left of the Artboard Navigation menu. You can use these to navigate to the first ([K]), previous ([◀]), next ([▶]), and last ([▶I]) artboards.

7 Click the Previous navigation button ([◀]) to view the previous artboard (Artboard 1) in the Document window.

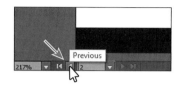

8 Choose View > Fit Artboard In Window to make sure that the first artboard (Artboard 1) fits in the Document window.

Another method for navigating multiple artboards is to use the Artboards panel. Next, you will open the Artboards panel and navigate the document.

9 Choose Window > Artboards to expand the Artboards panel on the right side of the workspace.

The Artboards panel lists all artboards in the document. This panel allows you to navigate between artboards, rename artboards, add or delete artboards, edit artboard settings, and more.

Next, you will focus on navigating the document using this panel.

10 Double-click the number 2 in the Artboards panel. This fits Artboard 2 in the Document window.

11 Double-click the number 1 to the left of Artboard 1 in the Artboards panel to show the first artboard in the Document window.

Notice that when you double-click to navigate to an artboard, that artboard fits in the Document window.

● **Note:** Double-clicking the artboard name in the Artboards panel allows you to change the name of the artboard. Clicking the artboard icon (▦) or (▣) to the right of the artboard name in the panel allows you to edit artboard options.

12 Click the Artboards panel icon (▦) in the dock to collapse the Artboards panel.

Artboard overview

Artboards represent the regions that can contain printable artwork (similar to pages in a program like Adobe InDesign). You can use artboards to crop areas for printing or placement purposes. Multiple artboards are useful for creating a variety of things, such as multiple-page PDFs, printed pages with different sizes or different elements, independent elements for websites, video storyboards, or individual items for animation in Adobe Flash® or Adobe After Effects.

A. *Printable area* is bounded by the innermost dotted lines and represents the portion of the page on which the selected printer can print.

B. *Nonprintable area* is between the two sets of dotted lines representing any nonprintable margin of the page. This example shows the nonprintable area of an 8.5" x 11" page for a printer that cannot print to the edge of the page.

C. *Artboard* is bounded by solid lines and represents the entire region that can contain printable artwork.

D. *Bleed area* is the amount of artwork that falls outside of the printing bounding box, or outside the crop area and trim marks.

E. *Canvas* is the area outside the artboard that extends to the edge of the 227" square window. Objects placed on the canvas are visible on-screen, but they do not print.

—From Illustrator Help

Using the Navigator panel

The Navigator panel is another way to navigate a document with a single artboard or multiple artboards. This is useful when you need to see all artboards in the document in one window and to edit content in any of those artboards in a zoomed-in view.

1   Choose Window > Navigator to open the Navigator panel. It is in a free-floating group of two panels in the workspace.

2   In the Navigator panel, type **50%** in the Zoom box in the lower-left corner of the panel and press Enter or Return to decrease the level of magnification.

● **Note:** You can also drag the slider in the Navigator panel to change the view of your artwork. Pause for a moment after dragging to allow the panel to catch up.

The red box in the Navigator panel, called the *proxy view area*, becomes larger, indicating the area of the document that is being shown. Depending on the zoom percentage, you may or may not see the proxy view area yet, but you will in the next few steps.

3 Click the larger mountain icon (⛰) in the lower-right corner of the Navigator panel several times to zoom in to the brochure until the percentage in the Navigator panel shows approximately 150%.

● **Note:** The percentage and proxy view area in your Navigator panel may appear differently in this section. That's okay.

4 Position the pointer inside the proxy view area of the Navigator panel. When the pointer becomes a hand (✋), drag to pan to different parts of the artwork. Try dragging the proxy view area over the postcard in the Navigator panel preview.

5 In the Navigator panel preview area at the top of the panel, move the pointer outside of the proxy view area (red box) and click. This moves the box and displays a different area of the artwork in the Document window.

6 Choose View > Fit Artboard In Window.

7 Click the Navigator panel menu icon (▤) and deselect View Artboard Contents Only so that you see any artwork that is on the canvas, as well. Notice the logo on the canvas in the panel.

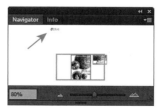

● **Note:** You may need to adjust the slider in the Navigator panel to see the logo in the proxy view area.

8   Close the Navigator panel group by clicking the Close button (X) in upper-left corner (Mac OS) or the upper-right corner (Windows).

Arranging multiple documents

When you open more than one Illustrator file, the Document windows are tabbed. You can arrange the open documents in other ways, such as side by side, so that you can easily compare or drag items from one document to another. You can also use the Arrange Documents window to quickly display your open documents in a variety of configurations.

You should currently have two Illustrator files open: businesscard.ai and L1_start2.ai. Each file has its own tab at the top of the Document window. These documents are considered a group of Document windows. You can create document groups to loosely associate files while they are open.

1   Click the businesscard.ai document tab to show businesscard.ai in the Document window.

● **Note:** Be careful to drag directly to the right. Otherwise, you could undock the Document window and create a new group. If that happens, choose Window > Arrange > Consolidate All Windows.

2   Click and drag the businesscard.ai document tab to the right of the L1_start2.ai document tab.

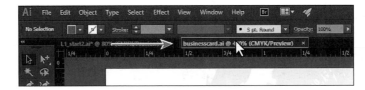

Dragging the document tabs allows you to change the order of the documents. This can be very useful if you use the document shortcuts to navigate to the next or previous document.

▶ **Tip:** You can cycle between open documents by pressing Command+~ (next document), Command+Shift+~ (previous document) (Mac OS) or Ctrl+F6 (next document), Ctrl+Shift+F6 (previous document) (Windows).

These two documents are marketing pieces for the same company. To see both of them at one time, you can arrange the Document windows by cascading the windows or tiling them. *Cascading* allows you to cascade (stack) different document groups. *Tiling* shows multiple Document windows at one time, in various arrangements.

Next, you will tile the open documents so that you can see them both at one time.

3   *Windows users skip to the next step.* On the Mac OS, choose Window > Application Frame. Then, click the green button (green by default) in the upper-left corner of the Application window so that it fits as well as possible.

Mac OS users can use the Application frame to group all the workspace elements in a single, integrated window, similar to working in Windows. If you move or resize the Application frame, the elements respond to each other so that they don't overlap.

4 Choose Window > Arrange > Tile.

This shows both Document windows arranged in a pattern.

5 Click in each of the Document windows to activate the documents and choose View > Fit Artboard In Window for each of the documents. Also, make sure that Artboard 1 is showing for each document in the Document window.

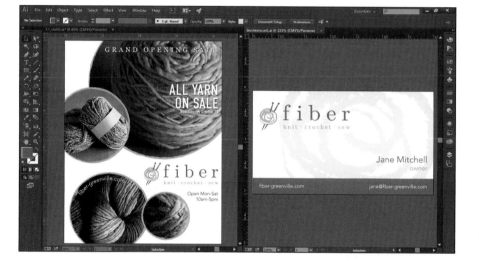

● **Note:** Your documents may be tiled in a different order. That's okay.

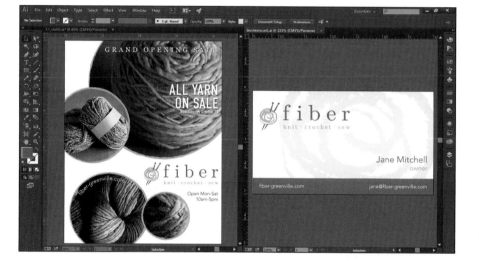

With documents tiled, you can drag the dividing line between each of the Document windows to reveal more or less of a particular document. You can also drag objects between documents, which copies them from one document to another.

To change the arrangement of the tiled windows, it's possible to drag document tabs to new positions. However, it's easier to use the Arrange Documents window to quickly arrange open documents in a variety of configurations.

6 Click the Arrange Documents button (▦▾) in the Application bar to display the Arrange Documents window. Click the Consolidate All button (▢) to bring the documents back together.

7 Click the Arrange Documents button (▦▾) in the Application bar to display the Arrange Documents window again. Click the 2-Up vertical button (▥) in the Arrange Documents window.

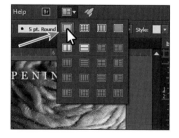

● **Note:** On the Mac OS, the menu bar is above the Application bar. Also, depending on the resolution of your screen, the Windows menus may appear in the Application bar.

Tip: You can also choose Window > Arrange > Consolidate All Windows to return the two documents to tabs in the same group.

8 Click to select the businesscard.ai tab, if it is not already selected. Then, click the Close button (X) on the businesscard.ai document tab to close the document. If a dialog box appears asking you to save the document, click Don't Save (Mac OS) or No (Windows).

9 Choose File > Close to close the L1_start2.ai document without saving.

Finding resources for using Illustrator

For complete and up-to-date information about using Illustrator panels, tools, and other application features, visit the Adobe website. By choosing Help > Illustrator Help, you'll be connected to the Illustrator Help website, where you can search Illustrator Help and support documents, as well as other websites relevant to Illustrator users. Community Help brings together active Adobe product users, Adobe product team members, authors, and experts to give you the most useful, relevant, and up-to-date information about Adobe products.

If you choose Help > Illustrator Help, you can also download a PDF of the Illustrator Help content by clicking the download link for your version.

Syncing with the Adobe Creative Cloud

The Sync Settings feature enables individual users to sync their preferences, presets, and libraries to the Adobe Creative Cloud. This means that if you use two computers, say, one at home and the other at work, the Sync Settings feature makes it easy for you to keep those settings synchronized across both computers. Also, if you have replaced your old computer with a new one and have reinstalled Illustrator, this friendly feature will let you bring back all those settings you took so much time to set up.

The syncing happens via your Adobe Creative Cloud account. All the settings are uploaded to your Creative Cloud account, and then are downloaded and applied on the other computer.

You need to initiate the sync manually; it does not happen automatically and it cannot be scheduled. For more information on syncing, see the "Sync settings using Adobe Creative Cloud" section in the Getting Started section of this book.

Review questions

1 Describe two ways to change the view of a document.

2 How do you select a tool in Illustrator?

3 Describe three ways to navigate among artboards in Illustrator.

4 How do you save panel locations and visibility preferences?

5 Describe how arranging Document windows can be helpful.

Review answers

1 You can choose commands from the View menu to zoom in or out of a document or to fit it to your screen; you can also use the Zoom tool (🔍) in the Tools panel and click or drag over a document to enlarge or reduce the view. In addition, you can use keyboard shortcuts to magnify or reduce the display of artwork. You can also use the Navigator panel to scroll artwork or to change its magnification without using the Document window.

2 To select a tool, you can either click the tool in the Tools panel or press the keyboard shortcut for that tool. For example, you can press V to select the Selection tool (▶) from the keyboard. Selected tools remain active until you click a different tool.

3 To navigate among artboards in Illustrator, you can choose the artboard number from the Artboard Navigation menu at the lower-left of the Document window; you can use the Artboard Navigation arrows in the lower-left of the Document window to go to the first, previous, next, and last artboards; you can use the Artboards panel to navigate to an artboard; or you can use the Navigator panel to drag the proxy view area to navigate between artboards.

4 You can save panel locations and visibility preferences by choosing Window > Workspace > New Workspace to create custom work areas and to make it easier to find the controls that you need.

5 Arranging Document windows allows you to tile windows or to cascade document groups. This can be useful if you are working on multiple Illustrator files and you need to compare or share content among them.

2 TECHNIQUES FOR SELECTING ARTWORK

Lesson overview

In this lesson, you'll learn how to do the following:

- Differentiate between the various selection tools and use different selection techniques.

- Recognize Smart Guides.

- Save selections for future use.

- Use tools and commands to align shapes and points to each other and the artboard.

- Group and ungroup items.

- Work in Isolation mode.

- Arrange content.

- Select objects that are behind other objects.

- Hide and lock items for organizational purposes.

 This lesson takes approximately 60 minutes to complete.

Download the project files for this lesson from the Lesson & Update Files tab on your Account page at www.peachpit.com and store them on your computer in a convenient location, as described in the Getting Started section of this book.

Your Account page is also where you'll find any updates to the chapters or to the lesson files. Look on the Lesson & Update Files tab to access the most current content.

Selecting content in Adobe Illustrator is one of the
more important things you'll do. In this lesson, you
learn how to locate and select objects using the
Selection tools; protect other objects by grouping,
hiding, and locking them; align objects to each other
and the artboard; and much more.

Getting started

When changing colors or size and adding effects or attributes, you must first select the object to which you are applying the changes. In this lesson, you will learn the fundamentals of using the selection tools. More advanced selection techniques using layers are discussed in Lesson 8, "Organizing Your Artwork with Layers."

● **Note:** If you have not already downloaded the project files for this lesson to your computer from your Account page, make sure to do so now. See "Getting Started" at the beginning of the book.

1 To ensure that the tools and panels function exactly as described in this lesson, delete or deactivate (by renaming) the Adobe Illustrator CC preferences file. See "Restoring default preferences" in the Getting Started section at the beginning of the book.

2 Start Adobe Illustrator CC.

3 Choose File > Open, and open the L2start.ai file in the Lesson02 folder, located in the Lessons folder on your hard disk. Choose View > Fit All In Window.

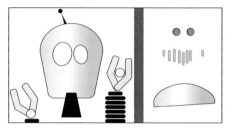

● **Note:** On Mac OS, you may need to choose Window > Arrange > Tile to maximize the size of the Document window after resetting the workspace.

4 Choose Window > Workspace > Essentials, make sure it's selected, and then choose Window > Workspace > Reset Essentials to reset the workspace.

Selecting objects

Whether you are creating artwork from scratch or editing existing artwork in Illustrator, you will need to become familiar with selecting objects. There are many methods and tools for doing this, and in this section, you'll explore the most widely used, which includes the Selection (▶) and Direct Selection (▷) tools.

Using the Selection tool

The Selection tool (▶) in the Tools panel lets you select, move, and resize entire objects. In this first section, you'll become familiar with the tool.

1 Select the Selection tool (▶) in the Tools panel, if it's not already selected. Move the pointer over different shapes on the artboards, without clicking.

The icon that appears as you pass over objects (▶.) indicates that there is an object that can be selected under the pointer. When you hover over an object, that object is also outlined in a color like blue (in this instance).

2 Select the Zoom tool (🔍) in the Tools panel, and drag a marquee around the two red circles on the artboard on the right to zoom in.

3   Select the Selection tool in the Tools panel, and then position the pointer over the black edge of the red circle on the left. A word such as "path" or "anchor" may appear, because Smart Guides are turned on by default.

Smart Guides are temporary snap-to guides that help you align, edit, and transform objects or artboards. You'll learn more about Smart Guides in Lesson 3, "Using Shapes to Create Artwork for a Postcard."

4   Click anywhere in the red circle on the left to select it. A bounding box with eight handles appears.

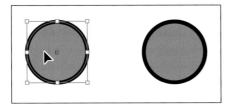

The bounding box is used when making changes to objects, such as resizing or rotating them. The bounding box also indicates that an item is selected and ready to be modified, and the color of the bounding box indicates which layer the object is on. Layers are discussed more in Lesson 8.

5   Using the Selection tool, click in the red circle on the right. Notice that the left red circle is now deselected and only the right circle is selected.

6   Hold down the Shift key, and click the left red circle to add it to the selection. Both red circles are now selected, and a larger bounding box surrounds them.

● **Note:** To select an item without a fill, you can click the stroke (the edge), or drag a selection marquee across the object.

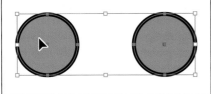

7   Reposition the circles anywhere in the document by clicking inside either selected circle (in the red area) and dragging. Because both circles are selected, they move together.

As you drag, you may notice the green lines that appear. These are called *alignment guides* and are visible because Smart Guides are turned on (View > Smart Guides). As you drag, the objects are aligned to other objects on the artboard. Also notice the measurement label (gray box) next to the pointer that shows the object's distance from its original position. Measurement labels also appear because Smart Guides are turned on.

8   Deselect the circles by clicking the artboard where there are no objects or by choosing Select > Deselect.

9 Revert to the last saved version of the document by choosing File > Revert. In the dialog box that appears, click Revert.

Using the Direct Selection tool

The Direct Selection (🔾) tool selects anchor points or path segments within an object so that it can be reshaped. Next, you will become familiar with selecting anchor points and path segments using the Direct Selection tool.

1 Choose View > Fit All In Window.

2 Select the Zoom tool (🔍) in the Tools panel, and drag a marquee around the series of orange shapes below the red circles you selected previously to zoom in.

▶ **Tip:** You can also click in the middle of a shape to select it and to see the anchor points around its edge. This can be an easy way to see where the points are, and then you can click a point to select it.

3 Select the Direct Selection tool (🔾) in the Tools panel. Without clicking, position the pointer over the top edge of one of the orange shapes. Move the pointer along the top edge of the shape until the word "anchor" appears by the pointer.

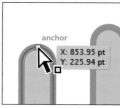

When the Direct Selection tool is over an anchor point of a path or object, the word "anchor" appears. In Illustrator, as you draw, you create paths that are made up of anchor points and paths. Anchor points are used to control the shape of the path. The "anchor" label is showing because Smart Guides are turned on (View > Smart Guides). Also notice the little white box to the right of the pointer. The small dot that appears in the center of the white box indicates that the cursor is positioned over an anchor point.

4 Click to select that anchor point.

Notice that only the anchor point you selected is solid, indicating that it is selected, and the other anchor points in the shape are hollow, indicating that they are not selected. Also notice the small blue lines extending from the selected anchor point. These are called direction lines. At the end of the direction lines are

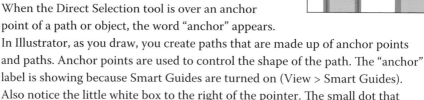

direction points. The angle and length of the direction lines determine the shape and size of the curved segments. Moving the direction points can reshape the path.

● **Note:** The gray measurement label that appears as you drag the anchor point has the values dX and dY. *dX* indicates the distance that the pointer has moved along the x axis (horizontal), and *dY* indicates the distance that the pointer has moved along the y axis (vertical).

5 With the Direct Selection tool still selected, drag the selected anchor point up to edit the shape of the object.

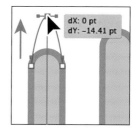

6 Try clicking another point on the edge of the shape, and notice that the previous point is deselected.

7 Revert to the last saved version of the file by choosing File > Revert. In the Revert dialog box, click Revert.

Exploring selection and anchor point preferences

To display selection and anchor point preferences, choose Illustrator > Preferences > Selection & Anchor Display (Mac OS) or Edit > Preferences > Selection & Anchor Display (Windows). You can change the size of anchor points (called *anchors* in the dialog box) or the display of the direction lines (called *handles* in the dialog box).

As you move the pointer over anchor points in your artwork, they are highlighted. You can also turn off the highlighting of anchor points as the pointer hovers over them. Highlighting anchor points makes it easier to determine which point you are about to select. You will learn more about anchor points and anchor point handles in Lesson 5, "Creating an Illustration with the Drawing Tools."

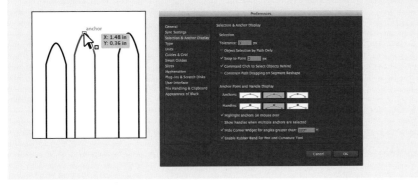

Creating selections with a marquee

Another way to select content is by dragging a marquee around the objects that you want to select, which is what you'll do next.

1   Choose View > Fit All In Window.

2   Select the Zoom tool (🔍) in the Tools panel, and click three times, slowly, on the red circles.

3   Select the Selection tool (▶) in the Tools panel. Position the pointer above and to the left of the leftmost red circle, and then drag downward and to the right to create a marquee that overlaps just the tops of the circles.

▶ **Tip:** When dragging with the Selection tool (▶), you need to encompass only a small part of an object to select it.

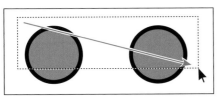
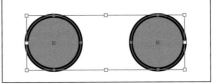

4   Choose Select > Deselect, or click where there are no objects.

Now you'll use the Direct Selection tool to select multiple anchor points in the red circles by dragging a marquee around anchor points.

5   Select the Direct Selection tool (⟨⟩) in the Tools panel. Starting off the top, left of the leftmost red circle (see the figure), drag across the top edges of the two circles. Only the top anchor points become selected.

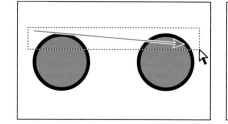
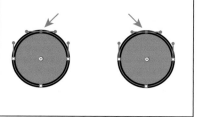

● **Note:** Selecting points using this method might take some practice. You'll need to drag across only the points you want selected; otherwise, more points will be selected. You can always click away from the objects to deselect them and then try again.

6   Click one of the selected anchor points, and drag to see how the anchor points reposition together.

You can use this method when selecting points so that you don't have to click exactly on the anchor point that you want to select.

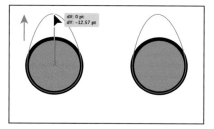

7   Revert to the last saved version of the file by choosing File > Revert. In the dialog box that appears, click Revert.

Creating selections with the Magic Wand tool

You can use the Magic Wand tool (✣) to select all objects in a document that have the same attributes, like a color fill. The fill is a color applied to the inside of an object. You can customize the Magic Wand tool to select objects based on options, like stroke weight, stroke color, and more, by double-clicking the Magic Wand tool in the Tools panel. You can also change the tolerances (range) used to identify similar objects.

1   Select the Selection tool (▶) and click in a blank area of the smaller artboard on the right. This makes that artboard the active artboard.

2   Choose View > Fit Artboard In Window.

3   Select the Magic Wand tool (✣) in the Tools panel. Click one of the red circles on the right artboard, and notice that the other red circle becomes selected as well. No bounding box (a box surrounding the two shapes) appears, because the Magic Wand tool is still selected.

4   Holding down the Shift key, notice that the pointer has a plus sign (+) next to it. Click one of the orange shapes (below the red shapes) with the Magic Wand tool, and then release the key.

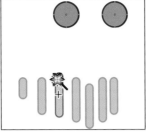

This adds all of the shapes filled with that same orange color to the selection.

5   With the Magic Wand tool still selected, hold down the Option (Mac OS) key or Alt (Windows) key and notice that a minus sign (−) appears next to the pointer. Click one of the orange shapes to deselect all of the shapes with that same fill, and then release the key. The red circles should still be selected.

6   Choose Select > Deselect, or click where there are no objects.

Selecting similar objects

You can also select objects based on similar fill color, stroke color, stroke weight, and more, using the Select Similar Objects button or the Select > Same command. The stroke of an object is the outline (border), and the stroke weight is the width of the stroke. Next, you will select several objects with the same fill and stroke applied.

1   Select the Selection tool (▶) and click to select one of the red circles.

2   Click the arrow to the right of the Select Similar Objects button (▨ ▾) in the Control panel to show a menu. Choose Fill Color to select all objects on any artboard with the same fill color (red) as the selected object.

Notice that the circles with the same red-colored fill are selected.

3   Click to select one of the orange shapes, and then choose Select > Same > Fill & Stroke.

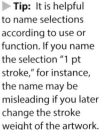

All of the orange-filled shapes with the same stroke and fill and are now selected.

If you know that you may need to reselect a series of objects again, like the orange objects, you can save the selection you make so that you can easily recall it later. That's what you'll do next.

4   With the orange shapes still selected, choose Select > Save Selection. Name the selection **RobotMouth** in the Save Selection dialog box, and click OK so that you'll be able to choose this selection at a later time.

5   Choose Select > Deselect.

▶ **Tip:** It is helpful to name selections according to use or function. If you name the selection "1 pt stroke," for instance, the name may be misleading if you later change the stroke weight of the artwork.

Selecting in Outline mode

By default, Adobe Illustrator displays all artwork with their paint attributes, like fill and stroke, showing. However, you can choose to display artwork so that only its outlines (or paths) are visible. The next method for selecting involves viewing artwork in Outline mode and can be very useful if you want to select objects within a series of stacked objects.

1   Choose View > Fit Artboard In Window to fit the artboard with the orange shapes into the Document window.

2   With the Selection tool (▶), click within the gray half-circle shape at the bottom of the artboard to select it. This will become the body of the robot.

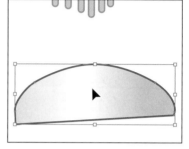

Since the shape has a fill (a color, pattern, or gradient filling the inside an object), you can click anywhere within the bounds of the object to select it.

3   Choose Select > Deselect, to deselect the shape.

4   Choose View > Outline to view the artwork as outlines.

5   With the Selection tool, click inside that same half-circle shape.

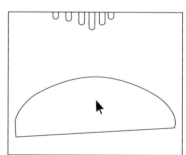

Notice that you cannot select the object using this method. Outline mode displays artwork as outlines with no fill. To select in Outline mode, you can click the edge of the object or drag a marquee across the shape to select it.

6   Click the Previous artboard button (◀) in the lower-left corner of the Document window to fit the first artboard in the window.

7   On the left artboard, with the Selection tool selected, drag a marquee across the right (smaller) ellipse that makes the robot's eye. Press the Left Arrow key several times to move the ellipse so that it almost touches the ellipse to the left.

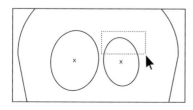
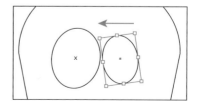

8   Choose View > Preview to see the artwork.

Aligning objects

Illustrator makes it easy to align or distribute multiple objects relative to each other, the artboard, or a key object. In this section, you'll explore the different options for aligning objects.

Aligning objects to each other

The simplest type of alignment is aligning objects to each other, and that's what you'll do next.

1 Choose Select > RobotMouth to reselect the orange shapes.

2 Click the Next artboard button () in the lower-left corner of the Document window to fit the artboard with the orange and red shapes in the window.

3 Select the Zoom tool () in the Tools panel, and drag a marquee around the series of orange-filled shapes to zoom in.

4 Choose Align To Selection from the Align To button () in the Control panel, if it's not already selected, to ensure that the selected objects are aligned to each other.

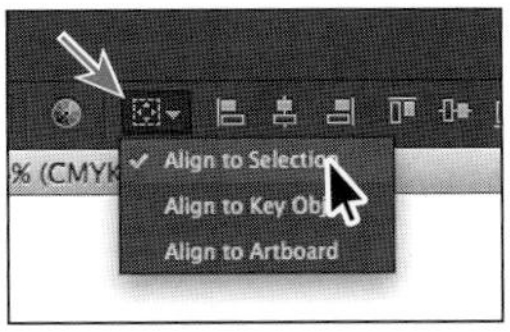

5 Click the Vertical Align Bottom button () in the Control panel.

Notice that the bottom edges of all the orange objects move to align with the lowest orange object.

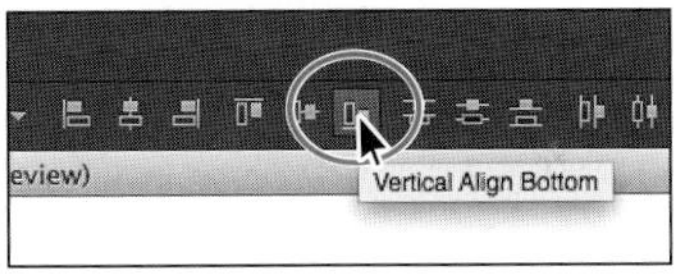

Note: The Align options may not appear in the Control panel. If you don't see the Align options, click the word "Align" in the Control panel to open the Align panel. The number of options displayed in the Control panel depends on your screen resolution.

6 Choose Edit > Undo Align to return the objects to their original positions. Leave the objects selected for the next section.

Aligning to a key object

A *key object* is an object that you want other objects to align to. You specify a key object by selecting all the objects you want to align, including the key object, and then clicking the key object again. When selected, the key object has a thick outline, and the Align To Key Object icon () appears in the Control panel and the Align panel. Next, you will align the orange shapes.

Note: The key object outline color is determined by the layer color that the object is on.

Tip: In the Align panel, you can choose Show Options from the panel menu () and then choose Align To Key Object from the Align To option. The object that is in front becomes the key object.

1 With the orange shapes still selected, click the leftmost shape with the Selection tool ().

The thick blue outline indicates that the leftmost shape is the key object that other objects will align to.

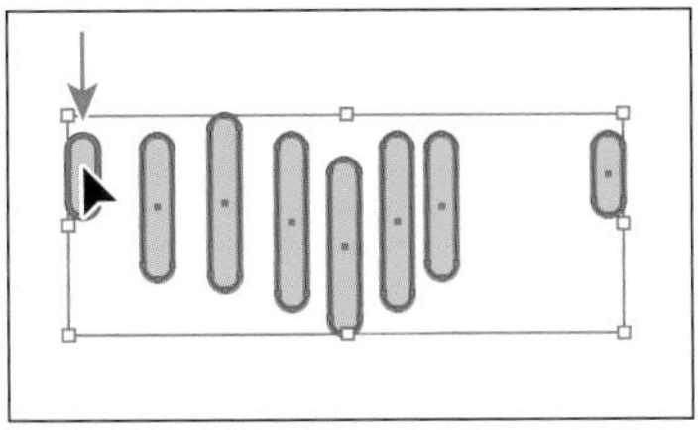

Note: To stop aligning and distributing relative to an object, click the object again to remove the blue outline, or choose Cancel Key Object from the Align panel menu (⊟).

2   Click the Vertical Align Top button (⬛) in the Align options in the Control panel. Notice that all of the orange shapes move to align to the top edge of the key object.

3   Choose Select > Deselect.

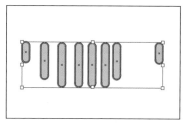

Aligning anchor points

Next, you'll align two anchor points to each other using the Align options. Like setting a key object in the previous section, you can also set a key anchor point that other anchor points will align to.

1   Choose View > Fit Artboard In Window.

2   Select the Direct Selection tool (▷), and click the lower-left point of the gray half-circle at the bottom of the artboard. Shift-click to select the lower-right point of the same gray half-circle.

You select the points in a specific order because the last selected anchor point is the key anchor point. Other points align to this point.

3   Click the Vertical Align Top button (⬛) in the Control panel. The first anchor point selected aligns to the second anchor point selected.

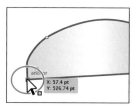 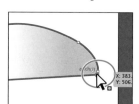 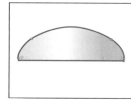

Select the first point.   Select the second point.   After aligning the points.

4   Choose Select > Deselect.

Distributing objects

Distributing objects using the Align panel enables you to select multiple objects and to distribute the spacing between those objects equally. Next, you will make the spacing between the orange shapes even, using a distribution method.

Note: Using the Horizontal or Vertical Distribute Center buttons distributes the spacing equally between the *centers* of the objects. If the selected objects are not the same size, unexpected results may occur.

1   Select the Selection tool (▶) in the Tools panel. Choose Select > RobotMouth to reselect all of the orange shapes.

2   Click the Horizontal Distribute Center button (⬛) in the Control panel.

Distributing moves all of the orange shapes so that the spacing between the *center* of each of them is equal.

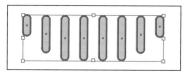

3   Choose Edit > Undo Align.

4   Choose Select > Deselect.

5   Choose View > Zoom In, twice, to zoom in to the orange shapes.

6   With the Selection tool selected, hold
    down the Shift key and click/drag the
    rightmost orange shape slightly to the
    left. Stop dragging just before the shape
    touches the orange shape to its left. Release
    the mouse button and then the key.

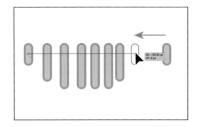

    The Shift key keeps the shape aligned
    vertically with the other shapes.

7   Choose Select > RobotMouth to select all of
    the orange shapes again, and then click the
    Horizontal Distribute Center button (▥)
    again. Notice that, with the rightmost shape
    repositioned, the objects move to redistribute
    the spacing between the centers.

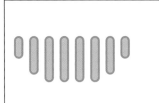

8   Choose Select > Deselect.

● **Note:** When
distributing objects
horizontally, make sure
that the leftmost and
rightmost objects are
where you want them,
and then distribute the
objects between them.
For vertical distribution,
position the topmost
and bottommost
objects, and then
distribute the objects
between them.

Aligning to the artboard

You can also align content to the artboard rather than to a selection or a key object.
Aligning to the artboard aligns each selected object separately to the artboard. Next,
you'll get the gray half-circle shape on the artboard with the rest of the robot and
align it to the bottom, center of the artboard.

1   With the Selection tool (▶) selected, click the gray half-circle shape at the
    bottom of the artboard to select it. Choose Edit > Cut.

2   Click the Previous artboard button (◀) in the lower-left corner of the Document
    window to navigate to the first (left) artboard in the document, which contains
    the robot head.

3   Choose Edit > Paste to paste the gray half-circle.

4   Click the Align To Selection button (▦▾) in the Control panel, and choose
    Align To Artboard in the menu that appears. Selected content will now align to
    the artboard.

▶ **Tip:** If you need a
refresher on the Align
To Selection button,
refer back to the
"Aligning objects to
each other" section.

5   Click the Horizontal Align Center button
    (▤) (just in case), and then click the
    Vertical Align Bottom button (▥) to align
    the selection to the horizontal center and
    vertical bottom of the artboard.

6   Choose Select > Deselect.

Working with groups

You can combine objects into a group so that the objects are treated as a single unit. This way, you can move or transform a number of objects without affecting their individual attributes or relative positions.

Grouping items

Next, you will select multiple objects and create a group from them.

1 Choose View > Fit All In Window to see both artboards.

2 Choose Select > RobotMouth to reselect the series of orange shapes.

Tip: One way to select the objects in a group individually is to select the group and then choose Object > Ungroup. This ungroups them permanently.

3 Choose Object > Group, and notice that the word "Group" appears in the Selection Indicator on the left side of the Control panel with the shapes still selected.

4 Choose Select > Deselect.

5 With the Selection tool (▶) selected, click one of the orange shapes in the group. Because they are grouped together, all are now selected.

6 Drag the group of orange shapes onto the robot head (below the eyes).

7 Choose Select > Deselect.

Working in Isolation mode

Isolation mode isolates groups or sublayers so that you can easily select and edit specific objects or parts of objects without having to ungroup the objects. When in Isolation mode, all objects outside of the isolated group are locked and dimmed so that they aren't affected by the edits you make.

Next, you will edit a group using Isolation mode.

1 With the Selection tool (▶), click the robot's hand at the end of the longer arm. You will see that it selects a group of shapes that make up the hand.

Tip: To enter Isolation mode, you can also select a group with the Selection tool, and then click the Isolate Selected Object button (▣) in the Control panel.

2 Double-click a shape in that hand to enter Isolation mode.

3 Choose View > Fit Artboard In Window, and notice that the rest of the content in the document appears dimmed (you can't select it).

At the top of the Document window, a gray bar appears with the words "Layer 1" and "<Group>." This indicates that you have isolated a group of objects that is on Layer 1. You will learn more about layers in Lesson 8.

4 Choose View > Smart Guides to turn them off. This way, when you drag content, it won't snap to other content.

5 Drag the light-gray circle down to approximately match the position of the circle shape in the other hand.

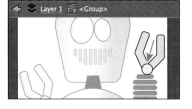

When you enter Isolation mode, groups are temporarily ungrouped. This enables you to edit objects in the group or to add new content without having to ungroup.

6 Double-click outside of the shapes within the group to exit Isolation mode.

7 Click to select the circle shape. Notice that it is once again grouped with the rest of the shapes in the hand, and you can also select other objects.

8 Choose Select > Deselect.

▶ **Tip:** To exit Isolation mode, you can also click the gray arrow in the upper-left corner of the Document window, or deselect all content and click the Exit Isolation Mode button (◄) in the Control panel. You can also press the Escape key when in Isolation mode or double-click a blank area of the Document window to exit Isolation mode.

Creating a nested group

Groups can also be *nested*—grouped within other objects or grouped to form larger groups. Nesting is a common technique used when designing artwork. It's a great way to keep associated content together.

In this section, you will explore how to create a nested group.

1 With the Selection tool (▶), drag a marquee across the series of black shapes below the hand that make up the longer arm of the robot.

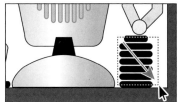

2 Choose Object > Group.

3 With the Selection tool, Shift-click the hand above the arm to select that group as well. Choose Object > Group.

You have created a *nested group*—a group that is combined with other objects or groups to form a larger group.

4 Choose Select > Deselect.

5 With the Selection tool, click one of the grouped objects in that same arm. All objects in the nested group become selected.

6 Click a blank area on the artboard to deselect the objects.

Next, you will explore the Group Selection (▶+) tool.

7   Hold down the Direct Selection tool ( ) in the Tools panel to reveal more tools. Click the Group Selection tool (⁺) to select it. The Group Selection tool adds the object's parent group(s) to the current selection.

8   Click one of the shapes in the same robot hand to select it. Click again, on the same shape, to select the object's parent group (the group of hand shapes). Click once more, on that same shape, to select the group composed of the hand and arm. The Group Selection tool adds each group to the selection in the order in which it was grouped.

 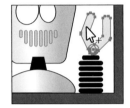 

Click once. | Click twice to select the parent group. | Click a third time to select all artwork in the nested group.

9   Choose Select > Deselect.

● **Note:** To ungroup ALL of the selected objects, even the hand and arm shapes, you would choose Object > Ungroup twice.

10 With the Selection tool, click any of the objects in the nested group to select the group. Choose Object > Ungroup to ungroup the objects.

11 Choose Select > Deselect.

12 Click to select the hand. Notice that it is still a group of objects.

Exploring object arrangement

▶ **Tip:** To learn more about objects and stacking order, see the PDF "Stack_order.pdf" in the Lessons > Lesson_extras folder.

As you create objects, Illustrator stacks them in order on the artboards, beginning with the first object created. The order in which objects are stacked (called *stacking order*) determines how they display when they overlap. You can change the stacking order of objects in your artwork at any time, using either the Layers panel or Object > Arrange commands.

Arranging objects

Next, you will work with the Arrange commands to change how objects are stacked.

1   Choose View > Fit All In Window to see both artboards in the document.

2   With the Selection tool ( ) selected, click to select the black shape below the robot's head (the robot's "neck").

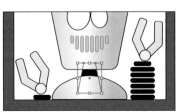

3   Choose Object > Arrange > Send To Back to send the shape behind the robot's head.

4 Click to select either of the red circles on the right artboard.

5 Drag the selected circle on top of the smaller eye for the robot. Release the mouse, and notice that the red circle disappears, but it's still selected.

It went behind the ellipse (the eye) because it was probably created before the eye shape, which means it is lower in the stacking order.

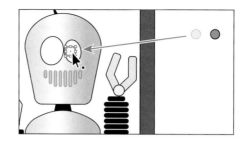

6 With the red circle still selected, choose Object > Arrange > Bring to Front. This brings the red circle to the front of the stack, making it the topmost object.

Selecting objects behind

When you stack objects on top of each other, sometimes it becomes difficult to select objects that are underneath other objects. Next, you will learn how to select an object through a stack of objects.

1 With the Selection tool (), select the other red circle on the right artboard, drag it onto the larger robot eye shape on the left artboard, and then release the mouse.

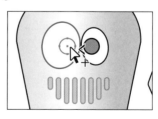

Notice that this circle disappears like the other, but is still selected. This time, you will deselect the circle and then reselect it using another method.

2 Choose Select > Deselect, and the red circle is no longer selected.

3 With the pointer positioned over the location of the second red circle you just deselected, the one behind the eye shape, hold down the Command (Mac OS) or Ctrl (Windows) key and click until the circle is selected again (this may take several clicks).

4 Choose Object > Arrange > Bring To Front to bring the circle on top of the eye.

5 Choose Select > Deselect.

● **Note:** You may see an angle bracket displayed with the pointer ().

● **Note:** To select the hidden red circle, make sure that you click where the circle and the eye overlap. Otherwise, you won't be able to select the red circle.

Hiding and locking objects

Tip: To learn more selection techniques, see the PDF named "Selections.pdf" in the Lesson_extras folder in the Lessons folder.

When working on complex artwork, it may become more difficult to make selections. In this section, you'll learn how to lock and hide content to make selecting objects easier.

1 Choose View > Fit Artboard In Window.

2 Choose Object > Show All to reveal a mask over the robot's eyes. Choose Object > Arrange > Bring To Front to bring the mask to the front.

3 With the Selection tool (▶), click to attempt to select one of the eyes.

   Notice that you can't, since the mask is on top of them. In order to access the eyes, you could use one of the methods we previously discussed or use one of two other methods: hide or lock.

4 With the mask still selected, choose Object > Hide > Selection, or press Command+3 (Mac OS) or Ctrl+3 (Windows). The mask is hidden so that you can more easily select other objects. (This is how we hid the mask when we set up the file.)

5 Click to select one of the red circles in the eyes, and move it.

6 Choose Object > Show All to show the mask again.

7 With the mask selected, choose Object > Lock > Selection, or press Command+2 (Mac OS) or Ctrl+2 (Windows).

   The mask is still visible, but you cannot select it.

8 With the Selection tool, click to select one of the eye shapes.

9 Choose Object > Unlock All, and then choose Object > Hide > Selection to hide the mask again.

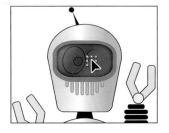

10 Choose View > Smart Guides to turn them on.

11 Choose File > Save, to save the file, and then choose File > Close.

Review questions

1 How can you select an object that has no fill?

2 Explain two ways you can select an item in a group without choosing Object > Ungroup.

3 Of the two Selection tools (Selection [➤] and Direct Selection [➤]), which allows you to edit the individual anchor points of an object?

4 What should you do after creating a selection that you are going to use repeatedly?

5 Sometimes you are unable to select an object because it is underneath another object. Explain two ways to get around this issue.

6 To align objects to the artboard, what do you need to first select in the Align panel or Control panel before you choose an alignment option?

Review answers

1 You can select an object that has no fill by clicking the stroke or by dragging a marquee across any part of the object.

2 Using the Group Selection tool (➤⁺), you can click once to select an individual item within a group. Click again to add the next grouped items to the selection. Read Lesson 8, "Organizing Your Artwork with Layers," to see how you can use layers to make complex selections. You can also double-click the group to enter Isolation mode, edit the shapes as needed, and then exit Isolation mode by pressing the Escape key or by double-clicking outside of the group.

3 Using the Direct Selection tool (➤), you can select one or more individual anchor points and make changes to the shape of an object.

4 For any selection that you anticipate using again, choose Select > Save Selection. Name the selection so that you can reselect it at any time from the Select menu.

5 If your access to an object is blocked, you can choose Object > Hide > Selection to hide the blocking object. The object is not deleted. It is just hidden in the same position until you choose Object > Show All. You can also use the Selection tool (➤) to select an object that's behind other objects by pressing the Command (Mac OS) or Ctrl (Windows) key, and then clicking on the overlapping objects until the object you want to select is selected.

6 To align objects to an artboard, first select the Align To Artboard option.

3 USING SHAPES TO CREATE ARTWORK FOR A POSTCARD

Lesson overview

In this lesson, you'll learn how to do the following:

- Create a document with multiple artboards.

- Use tools and commands to create basic shapes.

- Understand Live Shapes.

- Scale and duplicate objects.

- Join and outline objects.

- Edit strokes with the Width tool.

- Work with the Shape Builder tool.

- Work with Pathfinder commands to create shapes.

- Work with drawing modes.

- Use Image Trace to create shapes.

 This lesson takes approximately 90 minutes to complete.

Download the project files for this lesson from the Lesson & Update Files tab on your Account page at www.peachpit.com and store them on your computer in a convenient location, as described in the Getting Started section of this book.

Your Account page is also where you'll find any updates to the chapters or to the lesson files. Look on the Lesson & Update Files tab to access the most current content.

You can create documents with multiple artboards and many kinds of objects by starting with a basic shape, and then editing it to create new shapes. In this lesson, you'll create a new document, and then create and edit some basic shapes for a postcard.

Getting started

In this lesson, you'll explore the different methods for creating artwork using the shape tools and various creation methods to create artwork for a postcard.

1 To ensure that the tools and panels function exactly as described in this lesson, delete or deactivate (by renaming) the Adobe Illustrator CC preferences file. See "Restoring default preferences" in the Getting Started section at the beginning of the book.

2 Start Adobe Illustrator CC.

● **Note:** If you have not already downloaded the project files for this lesson to your computer from your Account page, make sure to do so now. See the "Getting Started" section at the beginning of the book.

● **Note:** In Mac OS, when opening lesson files, you may need to click the round, green button in the upper-left corner of the Document window to maximize the window's size.

3 Choose File > Open. Locate the file named L3_end.ai, which is in the Lesson03 folder in the Lessons folder that you copied onto your hard disk. These are the finished illustrations that you will create in this lesson.

4 Choose View > Fit All In Window and leave the file open for reference, or choose File > Close.

Creating a new document

You will now create a document for the postcard that will have two artboards, each with content that you will later combine.

1 Choose File > New to open a new, untitled document. In the New Document dialog box, change the following options:

-   Name: **Postcard**
-   Profile: Choose **Print** (the default setting).
-   Number Of Artboards: **2** (to create two artboards). (When you change the number of artboards, the Profile changes to [Custom].)
-   Arrange By Row (⮕): **Selected**
-   Make sure that the Left To Right Layout arrow (⮕) is showing.

Next, you'll jump to the units so that the rest of the changes are in inches.

-   Units: **Inches**
-   Spacing: **1** (The spacing value is the distance between each artboard.)
-   Width: **6 in** (You don't need to type the **in** for inches, since the units are set to inches.)
-   Height: **4 in**

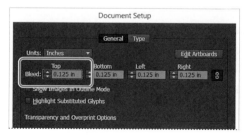

Note: You can set up a document for different kinds of output, such as print, Web, video, and more, by choosing a Profile. For example, if you are designing a Web-page mockup, you can use a Web document profile, which automatically displays the page size and units in pixels, changes the color mode to RGB, and changes the raster effects to Screen (72 ppi).

2 Click OK in the New Document dialog box.

3 Choose File > Save As. In the Save As dialog box, ensure that the name of the file is **Postcard.ai** (Mac OS) or **Postcard** (Windows), and choose the Lesson03 folder. Leave the Format option set to Adobe Illustrator (ai) (Mac OS) or Save As Type option set to Adobe Illustrator (*.AI) (Windows), and click Save. In the Illustrator Options dialog box, leave the Illustrator options at their default settings and click OK.

▶ **Tip:** To learn more about the New Document dialog options, search for "New document dialog" in Illustrator Help (Help > Illustrator Help).

4 Click the Document Setup button in the Control panel.

The Document Setup dialog box is where you can change the artboard size (by clicking the Edit Artboards button), units, bleeds, and more, after a document is created.

Note: If the Document Setup button does not appear in the Control panel, it may mean that content in the document is selected. You can also choose File > Document Setup.

5 In the Bleed section of the Document Setup dialog box, change the value in the Top field to **0.125 in**, either by clicking the Up Arrow to the left of the field once or by typing the value, and all four fields change. Click OK.

Notice the red line that appears around both artboards. The red line indicates the bleed area. Typical bleeds for printing are about 1/8 of an inch, but it can depend on the printing vendor.

Note: You could have set up the bleeds when you first set up the document in the New Document dialog box by choosing File > New.

Working with basic shapes

In the first part of this lesson, you'll create some lamps for the postcard using basic shapes, like rectangles, ellipses, rounded rectangles, and polygons. You'll begin this exercise by setting up the workspace.

1 Choose Window > Workspace > Essentials (if it's not already selected), and then choose Window > Workspace > Reset Essentials.

▶ Tip: You can also show/hide rulers by pressing Command+R (Mac OS) or Ctrl+R (Windows).

2 Choose View > Rulers > Show Rulers to display rulers along the top and left side of the Document window (if they are not already showing).

The ruler units are inches because you specified them in the New Document dialog box. You can change the ruler units for all documents or for the current document only. The ruler unit shows when measuring objects, moving and transforming objects, setting grid and guide spacing, and creating shapes. It does not affect the units used in the Character, Paragraph, and Stroke panels. The units used in these panels can be changed by choosing (Illustrator > Preferences > Units [Mac OS] or Edit > Preferences > Units [Windows]).

Creating rectangles

● Note: As you go through this section, know that you don't have to match the sizes of the drawn shapes exactly. They are just there as a guide.

First, you'll create a series of rectangles that will be the start of a lamp on the postcard. Rectangles and rounded rectangles are considered Live Shapes. This means that attributes like width, height, rotation, corner radius, and corner style are still editable later and are retained even if you scale or rotate the shape.

1 Make sure that the number 1 is showing in the Artboard Navigation area in the lower-left corner of the Document window, which indicates that the first artboard is showing. Choose View > Fit Artboard In Window.

2 Select the Rectangle tool (▨) in the Tools panel. Position the pointer anywhere in the artboard, and click and drag down and to the right. As you drag, notice the gray tool tip that appears indicating width and height. Drag until the rectangle is approximately 1.5 in wide and has a height of 1 in, as seen in the tool tip next to the cursor.

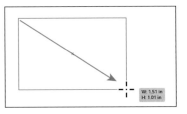

As you drag to create shapes, the tool tip that appears next to the pointer is called the *measurement label* and is a part of the Smart Guides (View > Smart Guides), which will be discussed later in this lesson. When you release the mouse button, the rectangle is selected. Also, by default, shapes are filled with a white color and have a black stroke (border). A shape with a fill can be selected and moved by first positioning the pointer anywhere inside the shape and then clicking and dragging.

After drawing a shape, you can easily edit its size, position, and more using any number of methods.

3   Choose Window > Transform. In the Transform panel that appears, change the size of the selected object by typing **0.9** for the width (W:) and **0.35** for the height (H:). Typing the **in** for inches isn't necessary; it is added automatically.

From the Transform panel, you can change the appearance of your Live Rectangle, including its dimensions, rotation, and corner properties. The center point of the rectangle lets you drag to align the object with other elements in your artwork.

4   Change the X value to **4.9** and the Y value to **3.6** to move the rectangle *relative to* the upper-left corner of the artboard. Press Enter or Return after typing in the Y value to accept it.

Tip: Holding down the Option (Mac OS) or Alt (Windows) key as you drag with the Rectangle, Rounded Rectangle, or Ellipse tool draws a shape from its center point rather than from its upper-left corner. Holding down the Shift key as you draw with the Rectangle, Rounded Rectangle, or Ellipse tool selected draws a shape in perfect proportion (a square, rounded corner square, or circle).

Tip: If you would like the Transform panel to open every time you create a rectangle or rounded rectangle, you can choose Show On Rectangle Creation in the Transform panel menu (▾≣) to toggle it on and off.

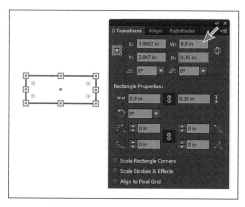

Change the width and height.

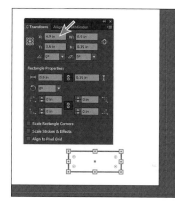

Change the position.

5   With the new rectangle still selected, click the Fill color (▢▾) in the Control panel to open the Swatches panel. When you position the pointer over colors in the panel, a tool tip with the color name appears. We chose a yellow/green swatch with the tool tip that shows "C=20 M=0 Y=100 K=0."

6   Press the Escape key to hide the Swatches panel.

Next, you will create another rectangle by entering values (like Width and Height) rather than by drawing it. Using any of the shape tools, you can either draw a shape or click on the artboard with a shape tool selected to enter values in a dialog box. This rectangle will become another part of the lamp.

7   With the Rectangle tool still selected, position the pointer above the rectangle you drew on the artboard and click.

The Rectangle dialog box appears. In the Rectangle dialog box, the width and height values that you see match the last shape drawn.

▶ **Tip:** You also could have simply copied and pasted the original rectangle and changed its size and position. You can also Option-drag (Mac OS) or Alt-drag (Windows) a shape to create a copy.

8 In the Rectangle dialog box, change the Width to **0.6 in**, press the Tab key, and change the Height to **0.1**. Click OK.

Notice that the new rectangle has the same fill color and stroke as the previous shape you drew.

9 Select the Selection tool (▸) in the Tools panel. Drag the new rectangle about halfway up the artboard, above the first rectangle you drew.

This is just to get the shape out of the way of some new shapes you will be creating.

10 With the new rectangle still selected, click the Fill color in the Control panel to open the Swatches panel. Choose the yellow swatch with the tool tip that shows "C=5 M=0 Y=90 K=0." Press the Escape key to hide the Swatches panel.

Working with the document grid

The grid allows you to work more precisely by creating a series of non-printing horizontal and vertical guides behind your artwork in the Document window that objects can snap to. To turn the grid on and use its features, do the following:

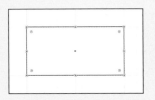

- To show the grid, choose View > Show Grid. To hide the grid, choose View > Hide Grid.

- To snap objects to the gridlines, choose View > Snap To Grid, select the object you want to move, and drag it to the desired location. When the object's boundaries come within 2 pixels of a gridline, it snaps to the point.

- To specify grid properties such as the spacing between gridlines, grid style (lines or dots), grid color, or whether grids appear in the front or back of artwork, choose Illustrator > Preferences > Guides & Grid (Mac OS) or Edit > Preferences > Guides & Grid (Windows).

—From Illustrator Help

Creating a rounded rectangle

Next, you'll create a rectangle with rounded corners for another part of the illustration. You'll also round the corners of one of the existing rectangles. This involves working with Live Corners.

1 Select the Zoom tool (🔍) in the Tools panel, and click once, on the smaller rectangle you created.

2 Click and hold down the mouse button on the Rectangle tool (■), and select the Rounded Rectangle tool (⬭) in the Tools panel.

3 Position the pointer below the smaller rectangle. Click and drag down and to the right until the rectangle has an approximate width of 0.45 inches and a height of 0.2 inches, but *do not release the mouse button yet*. With the mouse button still held down, press the Down Arrow key a few times to see the corner radius become less rounded (the R value in the tool tip). Press the Up Arrow key to see the corner become more rounded. Don't worry about the R (radius) value in the tool tip since we can edit it later, and release the mouse button.

▶ **Tip:** You can also press and hold the Down Arrow or Up Arrow key to change the corner radius faster.

● **Note:** The values you see in the measurement label may not be the same as you see in the figure, and that's okay.

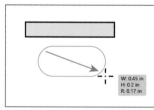

Draw the rounded rectangle.

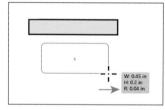

Change the corner radius.

4 With the new rectangle still selected, click the Fill color in the Control panel to open the Swatches panel. Choose the yellow swatch with the tool tip that shows "C=20 M=0 Y=100 K=0." Press the Escape key to hide the Swatches panel.

5 With the rounded rectangle selected, change the upper-left corner radius to **0.05** in by typing the value into the field in the Transform panel. Click in another field, or press the Tab key to see the other corners change as well. The Link Corner Radius Value button (🔗) is on by default.

▶ **Tip:** You can also edit the corner radius and type for all corners at once in the Control panel.

By default, the corners are rounded, but you will see shortly that you can choose from three corner types.

Next, you'll use Smart Guides to help you align the rounded rectangle to the smaller rectangle.

▶ **Tip:** The color of the Smart Guides can be changed from green to another color by choosing Illustrator > Preferences > Smart Guides (Mac OS) or Edit > Preferences > Smart Guides (Windows).

6 Select the Selection tool (▶) in the Tools panel. Drag the rounded rectangle up so that it's centered horizontally with the rectangle above it and so that its top edge snaps to the bottom of that same rectangle, as shown in the figure. When the word "intersect" and the green line(s) appear (Smart Guides), release the mouse button.

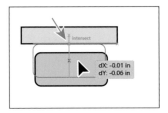

7 With the rounded rectangle selected, click and drag the right, middle bounding point to the right. As you drag, press the Option (Mac OS) or Alt (Windows) key. This allows you to resize from the center of the shape. Drag until the width is approximately 0.5 in, release the mouse button, and then release the modifier key.

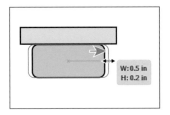

Editing the corners of a Live Shape

After creating a rectangle or rounded rectangle, you can later easily edit the corner radius and the corner type. Next, you will edit the corner radius and type of the larger rectangle you drew.

1 With the Selection tool (▶) selected, click to select the larger rectangle beneath the other two shapes, and notice that the shape has four corner widgets that you can drag to edit all of the corners at one time (an arrow is pointing to one in the figure). You may need to scroll down in the Document window to see it.

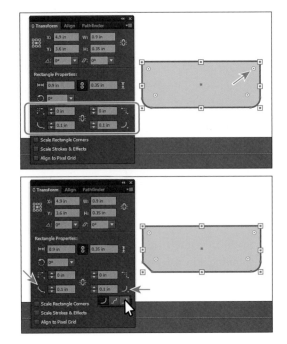

▶ **Tip:** In the Transform panel, with a Live Shape selected, you will see the Scale Rectangle Corners option. With this option selected, if you were to scale the Live Shape larger or smaller, the corner radius would scale as well. Otherwise, without the option selected, the corner radius would stay the same.

2 In the Transform panel, click the Link Corner Radius Values button (🔗) to turn it off. That way you can edit the corners independently. Change the lower-left and lower-right radius values to **0.1 in.**

3 In the Transform panel, click the lower-left Corner Type button and select the Chamfer option to edit the type of corner. Do the same for the lower-right corner type (shown in the figure).

Another method for editing the corners of a Live Shape involves editing the corner widgets directly on the selected shape(s), which is what you'll do next. You may want to zoom in further to the selected rectangle.

4   Choose Select > Deselect.

5   Select the Direct Selection tool (◄) and drag a marquee across the top half of the rectangle to select the top two corner points.

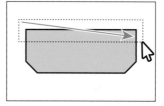

Notice that there are now two corner widgets showing, one for each of the selected anchor points. Using the following method allows you to edit the corner radius and type for only the selected anchor points in one shape or across multiple shapes.

6   Click either corner widget and drag it toward the center of the shape without worrying about how much right now. The corners of a drawn shape are referred to as Live Corners.

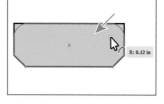

If you were drag too far, you would see a bold red line appear, indicating that you can drag no further.

7   Double-click either corner widget to open the Corners dialog box. In the dialog box, change the Radius value to **0.15 in** and click OK.

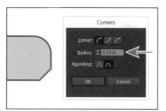

▶ **Tip:** You can Option-click (Mac OS) or Alt-click (Windows) a corner widget in a shape to cycle through the different corner types.

The Corners dialog box allows you to edit the corner type and radius, but it also has an extra option called Rounding for setting absolute versus relative rounding. Absolute means the rounded corner is exactly the radius value. Relative makes the radius value based on the angle of the corner point.

8   Click the word Corners in the Control panel to show the same Corners options as a menu. Change the Corner Radius value to **0** (zero) and click away from the shape to deselect it.

Setting the radius to 0 (zero) for the selected anchor points is one way of removing the corner radius from the selected anchor points.

9   Choose View > Fit Artboard In Window.

10 Choose File > Save and leave the Transform panel open.

Creating an ellipse

Next, you'll draw an ellipse using the Ellipse tool (⬤) to make up the next part of the lamp. The Ellipse tool can draw perfect circles when you press and hold the Shift key as you draw, or it can draw an ellipse without a modifier key.

1   Click and hold down the mouse button on the Rounded Rectangle tool (▣) in the Tools panel, and select the Ellipse tool (⬤).

2   Choose View > Smart Guides to turn them off. Next, you will create a shape with no Smart Guides turned on to see the difference.

3   Position the pointer over a blank area of the artboard. Begin dragging down and to the right to draw a circle that isn't very large (see the figure).

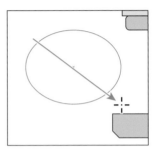

Notice that you cannot see the size of the circle in the measurement tool tip, since the tool tip is part of the Smart Guides that were turned off. The green alignment guides are also not showing, since the shape is not snapping to other content on the artboard. Smart Guides can be useful in certain situations, such as when more precision is necessary, and can be toggled on and off when needed.

● **Note:** An ellipse is not a Live Shape like a rectangle or rounded rectangle, so you will see "No Shape Properties" in the Transform panel.

4   Select the Selection tool (▶), and in the Transform panel, ensure that the Constrain Width And Height Proportions is turned off. Change the Width to **1.35 in** and the Height to **1.2 in**.

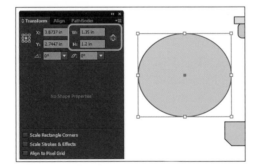

5   Choose View > Hide Bounding Box.

The bounding box, as you saw in previous lessons, allows you to transform the shape. With the bounding box not showing, you can drag the shape by an edge or an anchor point without transforming it.

6   Choose View > Smart Guides to turn them back on.

2 Click and drag slowly to the right to create a star shape. Notice that as you move the pointer, the star changes size and rotates freely. Without releasing the mouse button, stop dragging and press the Down Arrow key once (to decrease the number of points on the star to four). Drag the mouse until you see a width of approximately 0.5 in and stop dragging. Release the mouse button.

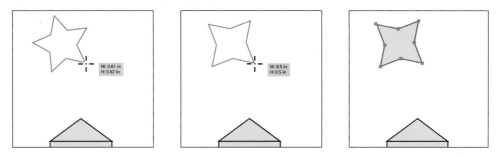

3 Delete the star you just created.

Next, you will create a star that is straight (constrained), and has arms that are a little longer. This requires that you edit the star you create using two keyboard modifiers.

4 Click and drag slowly to the right to create a star shape. Notice that it has the same number of points as the last star you created (four). Drag until you see a width of approximately 0.5 in, then press the Command (Mac OS) or Ctrl (Windows) key, and continue dragging to the right. This keeps the inner radius constant, making the arms longer. Drag until you see a width of approximately 0.65 in and stop dragging, *without releasing the mouse button*. Release the Ctrl or Command key, but not the mouse. Hold down the Shift key, and ensure that the star has a width of about 0.8 in. Release the mouse button, and then release the Shift key, and you should see a star.

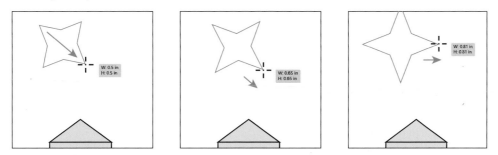

The next time you draw a star, it will have the same settings. If you want to practice creating another star, try using the keyboard modifiers you've explored. Remember, do not release the mouse button until you are sure you are finished drawing the star. If you do try a few more, delete them and then select the star you made in this step before moving on. Your star doesn't have to exactly match the stars in the figures.

▶ **Tip:** You can also click in the Document window with the Star tool (⭐) and edit the options in the Star dialog box instead of drawing it.

5   Change the Stroke weight of the selected star, to the right of the word "Stroke" in the Control panel, to **0**.

6   Change the Fill color in the Control panel to the orange color with the tool tip "C=0 M=80 Y=95 K=0." Press the Escape key to hide the Swatches panel.

7   Select the Selection tool (➤) and Option-drag (Mac OS) or Alt-drag (Windows) to create a copy of the star (see the following figure). Release the mouse button and then the key.

8   Change the Fill color of the copy in the Control panel to the red color with the tool tip "C=15 M=100 Y=90 K=10."

9   Choose Select > Deselect.

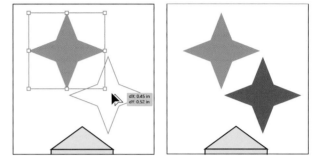

Changing stroke width and alignment

So far in this lesson, you've edited the fill of shapes, but haven't touched the strokes (a visible outline or border of an object or path). Every shape and path, by default, is created with a 1-point black stroke. You can easily change the color of a stroke or the weight of a stroke to make it thinner or thicker. Strokes are also aligned to the center of a path edge by default, but you can change the alignment as well using the Stroke panel.

1   Click to select the bottom rectangle beneath the circle.

●**Note:** You can also open the Stroke panel by choosing Window > Stroke, but you may need to choose Show Options from the panel menu (▾).

2   Select the Zoom tool (🔍) in the Tools panel, and click that rectangle once to zoom in. You may need to move the Transform panel out of your way.

3   Click the word "Stroke" in the Control panel to open the Stroke panel. In the Stroke panel, change the Stroke weight to **5 pt**. Notice that the stroke of the rectangle is centered on the edge of the shape by default.

4   Click the Align Stroke To Inside button (▣) in the Stroke panel. This aligns the stroke to the inside edge of the rectangle.

●**Note:** Going forward, you will find that by opening a panel in the Control panel (such as the Stroke panel in this step), you will need to hide it before moving on. You can do this by pressing the Escape key.

5   With the rectangle still selected, click the Stroke color in the Control panel (to the left of the word "Stroke"), and change the stroke color to the yellow used earlier, the one with the tool tip "C=5 M=0 Y=90 K=0." Press the Escape key to hide the panel.

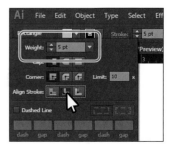

6 Press Shift+X to swap the stroke and fill colors.

7 Choose Select > Deselect.

● **Note:** If pressing Shift+X doesn't work, you can also click the Swap Fill And Stroke arrow (⬚) toward the bottom of the Tools panel.

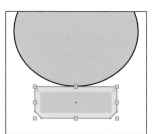 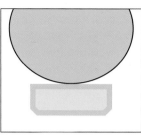

8 Choose File > Save.

About aligning strokes

If an object is a closed path (such as a square), you can select an option in the Stroke panel to align the stroke along the path to the center (default), inside, or outside:

Align Stroke To Center   Align Stroke To Inside   Align Stroke To Outside

Working with lines

Next, you'll work with straight lines and line segments, known as *open paths*, to create another lamp. Shapes can be created in many ways in Illustrator, and the simpler way is usually better.

1 Choose View > Fit Artboard In Window.

2 Select the Zoom tool (🔍) in the Tools panel, and click once in the empty area near the upper-left corner of the artboard to zoom in.

3 Choose Reset Essentials from the workspace switcher in the Application bar.

So far, you've been working in the default Preview mode, which lets you see how objects are painted with fill and stroke colors. If paint attributes seem distracting, you can work in Outline mode, which you'll do next.

4 Choose View > Outline to switch from Preview to Outline mode.

● **Note:** Outline mode temporarily removes all paint attributes, such as colored fills and strokes, to speed up selecting and redrawing artwork. You can't select or drag shapes by clicking in the middle of a shape, because the fill temporarily disappears.

5 Click and hold down the mouse button on the Star tool (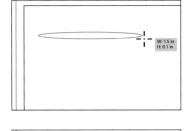) in the Tools panel, and select the Ellipse tool ( ). In a blank area near the top of the artboard, draw an ellipse that has a width of 1.5 in and a height of 0.1 in, as shown in the measurement label that appears.

Note: When you drag to select, make sure that you do not drag across the points on the left and right ends of the ellipse.

6 Select the Direct Selection tool ( ) in the Tools panel. Drag across the top anchor point to select it. See the figure for where to create the selection.

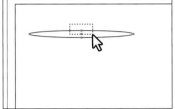

Dragging across a path will select the line segment and anchor points associated with it. If you drag across an anchor point in a path, you also select the line segments on either side of the anchor point.

Tip: Another method for cutting a path is to use either the Scissors tool or the Knife tool. You will learn about using the Scissors tool ( ) and Knife tool ( ) for cutting paths in Lesson 5, "Creating an Illustration with the Drawing Tools."

7 Choose Edit > Cut, and then choose Edit > Paste In Front to create a new path that is directly on top of the original.

This copies and pastes only the top half of the ellipse as a single path, because that is what you selected with the Direct Selection tool.

8 Select the Selection tool ( ), and select the bottom half of the shape. Press Shift+Down Arrow five times to move the line down.

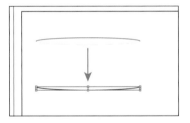

Pressing an arrow key will move a selected object 1 pt, by default. Pressing Shift+arrow will move an object 10 pts per arrow keypress.

9 Choose View > Fit Artboard In Window.

10 Select the Line Segment tool ( ) in the Tools panel. Position the point over the center of the path you just moved down (see the red X in the figure). When the word "anchor" appears, press the Shift key and drag down until you see roughly D: 2.5 in. The "D:" in the measurement label is Distance. Release the mouse button and then the Shift key.

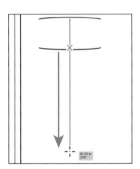

11 With the line selected, change the Stroke weight to **9 pt** and change the Stroke color to Black in the Control panel.

12 Choose Select > Deselect, and then choose File > Save.

Joining paths

Suppose you draw a "U" shape and later decide you want to close the shape, essentially joining the ends of the "U" with a straight path. If you select the path, you can use the Join command to create a line segment between the end points, closing the path. When more than one open path is selected, you can join them together to create a closed path. You can also join the end points of two separate paths. Next, you will join the two paths to create a single closed path.

1   Select the Selection tool (▶) in the Tools panel. Drag a selection marquee across the two paths. Make sure not to select the line you just drew.

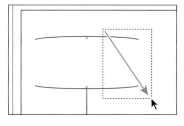

2   Choose Object > Path > Join. Notice that the anchor points on the left side of the paths are now joined with a path.

3   Choose Object > Path > Join once more.

4   Choose Select > Deselect to see the closed path.

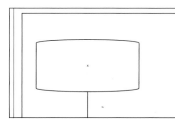

When you apply the Join command to two or more open paths, Illustrator first looks for and joins the paths that have end points stationed closest to each other. This process is repeated every time you apply the Join command until all paths are joined.

> **Tip:** If you want to join specific anchor points from separate paths, select the anchor points and press Command+J (Mac OS) or Ctrl+J (Windows).

> **Tip:** In Lesson 5, "Creating an Illustration with the Drawing Tools," you'll learn about the Join tool (✖), which allows you to join two paths at a corner, keeping the original curve intact.

> ● **Note:** If you only want to fill the shape with a color, it is not necessary to join the path to make a closed path. An open path can have a color fill. It is, however, necessary to join a path if you want a stroke to appear around the entire fill area.

5   Choose View > Preview.

6   Click the joined path to select it and press the letter D to apply the default black 1 pt stroke and white fill. Change the Stroke weight in the Control panel to **2 pt**.

7   Select the Ellipse tool (⬭) in the Tools panel and click the artboard. In the Ellipse dialog box, change the Width to **1.1** and the Height to **0.35**. Click OK.

8   Change the Fill color to Black and change the Stroke weight to **0** in the Control panel.

> ● **Note:** On Windows, if your machine supports it, you may see View > Preview On CPU instead of View > Preview.

9　Press the letter V to select the Selection tool. Drag the ellipse from the center to the bottom of the vertical path you drew. Snap the center to the bottom of the path.

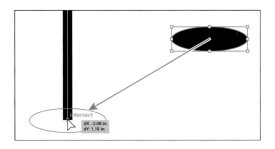

Don't worry if the bottom of the lamp is off the bottom of the artboard. Later, you will align all of the lamps to each other.

Open path vs. closed path

As you draw, you create a line called a *path*. A path is made up of one or more straight or curved segments. The beginning and end of each segment is marked by anchor points, which work like pins holding a wire in place. A path can be closed (for example, a circle), or open, with distinct endpoints (for example, a wavy line).

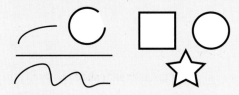

Open paths.   Closed paths.

Both open and closed paths can have fills applied to them.

—From Illustrator Help

Editing and combining paths and shapes

In Illustrator, you can edit and combine paths and shapes in different ways to achieve what you want. This includes working with the Width tool (🖋), outlining strokes, the Shape Builder tool (🖱), Pathfinder effects, and the Eraser tool (🩹), among other features you will explore in Lesson 4, "Transforming Artwork."

Using the Width tool

Not only can you adjust the stroke weight and the alignment of the stroke, but you can also alter regular stroke widths either by using the Width tool (🖋) or by applying width profiles to the stroke. This allows you to create a variable width along the stroke of a path.

Next, you will use the Width tool to create the base for another new lamp.

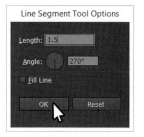

1 Select the Line Segment tool (╱) in the Tools panel, and click roughly in the center of the artboard. In the Line Segment Tool Options dialog box, change the length to **1.5** and leave the rest of the settings at their defaults. Click OK to create a line.

2 Make sure that the Stroke color of the line is Black, the Fill color is None (important), and that the Stroke weight is **1 pt** in the Control panel.

3 Select the Zoom tool (🔍) in the Tools panel and click twice, *slowly*, on the line to zoom in.

4 Select the Width tool (🖉) in the Tools panel. Position the pointer over the middle of the line, and notice that the pointer has a plus symbol next to it (▶₊), indicating that if you click and drag, you can edit the stroke. Click and drag to the right, away from the line. Notice that, as you drag, you are stretching the stroke to the left and right equally. Release the mouse when the measurement label shows Side 1 and Side 2 at approximately 0.29 in.

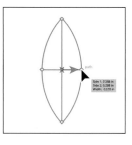

The new point that is filled with blue on the original line is called the width point. The lines extending from the width point are the *handles*. Width points created at a corner or at a direct-selected anchor point stick to the anchor point during basic editing of the path.

5 Click in a blank area of the artboard to deselect the path. Position the pointer over the path again and the new width point you just created will appear (an arrow is pointing to it in the figure). The width point you see in line with the pointer is where a new point would be created if you were to click. Position the pointer over the original width point and when you see lines extending from it and the pointer changes (▶ᵜ), drag it up a bit.

▶ **Tip:** If you select a width point by clicking on it, you can press Delete to remove it. If there was only one width point on a stroke, removing that point would remove the width completely.

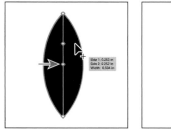

Aside from clicking and dragging to add a width point to a path, you can also double-click and enter values in a dialog box. That's what you'll do next.

6 Position the pointer over the top anchor point of the line, and notice that the pointer has a wavy line next to it (↘︎) and the word "anchor" appears. Double-click on the point to create a new width point and to open the Width Point Edit dialog box.

7 Change the Side 1 width to **0.2 in** and change Side 2 to **0.2 in** as well, and click OK.

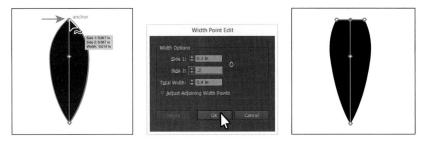

The Width Point Edit dialog box allows you to adjust the sides together or separately, using more precision. Clicking the Adjust Widths Proportionately button (▦) would link Side 1 with Side 2 so that they adjust together, in proportion. Also, if you select the Adjust Adjoining Width Points option, any changes you make to the selected width point affect neighboring width points as well.

8 Double-click the bottom anchor point of the path and repeat step 7 above to make the stroke width the same at the top and bottom of the path.

You can also duplicate a width point if you like, which is what you'll do next.

▶ Tip: You can drag one width point on top of another width point to create a discontinuous width point. If you double-click a discontinuous width point, the Width Point Edit dialog box allows you to edit both width points.

9 Position the pointer over the bottom anchor point of the line. Press the Option (Mac OS) or Alt (Windows) key, and drag up to duplicate the width point. Use the figure below to see roughly how far to drag. Release the mouse button, and then release the modifier key.

10 Position the pointer over the right end of the width point handle and drag to the right until you see a Side 1 and Side 2 of roughly 0.42 in.

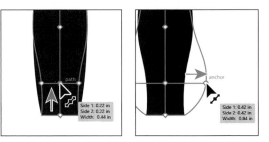

▶ Tip: If you Option-drag (Mac OS) or Alt-drag (Windows) a width point handle, you will adjust only the side you are dragging.

11 Position the pointer over the edge of the stroke above the last point (indicated by the red X in the figure). Click and drag to the left until you see a Side 1 width of approximately 0.24 in.

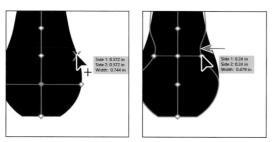

● **Note:** You don't have to position the pointer over the center of the line and drag to create another width point. You can also drag from anywhere in the stroke area.

12 Position the pointer between the top width point and the second width point from the top. See the red X in the figure for help. Click and drag to the left until you see a Side 1 width of approximately 0.14 in.

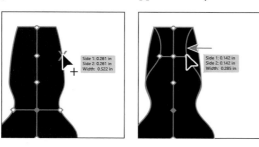

13 Select the Rectangle tool (▨) in the Tools panel. In the blank area above the lamp you just created, click to open the Rectangle dialog box. Change the Width to **1.5 in** and the Height to **0.8 in**. Click OK.

14 Change the Fill color to an orange with a tool tip of "C=0 M=80 Y=95 K=0" in the Control panel. Change the Stroke color to the same orange with a Stroke weight of **1 pt**.

15 Select the Selection tool (▸) and drag the rectangle so that it is centered with the lamp body and covers the very top. See the figure for placement help.

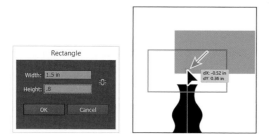

Next, you will use the Width tool to edit one side of the stroke, rather than both, as you've been doing.

16 With the rectangle still selected, select the Width tool in the Tools panel. Option-drag (Mac OS) or Alt-drag (Windows) the top, middle of the stroke up until you see a value of approximately 0.1 in for Side 1 in the measurement label. Release the mouse button and then the key.

17 Do the same for the bottom of the rectangle—but dragging down with the Option (Mac OS) or Alt (Windows) key held down.

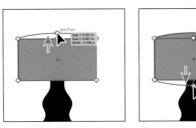

Saving width profiles

After defining the stroke width, you can save the variable width profile from the Stroke panel or the Control panel by selecting a modified stroke and then clicking the Add To Profiles button at the bottom of the Variable Width Profiles menu in the Control panel or the Profile menu at the bottom of the Stroke panel.

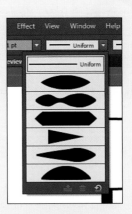

Width profiles can be applied to selected paths by choosing them from the Variable Width Profile menu in the Control panel or the Profile menu in the Stroke panel. When a stroke with no variable width is selected, the list displays the Uniform option. You can also select the Uniform option to remove a variable width profile from an object. To restore the default width profile set, click the Reset Profiles button at the bottom of the Profile menu.

If you apply a variable width profile to a stroke, it is indicated with an asterisk (*) in the Appearance panel.

—From Illustrator Help

Outlining strokes

Paths, such as a line, can show a stroke color but not a fill color by default. If you create a line in Illustrator and want to apply both a stroke and a fill, you can outline the stroke, which converts the line into a closed shape (or compound path). By outlining the stroke, you can no longer edit the path using the Width tool ( ).

Next, you will outline the stroke of the lamp you just created with the Width tool.

1 With the Selection tool (🖢), select the black path you edited with the Width tool (🐾) and choose Object > Path > Outline Stroke.

   This creates a filled shape that is a closed path.

2 With the new shape selected, click the Fill color in the Control panel and change the color to the yellow/green that shows "C=20 M=0 Y=100 K=0" in the tool tip.

3 Shift-click the orange lampshade and choose Object > Group.

4 Choose Select > Deselect, and then choose File > Save.

5 Choose View > Fit Artboard In Window.

● **Note:** If you outline the stroke and it shows as "Group" in the Selection Indicator on the left end of the Control panel, then there was a fill set on the line. If the artwork is a group, choose Edit > Undo Outline Stroke, apply a fill of None to the path, then try again.

Working with the Shape Builder tool

In Illustrator, you can combine vector objects to create shapes in a variety of ways. The resulting paths or shapes differ depending on the method you use to combine the paths. The first method you will learn for combining shapes involves working with the Shape Builder tool. This tool allows you to visually and intuitively merge, delete, fill, and edit overlapping shapes and paths directly in the artwork. Using the Shape Builder tool (◓), you'll create a lampshade for the lamp on the right.

1 With the Selection tool (🖢) selected, Shift-click both star shapes. Choose Object > Hide > Selection to temporarily hide them.

2 Select the Rectangle tool (▯) in the Tools panel. Near the top edge of the artboard on the right, above the yellow/green lamp shapes, click to open the Rectangle dialog box. Change the Width to **2 in** and the Height to **1.2 in**. Click OK.

3 Change the Fill color of the rectangle to an orange with a tool tip of "C=0 M=80 Y=95 K=0" in the Control panel, if necessary.

4 Click the artboard again to open the Rectangle dialog box. Ensure that the Width is still 2 in and change the Height to **0.15 in**. Click OK. Change the fill of the smaller rectangle to Black in the Control panel.

5 With the Selection tool, drag the smaller rectangle so that its top edge snaps to the bottom of the first rectangle and aligns to its center.

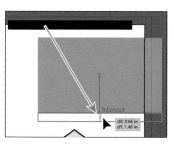

● **Note:** You may find that the rectangles are snapping to other content as well. In that case, you can either use Align options or move both rectangles away from other objects.

6   Click to select the yellow triangle at the top of the lamp shapes on the right. Choose Edit > Copy and then Edit > Paste.

7   In the Transform panel (Window > Transform), change the Width to **2 in** and the Height to **2 in**.

8   With the Selection tool, drag the triangle so that its bottom edge aligns with the bottom of the larger rectangle and is centered vertically with it.

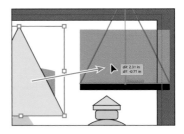

9   Drag across all three shapes to select them.

In order to edit shapes with the Shape Builder tool (⬚), they need to be selected.

Using the Shape Builder tool, you will now combine, delete, and paint these shapes.

10 Select the Shape Builder tool (⬚) in the Tools panel. Position the pointer below the shapes, and drag from the red X in the figure up into the larger rectangle. Release the mouse button to combine the shapes.

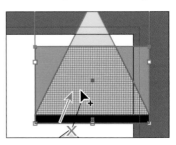

▶ **Tip:** You can also press the Shift key and drag a marquee across a series of shapes to combine them. Pressing Shift+Option (Mac OS) or Shift+Alt (Windows) and dragging a marquee across selected shapes with the Shape Builder tool (⬚) selected allows you to delete a series of shapes within the marquee.

When you select the Shape Builder tool, the overlapping shapes are divided into separate objects temporarily. As you drag from one part to another, a red outline appears, showing you what the final shape outline will look like when it merges the shapes together.

▶ **Tip:** You can also press the Option (Mac OS) or Alt (Windows) key and drag through a series of shapes to delete them all at once.

11 With the shapes still selected, hold down the Option (Mac OS) or Alt (Windows) key. Notice that, with the modifier key held down, the pointer shows a minus sign (▶_). Click each shape indicated in the figure with a red X to delete them.

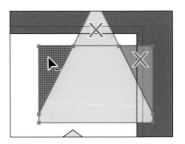

▶ **Tip:** You can also apply fills to any of the selected shapes with the Shape Builder tool by selecting the fill color first and then clicking the shape.

12 With the shape still selected, select the Selection tool (▶). Change the Fill color in the Control panel to a light gray, with the tool tip showing "C=0 M=0 Y=0 K=10." Press the Escape key to hide the panel. Change the Stroke weight to **0**.

13 Choose Select > Deselect.

14 Choose Object > Show All to show the star shapes that are now behind the lampshade.

15 With the stars selected, choose Object > Arrange > Bring To Front.

16 With the Selection tool, Shift-drag a corner to make them small enough to fit on the gray lampshade. Position them like you see in the figure.

17 Shift-click the gray lampshade and stars to select all three objects, and choose Object > Group.

18 Choose Select > Deselect, and then choose File > Save.

Shape Builder tool options

You can set up and customize various options such as gap detection, coloring source, and highlighting to get the required merging capability and better visual feedback.

Double-click the Shape Builder Tool icon (🖱️) in the Tools panel to set these options in the Shape Builder Tool Options dialog box.

—From Illustrator Help

Working with the Pathfinder panel

The bottom row of buttons in the Pathfinder panel, called *Pathfinder effects*, lets you combine shapes in many different ways to create paths or compound paths by default. When a Pathfinder effect (such as Merge) is applied, the original objects selected are permanently transformed. If the effect results in more than one shape, they are grouped automatically.

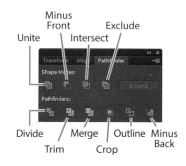

Pathfinder effects in the Pathfinder panel

Next, you will finish the yellow/green lamp using Pathfinder effects.

1 Choose Window > Pathfinder to open the Pathfinder panel group.

2 With the Selection tool (▶), hold down the Shift key and click the small yellow triangle and the small rectangle beneath the lamp shade to select both objects.

3   With the shapes selected, in the Pathfinder panel, click the Merge button (■) to combine the shapes into one.

    With the new shape selected, notice the word "Path" on the left side of the Control panel.

4   Choose Select > Deselect, and then choose File > Save.

Shape modes in the Pathfinder panel

The buttons in the top row of the Pathfinder panel, called *shape modes*, create paths just like the Pathfinder effects, but they can also be used to create compound shapes. When several shapes are selected, clicking a shape mode while pressing the Option (Mac OS) or Alt (Windows) key creates a compound shape rather than a path. The original underlying objects of compound shapes are preserved. As a result, you can still select each original object within a compound shape. Using a shape mode to create a compound shape can be useful if you think that you may want to retrieve the original shapes at a later time.

Next, you will use shape modes to finish the yellow/green lamp.

1   Select the Zoom tool (🔍), and click several times on the rectangle at the bottom of the yellow/green lamp to zoom in.

2   Select the Rectangle tool (■) in the Tools panel. Draw a rectangle that has an approximate width of 0.5 in and a height of 0.1 in.

3   With the Selection tool (▶), Shift-click the bottom yellow/green rectangle with the chamfered corners to select both shapes. Release the Shift key. Click again on the larger shape to make it the key object for alignment.

4   Click the Horizontal Align Center button (■) and the Vertical Align Bottom button (■) in the Control panel to align the two shapes.

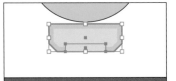

5   With the objects selected, hold down the Option (Mac OS) or Alt (Windows) key and click the Minus Front button (■) in the Shape Modes section of the Pathfinder panel.

    This creates a compound shape that traces the outline where the two objects overlap. You will still be able to edit both shapes separately.

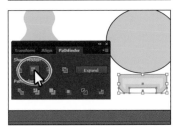

▶ **Tip:** To edit the original shapes in a compound shape like this one, you can also select them individually with the Direct Selection tool (▶).

6   Choose Select > Deselect to see the final shape.

7   With the Selection tool, double-click the same shape to enter Isolation mode.

8   Choose View > Outline so that you can see the two shapes.

9   Click the edge of the smaller rectangle to
    select it. Option-drag (Mac OS) or Alt-drag
    (Windows) the right, middle bounding point
    of the smaller rectangle bounding box to
    the left to make it a bit narrower. Drag until
    the measurement tool tip shows a width of
    approximately 0.4 in. Release the mouse button and then the key.

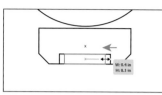

● **Note:** It is easier to
resize a shape precisely
if you zoom in. You
can also change the
width and height of the
selected shape in the
Transform panel.

10 Press the Escape key to exit Isolation mode.

    Because you entered Outline mode while in Isolation mode, exiting Isolation
    mode switches back to Preview mode automatically.

You will now expand the window shape. Expanding a compound shape maintains
the shape of the compound object, but you can no longer select or edit the
original objects. You will typically expand an object when you want to modify the
appearance attributes and other properties of specific elements within it.

11 Click away from the shape to deselect it, and
    then click to select it again. Click the Expand
    button in the Pathfinder panel. Close the
    Pathfinder panel group.

12 Choose Select > Deselect.

13 Choose View > Fit Artboard In Window, and
    then choose File > Save.

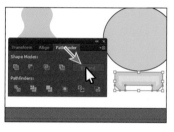

Using the Eraser tool

The Eraser tool (🖊) lets you erase any area of your vector artwork, regardless of the
structure. You can use the Eraser tool on paths, compound paths, paths inside Live Paint
groups, and clipping content. Next, you'll use the Eraser tool to edit one of the lampshades.

1   With the Selection tool (▶), select the white lampshade on the left side of
    the artboard.

    By selecting the white lampshade, you'll erase only that shape and nothing else.
    If you leave all objects deselected, you can erase any object that the tool touches,
    across all layers.

2   Double-click the Eraser tool (🖊) in the
    Tools panel to edit the tool properties.
    In the Eraser Tool Options dialog box,
    change the Size to **4 pt**. Click OK.

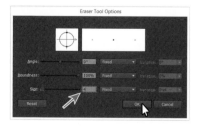

Eraser Tool Options

▶ **Tip:** With the Eraser
tool (🖊) selected
and the pointer on
the artboard, you can
press and hold the
Right Bracket key (])
for a second or two to
increase the diameter of
the eraser. If you make it
too large, you can press
the Left Bracket key ([)
to make it smaller.

Tip: If you press the Shift key and drag across content, you will constrain the Eraser tool ( ) to a vertical, horizontal, or diagonal line.

Tip: If you press the Option (Mac OS) or Alt (Windows) key, you will be able to drag a marquee across content to erase it.

3 Position the pointer off the upper-left corner of the white rectangle (where you see the red X in the figure). Click and drag diagonally across the rectangle. When you release the mouse button, the rectangle is cut in two and the two paths are closed shapes.

● **Note:** You cannot erase images, text, symbols, graphs, or gradient mesh objects.

4 Try dragging across the lampshade some more to create an effect like you see in the figure below.

5 Choose Object > Group, and then choose Select > Deselect.

6 Select the Selection tool and drag across the lampshade you just created, the line, and the ellipse beneath it to select all *three* objects that make up that lamp. Choose Object > Group.

7 Choose Select > Deselect, and then choose File > Save.

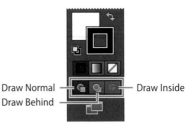

Working with drawing modes

● **Note:** To learn more about clipping masks, see Lesson 14, "Using Illustrator CC with Other Adobe Applications."

Illustrator has three different drawing modes available that are found at the bottom of the Tools panel: Draw Normal, Draw Behind, and Draw Inside. Drawing modes allow you to draw shapes in different ways. The three drawing modes are:

- **Draw Normal mode:** You start every document by drawing shapes in Normal mode, which stacks shapes on top of each other.

- **Draw Behind mode:** This mode allows you to draw objects behind other objects without choosing layers or paying attention to the stacking order.

- **Draw Inside mode:** This mode lets you draw objects or place images inside other objects, including live text, automatically creating a clipping mask of the selected object.

Working with Draw Behind mode

Throughout this lesson, you've been working in the default Draw Normal mode. Next, you'll draw a rectangle that will cover the artboard and go behind the rest of the content using Draw Behind mode.

1   Click the Draw Behind button () at the bottom of the Tools panel.

As long as this drawing mode is selected, every shape you create using the different methods you've learned will be created behind the other shapes on the page. The Draw Behind mode also affects placed content (File > Place).

2   Select the Rectangle tool (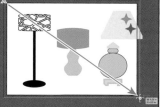) in the Tools panel. Position the pointer off the upper-left corner of the artboard in the corner of the red bleed guides. Click and drag off the lower-right side of the artboard to the corner of the red bleed guides.

3   With the new rectangle selected, click the Fill color in the Control panel and change the fill color to a red with the tool tip values "C=15 M=100 Y=90 K=10." Press the Escape key to hide the Swatches panel.

4   Change the Stroke weight to **0** in the Control panel.

5   Choose Object > Lock Selection.

6   Click the Draw Normal button (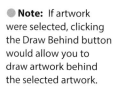) at the bottom of the Tools panel.

Note: If the Tools panel you see is displayed as a single column, you can click the Drawing Modes button () at the bottom of the Tools panel and choose Draw Behind from the menu that appears.

Note: If artwork were selected, clicking the Draw Behind button would allow you to draw artwork behind the selected artwork.

Using the Draw Inside mode

Next, you will learn how to draw a shape inside of another using the Draw Inside drawing mode. This can be useful if you wanted to hide (mask) part of artwork.

1   Select the Selection tool (⬥) in the Tools panel. Click to select the yellow/green ellipse of the rightmost lamp.

2   Click the Draw Inside button (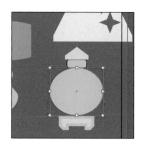), near the bottom of the Tools panel.

This button is active when a single object is selected (path, compound path, or text), and it allows you to draw within the selected object only. Every shape you create will now be drawn inside of the selected shape (the circle). Notice that the ellipse has a dotted open rectangle around it, indicating that, if you draw, paste, or place content, it will be inside of the circle, even if you were to choose Select > Deselect.

3 Select the Ellipse tool (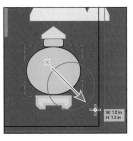) in the Tools panel. Position the pointer near the center of the yellow/green ellipse, press the Shift key, and draw a circle that has a width and height of 1.2 in. Release the mouse button and then the key.

4 Change the Fill color of the new circle to the yellow with the tool tip that shows "C=5 M=0 Y=90 K=0."

5 Change the Stroke weight to **0** in the Control panel.

● **Note:** If you draw a shape outside of the original yellow/green ellipse shape, it will seem to disappear. That is because the yellow/green ellipse is masking all shapes drawn inside of it; so only shapes positioned inside of the ellipse bounds will appear.

6 Choose Select > Deselect.

Notice that the ellipse still has the dotted open rectangle around it, indicating that Draw Inside mode is still active.

When you are finished drawing content inside of a shape, you can click the Draw Normal button (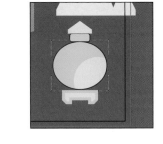) so that any new content you create will be drawn normally (stacked rather than drawn inside). Right now, if you were to attempt to select the ellipse or the circle inside of it, you would select the ellipse. If you move the ellipse, the shape inside goes with it. If you resize or reshape the yellow/green ellipse, the shape inside will resize or reshape.

▶ **Tip:** You can also toggle between the available Drawing Modes by pressing Shift+D.

7 Click the Draw Normal button at the bottom of the Tools panel.

This ensures that any new content you create will not be drawn inside of the yellow/green ellipse.

Editing content drawn inside

Next, you will edit the circle inside of the yellow/green ellipse to see how you can later edit content drawn inside.

1 Select the Selection tool (▶), and click to select the yellow circle (that is inside of the yellow/green ellipse). Notice that it selects the yellow/green ellipse instead.

The yellow/green ellipse is now a mask, also called a *clipping path*. The ellipse and the circle together make a clip group and are now treated as a single object. If you look on the left end of the Control panel, you will see "Clip Group" and two buttons that allow you to edit either the clipping path (the yellow/green ellipse) or the contents (the yellow circle).

▶ **Tip:** You can separate the shapes by right-clicking on the shapes and choosing Release Clipping Mask. This would make two shapes, stacked one on another.

2 Click the Edit Contents button () on the left end of the Control panel to select the yellow circle.

▶ **Tip:** You can also double-click the yellow circle to enter Isolation mode and press the Escape key to exit.

3 Drag the yellow circle from within the yellow fill color up to match the figure as best you can.

4 Click the Edit Clipping Path button (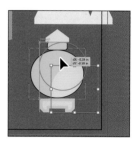) on the left end of the Control panel to select the yellow/green ellipse.

Tip: Sometimes it can be helpful to choose View > Outline, to more easily see and select shapes when in Isolation mode.

5 Change the Stroke weight to **0** in the Control panel.

   If you find it difficult to change the Stroke weight to **0** (zero), try changing it to another value first, and then **0**.

6 Choose Select > Deselect.

Next, you will assemble the yellow/green lamp by dragging shapes. Make sure that you keep the shapes aligned horizontally with each other using the Smart Guides for alignment.

7 Drag the shape below the clip group (circle) up to match the first part of the following figure (below).

8 Click to select the yellow/green rounded rectangle above the clip group (the circle).

9 Change the Stroke weight to **0** in the Control panel.

10 Drag that same rounded rectangle and the shape above it down to match the middle part of the following figure (you will need to select both).

11 Drag the lampshade over the top of the lamp to match the figure.

12 Drag across all of the shapes in the lamp to select them, and choose Object > Group.

13 Choose Select > Deselect, and then choose File > Save.

Using Image Trace to create shapes

In this part of the lesson, you will learn how to work with the Image Trace command. Image Trace traces existing artwork, like a raster picture from Adobe Photoshop. You can then convert the drawing to vector paths or a Live Paint object. This can be useful for turning a drawing into vector art, tracing raster logos, tracing a pattern or texture, and much more.

1   With the Selection tool (⬆) selected, click the Next artboard button (▶) in the status bar in the lower-left corner of the Document window to navigate to the second artboard.

2   Choose File > Place. In the Place dialog box, select the Logo.png file in the Lessons > Lesson03 folder on your hard disk, and click Place (shown in the figure). Click on the left edge of the artboard to place the image. The image will be larger than the artboard, but that's okay.

With the placed image selected, the Control panel options change. You can see the words "Linked File" on the left side of the Control panel, and you can see the name Logo.png and the resolution (PPI: 72), as well as other information.

▶ **Tip:** You will learn more about placing images in Lesson 14, "Using Illustrator CC with Other Adobe Applications."

▶ **Tip:** Tracing a larger image or higher-resolution image will most likely result in better results.

3   Click the Image Trace button in the Control panel. The tracing results you see may differ slightly from the figure, and that's okay.

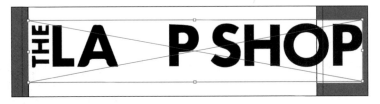

This converts the image into an image tracing object using the default tracing options. That means that you can't edit the vector content yet, but you can change the tracing settings or even the original placed image and then see the updates.

● **Note:** You can also choose Object > Image Trace > Make, with raster content selected, or begin tracing from the Image Trace panel (Window > Image Trace).

4   Choose 6 Colors from the Preset menu on the left end of the Control panel.

Illustrator comes with preset tracing options that you can apply to your image tracing object. You can then make changes to the tracing settings, if need be, using the default preset as a starting point.

5 Choose Outlines With Source Image from the View menu in the Control panel, and take a look at the image. Choose Tracing Result from that same menu.

An image tracing object is made up of the original source image and the tracing result (which is the vector artwork). By default, only the tracing result is visible. However, you can change the display of both the original image and the tracing result to best suit your needs.

6 Choose Window > Image Trace to open the Image Trace panel. In the panel, click the Auto-Color button (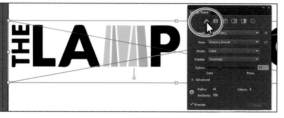) at the top of the panel.

▶ **Tip:** The Image Trace panel can also be opened with traced artwork selected, by clicking the Image Trace Panel button (▤) in the Control panel.

The buttons along the top of the Image Trace panel are saved settings for converting the image to grayscale, black and white, and more. Below the buttons at the top of the Image Trace panel, you will see the Preset and View options. These are the same as those in the Control panel. The Mode option allows you to change the color mode of resulting artwork (color, grayscale, or black and white). The Palette option is also useful for limiting the color palette or for assigning colors from a color group.

7 Press and hold the eye icon (👁) to the right of the View menu in the Image Trace panel to see the source image on the artboard. Release the mouse button.

8 In the Image Trace panel, click the toggle arrow to the left of the Advanced options to reveal them. Change only the following options, using the values as a starting point:

- Colors: **3**
- Paths: **80%**
- Corners: **90%**
- Noise: **10 px**
- Snap Curves To Lines: **Selected**
- Ignore White: **Selected**

Note: By selecting the Snap Curves To Lines option, the small yellow/green lamp pull cord no longer has rounded corners. You can fix that yourself using the drawing tools after you learn more about them in Lesson 5, "Creating an Illustration with the Drawing Tools."

The type in the logo isn't perfect yet. You can clean up the type (see the sidebar "Cleaning up traced artwork") or find out the original font used and replicate it.

9 Close the Image Trace panel.

10 With the logo image tracing object still selected, click the Expand button in the Control panel. The logo is no longer an image tracing object but is composed of shapes and paths that are grouped together.

11 With the Selection tool, double-click the logo to enter Isolation mode. Click one of the black letters to select it. Choose Select > Same > Fill Color to select all of the black letters. Change the Fill color to White in the Control panel. Press the Escape key to hide the Swatches panel.

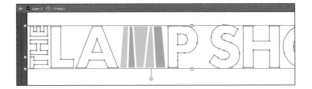

12 Press the Escape key to exit isolation mode. Choose Select > Deselect, and then click to select the logo group.

13 Choose Object > Transform > Scale. In the Scale dialog box, change the Uniform value to **48** and click OK. This will scale the logo so you can place it into the previous artboard.

14 Choose View > Fit All In Window to see both artboards. Drag the logo into the upper-right corner of the first artboard (with the lamps on it). See the figure for placement.

15 Drag the lamps into position like you see in the figure.

16 Choose File > Save, and then choose File > Close.

Cleaning up traced artwork

After tracing, you may need to clean up the resulting vector artwork. Using the Object > Path > Simplify command, you can simplify selected paths.

For instance, for the logo you traced, you could double-click the logo after it's been expanded and painted, and select a few of the letters. You can then choose Object > Path > Simplify to change the path settings in the Simplify dialog box. You can apply the Simplify command to other parts of the logo as well. By aligning points and editing paths using the drawing tools, you can turn the raster logo into a viable vector logo.

Review questions

1 What are the basic tools for creating shapes?

2 What is a Live Shape?

3 How do you select a shape with no fill?

4 How do you change the number of sides on a polygon as you draw?

5 Name two ways you can combine several shapes into one.

6 How can you convert a raster image to editable vector shapes?

Review answers

1 There are six shape tools: Rectangle, Rounded Rectangle, Ellipse, Polygon, Star, and Flare. As explained in Lesson 1, "Getting to Know the Work Area," to tear off a group of tools from the Tools panel, position the pointer over the tool that appears in the Tools panel and hold down the mouse button until the group of tools appears. Without releasing the mouse button, drag to the triangle on the right side of the group, and then release the mouse button to tear off the group.

2 After you draw a rectangle or rounded rectangle using the shape tool, you can continue to modify its properties such as width, height, rounded corners, corner types, and radii (individually or collectively). This is what is known as a Live Shape. These shape properties are editable using the Transform panel, which has a separate Rectangle Properties section, or directly on the art.

3 Items that have no fill can be selected by clicking the stroke or by dragging a selection marquee across the item.

4 To change the number of sides on a polygon as you draw, select the Polygon tool () in the Tools panel. Start dragging to draw the shape, and press the Down Arrow key to reduce the number of sides and the Up Arrow key to increase the number of sides.

5 Using the Shape Builder tool (), you can visually and intuitively merge, delete, fill, and edit overlapping shapes and paths directly in the artwork. You can also use the Pathfinder effects to create new shapes out of overlapping objects. You can apply Pathfinder effects by using the Effects menu or the Pathfinder panel.

6 You can convert a raster image to editable vector shapes by tracing it. To convert the tracing to paths, click Expand in the Control panel or choose Object > Image Trace > Expand. Use this method if you want to work with the components of the traced artwork as individual objects. The resulting paths are grouped.

4 TRANSFORMING ARTWORK

Lesson overview

In this lesson, you'll learn how to do the following:

- Add, edit, rename, and reorder artboards in an existing document.

- Navigate artboards.

- Work with rulers and guides.

- Move, scale, and rotate objects using a variety of methods.

- Reflect, shear, and distort objects.

- Position objects with precision.

- Position and align content with Smart Guides.

- Use the Free Transform tool to distort an object.

- Create a PDF.

This lesson takes approximately 60 minutes to complete.

Download the project files for this lesson from the Lesson & Update Files tab on your Account page at www.peachpit.com and store them on your computer in a convenient location, as described in the Getting Started section of this book.

Your Account page is also where you'll find any updates to the chapters or to the lesson files. Look on the Lesson & Update Files tab to access the most current content.

You can modify objects in many ways as you create artwork, by quickly and precisely controlling their size, shape, and orientation. In this lesson, you'll explore creating and editing artboards, the various Transform commands, and specialized tools, while creating several pieces of artwork.

Getting started

In this lesson, you'll create content and use it in a ticket for a sporting event. Before you begin, you'll restore the default preferences for Adobe Illustrator and then open a file containing the finished artwork to see what you'll create.

1 To ensure that the tools and panels function exactly as described in this lesson, delete or deactivate (by renaming) the Adobe Illustrator CC preferences file. See "Restoring default preferences" in the Getting Started section at the beginning of the book.

● **Note:** If you have not already downloaded the project files for this lesson to your computer from your Account page, make sure to do so now. See the "Getting Started" section at the beginning of the book.

2 Start Adobe Illustrator CC.

3 Choose File > Open, and open the L4_end.ai file in the Lessons > Lesson04 folder on your hard disk.

This file contains the three artboards that make up the front, back, and inside of a folding ticket for a sporting event.

4 Choose View > Fit All In Window, and leave the artwork onscreen as you work. If you don't want to leave the file open, choose File > Close (without saving).

To begin working, you'll open an existing art file.

5 Choose File > Open to open the L4_start.ai file in the Lesson04 folder, located in the Lessons folder on your hard disk.

● **Note:** If you don't see "Reset Essentials" in the Workspace menu, choose Window > Workspace > Essentials before choosing Window > Workspace > Reset Essentials.

6 Choose File > Save As. In the Save As dialog box, name the file **Ticket.ai**, and navigate to the Lesson04 folder. Leave the Format option set to Adobe Illustrator (ai) (Mac OS) or Save As Type option set to Adobe Illustrator (*.AI) (Windows), and then click Save. In the Illustrator Options dialog box, leave the Illustrator options at their default settings, and then click OK.

7 Choose Window > Workspace > Reset Essentials.

Working with artboards

Artboards represent the regions that can contain printable artwork, similar to pages in Adobe InDesign. You can use multiple artboards for creating a variety of things, such as multiple-page PDF files, printed pages with different sizes or different elements, independent elements for websites, or video storyboards, for instance.

Adding artboards to the document

You can add and remove artboards at any time while working in a document. You can create artboards in different sizes, resize them with the Artboard tool (⊞) or Artboards panel (▥), and position them anywhere in the Document window. All artboards are numbered and can have a unique name assigned to them.

Next, you will add two more artboards to the document. Since this is a ticket for a sporting event that will fold, each artboard will be a different face of the ticket (front, inside, and back).

1   Choose View > Fit Artboard In Window, then press Command+− (Mac OS) or Ctrl+− (Windows) to zoom out.

2   Press the spacebar to temporarily access the Hand tool (✋). Drag the artboard to the left to see more of the darker canvas off the right side of the artboard.

3   Select the Artboard tool (⊞) in the Tools panel. Position the Artboard tool pointer to the right of the existing artboard and in line with its top edge (a green alignment guide appears). Drag down and to the right to create an artboard that is 3.5 in (width) by 6 in (height). The measurement label indicates the artboard size.

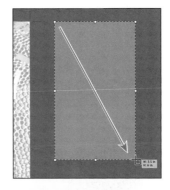

> **Tip:** If you find it difficult to make the width value exactly 3.5 in, you can always change the W: (width) value in the Control panel, after you finish drawing the artboard.

▶ **Tip:** If you zoom in on an artboard, the measurement label has smaller increments.

4   Click the Artboards panel icon (▥) on the right side of the workspace to show it.

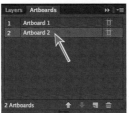

The Artboards panel allows you to see how many artboards the document currently contains. It also allows you to reorder, rename, add, and delete artboards and to choose many other options related to artboards. Notice that Artboard 2 is highlighted in the panel. The active artboard is always highlighted in this panel.

Next, you will create a copy of an artboard using this panel.

5 Click the New Artboard button (⬚) at the bottom of the panel to create a copy of Artboard 2, called Artboard 3. The copy is placed to the right of Artboard 2 in the Document window.

▶ **Tip:** You can also create a new artboard by clicking the New Artboard button (⬚) in the Control panel. This allows you to create a duplicate of the last selected artboard. After clicking the button, position the pointer in the canvas area and click to create a new artboard.

6 Choose View > Fit All In Window to see all of your artboards and leave the Artboard tool selected.

Editing artboards

After creating artboards, you can edit or delete artboards at any time by using the Artboard tool (⬚), menu commands, or the Artboards panel. Next, you will reposition and change the sizes of several of the artboards using multiple methods.

1 Press Command+– (Mac OS) or Ctrl+– (Windows) *twice* to zoom out further.

2 With the Artboard tool (⬚) still selected, drag Artboard 3 from the center, to the left of the original (larger) artboard. You can reposition artboards at any time and even overlap them, if necessary.

▶ **Tip:** With the Artboard tool (⬚), you can also copy an artboard by holding down the Option (Mac OS) or Alt (Windows) key and dragging away from the original artboard. When creating new artboards, you can place them anywhere—you can even overlap them.

3 With the Artboard tool selected, drag the bottom-center bounding point of the artboard down until the height is 8 in, as shown in the measurement label. The bottom will snap to the bottom of the larger artboard to its right and a green alignment (smart) guide will appear.

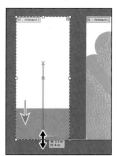

▶ **Tip:** To delete an artboard, select the artboard with the Artboard tool (⬚) and either press Delete, click the Delete Artboard button (🗑) in the Control panel, or click the Delete icon (☒) in the upper-right corner of an artboard. You can delete all but one artboard.

Another way to resize an artboard is to do so by entering values in the Control panel, which is what you'll do next.

4   Click Artboard 2, to the right of the larger artboard in the middle. "Artboard 2" will be highlighted in the Artboards panel. Select the upper-middle point in the reference point locator () in the Control panel. Change the height to **8** in the Control panel and press Enter or Return to accept the value.

▶ **Tip:** With the Artboard tool (⌗) selected, you can press the Shift key to resize an artboard proportionally or press the Option (Mac OS) or Alt (Windows) key and drag to resize an artboard from its center.

Selecting the upper-middle point allows you to resize an artboard from the top, center of the artboard. By default, artboards are resized from their center.

In the Control panel, with the Artboard tool selected, you will see many options for editing the currently active artboard. The Preset menu lets you change a selected artboard to a set size. Notice that the sizes in the Preset menu include typical print, video, tablet, and Web sizes. You can also fit the artboard to the artwork bounds or the selected art, which is a great way to fit an artboard to a logo, for instance. Other options in the Control panel include the ability to switch orientation, rename or delete the artboard, even show other helpful guides like a center point or video-safe areas.

● **Note:** If you don't see the Width (W) and Height (H) fields in the Control panel, click the Artboard Options button (▤) in the Control panel and enter the values in the dialog box that appears.

▶ **Tip:** You can see the Constrain Width and Height Proportions icon (▨) in the Control panel, between the Width and Height fields. This icon, if selected (▨), allows the width and height to change in proportion to each other.

5   Select the Selection tool (▶), and choose View > Fit All In Window.

Notice the *very* subtle black outline around Artboard 2, with "2" showing in the Artboard Navigation menu (lower-left corner of the Document window), and "Artboard 2" highlighted in the Artboards panel, all of which indicate that Artboard 2 is the currently active artboard. There can only be one active artboard at a time. Commands such as View > Fit Artboard In Window apply to the active artboard.

Renaming artboards

By default, artboards are assigned a number and a name. When you navigate the artboards in a document, it can be helpful to name them. Next, you are going to rename the artboards so that the names are more useful.

1   In the Artboards panel, double-click the name "Artboard 1." Change the name to **Inside**, and press Enter or Return.

▶ **Tip:** You can also change the name of an artboard by double-clicking the Artboard tool (⌗) in the Tools panel. Doing so changes the name for the currently active artboard in the Artboard Options dialog box. You can make an artboard the currently active artboard by clicking it with the Selection tool (▶).

You will now rename the rest of the artboards.

2   Double-click the Artboard Options icon () to the right of the name "Artboard 2" in the Artboards panel. This opens the Artboard Options dialog box.

> **Tip:** The Artboard Options icon (▣) appears to the right of the name of each artboard in the Artboards panel. It not only allows access to the artboard options for each artboard but also indicates the orientation (vertical or horizontal) of the artboard. You only need to single-click the icon when the artboard name is highlighted in the panel.

3   In the Artboard Options dialog box, change the Name to **Back** and click OK.

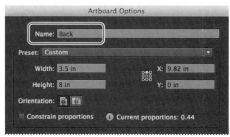

The Artboard Options dialog box has a lot of extra options as well as a few we've already seen, like width and height.

4   Double-click the name "Artboard 3" in the panel, and change the name to **Front**. Press Enter or Return to accept the name.

5   Choose File > Save, and keep the Artboards panel showing for the next steps.

Reordering artboards

When you navigate your document, the order in which the artboards appear can be important, especially if you are navigating the document using the Next artboard (▶) and Previous artboard (◀) buttons. By default, artboards are ordered according to the order in which they are created, but you can change that order. Next, you will reorder the artboards in the Artboards panel.

1   With the Artboards panel still open, double-click the number 1 to the left of the name "Inside" in the panel. This makes the artboard named "Inside" the active artboard and fits it in the Document window.

> **Tip:** You can also reorder the artboards by selecting an artboard in the Artboards panel and clicking the Move Up (⬆) or Move Down (⬇) button at the bottom of the panel.

2   Click and drag the "Front" artboard name up until a line appears above the artboard named "Inside." Release the mouse button.

This moves the artboard up in order so that it becomes the first artboard in the list.

3   Double-click to the right or left of the name "Front" in the Artboards panel to fit that artboard in the Document window, if necessary.

4 Click the Next artboard button (▶) in the lower-left corner of the Document window to navigate to the next artboard (Inside). This fits the Inside artboard in the Document window.

If you had not changed the order, the next artboard would have been dimmed since it was the last artboard in the Artboards panel (there was no artboard after it).

5 Choose File > Save.

Now that the artboards are set up, you will concentrate on transforming artwork to create the content for your project.

Editing document setup options

When working with artboards for the current document, you can change default setup options, like units of measure, bleed guides, type settings (such as language), and more in the Document Setup dialog box. To access the Document Setup dialog box, you can either choose File > Document Setup, or, if nothing is selected in the Document window, click the Document Setup button in the Control panel.

There are two sets of options in the Document Setup dialog box that will be worth exploring: General and Type. In the General options, you can change the units and set bleed guides, among a host of other options.

Transforming content

Transforming content allows you to move, rotate, reflect, scale, shear, and either free distort or perspective distort objects. Objects can be transformed using the Transform panel, selection tools, specialized tools, Transform commands, guides, Smart Guides, and more. For the remainder of the lesson, you will transform content using a variety of methods and tools.

Working with rulers and guides

Rulers help you accurately place and measure objects. They appear at the top and left in the Document window and can be shown and hidden. *Guides* are non-printing lines created from the rulers that help you align objects. Next, you will create a few guides based on ruler measurements so that later you can more accurately align content.

1   Choose View > Rulers > Show Rulers, if you don't see the rulers.

2   Choose View > Fit All In Window.

3   With the Selection tool ( ) selected, click each of the artboards and, as you do, look at the horizontal and vertical rulers. Notice that the 0 (zero) for each ruler is always in the upper-left corner of the active (selected) artboard.

    The point on each ruler (horizontal and vertical) where the 0 appears is called the *ruler origin*. By default, the ruler origin is in the upper-left corner of the active artboard. As you can see, the 0 point on both rulers corresponds to the edges of the active artboard.

    There are two types of rulers in Illustrator: *artboard rulers* and *global rulers*. Artboard rulers, which are the default rulers that you are seeing, set the ruler origin at the upper-left corner of the *active* artboard. Global rulers set the ruler origin at the upper-left corner of the *first* artboard, or the artboard that is at the top of the list in the Artboards panel, no matter which artboard is active.

    ● **Note:** You could switch between artboard and global rulers by choosing View > Rulers > and selecting Change To Global Rulers or Change To Artboard Rulers, (depending on which option is currently chosen), but don't do that now.

4   Click the leftmost artboard, called "Front."

5   Open the Layers panel by choosing Window > Layers, and select the layer named Edit.

6 Shift-drag from the left vertical ruler right to create a vertical guide at 1 inch on the horizontal ruler (the ruler above the artboard) on the "Front" artboard. Release the mouse button, and then release the Shift key.

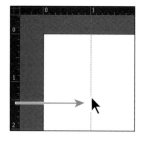

Dragging with the Shift key pressed "snaps" guides to the measurements on the ruler. The guide is selected and when selected, its color matches the color of the layer that it's associated with (red in this case). By default, guides that are not selected are aqua in color.

● **Note:** Guides are similar to drawn objects in that they can be selected like a drawn line, and they can be deleted by pressing the Backspace or Delete key, and they also are on the active layer in the Layers panel.

7 With the guide still selected (it should be red in color), change the X value in the Control panel to **0.25 in**, and press Enter or Return.

▶ **Tip:** To change the units for a document, you can right-click either ruler and choose the new units.

On the horizontal ruler, measurements to the right of 0 (zero) are positive and to the left are negative. On the vertical ruler, measurements below 0 (zero) are positive and above are negative.

● **Note:** If you don't see the X value, you can click the word "Transform" in the Control panel or open the Transform panel (Window > Transform).

8 Position the pointer in the upper-left corner of the Document window, where the rulers intersect (▓), and drag the pointer to the lower-left corner of the artboard. When the word "intersect" appears, release the mouse button.

As you drag, a crosshair in the window and in the rulers indicates the changing ruler origin. This sets the ruler origin (0,0) to the lower-left corner of the artboard. This can be very useful when you need to place content a set distance from the bottom edge of the artboard, for instance.

▶ **Tip:** If you Command-drag (Mac OS) or Ctrl-drag (Windows) from the ruler intersect, you create a horizontal and vertical guide that intersects where you release the mouse button and then release the Ctrl or Command key.

Next, you'll add a guide using a different method that can sometimes be faster.

9 Select the Zoom tool (🔍) and click several times, slowly, on the lower-left corner of the artboard until you see 1/4-inch measurements on the ruler. We had to click at least four times.

10 Shift-double-click the vertical ruler at the 1/4-inch mark (the ruler to the left of the artboard), *above* the 0 on the ruler. This creates a guide that crosses the bottom edge of the artboard at –0.25 in from the bottom.

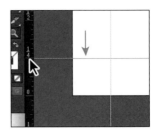

11 Position the pointer in the upper-left corner of the Document window, where the rulers intersect (■), and double-click to reset the ruler origin.

12 Choose View > Guides > Lock Guides to prevent them from being accidentally moved.

The guides are no longer selected and are aqua in color by default.

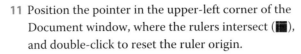

▶ **Tip:** You can also hide and show guides by pressing Command+; (Mac OS) or Ctrl+; (Windows).

13 Choose View > Fit All In Window.

14 With the Selection tool (▶) selected, select the white text "ALL CITY."

15 Choose View > Hide Edges so you only see the bounding box of the grouped paths.

This hides the inside edges of the shapes, but not the bounding box. It can make it easier to move and position the artwork.

16 Drag the text group into the lower-left corner of the artboard with the guides. When the left and bottom edges snap to the guides, release the mouse button.

Positioning objects precisely

At times, you may want to position objects more precisely—either relative to other objects or to the artboard. You could use the alignments options, like you saw in Lesson 2 "Techniques for Selecting Artwork," but you can also use Smart Guides and the Transform panel to move objects to exact coordinates on the x and y axes and to control the position of objects in relation to the edge of the artboard.

Next, you'll add content to the backgrounds of two artboards and then position that content precisely.

1 Press Command+− (Mac OS) or Ctrl+− (Windows) (or View > Zoom Out) *three times* to zoom out. You should see content off the bottom edge of the artboards.

2 Click the artboard with the guides on it (the artboard named Front) to ensure that it is the active artboard (check the origin of the rulers and make sure that 0,0 starts in the upper-left corner of the artboard).

3 With the Selection tool (▶), click to select the large background shape on the left, below the artboards (see the next figure for which shape).

4 Click the upper-left point of the reference point locator (▦) in the Control panel. Then, change the X value to **0** and the Y value to **0**.

● **Note:** Again, depending on the resolution of your screen, the Transform options may not appear in the Control panel. If they do not appear, you can click the word "Transform" to see the Transform panel, or you can choose Window > Transform.

The content should now be precisely positioned on the artboard, since it was the same size as the artboard to begin with.

5 In the Artboards panel, select the artboard named Back to make it the active artboard.

6 Select the group with the "City Arena" text in it below the artboards. You may need to either zoom out or scroll over and down to see it.

7 With the upper-left point of the reference point locator (▦) selected in the Control panel, change the X value to **0** and the Y value to **0**.

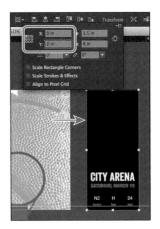

Next, you will use Smart Guides to move content. When moving objects with Smart Guides turned on (View > Smart Guides), measurement labels appear next to the pointer and display the distance (X and Y) from the object's original location. You will use these to make sure that an object is a certain distance from the edge of the artboard.

8 With the Selection tool, click to select the basketball hoop with net below the artboards. With the upper-left point of the reference point locator (▦) in the Control panel selected, change the X value to **0** and the Y value to **0**.

9 Choose View > Fit Artboard In Window.

10 Using the Selection tool, position the pointer over the selected basketball hoop with net and drag the group down and to the right. As you drag, press the Shift key to constrain the movement to 45°. When the measurement label shows approximately dX: 0.25 in and dY: 0.25 in, release the mouse button, and then the Shift key. Leave the artwork selected.

The dX indicates the distance moved along the x axis (horizontally), and dY indicates the distance moved along the y axis (vertically). Don't worry if you can't get the exact values, it's difficult when zoomed out so far. Also, because there is other content on the canvas, Smart Guides are attempting to snap to it. You can always change the X and Y values in the Control panel or Transform panel.

● **Note:** You can also choose Illustrator > Preferences > Smart Guides (Mac OS) or Edit > Preferences > Smart Guides (Windows) and deselect the Measurement Labels option to turn off just the measurement labels when Smart Guides are on.

11 Choose File > Save.

Scaling objects

So far in this book, you've scaled most content with the selection tools. In this lesson, you'll use several other methods to scale objects.

1   With the artwork (basketball hoop and net) still selected, ensure that the upper-left point of the reference point locator (▦) is selected in the Control panel. Click to select the Constrain Width And Height Proportions icon (▣) located between the W and H fields. Change the Width (W:) to **255%**. Press Enter or Return to accept the value.

● **Note:** The figure shows the Width value before pressing Enter or Return.

When typing values to transform content, you can type different units such as percent (%) or pixels (px) and they will be converted to the default unit, which is inches (in) in this case.

2   Choose View > Fit All In Window.

3   Press Command+– (Mac OS) or Ctrl+– (Windows) (or View > Zoom Out) *twice* to zoom out. You should see content off the bottom edge of the artboards again. You may need to scroll down to see all of the content.

4   Select the basketball and double-click the Scale tool (▦) in the Tools panel.

5   In the Scale dialog box, change Uniform to **61%**. Toggle Preview on and off to see the change in size. Click OK.

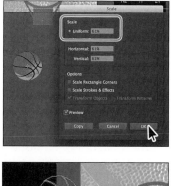

▶ **Tip:** You could also choose Object > Transform > Scale to access the Scale dialog box.

6   Select the Selection tool (▶) and drag the basketball onto the first artboard named "Front," like you see in the figure.

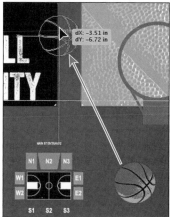

7   Select the basketball court group (without the numbers on it) *below the larger artboard*. Notice that the Stroke weight in the Control panel shows as 1 pt.

8   Select the Zoom tool (🔍) in the Tools panel and click several times, *slowly*, to zoom in to it.

9   Choose View > Show Edges.

10 Open the Transform panel by clicking the X, Y, W, or H link in the Control panel (or the word "Transform" if that appears in the Control panel). Select Scale Strokes & Effects.

11 In the Control panel, either click the word "Transform" to reveal the Transform panel, or click the center reference point of the reference point locator (▦) in the Control panel. Ensure that the Constrain Width And Height Proportions is set (⬚), and type **3.5** in the Width (W) field, and then press Enter or Return to increase the size of the artwork. Notice that the Stroke weight has scaled as well, and is now 2 pt. Leave the artwork selected.

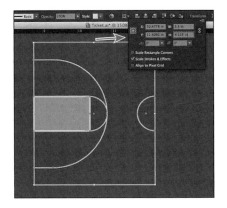

By default, strokes and effects, like drop shadows, are not scaled along with objects. For instance, if you enlarge a circle with a 1 pt stroke, the stroke remains 1 pt. But by selecting Scale Strokes & Effects before you scale—and then scaling the object—that 1 pt stroke would scale (change) relative to the amount of scaling applied to the object.

Reflecting objects

When you *reflect* an object, Illustrator flips the object across an invisible vertical or horizontal axis. In a similar way to scaling and rotating, when you reflect an object, you either designate the reference point or use the object's center point, by default.

Next, you'll use the Reflect tool (▷◁) to flip the basketball court artwork 90° across the vertical axis and copy it.

1 Select the Reflect tool (▷◁), which is nested within the Rotate tool (⟲) in the Tools panel. Click the right edge of the basketball court group (the word "anchor" or "path" may appear).

This sets the invisible axis that the shape will reflect around on the right edge of the selected artwork, rather than on the center, which is the default.

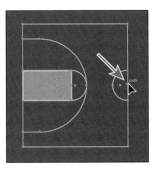

▶ **Tip:** You can reflect and copy in one step. With the Reflect tool (▷◁) selected, Option-click (Mac OS) or Alt-click (Windows) to set a point to reflect around and to open the Reflect dialog box, in one step. Select Vertical, and then click Copy.

2 With the basketball court artwork still selected, position the pointer off the right edge and drag clockwise. As you are dragging, hold down the Shift+Option (Mac OS) or Shift+Alt (Windows) keys. When the measurement label shows −90°, release the mouse button and then release the modifier keys.

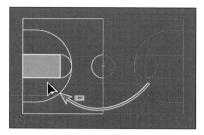

The Shift key constrains the rotation to 45° as the artwork is reflected, and the Option (Alt) key will copy the artwork. Leave the new court artwork where it is for now. You'll move it later.

3   Select the Selection tool (▶) and drag across both groups, then choose Object > Group.

Distorting objects with effects

You can distort the original shapes of objects in different ways, using various tools. Now you'll distort the basketball net using the Pucker & Bloat effect. These are different types of transformations because they are applied as effects, which means you could ultimately edit the effect later or remove it in the Appearance panel.

● **Note:** To learn more about effects, see Lesson 11, "Exploring Creative Uses of Effects and Graphic Styles."

1   Choose "2 Inside" from the Artboard Navigation menu to fit the larger artboard in the Document window.

2   Click the Layers panel icon () to open the panel, and then click the visibility column (an arrow is pointing to it in the figure) to the left of the Net layer name to show that content, and click the eye icon (👁) to the left of the Background layer to hide its contents.

You are going to create a net for the basketball hoop that is already on the artboard.

3   Click to select the red triangle shape. Choose Effect > Distort & Transform > Pucker & Bloat.

4   In the Pucker & Bloat dialog box, select Preview and drag the slider to the left to change the value to roughly **–20%**, which distorts the triangle. Click OK.

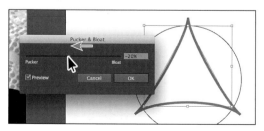

▶ **Tip:** To access the Rotate dialog box, you can also double-click the Rotate tool (⟳) in the Tools panel. The Transform panel (Window > Transform) also has a rotate option.

5 Drag across the triangle and circle to select them both. Choose Object > Transform > Rotate. In the Rotate dialog box, change the Angle to **30**, select Preview, and then click Copy. You will learn more about rotating artwork in the next section.

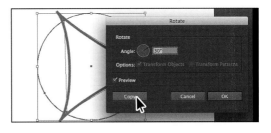

6 Choose Object > Transform > Transform Again to repeat the transformation on the selected shapes.

7 Press Command+D (Mac OS) or Ctrl+D (Windows) once to apply the transformation one more time.

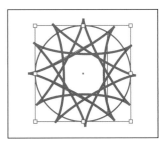

8 Choose Select > Deselect, and then drag across the edge of the circle (see the figure below) to select all of the copies and press Delete.

9 Drag across the triangles to select them all and choose Object > Group.

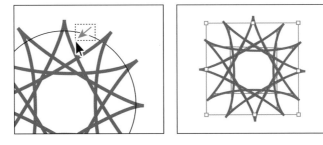

10 Drag the group down onto the basketball hoop and visually center-align them. Change the Stroke color to White in the Control panel.

11 In the Layers panel, click the visibility column to the left of the Background and the Text layers to show the content for each.

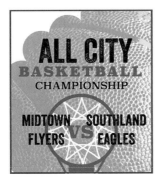

Next, you will apply a Free Distort effect to artwork.

12 Choose "3 Back" from the Artboard Navigation menu and select the basketball net.

13 Choose Effect > Distort & Transform > Free Distort.

14 In the Free Distort dialog, box drag the lower-left and lower-right points so they match the figure. Click OK.

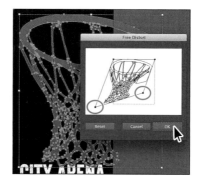

▶ **Tip:** Later in this lesson, you will learn about the Free Transform tool () that has a free distort option. Applying a free distort via the Free Transform tool is permanent and affects the underlying artwork, whereas the Free Distort effect can be edited and even removed later because it's an effect.

Rotating objects

You rotate objects by turning them around a designated reference point. There are lots of ways to do this, including methods that range from more precise to more free-form rotation.

First, you'll rotate the basketball manually, using the Selection tool.

1 Choose "1 Front" from the Artboard Navigation menu in the lower-left corner of the Document window.

2 With the Selection tool (▶), select the basketball. Option-drag (Mac OS) or Alt-drag (Windows) the basketball up and to the left to create a copy. When the artwork is positioned like you see in the figure, release the mouse button and then the modifier key.

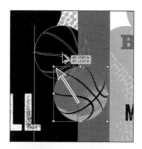

3 Position the pointer just off either the upper-right or lower-right corner points of the bounding box of the basketball you just created and when the pointer changes to rotate arrows (↘), drag in a counterclockwise fashion (up). When the measurement label shows *approximately* 15°, release the mouse button.

▶ **Tip:** You can press the Shift key as you rotate artwork with the Rotate tool (↻) or Selection tool (▶) to constrain the rotation to 45°. Remember to release the mouse button before the key.

Next, you'll rotate content using the Rotate tool (↻) and learn how this method can be different from rotating with the Selection tool.

4 With the Selection tool, Option-drag (Mac OS) or Alt-drag (Windows) the selected basketball up and to the left to create another copy. When the artwork is positioned like you see in the following figure, release the mouse button and then the modifier key.

▶ **Tip:** To rotate the object around a different reference point, click once anywhere in the document window to reposition the reference point. Then move the pointer away from the reference point and drag in a circular motion.

5 Select the Rotate tool (⟳) in the Tools panel (it's under the Reflect tool). Notice the rotate-around point in the center of the basketball artwork. The Rotate tool allows you to rotate the object around a different reference point. Position the pointer to the right of the basketball, and drag counterclockwise (up) until the measurement label shows approximately 15°, and then release the mouse button.

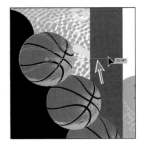

▶ **Tip:** If you select an object and then select the Rotate tool (⟳), you can Option-click (Mac OS) or Alt-click (Windows) anywhere on the object (or artboard) to set a reference point and to open the Rotate dialog box in one step.

Next, you will rotate each basketball in place using the Transform Each command.

6 With the Selection tool, Option-drag (Mac OS) or Alt-drag (Windows) the selected basketball up and to the left to create a final copy. When the artwork is positioned like you see in the following figure, release the mouse button and then the modifier key.

▶ **Tip:** You can choose Object > Transform > Transform Each to rotate several selected objects separately, and around the center of each.

7 With the last basketball selected, double-click the Rotate tool in the Tools panel. In the Rotate dialog box that appears, the last rotation value should be the value set for the Angle value. It should be approximately 15°. Make sure it's **15**° and click OK.

▶ **Tip:** After transforming content using various methods, including rotation, you will notice that the bounding box is now rotated. You can choose Object > Transform > Reset Bounding Box to reset the bounding box around the artwork again.

8 Choose File > Save.

Shearing objects

Shearing an object slants, or skews, the sides of the object along the axis you specify, keeping opposite sides parallel and making the object asymmetrical.

Next, you'll copy artwork and apply shear to it.

1 Choose View > Fit All In Window.

2 Press Command+– (Mac OS) or Ctrl+– (Windows) (or View > Zoom Out) *twice* to zoom out. You should see content off the bottom edge of the artboards again.

3 Select the Selection tool (➤). Click to select the grouped content below the first artboard that contains the "N1," "N2," etc.

4 Choose Edit > Cut, and then choose "3 Back" from the Artboard Navigation menu in the lower-left corner of the Document window.

5 Select the basketball net and choose Object > Hide > Selection.

6 Choose Edit > Paste to paste a copy in the center of the artboard.

7 Begin dragging the group of content up, and as you drag, press the Shift key to constrain the movement. Drag it up until it looks something like you see in the figure. Release the mouse button and then the Shift key.

8 Choose Object > Ungroup and the Select > Deselect.

9 Press Command++ (Mac OS) or Ctrl++ (Windows) once to zoom in to the artboard.

10 Select the gray square beneath the "N1" text. Select the Shear tool (↗), nested within the Scale tool (◲) in the Tools panel. Position the pointer above the shape; press the Shift key and drag to the left. The Shift key constrains the artwork to its original width.

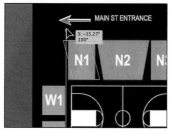

If you were shearing a single object and precision didn't matter, you could leave the object as is. But this artwork requires the shapes beneath "N1" and "N3" to have the same shearing applied.

11 Choose Edit > Undo Shear.

12 With the rectangle still selected, double-click the Shear tool. In the Shear dialog box, change the Shear Angle to **170**, select Preview, and click OK.

13 With the Selection tool, select the gray rectangle beneath the "N3" text. Double-click the Shear tool in the Tools panel and change the Shear Angle to **−170**, select Preview, and click OK. Leave the rectangle selected.

▶ **Tip:** You can also apply shear numerically in the Transform panel (Window > Transform) or in the Shear dialog box (Object > Transform > Shear).

14 Select the Selection tool, and with the Shift key pressed, select the gray rectangles behind the "N1" and "N2" text to select all three.

15 Choose Object > Group.

16 Select the Rotate tool ( ) and position the pointer over the center of the circle below (circled in the figure). When the green word "center" appears, Option-click (Mac OS) or Alt-click (Windows). In the Rotate dialog box, change the Angle to **180** and click Copy.

17 Choose Object > Show All to show the basketball net you hid earlier.

18 Choose Select > Deselect, and then choose File > Save.

Transforming with the Free Transform tool

The Free Transform tool (⬚) is a multipurpose tool that allows you to distort an object, combining functions like moving, scaling, shearing, rotating, and distorting (perspective or free). The Free Transform tool is also touch-enabled, which means you can control transformation using touch controls on certain devices. For more information on touch controls, see the sidebar at the end of this section.

● **Note:** To learn more about the options for the Free Transform tool, search for "Free Transform" in Adobe Help (Help > Illustrator Help).

1 Select the Selection tool (▶) in the Tools panel. Press the Spacebar to access the Hand tool (✋) temporarily. Drag up so you can see the basketball court artwork beneath the artboards.

2 Click to select the basketball court group, and then select the Free Transform tool (⬚) in the Tools panel.

After selecting the Free Transform tool, the Free Transform widget appears in the Document window. This widget, which is free-floating and can be repositioned, contains options to change how the Free Transform tool works. By default, the Free Transform tool allows you to move, shear, rotate, and scale objects. By selecting other options, like Perspective Distort, you can change how the tool transforms content.

Constrain

Free Transform

Selected Action (light-gray background)

Perspective Distort

Free Distort

First, you'll change the width of the selected artwork using the Free Transform tool.

3 Position the pointer over the left middle point of the artwork bounding box, and the pointer changes its appearance (⤢), indicating that you can shear or distort. Begin dragging to the right. As you drag, press the Option (Mac OS) or Alt (Windows) key to change both sides at once. Notice that you can't drag the artwork up or down—the movement is constrained to horizontal by default. When a width of *approximately* 3.7 in shows in the measurement label, release the mouse button and then the key.

● **Note:** If you were to drag the side bounding point up first to distort the artwork by shearing, the movement wouldn't be constrained and you could move in any direction.

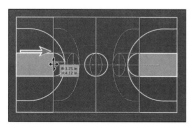

Next, you will rotate with the Free Transform tool around a specific point.

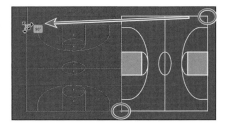

▶ **Tip:** You can also drag the reference point to a location. You can double-click the reference point to reset its position.

4   Position the pointer over the lower-left corner and double-click when the pointer looks like this (✛). This moves the reference point and ensures that the artwork will rotate around it. Press the Shift key and drag the upper-right corner in a counterclockwise fashion until you see 90° in the measurement label. Release the mouse button and then the Shift key.

● **Note:** If you find that, by trying to rotate, you are instead scaling, stop dragging and choose Edit > Undo Scale and try again.

● **Note:** The Constrain option cannot be selected when the Perspective Distort option is selected.

Like other transform tools, by holding down the Shift key while dragging with the Free Transform tool, you can constrain the movement for most of the transformations. If you don't want to hold down the Shift key, you can also select the Constrain option in the Free Transform widget before transforming, to constrain movement automatically. After dragging, the Constrain option is deselected.

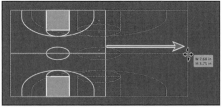

5   Position the pointer over the right middle point of the artwork bounding box, and drag to the right. Drag until a width of approximately 7.7 in shows in the measurement label.

6   With the Free Transform tool still selected, click the Perspective Distort option in the Free Transform widget (circled in the figure below).

With this option selected, you can drag a corner point of the bounding box to distort the perspective.

● **Note:** The Free Distort option of the Free Transform tool (◻) allows you to freely distort the selected content by dragging one of the corner bounding points.

7   Position the pointer over the upper-left corner of the bounding box, and the pointer changes in appearance (◹). Drag to the right until it looks like the figure.

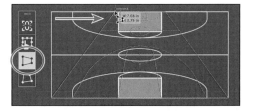

8   Change the Opacity to **60%** in the Control panel.

9   Press Command+– (Mac OS) or Ctrl+– (Windows) several times to zoom out, until you see the artboard with the basketballs on it.

10 Select the Selection tool and drag the artwork onto the artboard similar to what you see in the figure.

● **Note:** If the artwork appears on top of the text, choose Object > Arrange > Send To Back as many times as necessary to arrange it behind the text.

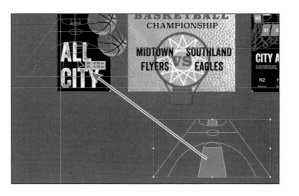

11 Select the Artboard tool (⊞) in the Tools panel. Drag the 1 Front artboard to the left until the basketball court is no longer overlapping the artboard to the right.

● **Note:** When you drag an artboard with content on it, the art moves with the artboard, by default. If you want to move an artboard but not the art on it, select the Artboard tool (⊞) and then click to deselect Move/Copy Artwork With Artboard (⬚) in the Control panel.

▶ **Tip:** You could also simply mask the content that is outside of the artboard. You will learn about clipping masks in Lesson 14, "Using Illustrator CC with Other Adobe Applications."

12 Choose View > Fit All In Window and then choose Choose File > Save.

The Free Transform tool and touch-enabled devices

In Illustrator CC, the Free Transform tool is touch-enabled. This means that, if you are using either a Windows 7– or 8–based touchscreen PC or a Touchscreen device like Wacom Cintiq 24HD Touch, you can utilize certain touch-enabled features.

Here are a few noteworthy examples:

• You can touch and drag from the center of an object and move the reference point.

• Double tapping on any of the corner points moves the reference point for the object to that point.

• Double tapping on the reference point resets it to the default position (if it's not already there).

• To constrain movement, you can tap the Constrain option in the widget before transforming.

Creating a PDF

Portable Document Format (PDF) is a universal file format that preserves the fonts, images, and layout of source documents created on a wide range of applications and platforms. Adobe PDF is the standard for the secure, reliable distribution and exchange of electronic documents and forms around the world. Adobe PDF files are compact and complete, and can be shared, viewed, and printed by anyone with free Adobe Reader® software.

You can create different types of PDF files from within Illustrator. You can create multipage PDFs, layered PDFs, and PDF/x-compliant files. Layered PDFs allow you to save one PDF with layers that can be used in different contexts. PDF/X compliant files ease the burden of color, font, and trapping issues in printing. Next, you will save this project as a PDF so that you can send it to someone else to view.

1   Choose File > Save As. In the Save As dialog box, choose Adobe PDF (pdf) from the Format menu (Mac OS) or Adobe PDF (*.PDF) from the Save As Type menu (Windows). Navigate to the Lessons > Lesson04 folder, if necessary. Notice that you have the option, at the bottom of the dialog box, to save all of the artboards in the PDF or a range of artboards. Click Save.

● **Note:** If you want to learn about the options and other presets in the Save Adobe PDF dialog box, choose Help > Illustrator Help and search for "Creating Adobe PDF files."

2   In the Save Adobe PDF dialog box, click the Adobe PDF Preset menu to see all of the different PDF presets available. Ensure that [Illustrator Default] is chosen and click Save PDF.

There are many ways that you can customize the creation of a PDF. Creating a PDF using the [Illustrator Default] preset creates a PDF in which all Illustrator data is preserved. PDFs created with this preset can be reopened in Illustrator without any loss of data. If you are planning on saving a PDF for a particular purpose, such as viewing on the Web or printing, you may wish to choose another preset or adjust the options.

3   Choose File > Save, if necessary, and then choose File > Close.

Review questions

1 Name two ways to change the size of an existing active artboard.

2 How can you rename an artboard?

3 What is the *ruler origin*?

4 What is the difference between *artboard rulers* and *global rulers*?

5 Briefly describe what the Scale Strokes & Effects option does.

6 Name at least three transformations that can be applied with the Free Transform tool.

Review answers

1 To change the size of an existing artboard, you can double-click the Artboard tool (⊞) and edit the dimensions of the active artboard in the Artboard Options dialog box. Select the Artboard tool, position the pointer over an edge or corner of the artboard, and drag to resize. Select the Artboard tool, click an artboard in the Document window, and change the dimensions in the Control panel.

2 To rename an artboard, you can select the Artboard tool (⊞) and click within the bounds of an artboard to select it. Then, change the name in the Name field in the Control panel. You can also double-click the name of the artboard in the Artboards panel (▣) to rename it or click the Options button (▣) in the Artboards panel to enter the name in the Artboard Options dialog box.

3 The ruler origin is the point where 0 (zero) appears on each ruler. By default, the ruler origin is set to be 0 (zero) in the top-left corner of the active artboard.

4 There are two types of rulers in Illustrator: artboard rulers and global rulers. Artboard rulers, which are the default rulers, set the ruler origin at the upper-left corner of the active artboard. Global rulers set the ruler origin at the upper-left corner of the first artboard, no matter which artboard is active.

5 The Scale Strokes & Effects option, found in the Transform panel (or in Illustrator > Preferences > General [Mac OS] or Edit > Preferences > General [Windows]), scales any strokes and effects as the object is scaled. This option can be turned on and off, depending on the current need.

6 The Free Transform tool (⬚) can perform a multitude of transformation operations, including move, scale, rotate, shear, and distort (perspective distort and free distort).

5 CREATING AN ILLUSTRATION WITH THE DRAWING TOOLS

Lesson overview

In this lesson, you'll learn how to do the following:

- Draw curved and straight lines.

- Edit curved and straight lines.

- Draw with the Pen tool.

- Select and adjust curve segments.

- Add and delete anchor points.

- Convert between smooth points and corner points.

- Create dashed lines and add arrowheads.

- Cut paths with the Scissors and Knife tools.

- Draw and edit with the Pencil tool.

This lesson takes approximately 90 minutes to complete.

Download the project files for this lesson from the Lesson & Update Files tab on your Account page at www.peachpit.com and store them on your computer in a convenient location, as described in the Getting Started section of this book.

Your Account page is also where you'll find any updates to the chapters or to the lesson files. Look on the Lesson & Update Files tab to access the most current content.

Although the Pencil tool is preferable for drawing and editing free-form lines, the Pen tool and Curvature tool are excellent for drawing precisely, including drawing straight lines, Bezier curves, and complex shapes. You'll practice using the Pen tool, and then use all of these tools to create an illustration of a dish of ice cream.

Getting started

In the first part of this lesson, you'll ease into working with the Pen tool.

1   To ensure that the tools and panels function exactly as described in this lesson, delete or deactivate (by renaming) the Adobe Illustrator CC preferences file. See "Restoring default preferences" in the Getting Started section at the beginning of the book.

2   Start Adobe Illustrator CC.

● **Note:** If you have not already downloaded the project files for this lesson to your computer from your Account page, make sure to do so now. See the "Getting Started" section at the beginning of this book.

3   Open the L5_practice.ai file in the Lesson05 folder, located in the Lessons folder on your hard disk.

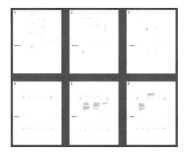

The document is made up of six artboards, numbered 1 through 6 (you most likely won't see all six, like in the figure). As you progress through the first part of this lesson, you will be asked to move to the next artboard.

4   Choose File > Save As. In the Save As dialog box, navigate to the Lesson05 folder and open it. Rename the file to **Practice.ai**. Choose Adobe Illustrator (ai) from the Format menu (Mac OS), or choose Adobe Illustrator (*.AI) from the Save As Type menu (Windows). Click Save and, in the Illustrator Options dialog box, leave the default settings, and then click OK.

Getting started with the Pen tool

The Pen tool (✐) is one of the main drawing tools that is used to create both free-form and more precise artwork and also plays a role in editing existing vector artwork. It's important to have an understanding of the Pen tool when working with Illustrator. Just know that it takes plenty of practice to feel comfortable with the tool.

In this first section, you'll begin to explore the Pen tool and, later in the lesson, you will create artwork using the Pen tool and other tools and commands. Next, you'll get ready to begin drawing.

● **Note:** If you don't see "Reset Essentials" in the menu, choose Window > Workspace > Essentials before choosing Window > Workspace > Reset Essentials.

1   Choose 1 from the Artboard Navigation menu in the lower-left corner of the Document window. Choose View > Fit Artboard In Window.

2   Choose Window > Workspace > Reset Essentials.

3   Choose View > Smart Guides to turn off the Smart Guides. Smart Guides can be useful when you draw, but you won't need them now.

4 In the Control panel, click Fill color and choose None (▢). Then, click the Stroke color and make sure that the Black swatch is selected.

5 Make sure the Stroke weight is 1 pt in the Control panel.

When you begin drawing with the Pen tool, it's usually best to have no fill on the path you create because the fill can cover the path you are trying to create. You can add a fill later, if necessary. Next, you'll draw a path in the work area of the artboard that looks like the zigzag path at the top of the artboard.

6 Select the Pen tool (✎) in the Tools panel. Position the pointer in the artboard area, and notice the asterisk next to the Pen icon (✎.), indicating that you are starting a path.

7 In the area labeled Work Area, click where the blue "start" square is, to set the first anchor point. Move the pointer to the right of the original point and you will see a line connecting the first point and the pointer, no matter where you move the pointer. This is called Pen tool preview (or Rubber Band). Later, as you create curved paths, it will make drawing them easier.

The asterisk has disappeared, indicating that you are now drawing a path.

8 Position the pointer down and to the right of the original point, and click to create the next anchor point in the path.

● **Note:** The first segment you draw is not visible until you click to create a second anchor point. If the path looks curved, you have accidentally dragged with the Pen tool; choose Edit > Undo Pen, and then click again.

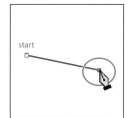

9 Click a third anchor point beneath the initial anchor point to create a zigzag pattern. Create a zigzag that has a total of six anchor points, which means you will click the artboard three more times.

One of the many benefits of using the Pen tool is that you can create custom paths and continue to edit the anchor points that make up the path. Notice that only the last anchor point is filled (not hollow like the rest of the anchor points), indicating that it is selected.

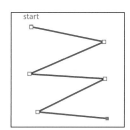

10 Choose Select > Deselect.

The type of anchor points you just created are called corner points. *Corner points* are not smooth like a curve; rather, they create an angle where the anchor point is. Now that you can create corner points, you will move on to adding other types of points like smooth points. But first, you will learn a few more techniques for selecting paths.

● **Note:** If you see a crosshair (-¦-) instead of the Pen icon (✎.), the Caps Lock key is active. Caps Lock turns tool icons into crosshairs for increased precision.

▶ **Tip:** You can turn off the Pen tool preview by choosing Illustrator > Preferences > Selection & Anchor Display (Mac OS) or Edit > Preferences > Selection & Anchor Display (Windows) to open the Preferences dialog box. In the dialog box, with the Selection & Anchor Display category options showing, deselect Enable Rubber Band for Pen and Curvature Tool.

Selecting paths

Back in Lesson 2 "Techniques for Selecting Artwork," you were introduced to selecting content with the Selection and Direct Selection tools. Next, you'll explore a few more options for selecting artwork with those same Selection tools.

Tip: You can also drag across a path to select it with the Selection tool.

1   Select the Selection tool ( ) in the Tools panel, and position the pointer directly over a straight line in the zigzag path. When the pointer shows a solid black box ( ) next to it, click.

This selects the path and all of the anchor points. You can tell the anchor points are selected because they become filled.

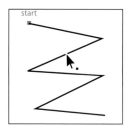

2   Drag from one of the straight lines in the path to a new location anywhere on the artboard. All the anchor points travel together, maintaining the zigzag path.

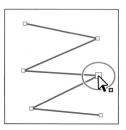

Tip: If the Pen tool ( ) were still selected, you could Command-click (Mac OS) or Ctrl-click (Windows) in a blank area of the artboard to deselect the path. This temporarily selects a Selection tool. When you release the Ctrl or Command key, the Pen tool is selected again.

3   Deselect the zigzag path in one of the following ways:

• With the Selection tool, click an empty area of the artboard.

• Choose Select > Deselect.

4   In the Tools panel, select the Direct Selection tool ( ) and when the pointer changes ( ), click the path to reveal all of the anchor points. Position the pointer over one of the anchor points and the anchor point will become larger than the others, and the pointer will show a small box with a dot in the center ( ) next to it (the following figure shows this). Both of these indicate that if you click, you will select the anchor point. Click to select the anchor point and the selected anchor point is filled (looks solid), whereas the deselected anchor points are still hollow.

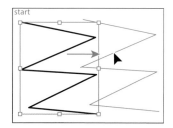

Note: When you position the pointer over a line segment that is not already selected, a black, solid square appears next to the Direct Selection tool pointer, indicating that you will select a line segment.

5   Drag the anchor point to the left a bit to reposition it.

The anchor point moves, but the others remain stationary. This is one method for editing a path, like you saw in Lesson 2.

6   Click in a blank area of the artboard to deselect.

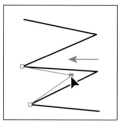

7 Position the Direct Selection pointer over a straight line segment in the middle of the zigzag shape. When the pointer changes (![pointer icon]), click to select. Choose Edit > Cut. This cuts only the selected segment from the zigzag.

● **Note:** If the entire zigzag path disappears, choose Edit > Undo Cut and try again.

8 Select the Pen tool (![pen icon]), and position the pointer over one of the end anchor points that was connected to the line segment that was cut. Notice that the Pen tool shows a forward slash (![pen slash icon]), indicating that if you click, you will continue drawing from that anchor point. Click the point.

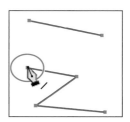

9 Position the pointer over the other anchor point that was connected to the cut line segment. The pointer now shows a merge symbol next to it (![pen merge icon]), indicating that you are connecting to another path. Click the point to reconnect the paths.

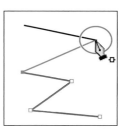

Constraining lines

In previous lessons, you learned that using the Shift key and Smart Guides in combination with shape tools constrains the shape of objects. The Shift key and Smart Guides can also constrain paths drawn with the Pen tool to create paths in angles of 45°. Next, you will learn how to draw straight lines and constrain angles as you draw.

1 Choose 2 from the Artboard Navigation menu in the lower-left corner of the Document window.

2 Choose View > Smart Guides to turn on the Smart Guides.

3 With the Pen tool (![pen icon]) selected, in the area labeled Work Area, click where the blue "start" square is to set the first anchor point.

   Don't worry if the Smart Guides are attempting to "snap" the anchor point you create to other content on the artboard, making it difficult to click directly on the "start" square. This is expected behavior and is sometimes why we turn off the Smart Guides when drawing.

4 Move the pointer to the right of the original anchor point approximately 1.5 in, as indicated by the measurement label. It doesn't have to be exact. A green alignment guide appears when the pointer is vertically aligned with the previous anchor point. Click to set another anchor point.

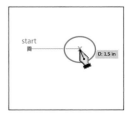

As you've learned in previous lessons, the measurement label and alignment guides are a part of the Smart Guides. When working with the Pen tool, you can achieve finer measurements in the measurement labels when you zoom in.

5 Click to set three more points, following the same generic shape as shown in the top half of the artboard.

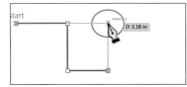

Notice the green alignment guides that appear as you draw. Sometimes they are helpful for aligning points, and sometimes they align to content that you don't necessarily want to align to.

6 Press the Shift key, and move the pointer to the right and down. When the measurement label shows 2 in, click to set an anchor point, and then release the modifier key.

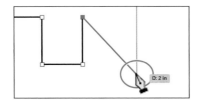

Notice that the new anchor point may not be where you clicked. That's because the line has been constrained to 45˚. Pressing the Shift key creates angled lines constrained to 45˚.

7 Position the pointer below the last point, and click to set the last anchor point for the shape.

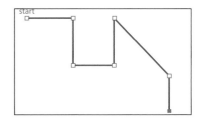

8 Choose Select > Deselect, and then choose File > Save.

Introducing curved paths

In this part of the lesson, you'll learn how to draw smooth, curved lines with the Pen tool. In vector drawing applications such as Illustrator, you draw a curve, called a Bezier curve, with anchor points and direction handles. By setting anchor points and dragging direction handles, you can define the shape of the curve. This type of anchor point, with direction handles, is called a *smooth point*. Although drawing curves this way can take some time to learn, it gives you the greatest control and flexibility in creating paths.

First, you'll just get the feel for how to create a curved path. The goal for this exercise is not to create anything specific but to get accustomed to the feel of creating Bezier curves.

1   Choose View > Smart Guides to deselect them.

2   Choose 3 from the Artboard Navigation menu in the lower-left corner of the Document window. You will draw in the area labeled Practice.

3   Press Z to switch to the Zoom tool (🔍) (or select it in the Tools panel), and click twice in the bottom half of the artboard to zoom in.

4   Select the Pen tool (✐) in the Tools panel. In the Control panel, make sure that the Fill color is None (▱) and the Stroke color is Black. Also, make sure the Stroke weight is still 1 pt in the Control panel.

5   With the Pen tool selected, click in a blank area of the artboard to create a starting anchor point.

6   Move the pointer away from the original point you created, and click and drag away from the point to create a curved path.

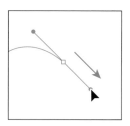

Notice that as you drag away from the point, direction handles appear. *Direction handles* consist of direction lines that end in round direction points. The angle and length of the direction handles determine the shape and size of the curve. Direction handles do not print and are not visible when the anchor point is inactive.

7   Move the pointer away from the anchor point you just created to see the Rubber Band (Pen tool preview). Move the pointer around a bit to see how it changes. Continue clicking and dragging in different areas to create a series of points.

8   Choose Select > Deselect. Leave the file open for the next section.

Components of a path

As you draw, you create a line called a path. A path is made up of one or more straight or curved segments. The beginning and end of each segment are marked by anchor points, which work like pins holding a wire in place. A path can be closed (for example, a circle) or open, with distinct endpoints (for example, a wavy line). You change the shape of a path by dragging its anchor points, the direction points at the end of direction lines that appear at anchor points, or the path segment itself.

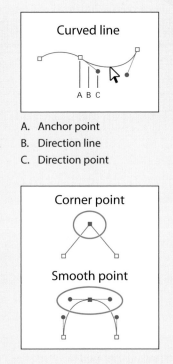

Curved line

A. Anchor point
B. Direction line
C. Direction point

Paths can have two kinds of anchor points: corner points and smooth points. At a corner point, a path abruptly changes direction. At a smooth point, path segments are connected as a continuous curve.

You can draw a path using any combination of corner and smooth points. If you draw the wrong kind of point, you can always change it.

—From Illustrator Help

Drawing a curve with the Pen tool

In this part of the lesson, you'll use what you just learned to trace a curved shape with the Pen tool.

1   Press the spacebar to temporarily select the Hand tool (✋), and drag down until you see the curve at the top of the artboard (on Artboard 3).

2   Select the Pen tool (✐) in the Tools panel. Click and drag from the "start" square, up to the gold dot, and then release the mouse button. This creates a direction line going in the same direction as the path.

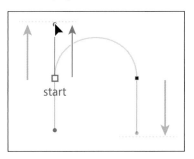

● **Note:** The artboard may scroll as you drag. If you lose visibility of the curve, choose View > Zoom Out until you see the curve and anchor point. Pressing the spacebar allows you to use the Hand tool to reposition the artwork.

3 Click the black point on the right side of the arch and drag down. Release the mouse button when the pointer reaches the gold dot and the path you are creating follows the arch.

If the path you created is not aligned exactly with the template, select the Direct Selection tool (⬠) and select the anchor points one at a time to show the direction handles. You can then adjust the direction handles using the Direct Selection tool until your path follows the template more accurately.

● **Note:** Pulling the direction handle longer makes a steeper slope; when the direction handle is shorter, the slope is flatter.

4 Select the Selection tool (▶), and click the artboard in an area with no objects, or choose Select > Deselect.

Deselecting the first path allows you to create a new path. If you click somewhere on the artboard with the Pen tool while the path is still selected, the path connects to the next point you draw.

5 Choose File > Save.

If you want to try drawing the curve for more practice, scroll down to the Practice area in the same artboard and trace the curve.

▶ **Tip:** To deselect objects, you can also press the Command (Mac OS) or Ctrl (Windows) key to temporarily switch to the Selection or Direct Selection tool, whichever was last used, then, click the artboard where there are no objects. Another way to end a path is to press the Escape key when you are finished drawing.

Drawing a series of curves with the Pen tool

Now that you've experimented with drawing a few curves, you will draw a shape that contains several continuous curves.

1 Choose 4 from the Artboard Navigation menu in the lower-left corner of the Document window. Select the Zoom tool (🔍), and click several times in the top half of the artboard to zoom in.

2 In the Control panel, make sure that the Fill color is None (⬜) and the Stroke color is Black. Also, make sure the Stroke weight is still 1 pt in the Control panel.

3 Select the Pen tool (✐). Click the blue "start" square, and drag up in the direction of the arch, stopping at the gold dot.

4 Position the pointer over the black square point to the right, click and drag down to the gold dot, adjusting the first arch with the direction handle before you release the mouse button.

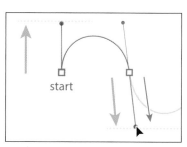

● **Note:** Don't worry if the path you draw is not exact. You can correct the line with the Direct Selection tool (⬠) when the path is complete.

5   Continue along the path, alternating between dragging up and down. Put anchor points only where there are black squares (points).

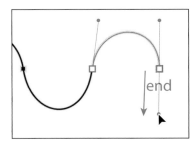

If you make a mistake as you draw, you can undo your work by choosing Edit > Undo Pen and then draw the last point again. Note that your direction lines may not match the figure at right, and that's okay.

6   When the path is complete, select the Direct Selection tool and click to select an anchor point.

When the anchor point is selected, the direction handles appear and you can readjust the curve of the path if necessary. With a curve selected, you can also change the stroke and fill of the curve. When you do this, the next line you draw will have the same attributes.

● **Note:** For more information about these attributes, see Lesson 6, "Using Color and Patterns to Enhance Signage."

If you want to try drawing the shape again for more practice, scroll down to the bottom half of the same artboard (labeled Practice) and trace the shape down there.

7   Choose File > Save.

Converting smooth points to corner points

When creating curves, the direction handles help to determine the shape and size of the curved segments, as you've already seen. Removing the direction lines from an anchor point can convert a smooth curve into a corner. In the next part of the lesson, you will practice converting between smooth points and corner points.

1   Choose 5 from the Artboard Navigation menu in the lower-left corner of the Document window.

On the top of the artboard, you can see the path that you will trace. You will use the top artboard as a template for the exercise, creating your paths directly on top of those. Use the Practice section at the bottom of the artboard for additional practice on your own.

2   In the top artboard, use the Zoom tool (🔍) and click several times to zoom in.

3   In the Control panel, make sure that the Fill color is None (▨) and the Stroke color is Black. Also, make sure the Stroke weight is still 1 pt in the Control panel.

● **Note:** Pressing the Shift key when dragging constrains the direction handles to multiples of 45°.

4   Select the Pen tool (✐), and pressing the Shift key, click the blue "start" square and drag up to the gold dot. Release the mouse button, and then release the Shift key.

5   Click the next black anchor point to the right, and pressing the Shift key, drag down to the red dot. When the curve looks correct, release the mouse button and then release the Shift key. Leave the path selected.

Now you need the curve to switch directions and create another arch. You will *split* the direction lines to convert a smooth point to a corner point.

6 Press the Option (Mac OS) or Alt (Windows) key, and position the pointer over either the last anchor point created or the bottom direction point. When a convert-point icon (^) appears next to the Pen tool pointer (⌕), click and drag a

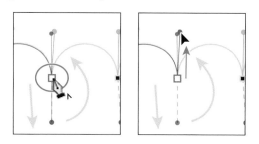

▶ **Tip:** After you draw a path, you can also select single or multiple anchor points and click the Convert Selected Anchor Points To Corner button (▣) or Convert Selected Anchor Points To Smooth button (▣) in the Control panel.

direction line up to the gold dot. Release the mouse button, and then release the modifier key. If you do not see the caret, you may create an additional loop.

You can practice adjusting the direction handles with the Direct Selection tool (▸) when the path is completed.

7 Position the Pen tool pointer over the next (third) black square point on the template path, and drag down to the red dot. Release the mouse button when the path looks similar to the template path.

8 Press the Option (Mac OS) or Alt (Windows) key and after the convert-point icon (^) appears, position the pointer over the anchor point or direction point and drag up to the gold dot. Release the mouse button, and then release the modifier key.

For the next (fourth) point, you will not release the mouse button to split the direction handles, so pay close attention.

9 For the fourth anchor point, click the next black square on the template path and drag down to the red dot until the path looks correct. This time, *do not release the mouse button.* Press the Option (Mac OS) or Alt (Windows) key, and drag up to the gold dot for the next

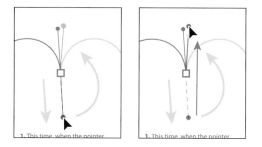

curve. Release the mouse button, and then release the modifier key.

10 Continue this process using the Option (Mac OS) or Alt (Windows) key to create corner points until the path is completed.

11 Use the Direct Selection tool to fine-tune the path, and then deselect the path.

If you want to try drawing the same shape for more practice, scroll down to the Practice area in the same artboard and trace the shape down there.

Combining curves and straight lines

Of course in the real world, when you draw with the Pen tool, you won't just create either curves or straight lines. In this next section, you'll learn how to go from curves to straight lines and from straight lines to curves.

1 Choose 6 from the Artboard Navigation menu in the lower-left corner of the Document window. Select the Zoom tool (🔍), and click several times in the top half of the artboard to zoom in.

2 Select the Pen tool (✏️). Click the blue "start" square, and drag up. Release the mouse button when the pointer reaches the gold dot.

3 Drag down from the second anchor point, and release the mouse button when the pointer reaches the gold dot and the arch matches the template. This method of creating a curve should be familiar to you by now.

If you were to click on the next black anchor point (don't), even pressing the Shift key (to produce a straight line), the path would be curved. The last point you created is a smooth anchor point and has a direction line after the point. The figure at right shows what the path would look like if you clicked with the Pen tool on the next point.

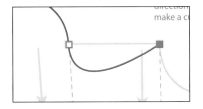

You will now continue the path as a straight line.

4 Position the pointer over the last point created (notice that the convert-point icon appears [^]), and click to delete the leading direction handle from the anchor point, as shown in the figure.

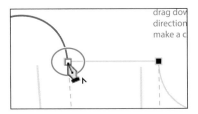

5 Press the Shift key, and click the next point in the template path to the right to set the next point, creating a straight segment.

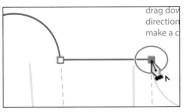

6 For the next arch, position the pointer over the last point created (notice that the convert-point icon appears [^]), and then drag down from that point to the gold dot. This creates a new direction line.

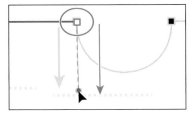

7 Click the next point, and drag up to complete the arch.

8 Click the last anchor point you just created to remove the direction line.

9 Shift-click the next point to create the second straight segment.

10 Click and drag up from the last point created to create a direction line, and then click and drag down on the end point to create the final arch.

If you want to try drawing the same shape for more practice, scroll down to the Practice area in the same artboard and trace the shape down there.

▶ **Tip:** Deselect before practicing with the next shape.

11 Choose File > Save, and then choose File > Close.

Creating the ice cream illustration

With a bit of Pen tool practice behind you, in this next part of the lesson, you'll create an illustration of a dish of ice cream. You'll use the new skills you learned in the previous exercises, and you'll also learn some additional techniques and tools.

1 Choose File > Open, and open the L5_end.ai file in the Lesson05 folder, located in the Lessons folder.

2 Choose View > Fit All In Window to see the finished artwork. (Use the Hand tool [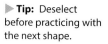] to move the artwork to where you want it.) If you don't want to leave the artwork open, choose File > Close.

3 Choose File > Open, and open the L5_start.ai file in the Lesson05 folder. Choose View > Fit All In Window.

4 Choose File > Save As, name the file **IceCream.ai**, and select the Lesson05 folder in the Save As dialog box.

Choose Adobe Illustrator (ai) from the Format menu (Mac OS) or choose Adobe Illustrator (*.AI) from the Save As Type menu (Windows), and click Save. In the Illustrator Options dialog box, leave the options set at the defaults, and then click OK.

Drawing the ice cream with the Pen tool

To start with, you'll draw an ice cream shape, which combines curves and corners. Just take your time as you practice with this shape, and use the guides provided to assist you in drawing it.

1 Choose View > Ice Cream to zoom in to the ice cream path to the right of the text "Flavor of the month."

2 In the Control panel, make sure that the Fill color is None (▱) and the Stroke color is Black.

3 Make sure the Stroke weight is **1 pt** in the Control panel.

▶ **Tip:** Don't forget, you can always undo a point you've drawn (Edit > Undo Pen) and then try again.

● **Note:** On Windows, you may need to scroll down in the panel menu.

● **Note:** You do not
have to start at the
blue square (point A)
to draw this shape. You
can set anchor points
for a path with the
Pen tool in a clockwise
or counterclockwise
direction.

4 With the Pen tool (⟋) selected, drag from
the blue square labeled A to the red dot
beneath it to set the starting anchor point
and direction of the first curve.

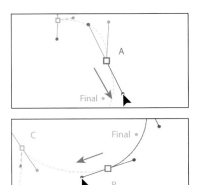

5 Continue on, dragging from point B to the
red dot, to create the first curve.

The next point you create will be
converted from a smooth point to a
corner point.

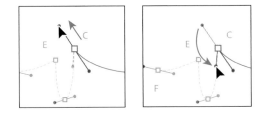

● **Note:** If you find
that the path you are
drawing has a fill of
white, some of the dots
in the template will be
hidden. You can always
change the fill to None
(☐) for the path you
are drawing.

6 Drag from point C to the red dot, but *don't release the mouse button yet*. With
the pointer over the red dot, hold down the Option (Mac OS) or Alt (Windows)
key and continue dragging from the red dot to the gold dot below the point.
Release the mouse button, and then release the modifier key. This splits the
direction handles.

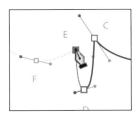

7 Drag from point D to the red dot. As you drag, pay attention to how the path
looks between points C and D.

8 Click point E, without dragging, to create a corner point with no direction lines.

You'll find that setting an anchor point without direction lines (a corner point)
allows you to set a point with no curve.

9 For points F and G, drag from each point to the red dot to create curves.

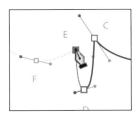 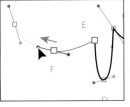 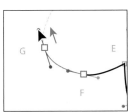

Click point E.   Create point F.   Create point G.

10 Drag from point H to the red dot, but don't release the mouse button yet.
When the pointer reaches the red dot, hold down the Option (Mac OS) or Alt
(Windows) key, and continue dragging from the red dot to the gold dot. Release
the mouse button, and then release the modifier key.

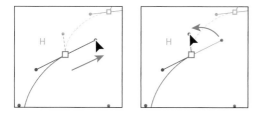

11 Drag from point I to the red dot, hold down the Option (Mac OS) or Alt (Windows) key, and continue dragging from the red dot to the gold dot. Release the mouse button, and then release the modifier key. This splits the direction handles.

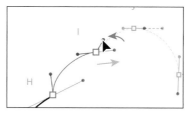

As you draw with the Pen tool, you may want to edit a curve you previously drew without ending the path you are drawing. Pressing a modifier key with the Pen tool selected, you can position the pointer over a previous path segment and drag to modify it, which is what you'll do next.

12 Position the pointer over the path between points H and I and press the Option (Mac OS) or Alt (Windows) key. The pointer changes appearance (▶.). Drag the path up and to the left to make the path have more curve, like you see in the figure. Release the mouse button and then the key. Now, you can continue drawing the path.

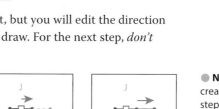

> **Tip:** You can also press the Option+Shift (Mac OS) or Alt+Shift (Windows) keys to constrain the handles to a perpendicular direction, which ensures that the handles are the same length.

For the next point, J, you will create a smooth point, but you will edit the direction handles independently using a modifier key as you draw. For the next step, *don't release the mouse button until you are told.*

13 Begin dragging from point J to the red dot on the right. As you drag, press and hold the Shift key to constrain the direction lines. When the pointer reaches the red dot, release the Shift key but not the mouse button. Press the Option (Mac OS) or Alt (Windows) key, and continue dragging the direction point (at the end of the direction line) from the red dot to the gold dot to make just that one direction handle longer. When the pointer reaches the gold dot, release the mouse button, and then release the key.

> ● **Note:** You could also create the point in this step by dragging with the Shift key pressed and releasing the mouse button when the pointer reaches the red dot. You could then position the Pen tool icon over the anchor point. When the convert-point icon (^) appears next to the pointer, you could drag out a new direction handle.

14 Continue drawing the point at K by first dragging from the anchor point to the red dot, and then pressing the Option (Mac OS) or Alt (Windows) key and dragging from the red dot to the gold dot.

Next, you'll complete the drawing of the ice cream by closing the path.

15 Position the Pen tool over the starting point A without clicking.

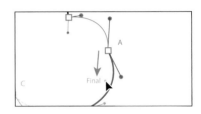

Notice that an open circle appears next to the Pen tool pointer ( ), indicating that the path will close if you were to click the anchor point (don't click yet). If you were to click and drag, the direction handles on either side of the point would move as a single straight line. We need to split the direction handles so the final point is a corner point.

▶ **Tip:** When creating a closing anchor point, you can press the spacebar to move the point.

16 Press the Option (Mac OS) or Alt (Windows) key with the pointer still over point A. Click and drag straight down and notice that a direction handle shows, but is going in the opposite direction (it's going up). Drag to the gold dot labeled "Final." Release the mouse button and then the key.

As you drag down, another direction line appears above the point. Without the modifier key, as you drag away from closing point, you are reshaping the path before and after the anchor point. Pressing the Option/Alt modifier key on the closing point allows you to edit the previous direction handle independently.

17 Command-click (Mac OS) or Ctrl-click (Windows) away from the path to deselect it, and then choose File > Save.

This is a shortcut method for deselecting a path while keeping the Pen tool selected. You could also choose Select > Deselect, among other methods.

Drawing the dish with the Curvature tool

With the Curvature tool ( ), you can draw and edit paths quickly and visually to create paths with smooth refined curves and straight lines. Using the Curvature tool, you can also edit paths while drawing or after the path is complete using the same tool.

In this section, you'll explore the Curvature tool while creating a dish for the ice cream you already drew.

1 Choose 2 Dish from the Artboard Navigation menu in the lower-left corner of the Document window. Choose View > Fit Artboard In Window (if necessary).

Looking at the template path, you will see a vertical red dotted line running through the A and I points. After you draw half of the ice cream dish, you will copy and reflect it around the red dotted line, then join the two halves together.

2 Select the Curvature tool (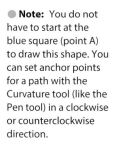) in the Tools panel. Click the blue square at point A to set the starting anchor point.

● **Note:** You do not have to start at the blue square (point A) to draw this shape. You can set anchor points for a path with the Curvature tool (like the Pen tool) in a clockwise or counterclockwise direction.

3 Press the Shift key, and click on point B (to the left of A). After clicking, release the key.

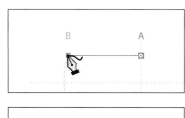

4 Move the pointer away from point B and notice the preview of the curve before and after point B.

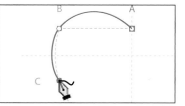

The Curvature tool works by creating anchor points where you click. The drawing curve will "flex" around the points dynamically. Direction handles are created when necessary to curve the path for you. If you were to click in this instance, the curve preview you see would become the drawn path.

5 Press the Shift key, and click point C to align the anchor points B and C. Release the Shift key after clicking and notice the new curved path.

6 Hover the pointer over point B and the pointer will change (⯈◉). Double-click to convert the smooth point to a corner point.

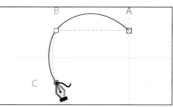

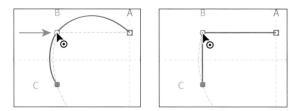

Double-clicking a point, which converts it to a corner point, has the effect of splitting the direction handles for the point.

7 Hover the pointer over point D and click to set the next point.

Notice that the path segments before and after point C are curved.

8 Hover the pointer over the anchor point at D. When the pointer changes () double-click to convert the point to a corner point.

The points you create with the Curvature tool can have three appearances, indicating it's current state: selected (●), corner point (not selected [◉]), and smooth point (not selected [○]).

9 Shift-click point E to create a point.

Notice that the path doesn't follow the dotted line of the template path between points D and E. As you draw with the Curvature tool, you can easily go back and make corrections, even adding and deleting points, and then continue drawing.

▶ **Tip:** If you click an existing point with the Curvature tool, it becomes selected (●). You can then press Delete or Backspace to remove it.

10 Hover the pointer over the path segment between the D and E points. When a plus (+) appears next to the pointer, click and drag to the left to create a point and curve the path. Drag to match the dotted template.

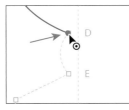 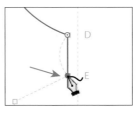 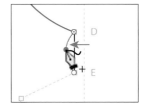

Convert D to a corner point. Create a point at E. Add a point to the path.

Now you can just continue drawing the path with the Curvature tool.

11 Option-click (Mac OS) or Alt-click (Windows) point F and notice that the path at point E is curved.

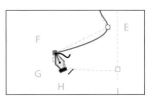

By Option-clicking (Mac OS) or Alt-clicking (Windows) when you create a point with the Curvature tool, you create a corner point instead of the default smooth point.

12 Option-click (Mac OS) or Alt-click (Windows) point E to make it a corner point.

13 Shift-click point G.

14 Click point H and then click point I.

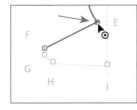 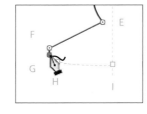 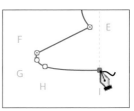

Convert E to a corner point. Shift-click point G. Create the last two points.

● **Note:** To close a path with the Curvature tool, hover the pointer over the first point you created in the path and a circle appears next to the pointer (✎₀). Click to close the path.

15 Press the Escape key to stop drawing and then choose Select > Deselect.

Finishing the ice cream dish

With one-half of the shape created, you will now create a copy, reflect the copy, and then join the two halves together to make a perfectly symmetrical closed shape—the ice cream dish. To learn more about reflecting objects, see Lesson 4, "Transforming Artwork."

The first step is to make sure that the first and last anchor points are lined up vertically with each other.

1 Select the Direct Selection tool (⬚), and click the last point you created (at point I). Shift-click the first point you created on the ice cream dish (at point A) to select both of the points at I and A.

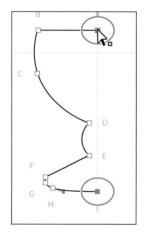

2 Click the Horizontal Align Center button (⬚) in the Control panel to align the points.

   Aligning the points isn't necessary to copy and join two halves, but aligning them will ensure that extra points won't be added when you join the halves together.

● **Note:** The Align options may not appear in the Control panel. You can either click the word "Align" in the Control panel or choose Window > Align to see the align options.

3 Select the Selection tool (⬚).

4 Choose Select > Deselect, and then click to select the entire path.

5 Choose View > Smart Guides to turn on the Smart Guides.

6 Position the pointer over the Rotate tool (⬚), click and hold down the mouse button to reveal more tools. Select the Reflect tool (⬚).

7 Click the Layers panel icon (⬚) to show the Layers panel. Click the eye icon (⬚) to the left of the layer named "template" to hide its contents. Click the Layers panel tab to hide the panel.

8 Position the pointer over the last (bottom) anchor point (I). When the word "anchor" appears, Option-click (Mac OS) or Alt-click (Windows).

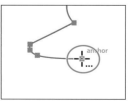

● **Note:** The modifier key sets the point that the shape will reflect around and opens the Reflect dialog box so you can copy the shape in one step.

9   In the Reflect dialog box that opens, select Vertical, if it's not already selected, and then click Copy.

10   Select the Selection tool, and choose Select > All On Active Artboard to select both halves.

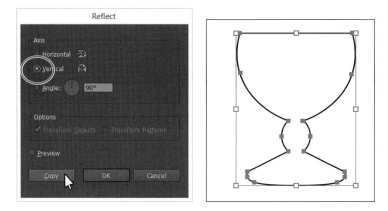

11   Press Command+J (Mac OS) or Ctrl+J (Windows) to join the two halves together into one closed path. Leave the path selected.

After doing this, it may not look like much has changed, when in fact both halves are combined into a single, closed path.

Editing curves

In this part of the lesson, you'll adjust curves you've drawn using several methods learned previously and a few new ones.

1   Choose Select > Deselect.

2   Select the Direct Selection tool (⟨⟩) and drag across the two points shown in the following figure to select them.

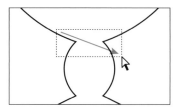

Notice that a Live Corners widget shows next to each of the anchor points. With both points selected, you can edit the radius of both by dragging one of the Live Corners widgets.

3   Drag the Live Corners widget on the right point to the right just a bit to make the path smoother. When the measurement label shows a radius of roughly 0.2 in, release the mouse button.

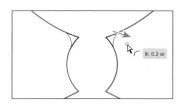

4   Choose View > Smart Guides to turn off the Smart Guides.

Next, you'll edit the ice cream shape you created earlier.

5   Choose View > Ice Cream.

Aside from zooming in on the ice cream path, the content from the template layer should be displayed as well, showing the guides you used to draw the path.

6   With the Direct Selection tool selected, click the ice cream path to select it. All of the anchor points will appear.

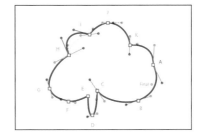

Clicking with the Direct Selection tool displays the direction handles for the selected line segment and lets you adjust the shape of individual curved segments. Clicking with the Selection tool (▶) selects the entire path.

7   Click the anchor point (J) that is at the top of the ice cream path to select it. Drag the point down just a bit until it roughly matches the figure.

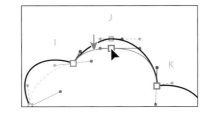

The points will be filled (not hollow) when selected.

▶ **Tip:** You can also press the arrow keys to nudge an anchor point in a direction. Pressing and holding down the Shift key and then pressing an arrow key moves the point ten times farther than pressing the arrow key without the modifier key.

8   Click the Layers panel icon (▨) to show the Layers panel. Click the eye icon (◉) to the left of the layer named "template" to hide its contents. Click the Layers panel tab to hide the panel.

● **Note:** The template layer was showing again after you chose View > Ice Cream because the visibility of layers is remembered when the view is saved.

9   With the Direct Selection tool, position the pointer over the path, like you see in the figure. Notice that the pointer changes appearance (▶.). This indicates that you can drag the path, which will adjust the anchor points as you drag. Drag the path up and to the left to make the curve a little more rounded. As you drag the path, notice that the direction handles are changing as well. This is an easy way to make edits to a path.

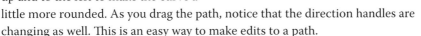

▶ **Tip:** As you are dragging a path with the Direct Selection tool, you can also press the Shift key to constrain the handles to a perpendicular direction, which ensures that the handles are the same length.

▶ **Tip:** If you wanted to adjust the direction handles instead of dragging the path, and wanted to see the direction handles for all of the selected points, you could click Show Handles For Multiple Selected Anchor Points (▨) in the Control panel.

10 Choose Select > Deselect, and then choose File > Save.

Deleting and adding anchor points

Most of the time, the goal of drawing paths with a tool like the Pen tool is to avoid adding more anchor points than necessary. You can, however, reduce a path's complexity or change its overall shape by deleting unnecessary points (and therefore gain more control over the shape), or you can extend a path by adding points to it. Next, you will delete and add anchor points to a path.

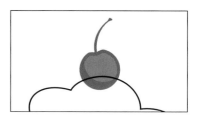

Note: If the cherry appears on top of other shapes on the page, select the cherry and then choose Object > Arrange > Send To Back.

1   Click the Layers panel icon (⬛) to show the Layers panel. Click the eye icon (👁) to the left of the layer named "cherry" to show its contents (shown in the figure). Click the Layers panel tab to hide the panel.

2   With the Direct Selection tool (▷) selected, click the edge of the ice cream path.

3   Select the Zoom tool (🔍) in the Tools panel, and click three times, slowly, on the cherry at the top of the ice cream path to zoom in.

4   Select the Pen tool (✒) in the Tools panel, and position the pointer over the ice cream path (see the figure). When a plus sign (+) appears to the right of the Pen tool pointer (✒₊), click to add another point to the path.

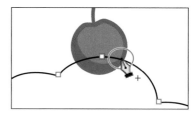

▶ **Tip:** When you press the Ctrl or Command key with the Pen tool selected, the last selected Selection tool (Selection or Direct Selection) is temporarily selected.

5   Select the Direct Selection tool, and drag the point up until it covers the cherry a bit. You're trying to make it look like the cherry was pushed into the ice cream.

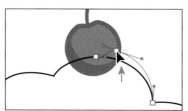

You could have simply selected the Direct Selection tool and dragged the path up, but we wanted to add specific anchor points to the path for later editing.

Next, you'll add another point and reposition it with the Pen tool.

6   Repeat steps 4 and 5 over the ice cream path on the left side of the cherry.

7   Choose Select > Deselect.

8   Press the spacebar to temporarily access the Hand tool (✋). Drag up in the Document window until you see the bottom of the ice cream path, and then release the spacebar.

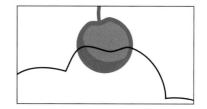

9   With the Selection tool, select the ice cream path.

10 Select the Pen tool in the Tools panel, and add points to the path on the right and left sides of the drip shape.

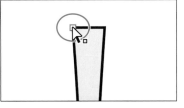

11 Position the Pen tool pointer over the bottom anchor point on that same drip. When a minus sign (−) appears next to the pointer (🖊_), click to delete the anchor point.

> **Tip:** With an anchor point selected, you can also click Remove Selected Anchor Points (✐) in the Control panel to delete the anchor point.

12 Choose Select > Deselect, and then choose File > Save.

Converting between smooth points and corner points

To more precisely control the path you create, you can convert points from smooth points to corner points and from corner points to smooth points, using several methods.

1 Choose 3 Spoon from the Artboard Navigation menu in the lower-left corner of the Document window.

2 Select the Direct Selection tool (▷), and position the pointer over the upper-left corner point on the spoon handle. When an open square with a dot in the center (▷□) appears next to the pointer, click the anchor point to select it.

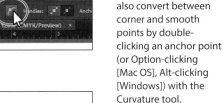

3 With the point selected, click the Convert Selected Anchor Points To Smooth button (◪) in the Control panel.

> **Tip:** You can also select multiple anchor points and convert them at the same time.

> **Tip:** You could also convert between corner and smooth points by double-clicking an anchor point (or Option-clicking [Mac OS], Alt-clicking [Windows]) with the Curvature tool.

● **Note:** If you don't drag directly from the end of the direction line, the shape may be deselected. You can click back on the anchor point to try again.

4 Drag the direction handle that's pointing down toward the center of the spoon. It doesn't have to match perfectly, but see the figure for roughly where to drag.

5 Repeat Steps 2–4 for the upper-right anchor point of the spoon handle.

Working with the Anchor Point tool

Next, you'll convert anchor points using the Anchor Point tool (⊾).

1. Choose 2 Dish from the Artboard Navigation menu in the lower-left corner of the Document window. Choose View > Fit Artboard In Window (if necessary).

2. Click the Layers panel icon (⬛) to show the Layers panel. Click the visibility column to the left of the layer named "template" to show its contents.

3. Select the Selection tool in the Tools panel and click the dish path to select it.

4. Position the pointer over the Pen tool (✐), click and hold down the mouse button to reveal more tools. Select the Anchor Point tool (⊾).

    You will also see the Add Anchor Point tool (⁺✐) and the Delete Anchor Point tool (⁻✐), which are specifically for adding or removing anchor points.

> **Tip:** If you position the Anchor Point tool pointer over the end of a direction handle that is split, you can press the Option (Mac OS) or Alt (Windows) key and when the pointer changes (▸), click to make the direction handles a single straight line again (not split).

5. Position the pointer over the C anchor point on the left side of the path. When the pointer looks like this ⊾, click and drag down. As you drag, press the Shift key. Drag down until the end of the opposite direction handle (that is pointing up) reaches point B (circled in red in the figure). Release the mouse button, and then release the key.

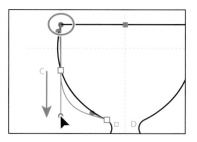

● **Note:** If the pointer looks like this ▸, don't drag. This means that the pointer is not over the anchor point and if you drag, you will reshape the curve.

With the Anchor Point tool, you can perform tasks like converting between smooth and corner points, edit direction handles, and more.

● **Note:** If the pointer looks like this (▸) when you click the point, try zooming in to the points and try again. That icon indicates clicking the end of a direction handle.

6. Click point B (left side) to convert the anchor point to a corner point.

    This is another way to convert an anchor point between smooth and corner. In order to convert an anchor point to a smooth point with the Anchor Point tool, you need to drag away from the point.

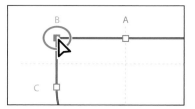

7. Position the pointer over the C anchor point *on the right side of the dish path,* and when the pointer looks like this ⊾, click and drag up. As you drag, press the Shift key. Drag up to snap to point B straight above it (on the right side). Release the mouse button and the release key.

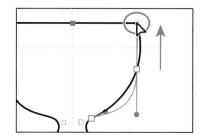

8 Click the upper-right corner point to convert it to a corner point.

9 Choose Select > Deselect, and then choose File > Save.

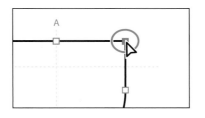

Cutting with the Scissors tool

There are several tools that allow you to cut and divide shapes. The Scissors tool (✂) splits a path at an anchor point or on a line segment, and the Knife tool (🔪) allows you to cut objects that automatically become closed paths. Next, you'll cut the ice cream dish path with the Scissors tool to reshape it.

1 Select the Selection tool (▶) in the Tools panel, and then choose Select > All On Active Artboard to select the dish path.

2 Choose View > Smart Guides to turn them on.

3 With the path selected, in the Tools panel, click and hold down the Eraser tool (⬭) and select the Scissors tool (✂). Position the pointer over point E (on the left), and when you see the word "anchor," click to cut the path at that anchor point. Go to the reflected side on the right, and click the same point. See the figure for where to click.

Note: If you click the stroke of a closed shape (a circle, for example) with the Scissors tool, it simply cuts the path so that it becomes open (a path with two end points).

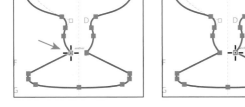

If you don't click directly on the path, you will see a warning dialog box. You can simply click OK and try again. Cuts made with the Scissors tool must be on a line or a curve rather than on an end point. When you click with the Scissors tool, a new anchor point appears and is selected.

4 Choose Select > Deselect.

5 Select the Selection tool, and click the bottom part of the dish path to select it. Press the Down Arrow key six times or so, to move the base down until you see a small gap between the two paths.

Tip: You can press Shift + arrow key (up or down) to move the artwork further.

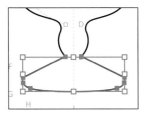
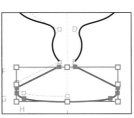

6   Choose Select > All On Active Artboard to select both paths.

7   Press Command+J (Mac OS) or Ctrl+J
    (Windows) once, and then press
    Command+J (Mac OS) or Ctrl+J
    (Windows) *again* to join the two open
    paths into one closed path. There should
    no longer be gaps between the cut paths.

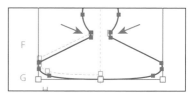

Creating a dashed line

Dashed lines apply to the stroke of an object and can be added to a closed path or an
open path. Dashes are created by specifying a sequence of dash lengths and the gaps
between them. Next, you'll create a line and add a dash to it.

1   Select the Zoom tool (🔍) in the Tools panel, and click twice, *slowly*, on the top
    of the cup path to zoom in.

2   Select the Line Segment tool (╱) in the Tools panel, and then choose
    Select > Deselect.

3   Position the pointer over the left side of
    the cup path, where the red horizontal
    dashed line is (see the red X in the figure).
    Click and drag to the right, and as you
    drag, press the Shift key. When the
    pointer reaches the other side of the shape
    and the word "intersect" displays, release
    the mouse, and then release the modifier key to create a straight line.

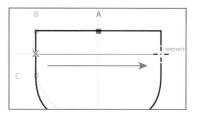

4   Choose View > Smart Guides to turn them off.

▶ **Tip:** The Preserves
Exact Dash And Gap
Lengths button (⊡)
allows you to retain the
appearance of the
dashes without aligning
to the corners or the
dash ends.

5   Click the word "Stroke" in
    the Control panel to show
    the Stroke panel. Change
    the following options in the
    Stroke panel:

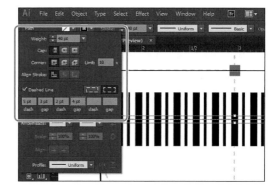

    •   Weight: **40 pt**

    •   Dashed Line: **Selected**
        (By default, this creates a
        repeating dash pattern of
        12 pt dash, 12 pt gap.)

    •   First Dash value: **5 pt** (This creates a 5 pt dash, 5 pt gap repeating pattern.)

    •   First Gap value: **3 pt** (This creates a 5 pt dash, 3 pt gap repeating pattern.)

    •   Change the next Dash value to **2 pt**, and change the next Gap value to **4 pt**.

    •   The values below Dashed Line should now be: 5 pt, 3 pt, 2 pt, 4 pt.

6   With the line still selected, change the Stroke color to the light-yellow swatch named "cup 65%" in the Control panel.

7   Select the Selection tool (▶), and click to select the cup shape.

8   Change the Stroke weight to **6 pt** in the Control panel. Change the fill color to the swatch named "cup" and the stroke color to the brown swatch named "cup stroke."

9   Click the word "Stroke" in the Control panel to reveal the Stroke panel. Click the Align Stroke To Outside button (▣).

10 Choose Select > All On Active Artboard, and then choose Object > Group.

● **Note:** If you find you cannot click the Align Stroke To Outside button (it's dimmed), the cup path may not be closed. With the cup path selected, choose Object > Join and try again.

Cutting with the Knife tool

Next, you'll cut the spoon in a straight line with the Knife tool (✐) to create two closed paths.

1   Choose 3 Spoon from the Artboard Navigation menu in the lower-left corner of the Document window.

2   Choose Select > All On Active Artboard. Artwork needs to be selected to cut it with the Knife tool.

3   Click and hold down the mouse on the Scissors tool (✂) and select the Knife tool (✐). Notice the Knife pointer (▸✐) in the Document window.

4   Position the pointer off the left side of the end of the spoon. Press and hold Option+Shift (Mac OS) or Alt+Shift (Windows), and drag all the way across the shape to cut in a straight line. See the figure for where to cut.

If you were to drag across a shape with the Knife tool without pressing a modifier key, you would find that the cut you make is very free-form and not straight at all.

▶ **Tip:** Pressing the Option key (Mac OS) or Alt key (Windows) allows you to cut in a straight line. Pressing the Shift key constrains to 45 degrees.

▶ **Tip:** Pressing the Caps Lock key will turn the Knife tool pointer into a more precise cursor (-¦-). This can make it easier to see where the cut will happen.

5   Choose Select > Deselect.

6   Select the Selection tool (↖), and drag the
    bottom part of the spoon path down a
    little bit to see that the spoon path is now
    cut into two closed paths.

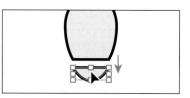

7   Choose Select > All On Active Artboard.

8   With the spoon shapes selected, choose
    Object > Transform > Rotate. In the
    Rotate dialog box, change the value to
    −45 and click OK.

9   Choose View > Fit All In Window.

Note: You may
need to collapse the
Libraries panel group if
it's showing.

10 With the Selection tool, drag the selected
    spoon shapes onto the ice cream path
    (see the figure), and choose Object >
    Arrange > Bring To Front.

11 Drag the cup group below the ice cream path and choose Object > Arrange >
    Send To Back. See the figure for position.

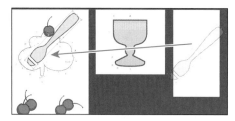

Drag the spoon and arrange it.   Drag the cup and arrange it.

12 Click the Layers panel icon (▩) to show the Layers panel, if necessary. Click the
    eye icon (◉) to the left of the layer named "template" to hide its contents.

13 Choose Select > Deselect, and then choose File > Save.

Adding arrowheads

You can add arrowheads to both ends of a path using the Stroke panel. There are
many different arrowhead styles to choose from in Illustrator, as well as arrowhead
editing options. Next, you'll add different arrowheads to a path.

1   Choose the 1 Ice Cream artboard from the Artboard Navigation menu in the
    lower-left corner of the Document window.

2   Choose View > Fit Artboard In Window, if necessary.

3   Select the Selection tool (↖), and click the black line below the orange text
    "THE MONTH."

4   Click the word "Stroke" in the
Control panel to open the Stroke
panel (or choose Window > Stroke).
In the Stroke panel, change the
following options:

- Stroke Weight: **50 pt**

- Choose **Arrow 20** from the
menu directly to the right of the
word "Arrowheads." This adds an arrowhead to the start (left end) of the line.

- Scale (beneath where you chose Arrow 20): **30%**

- Choose **Arrow 35** from the arrowheads menu to the far right of the word
"Arrowheads." This adds an arrowhead to the end of the line.

- Scale (beneath where you chose Arrow 35): **40%**

- Make sure that the Place Arrow Tip At End Of Path button (⬛) is selected.
The Align options allow you to adjust the path to align to the tip or the end of
the arrowhead.

5   Change the Stroke color of the selected path to the swatch named "cup stroke" in
the Control panel.

6   Click the larger spoon shape on the ice cream, and choose Object > Arrange >
Send To Back to send it behind all other shapes.

7   With the Selection tool selected, click the edge of the ice cream shape to select it.

8   Change the fill color to the pink swatch
with the tool tip "ice cream," change the
stroke color to the swatch with the tool
tip "cup stroke" in the Control panel,
and change the Stroke weight to **6 pt** in
the Control panel.

9   Choose Select > Deselect.

Drawing and editing with the Pencil tool

The Pencil tool (✏) lets you draw free-form open and closed paths that contain curves and straight lines. As you draw with the Pencil tool, anchor points are created on the path where necessary and according to the Pencil tool options you set. The path can easily be adjusted when the path is complete.

Next, you will draw and edit a few paths using the Pencil tool.

Tip: To draw a new path near the original without editing the original, you could double-click the Pencil tool to open the Pencil Tool Options dialog box. Deselect Edit Selected Paths, click OK, and then draw the new path.

Tip: When it comes to the Fidelity value, dragging the slider closer to Accurate usually creates more anchor points and more accurately reflects the path you've drawn. Dragging the slider toward Smooth makes fewer anchor points and a smoother, less complex path.

Note: If you see a crosshair (-¦-) instead of the Pencil icon (✏), the Caps Lock key is active. Caps Lock turns tool icons into crosshairs for increased precision.

1 Select the Zoom tool (🔍) in the Tools panel and click several times, slowly, on the bottom of the pink ice cream shape to zoom in.

2 Double-click the Pencil tool (✏) in the Tools panel. In the Pencil Tool Options dialog box, set the following options, leaving the rest at their default settings:

   - Drag the Fidelity slider all the way to the right to Smooth. This will reduce the number of points on a path drawn with the Pencil tool and make the path smoother.

   - Fill New Pencil Strokes: **Selected** (Without this option selected, which is the default, paths you draw will have no fill.)

   - Alt Key (Option key on Mac OS) Toggles To Smooth Tool: **Selected** (The Smooth tool is used to smooth the path after it is drawn.)

3 Click OK.

4 With the Pencil tool selected, position the pointer beneath the ice cream shape.

   The asterisk (*) that appears next to the pointer indicates that you are about to create a new path. If you don't see the asterisk, it means that you are about to redraw a shape that the pointer is near.

5 Draw a "drip" shape beneath the ice cream shape (see the figure for what to draw). When the pointer gets close to the start of the path, a small circle displays next to it (✏₀) to indicate that if you release the mouse button, the path will close. When you see the circle, release the mouse button to close the path.

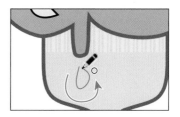

   Notice that as you are drawing, the path may not look perfectly smooth. After releasing the mouse button, the path is smoothed based on the Fidelity value that you set in the Pencil Tool Options dialog box.

6 With the new path still selected, position the Pencil tool over the bottom of the path and notice that the asterisk (*) disappears from the pointer, indicating that you are about to redraw the selected path. Try redrawing the drip. Make sure to start on the drip path and end on the drip path.

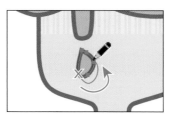

▶ **Tip:** You may find that it redraws the entire "drip" instead of editing it. You can zoom in to redraw a part of the path.

7 Press the Option (Mac OS) or Alt (Windows) key and the pointer will change to a circle. With the key held down, drag across the bottom of the drip shape, following loosely along the path, to smooth it. Release the key when done smoothing. You can try this a few times.

We selected the Alt Key (Option key on Mac OS) Toggles To Smooth Tool option in the Pencil Tool Options dialog box earlier. Rather than redrawing the path, it is simply smoothing it out with the modifier key held down.

8 Draw a "U" shape beneath the first drip shape, without closing it.

9 Click and hold down the mouse on the Pencil tool (✏) and select the Join tool (⤳).

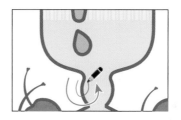

You can use the Join tool (⤳) to intelligently join paths that cross, overlap, or have open ends without affecting the original paths. Unlike the Join command (Object > Path > Join), you learned about in Lesson 3, the Join tool can trim overlapping paths as it joins and it doesn't simply create a straight line between the anchor points you are joining. The angle created by the two paths to be joined are taken into account.

10 With the Join tool selected, drag across the two ends of the "U" shaped path you created to join them.

When dragging (also called scrubbing) across paths, they will be either "extended and joined" or "trimmed and joined." In this example, the paths were extended and joined. The Join tool works on paths that are selected or not, but the result of joining is not selected, to continue working on more paths.

Aside from drawing more free-form paths, you can also create straight lines with the Pencil tool.

11 Click and hold down the mouse on the Join tool (✂) and select the Pencil tool (✏). Double-click the Pencil tool. In the Pencil Tool Options dialog box, deselect Fill New Pencil Strokes and click OK. This way you can draw a path with no fill.

12 Position the pointer above the end of the spoon that is sticking out of the ice cream shape (see red X in the following figure).

You are going to draw a shape with a flat side. Don't forget, you can always choose Edit > Undo Pencil and try again.

▶ **Tip:** You can also press Option+Shift (Mac OS) or Alt+Shift (Windows) as you draw with the Pencil tool to create a straight line that is constrained to 45°. If you press the Shift key before you start drawing a path with the Pencil tool, you can draw a straight line that is constrained to 45°.

13 Click and drag a small curve to the flat edge of the spoon shape. Without releasing the mouse button, press the Option (Mac OS) or Alt (Windows) key and drag a straight line that follows the flat edge of the spoon shape. Without releasing the mouse button, release the Option/Alt key and continue dragging to complete the shape as shown in the figure.

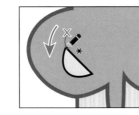 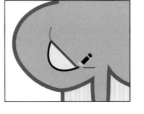 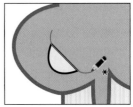

14 Choose View > Fit Artboard In Window.

15 Choose File > Save, and then choose File > Close.

Review questions

1   Describe how to draw straight vertical, horizontal, or diagonal lines using the Pen tool (✐).

2   How do you draw a curved line using the Pen tool?

3   How do you draw a corner point on a curved line?

4   Name two ways to convert a smooth point on a curve to a corner point.

5   Which tool would you use to edit a segment on a curved line?

6   How can you change the way the Pencil tool (✐) works?

Review answers

1   To draw a straight line, click with the Pen tool (✐) and then move the pointer and click again. The first click sets the starting anchor point, and the second click sets the ending anchor point of the line. To constrain the straight line vertically, horizontally, or along a 45° diagonal, press the Shift key as you click to create the second anchor point with the Pen tool.

2   To draw a curved line with the Pen tool, click to create the starting anchor point, drag to set the direction of the curve, and then click to end the curve.

3   To draw a corner point on a curved line, press the Option (Mac OS) or Alt (Windows) key and drag the direction handle on the end point of the curve to change the direction of the path. Continue dragging to draw the next curved segment on the path.

4   To convert a smooth point on a curve to a corner point, use the Direct Selection tool (▸) to select the anchor point, and then use the Anchor Point tool (⌐) to drag a direction handle to change the direction. Another method is to choose a point or points with the Direct Selection tool, and then click the Convert Selected Anchor Points To Corner button (⌐) in the Control panel.

5   To edit a segment on a curved line, select the Direct Selection tool and drag the segment to move it, or drag a direction handle on an anchor point to adjust the length and shape of the segment. Dragging a path segment with the Direct Selection tool or pressing the Option/Alt key and dragging a path segment with the Pen tool is another way to reshape a path.

6   To change the way the Pencil tool (✐) works, double-click the Pencil tool in the Tools panel to open the Pencil Tool Options dialog box. There you can change the smoothness, fidelity, and other options.

6 USING COLOR AND PATTERNS TO ENHANCE SIGNAGE

Lesson overview

In this lesson, you'll learn how to do the following:

- Understand color modes and the main color controls.

- Create, edit, and paint with colors using a variety of methods.

- Name and save colors, and build a color palette.

- Work with color groups.

- Use the Color Guide panel and the Edit Colors/Recolor Artwork features.

- Copy paint and appearance attributes from one object to another.

- Create and paint with patterns.

- Work with Live Paint.

This lesson takes approximately 90 minutes to complete.

Download the project files for this lesson from the Lesson & Update Files tab on your Account page at www.peachpit.com and store them on your computer in a convenient location, as described in the Getting Started section of this book.

Your Account page is also where you'll find any updates to the chapters or to the lesson files. Look on the Lesson & Update Files tab to access the most current content.

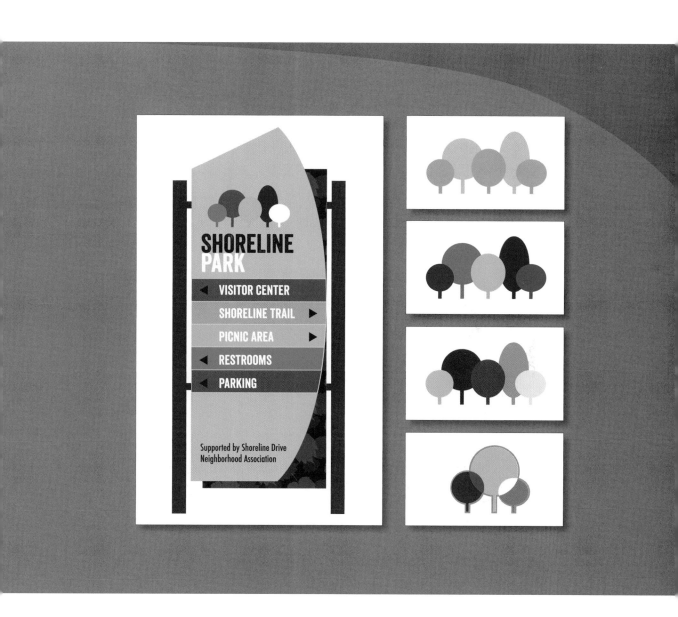

Spice up your illustrations with colors by taking advantage of color controls in Adobe Illustrator CC. In this information-packed lesson, you'll discover how to create and paint fills and strokes, use the Color Guide panel for inspiration, work with color groups, recolor artwork, create patterns, and more.

Getting started

In this lesson, you will learn about the fundamentals of color and create and edit colors for a park sign and logo, using the Color panel, Swatches panel, and more.

1 To ensure that the tools and panels function exactly as described in this lesson, delete or deactivate (by renaming) the Adobe Illustrator CC preferences file. See "Restoring default preferences" in the Getting Started section at the beginning of the book.

2 Start Adobe Illustrator CC.

● **Note:** If you have not already downloaded the project files for this lesson to your computer from your Account page, make sure to do so now. See the "Getting Started" section at the beginning of the book.

3 Choose File > Open, and open the L6_end.ai file in the Lesson06 folder, located in the Lessons folder, to view a final version of the park sign you will paint.

4 Choose View > Fit All In Window.

Leave the L6_end.ai file open for reference.

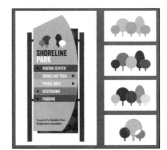

5 Choose File > Open. In the Open dialog box, navigate to the Lesson06 folder in the Lessons folder. Open the L6_start.ai file. This file has all of the pieces already in it; they just need to be painted.

● **Note:** In Mac OS, when opening lesson files, you may need to click the round, green button in the upper-left corner of the Document window to maximize the window's size.

6 Choose File > Save As. In the Save As dialog box, navigate to the Lesson06 folder and name it **ParkSign.ai**. Leave the Format option set to Adobe Illustrator (ai) (Mac OS) or the Save As Type option set to Adobe Illustrator (*.AI) (Windows), and click Save. In the Illustrator Options dialog box, leave the options at their default settings, and then click OK.

7 Choose Window > Workspace > Reset Essentials.

● **Note:** If you don't see "Reset Essentials" in the menu, choose Window > Workspace > Essentials before choosing Window > Workspace > Reset Essentials.

Understanding color

There are many ways to experiment with and apply color to your artwork in Adobe Illustrator CC. As you work with color, it's important to keep in mind the medium in which the artwork will be published, such as a print piece or a website. The colors you create need to be described in the correct way for the medium. This usually requires that you use the correct color mode and color definitions for your colors. The first part, color modes, will be described next.

Exploring color modes

Before starting a new illustration, you should decide which color mode the artwork should use, *CMYK* or *RGB*.

* **CMYK**—Cyan, magenta, yellow, and black are the colors used in four-color process printing. These four colors are combined and overlapped in a screen pattern to create a multitude of other colors. Select this mode for printing (in the New Document dialog box or the File > Document Color Mode menu).

* **RGB**—Red, green, and blue light are added together in various ways to create an array of colors. Select this mode if you are using images for onscreen presentations or the Internet.

When creating a new document, you select a color mode by choosing File > New and picking the appropriate profile, such as Print, which uses CMYK for the color mode. You can change the color mode by clicking the arrow to the left of Advanced and making a selection in the Color Mode menu.

▶ **Tip:** To learn more about color and graphics, search for "About color" in Illustrator Help (Help > Illustrator Help).

When a color mode is selected, the applicable panels open, displaying colors in the selected color mode. You can change the color mode of a document, after a file is created, by choosing File > Document Color Mode, and then selecting either CMYK Color or RGB Color in the menu.

Understanding the main color controls

In this lesson, you will learn about the traditional methods of coloring (also called *painting*) objects in Illustrator. This includes painting objects with colors and patterns using a combination of panels and tools, such as the Control panel, Color panel, Swatches panel, Color Guide panel, Color Picker, and the paint options in the Tools panel.

You'll begin by exploring some of more widely used options available for creating and applying color.

1 Click the L6_end.ai document tab at the top of the Document window.

2 Choose 1 from the Artboard Navigation menu in the lower-left corner of the Document window.

3 Select the Selection tool (▸), and click the large, light-brown shape in the sign behind the text "SHORELINE PARK."

● **Note:** Depending on your screen resolution, your Tools panel may either be a double or single column.

Objects in Illustrator can have a fill, a stroke, or both, as you've seen. At the bottom of the Tools panel, notice the Fill and Stroke boxes. The Fill box is brown for the selected object, and the Stroke box is None. Click the Stroke box, and then click the Fill box (making sure that the Fill box is the last selected). Notice that the box you click is brought to the front of the other. When a color is selected, it will apply to the fill or stroke of the selected object (whichever is in front).

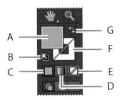

A. Fill box
B. Default Fill And Stroke button
C. Color button
D. Gradient button
E. None button
F. Stroke box
G. Swap Fill And Stroke button

▶ **Tip:** You can Shift-click the color spectrum bar at the bottom of the Color panel to rotate through different color modes, such as CMYK and RGB, or click the panel menu icon (▤) and choose a color mode.

4 Click the Color panel icon (◑) on the right side of the workspace, if it isn't open already. Click the double arrow to the left of the word "Color" in the panel tab until the panel looks like the figure below.

The Color panel displays the current fill and stroke of the selected content. The CMYK sliders in the Color panel show the percentages of cyan, magenta, yellow, and black used to create the selected color. The color spectrum bar at the bottom lets you quickly and visually select a fill or stroke color from a spectrum of colors.

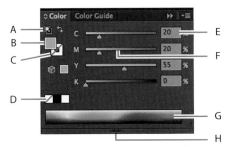

A. Default Fill And Stroke button
B. Fill box
C. Stroke box
D. None box
E. Color value
F. Color slider
G. Color spectrum bar
H. Drag to expand the color spectrum

5 Click the Swatches panel icon (▦) on the right side of the workspace.

You can name and save different types of colors, gradients, and patterns in the Swatches panel as swatches so that you can apply and edit them later. Swatches are listed in the Swatches panel in the order in which they were created, but you can reorder or organize the swatches into groups to suit your needs. All documents start with a set number of swatches, but any colors in the Swatches panel are available to the current document only (by default), since each document has its own defined swatches.

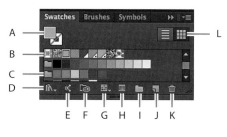

A. Fill and Stroke boxes

B. Swatch

C. Color group

D. Swatch Libraries menu

E. Open Color Themes panel

F. Libraries panel

G. Show Swatch Kinds menu

H. Swatch options

I. New Color group

J. New Swatch

K. Delete Swatch

L. List or Thumbnail view

6 Click the Color Guide panel icon (◣) on the right side of the workspace. Click the brown swatch in the upper-left corner of the panel to set the base color (labeled "A" in the figure below).

The Color Guide panel can provide color inspiration while you create your artwork. Either starting with the current color in the Fill box or by using an existing library of colors, it can help you pick color tints, analogous colors, and more. Those colors can then be applied directly to artwork using various methods, saved as swatches, or within groups, or edited using the Edit Colors feature.

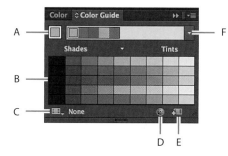

A. Set base color to the current color

B. Color variations

C. Limits the color group to colors in a swatch library

D. Edit Or Apply Colors button

E. Save Color Group to Swatch panel

F. Harmony Rules menu and active color group

7 Click the Color panel icon (▦). Using the Selection tool, click various shapes in the L6_end.ai file to see how their paint attributes are reflected in the Color panel and the Tools panel.

8 Leave the L6_end.ai file open for reference, or choose File > Close to close it without saving your changes (we closed it).

Working with color

As you will see in this section, Illustrator provides a lot of ways to arrive at the color you need. You'll start by applying an existing color to a shape, and then work your way through the most widely used ways to create and apply color.

● **Note:** Throughout this lesson, you'll be working on a document with a color mode that was set to CMYK when the document was created, which means that the majority of colors you create will, by default, be composed of cyan, magenta, yellow, and black.

Applying an existing color

As was mentioned previously, every new document in Illustrator has a series of default colors available for you to use in your artwork in the form of swatches in the Swatches panel. The first method of working with color you will explore is to paint a shape with an existing color.

1 Click the ParkSign.ai document tab at the top of the Document window, if you did not close the L6_end.ai document.

2 Choose 1 from the Artboard Navigation menu in the lower-left corner of the Document window (if it's not chosen already), and then choose View > Fit Artboard In Window.

3 Choose Window > Workspace > Reset Essentials.

4 With the Selection tool (▶), click to select the large red shape.

5 Click the Fill color in the Control panel, and the Swatches panel appears. Position the pointer over swatches in the list to reveal a tool tip with the swatch name. Click to apply the swatch named "Sign Bg." Press the Escape key to hide the Swatches panel.

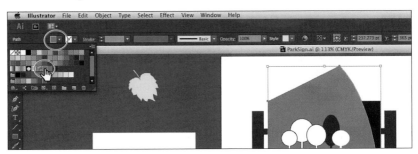

6 Choose Select > Deselect to ensure that nothing is selected.

Creating and saving a custom color as a swatch

At times, you may also need to create a custom color and save it for later use. Next, you'll create a color using the Color panel, and then you'll save that color as a swatch in the Swatches panel.

1   With the Selection tool ( ), click to select the white bar above the green bar, in the middle of the artboard (on the sign).

2   If the Color panel is not visible, click the Color panel icon ( ). Click the Color panel menu icon ( ) and choose CMYK from the menu (if it's not already selected).

Note: If the Color panel doesn't look like the following figure, choose Show Options from the Color panel menu.

3   In the Color panel, click the white Fill box (if it's not selected) to apply the color to the fill of the selected shape. Drag the bottom of the Color panel down to reveal more of the color spectrum bar. Click in the light-green part of the color spectrum to sample a light-green color and apply it to the fill.

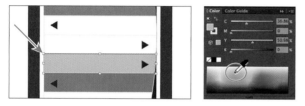

If artwork is selected when you create a color in the Color panel, the color is automatically applied.

4   Type the following values in the CMYK text fields: C=**42**, M=**0**, Y=**62**, K=**0**. This ensures that we are all using the same light-green color.

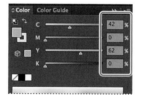

Now that you've created a color, you can save it as a swatch in the Swatches panel so that later you can edit or apply it elsewhere in this document.

Tip: Each CMYK value is a percentage of 100.

5   Click the Swatches panel icon ( ), and click the New Swatch button ( ) at the bottom of the panel to create a swatch from the color you just created.

6   In the New Swatch dialog box, name the color **Light Green** and, leaving the rest of the options as they are, click OK.

Notice that the new Light Green swatch is highlighted in the Swatches panel (it has a white border around it). That's because it is applied to the selected shape automatically. You may need to scroll in the Swatches panel to see it.

Tip: Naming colors can be an art form. You can name them according to their value (C=45, ...), appearance (Light Green), or a descriptive name like "text header," among other attributes.

7 With the Selection tool, select the third white tree from the left, on the top of the sign (see the following figure).

8 In the Swatches panel on the right, drag the bottom of the panel down to see more swatches. Ensure that the Fill box at the top of the panel is selected to paint the fill of the shape, and select the swatch named "Light Green" to apply it.

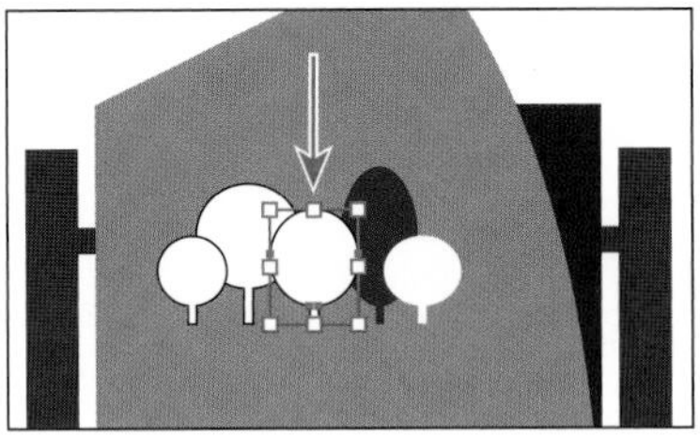

Select the tree.

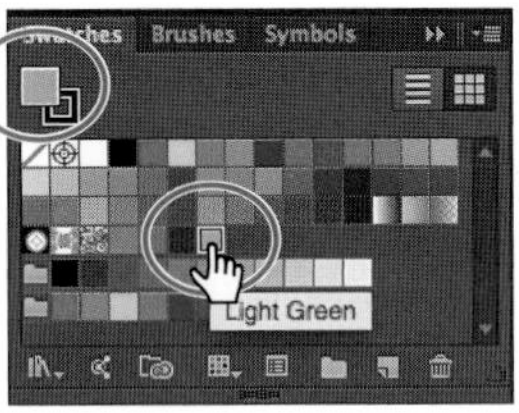

Apply the swatch.

When applying a swatch from the Swatches panel, it's always important to select the stroke or the fill first so that it paints the right part.

9 Click the Stroke box at the top of the Swatches panel to paint the stroke of the selected shape. Select the None swatch (☐) in the Swatches panel to remove the stroke.

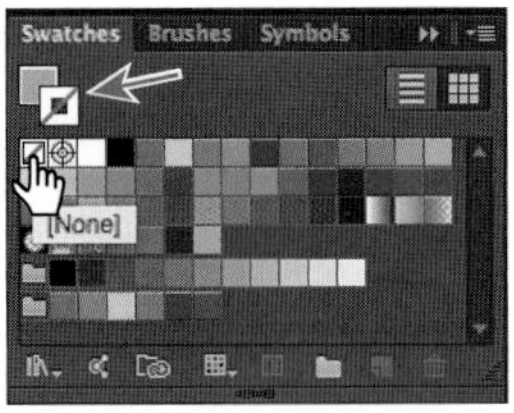

10 Choose Select > Deselect.

Creating a copy of a swatch

Next, you will create another swatch by copying and editing the Light Green swatch you made.

1 Click the Fill box at the top of the Swatches panel. This selects the Light Green swatch in the Swatches panel.

2 Click the New Swatch button (▣) at the bottom of the Swatches panel.

Clicking the New Swatch button creates a swatch from the fill or stroke color (whichever is active or up front at the top of the Swatches panel). If the None swatch is applied, you won't be able to click the New Swatch button (it'll be dimmed).

● **Note:** If the tree shape had still been selected, it would be filled with the new color.

3 In the New Swatch dialog box, change the name to **Orange** and change the values to C=**15**, M=**45**, Y=**70**, K=**0**. Click OK.

▶ **Tip:** In the New Swatch dialog box, the Color Mode menu lets you change the color mode of a specific color to RGB, CMYK, Grayscale, or another mode, when you create it.

4 With the Selection tool (↖), click the white bar above the Light Green-filled bar to select it. Click the Fill color in the Control panel, and click to select the color named "Orange."

Editing a swatch

After a color is created and saved in the Swatches panel, you can later edit that color if you need to. Next, you will edit the orange swatch that you created.

1 With the Selection tool (▶) selected, click to select the large brown sign shape you first applied a fill color to.

2 Make sure that the Fill box is selected in the Swatches panel, and then double-click the swatch named "Sign Bg" in the Swatches panel. In the Swatch Options dialog box, change the K value to **0**, select Preview to see the change, and then click OK.

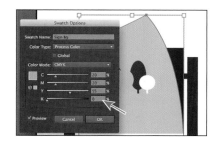

When you edit a swatch you created, if you want that edit to apply to other objects with that swatch color, they need to be selected. Otherwise, editing the swatch will not update the colored objects by default.

Creating and editing a global swatch

Next, you will create a color and make it a *global color*. When you edit a global color, all artwork with that swatch applied, regardless of whether it's selected, is updated.

1 With the Selection tool (▶), click to select the white bar above the orange bar.

2 In the Swatches panel, click the New Swatch button (▤) at the bottom of the panel. In the New Swatch dialog box, change the following options:

   • Swatch Name: **Forest Green**

   • Global: **Selected**

   • Change the CMYK values to C=**91**, M=**49**, Y=**49**, K=**0**

3 Click OK.

In the Swatches panel, notice that the new swatch is in the top row of colors, to the right of the white swatch. When you selected the shape, it was filled with white, so the white swatch was selected in the panel. When you click the New Swatch button to make a new color, it duplicates the selected swatch and puts the new swatch next to the original.

4 Click and drag the Forest Green swatch to the right of the Orange swatch to keep them together.

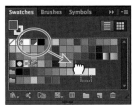

As you interact with the Forest Green swatch, notice the little white triangle in the lower-right corner. This indicates that it's a global swatch.

5 With the Selection tool, click the second white tree from the left (see the figure below). Make sure the Fill box is selected (active) in the Swatches panel and apply the new "Forest Green" swatch to the fill.

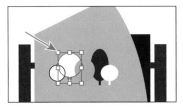

Select the tree.   Apply the swatch.

6 Change the Stroke weight in the Control panel to **0** by either typing in the value or by clicking the down arrow to remove it.

7 Choose Select > Deselect.

Now you'll see the power of a global swatch.

8 In the Swatches panel, double-click the "Forest Green" swatch. In the Swatch Options dialog box, change the K value to **24**, select Preview to see the changes (you may need to click in another field to see the change), and then click OK.

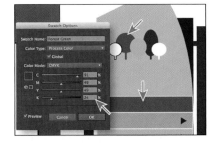

All of the shapes with the global swatch applied are updated, even though they weren't selected.

● **Note:** You can change an existing swatch into a global swatch, but it requires a bit more effort. You either need to select all of the shapes with that swatch applied before you edit the swatch and make it global, or you edit the swatch to make it global and then reapply the swatch to the content.

Using the Color Picker to create color

Another method for creating color is to use the Color Picker. The Color Picker lets you select color in a color field and in a spectrum by either defining colors numerically or by clicking a swatch, and it is found in other Adobe applications like InDesign and Photoshop. Next, you will create a color using the Color Picker and then save the color as a swatch in the Swatches panel.

1   With the Selection tool (⬤), click the bottom white bar on the sign.

2   Double-click the Fill box at the top of the Swatches panel to open the Color Picker.

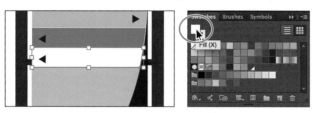

▶ **Tip:** You can also double-click the Fill box (or Stroke box) in the Color panel or at the bottom of the Tools panel to access the Color Picker.

In the Color Picker dialog box, the larger color field shows saturation (horizontally) and brightness (vertically) and is labeled "A" in the figure below. The color spectrum bar (labeled "B" in the figure) shows the hue.

3   In the Color Picker dialog box, click and drag in the color spectrum bar up and down to change the color range. Make sure that you wind up with the triangles in an orange/brown hue (it doesn't have to be exact).

4   Click and drag in the color field. As you drag right and left, you adjust the saturation, and as you drag up and down, you adjust the brightness. The color you create when you click OK (don't yet) appears in the New color rectangle, labeled "C" in the figure. Don't worry about matching the color in the figure yet.

▶ **Tip:** You can also change the color spectrum you see by selecting H, S, B, R, G, or B.

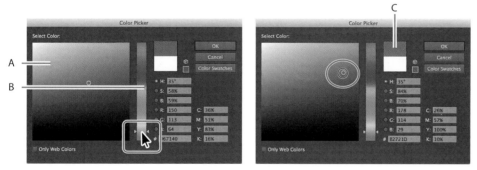

Drag in the color spectrum bar.   Drag in the color field.

5   In the CMYK text fields, change the values to: C=**40**, M=**65**, Y=**90**, and K=**33**. Click OK.

● **Note:** The Color Swatches button in the Color Picker shows you the swatches in the Swatches panel and the default color books (the sets of swatches that come with Illustrator), and it lets you select a color from one. You can return to the color spectrum by clicking the Color Models button and then editing the swatch color values, if necessary.

Next, you'll save the brown color that is applied to the bar as a swatch.

6   In the Swatches panel, click the New Swatch button (▣) at the bottom of the panel, and name the color **Dark Brown** in the New Swatch dialog box. Select Global, and then click OK to see the color appear as a swatch in the Swatches panel.

7   Choose Select > Deselect, and then choose File > Save.

Using Illustrator swatch libraries

Swatch libraries are collections of preset colors, such as Pantone and TOYO, and thematic libraries, such as Earthtone and Ice Cream. Illustrator has default swatch libraries that appear as separate panels when you open them, and these cannot be edited. When you apply color from a library to artwork, the color in the library becomes a swatch that is saved in that document only and appears in the Swatches panel. Libraries are a great starting point for creating colors.

Next, you will create a spot color, which prints using a spot ink, using a Pantone Plus library. You will then apply that color to a logo. When color is defined in Illustrator and later printed, the appearance of the color could vary. This is why most printers and designers rely on a color-matching system, like the PANTONE system, to help maintain color consistency and, in some cases, to give a wider range of colors.

● **Note:** Sometimes it's practical to use process (typically CMYK) and spot inks (PANTONE, for instance) in the same job. For example, you might use one spot ink to print the exact color of a company logo on the same pages of an annual report where photographs are reproduced using process color. You can also use a spot-color printing plate to apply a varnish over areas of a process color job. In both cases, your print job would use a total of five inks—four process inks and one spot ink or varnish.

Creating a spot color

In this section, you will see how to load a color library, such as the PANTONE color system, and how to add a PANTONE MATCHING SYSTEM (PMS) color to the Swatches panel.

1   In the Swatches panel, click the Swatch Libraries Menu button (▥) at the bottom of the panel. Choose Color Books > PANTONE+ Solid Coated.

    The PANTONE+ Solid Coated library appears in its own panel.

2   Type **755** in the Find field. As you type, the list is filtered, showing a smaller and smaller range of swatches. Type another **5** so that 7555 appears in the search field.

3   Click the swatch beneath the search field to add it to the Swatches panel. Click the X to the right of the search field to stop the filtering.

4   Close the PANTONE+ Solid Coated panel.

Open the color library.   Select the swatch after filtering the list.

● **Note:** When you exit Illustrator with the PANTONE library panel still open and then relaunch Illustrator, the panel does not reopen. To automatically open the panel whenever Illustrator opens, choose Persistent from the PANTONE+ Solid Coated panel menu (▤).

5   Choose 2 Artboard 2 from the Artboard Navigation menu in the lower-left corner of the Document window.

6   With the Selection tool (▸), click the first white-filled tree shape on the left. Make sure the Fill box is selected (active) in the Swatches panel and select the "PANTONE 7555 C" swatch to fill the shape.

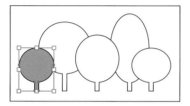 

▶ **Tip:** Now that you know a number of ways to apply a fill and stroke (the Swatches panel and Control panel), you can use either of those methods to apply color swatches going forward.

7   Change the Stroke weight to **0** in the Control panel.

8   Choose Select > Deselect, and then choose File > Save.

PANTONE swatches vs. other swatches in the Swatches panel

In the Swatches panel, you can identify spot-color swatches by the spot-color icon (▣) when the panel is in List view, or by the dot in the lower corner (▣) when the panel is in Thumbnail view. Process colors do not have a spot-color icon or a dot. To learn more about color libraries and spot colors, search for "About color" in Illustrator Help (Help > Illustrator Help).

Creating and saving a tint of a color

A *tint* is a mixture of a color with white to make the color lighter. You can create a tint from a global process color, like CMYK, or from a spot color.

Next, you will create a tint of the Pantone swatch.

1   With the Selection tool (➤), click the white tree shape just to the right of the tree shape filled with the Pantone color.

2   In the Swatches panel, apply the new Pantone color to the fill of the shape.

  ● **Note:** Don't forget, you need to make sure that the Fill box is selected in the Swatches panel to apply the color to the fill! Also, the Fill and Stroke boxes in the Tools panel, Color panel, and Swatches panel are linked together. When you change one, they all change.

● **Note:** You may need to choose Show Options from the Color panel menu to see the slider.

3   Click the Color panel icon (⬤) to expand the Color panel. Make sure that the Fill box is selected in the Color panel, and then drag the tint slider to the left to change the tint value to **70%.**

4   Click the Swatches panel icon (▦) on the right side of the workspace. Click the New Swatch button (🗋) at the bottom of the panel to save the tint. Notice the tint swatch in the Swatches panel. Position the pointer over the swatch icon to see its name, PANTONE 7555 C 70%.

Create the tint.   See the tint swatch in the panel.   Notice the result.

5   Change the Stroke weight to **0** in the Control panel for the selected tree shape.

6   For the remaining three tree shapes, apply the "PANTONE 7555 C" swatch, the tint swatch (PANTONE 7555 C 70%), and then the "PANTONE 7555 C" swatch to their fills, in that order.

7   Change the Stroke weight to **0** for each of the tree shapes.

8   Choose Select > Deselect, and then choose File > Save.

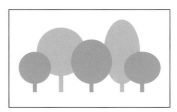

Adjusting colors

When working with colors, Illustrator offers an Edit Colors menu option (Edit > Edit Colors) that allows you to convert colors between color modes, blend colors, invert colors, and much more, for selected artwork. Next, you will change the trees logo with the PANTONE 7555 C color applied to use CMYK colors instead of Pantone.

1 While still on Artboard 2, choose Select > All On Active Artboard to select all of the shapes with the Pantone color and tint applied.

2 Choose Edit > Edit Colors > Convert To CMYK.

   The colors in the selected shapes are now composed of CMYK. Using this method for converting to CMYK does not affect the Pantone color swatches in the Swatches panel. It simply converts the selected *artwork* colors to CMYK. The swatches in the Swatches panel are no longer applied to the artwork.

   ● **Note:** Currently, Convert to RGB in the Edit Color menu is dimmed (you cannot select it). That's because the Document Color Mode is CMYK. To convert selected content color to RGB using this method, choose File > Document Color Mode > RGB Color.

Copying appearance attributes

At times you may want to simply copy appearance attributes, like character or paragraph formatting, fill, and stroke, from one object to another. This can be done with the Eyedropper tool (🖊) and can really speed up your creative process.

1 Choose 1 from the Artboard Navigation menu in the lower-left corner of the Document window to return to the artboard with the sign on it.

2 Using the Selection tool (▶), select the first white tree (on the left) at the top of the sign (the one with the stroke applied).

3 Select the Eyedropper tool (🖊) in the Tools panel. Click the green bar just above the bottom brown bar (see the figure).

   The tree has the attributes from the painted bar applied, including a cream-colored stroke.

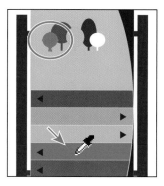

> **Tip:** You can double-click the Eyedropper tool in the Tools panel, before sampling, to change the attributes that the Eyedropper picks up and applies.

4 Click the Stroke color in the Control panel, and change the color to None (▢).

5 Choose Select > Deselect, and then choose File > Save.

Creating a color group

In Illustrator, you can save colors in color groups, which consist of related color swatches in the Swatches panel. Organizing colors by their use, such as grouping all colors for a logo, can be helpful for organization and more, as you'll soon see. Color groups cannot contain patterns, gradients, the None color, or Registration color.

Next, you will create a color group of some of the swatches you've created for the logo to keep them organized.

1   In the Swatches panel, click the swatch named "Aqua" to select it. Holding down the Shift key, click the swatch named "Forest Green" to the right to select five color swatches.

2   Command-click (Mac OS) or Ctrl-click (Windows) the orange swatch to remove it from the selection.

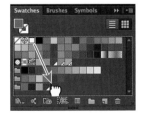

Note: If objects are selected when you click the New Color Group button, an expanded New Color Group dialog box appears. In this dialog box, you can create a color group from the colors in the artwork and convert the colors to global colors.

3   Click the New Color Group button (▦) at the bottom of the Swatches panel. Change the Name to **Tree Logo** in the New Color Group dialog box, and click OK to save the group.

4   With the Selection tool (▸) selected, click a blank area of the Swatches panel to deselect the color group you just created.

Each swatch in a color group can still be edited independently by double-clicking a swatch in the group and editing the values in the Swatch Options dialog box.

For the next step, you may want to drag the bottom of the Swatches panel down like we did, so that you can see all of the swatches in the panel.

5   Click the white swatch in the top row of the Swatches panel, and drag it to the right of the "Forest Green" swatch in the tree logo color group.

When dragging a color into a color group, make sure that you see a line appear on the right edge of the "Forest Green" swatch (see the figure). Otherwise, you may drag the white swatch to the wrong place. You can always choose Edit > Undo Move Swatches and try again. Aside from dragging colors in or out of a color group, you can rename a color group, reorder the colors in the group, and more.

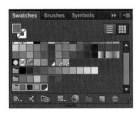
Note the new color group.

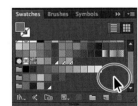
Deselect the swatches.

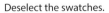
Drag the white swatch.

Working with color in the Color Guide panel

The Color Guide panel can provide you with color inspiration as you create your artwork. You can use it to pick color tints, analogous colors, and much more, and then apply them directly to artwork, edit them using several methods, or save them as a group in the Swatches panel.

Next, you will use the Color Guide panel to select different colors for a version of a tree logo, and then you'll save those colors as a color group in the Swatches panel.

1 Choose 3 Artboard 3 from the Artboard Navigation menu in the lower-left corner of the Document window.

2 With the Selection tool (▶), click the first tree on the left (with the aqua color fill). Make sure that the Fill box is selected in the Tools panel or Swatches panel.

3 Click the Color Guide panel icon (▨) on the right side of the workspace to open the panel. Click the Set Base Color To The Current Color button (▤) (see the following figure).

This allows the Color Guide panel to suggest colors based on the color showing in the Set Base Color To The Current Color button.

Next, you'll experiment with colors using Harmony Rules.

4 Choose Analogous from the Harmony Rules menu (circled in the figure) in the Color Guide panel.

A base group of colors is created to the right of the base color (aqua), and a series of tints and shades of those colors appears in the body of the panel.

● **Note:** The colors you see in the Color Guide panel may differ from what you see in the figure. That's okay.

▶ **Tip:** You can also choose a different color variation (different from the default Tints/Shades), such as "Show Warm/Cool," by clicking the Color Guide panel menu icon (▤) and choosing one.

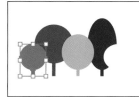

Select the tree.

Set the base color.

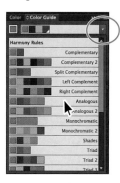

Choose the harmony rule.

There are lots of harmony rules to choose from, each instantly generating a color scheme based on any color you want. The base color you set (aqua) is the basis for generating the colors in the color scheme.

5 Click the Save Color Group To Swatch Panel button () at the bottom of the Color Guide panel to save the base colors (the five colors at the top) in the Swatches panel as a group.

6 Click the Swatches panel icon (). Scroll down to see the new group added.

 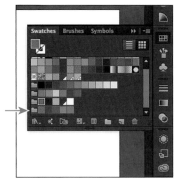

Save the new color group.   Note the saved color group.

Next, you'll experiment with the colors in the color group that you just created to create an alternate group of colors.

7 Choose Select > Deselect.

8 Click the Color Guide panel icon () to open the Color Guide panel.

● **Note:** If you choose a different color variation than the one suggested, your color will differ from those in the rest of this section.

9 In the list of swatches in the Color Guide panel, select the fifth color from the left, in the third row (see the figure).

If the tree were still selected, it would have been filled with the blue. You can apply or save any of the colors in the Color Guide panel as an individual swatch.

10 Click the Set Base Color To The Current Color button () (circled in the figure below) to ensure that all colors that the panel creates are based on that same blue.

11 Choose Complementary 2 from the Harmony Rules menu.

12 Click the Save Color Group To Swatch Panel button () to save the colors as a group in the Swatches panel.

13 Choose File > Save.

Editing a color group in the Edit Colors dialog box

When you create color groups in the Swatches panel or in the Color Guide panel, you can edit the swatches in the group either individually from the Swatches panel, or together. In this section, you will learn how to edit the colors of a color group in the Swatches panel using the Edit Color dialog box. Later, you will apply those colors to a version of the logo.

1 Choose Select > Deselect (if it's available), and then click the Swatches panel icon (▦) to show the panel.

   Deselecting right now is important! If artwork is selected when you edit the color group, the edits can apply to the selected artwork.

2 Click the Color Group icon (▤) to the left of the colors in the *bottom* color group (the one you just saved) to select the group.

3 Click the Edit Color Group button (◉) at the bottom of the Swatches panel to open the Edit Colors dialog box.

   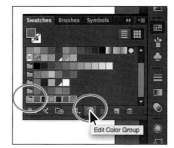

   The Edit Color Group button appears in multiple locations, like the Swatches and Color Guide panels. The Edit Colors dialog box allows you to edit a group of colors in various ways or even to create new color groups. On the right side of the Edit Colors dialog box, under the "Color Groups" section, all of the existing color groups in the Swatches panel are listed.

▶ **Tip:** With no artwork selected, you could also double-click the Color Group icon (the folder) to open the Edit Colors dialog box.

4 Select the name "Color Group 2" above the Color Groups if not already selected, on the right side of the dialog box (circled in the figure), and rename the group **Logo 2**. This is one way you can rename a color group.

   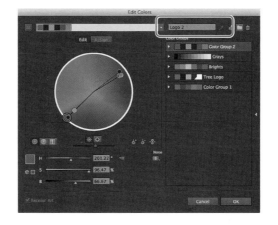

   Next, you will make a few changes to the colors in the "Logo 2" group. On the left side of the Edit Colors dialog box, you can edit the colors of each color group, either individually or together, and edit them visually or precisely using specific color values. In the color wheel, you'll see markers (circles) that represent each color in the selected group.

5   In the color wheel on the left side of the dialog box, drag the largest blue circle, called a *marker*, in the lower-left section of the color wheel, down and to the right just a little bit. The largest marker is the base color of the color group that you set in the Color Guide panel initially.

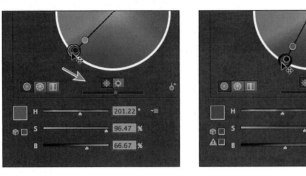

Drag the color marker.   The result.

Moving the color markers away from the center of the color wheel increases saturation, and moving them toward the center decreases saturation. Moving a color marker around the color wheel (clockwise or counterclockwise) edits the hue.

6   Drag the Adjust Brightness slider below the color wheel to the right, to brighten all the colors at once.

Next, you will edit the colors in the group independently, and then save the colors as a new named group.

7   Click the Unlink Harmony Colors button ( ) in the Edit Colors dialog box to edit the colors independently.

The lines between the color markers (circles) and the center of the color wheel become dotted, indicating that you can edit the colors independently.

Next, you will edit just one of the colors, since they are now unlinked, and you will edit that color by using specific color values rather than by dragging the color in the color wheel.

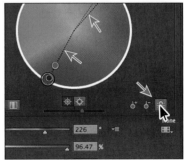

8 Click the Color Mode icon () to the right of the H, S, B values below the color wheel, and choose CMYK from the menu, if the CMYK sliders are not already visible.

9 Click to select the lightest orange marker in the color wheel, as shown in the figure. Change the CMYK values to C=**10**, M=**50**, Y=**100**, and K=**0**. Notice that the marker has moved in the color wheel, and it's the only one that moved. Leave the dialog box open.

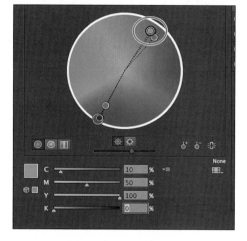

● **Note:** It's okay if the color markers in your Edit Colors dialog box are different from those shown in the figure.

10 Click the Save Changes To Color Group button (📥) in the upper-right corner of the Edit Colors dialog box to save the changes to the color group.

If you decide to make changes to colors in another color group, you can select the color group you want to edit on the right side of the Edit Colors dialog box and edit the colors on the left side. You can then save the changes to the group by clicking the Save Changes To Color Group button (📥) in the upper-right corner of the dialog box.

11 Click OK to close the Edit Colors dialog box.

The subtle changes to the colors in the group should show in the Swatches panel.

● **Note:** If a dialog box appears after clicking OK, click Yes to save the changes to the color group in the Swatches panel.

12 Choose File > Save.

Editing colors in artwork

You can also edit the colors in selected artwork using the Recolor Artwork command. It's really useful when global swatches weren't used in the artwork. Without using global colors in your artwork, updating a series of colors in selected artwork may take a lot of time.

Next, you will edit the colors for one of the logos that was created with colors that were not saved in the Swatches panel.

1   Choose 4 Artboard 4 from the Artboard Navigation menu in the lower-left corner of the Document window.

2   Choose Select > All On Active Artboard to select all of the artwork.

▶ **Tip:** You can also access the Recolor Artwork dialog box by selecting the artwork, and then choosing Edit > Edit Colors > Recolor Artwork.

3   Click the Recolor Artwork button (⬤) in the Control panel to open the Recolor Artwork dialog box.

The Recolor Artwork dialog box options allow you to edit, reassign, or reduce the colors in your selected artwork and to create and edit color groups. You'll probably notice that it looks an awful lot like the Edit Colors dialog box. The big difference is that instead of editing color and creating color groups to apply later, you are dynamically editing colors in the selected artwork.

4   In the Recolor Artwork dialog box, click the Hide Color Group Storage icon (◀) on the right side of the dialog box.

Like in the Edit Colors dialog box, all of the color groups in the Swatches panel appear on the right side of the Recolor Artwork dialog box (in the Color Groups storage area). In the Recolor Artwork dialog box, you can apply colors from these color groups to the selected artwork.

5   Click the Edit tab to edit the colors in the artwork using the color wheel.

6   Make sure that the Link Harmony Colors icon (⬛) is showing so that you can edit all of the colors independently.

The lines between the color markers (circles) and the center of the color wheel should be dotted. If it looks like this (⬛), click it to unlink.

When you created a color group, you worked with the color wheel and the CMYK sliders to edit color. This time, you will adjust color using a different method.

7   Click the Display Color Bars button (⬛) to show the colors in the selected artwork as bars. Click the cream color bar to select it.

8 At the bottom of the dialog box, change the CMYK values to C=**5**, M=**10**, Y=**40**, K=**0**. If the Recolor Artwork dialog box isn't in the way, you should see the artwork changing.

▶ **Tip:** If you want to return to the original logo colors, click the Get Colors From Selected Art button ().

9 Click the green color bar to select it instead of the cream color bar. With the pointer over the green color bar, right-click and choose Select Shade from the menu that appears. Click in the shade menu, and drag to change the color of the color bar.

Editing the colors as bars is just another way to view and edit the colors, and there are so many options for editing. To learn more about these options, search for "Color groups (harmonies)" in Illustrator Help (Help > Illustrator Help).

Click the cream color bar and edit it.

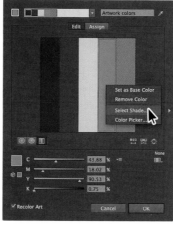
Choose Select Shade.

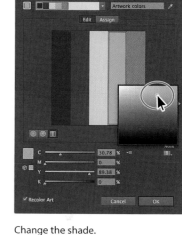
Change the shade.

10 Click OK in the Recolor Artwork dialog box.

11 Choose Select > Deselect, and then choose File > Save.

▶ **Tip:** You can save the edited colors as a color group by clicking the Show Color Group Storage icon (▶) on the right side of the dialog box, and then clicking the New Color Group button (▣).

● **Note:** When this book was written, the website was kuler.adobe.com.

Working with Adobe Color Themes

The Color Themes panel (Window > Color Themes) displays color themes you have created and synced with your account on the Adobe Color website (kuler.adobe.com). The Adobe ID used in Illustrator CC is automatically used to sign in to the Adobe Color website, and the Color Themes panel is refreshed with your Adobe Color themes. For more information about working with the Color Themes panel, search for "Color themes" in Illustrator Help (Help > Illustrator Help).

Assigning colors to your artwork

As you've seen, clicking the Recolor Artwork button (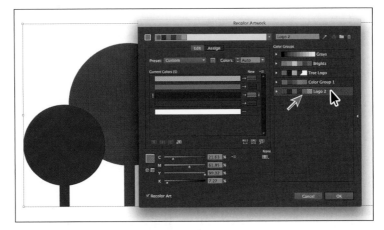) with artwork selected opens the Recolor Artwork dialog box. In the Recolor Artwork dialog box, you can edit colors in existing artwork, as you've seen, but you can also "assign" colors from an existing color group to your artwork. Next, you will assign a color group to create a version of the logo.

1 Choose 3 Artboard 3 from the Artboard Navigation menu in the lower-left corner of the Document window.

2 Choose Select > All On Active Artboard to select the logo trees.

3 Click the Recolor Artwork button (●) in the Control panel.

4 Click the Show Color Group Storage icon (▶) (the small arrow) on the right side of the dialog box to show the color groups, if they aren't already showing. Make sure that, in the top left of the dialog box, the Assign button is selected.

On the left side of the Recolor Artwork dialog box, notice that the five colors of the selected logo are listed in the Current Colors column, in what is called "hue-forward" sorting. That means they are arranged, from top to bottom, in the ordering of the color wheel: red, orange, yellow, green, blue, indigo, and violet.

● **Note:** If the colors of the logo do not change, make sure that Recolor Art is selected in the lower-left corner of the Recolor Artwork dialog box.

5 Under Color Groups in the Recolor Artwork dialog box, select the "Logo 2" color group you created earlier. The selected artwork on the artboard should change in color.

On the left side of the Recolor Artwork dialog box, notice that the colors of the color group named "Logo 2" are *assigned* to the colors in the logo. The Current Colors column shows what the color was in the logo, and an arrow to the right of each of those colors points to the New column, which contains what the color has become (or has been *reassigned to*). Notice that the white color has not been modified and that there is no arrow pointing to a color in the New column. That's because white, black, and grays are typically *preserved*, or unchanged.

6 Click the Hide Color Group Storage icon (◀) to hide the color groups. Drag the dialog box by the title bar at the top so that you can see the artwork.

7 Click the small arrow to the right of the dark-green bar in the Current Colors column (see the figure).

This tells Illustrator *not* to change that specific green color in the logo. You can see that reflected in the logo on the artboard.

Now suppose that you wanted to change the white color in the "Logo 2" color group. That's what you'll do next.

8 Click the line to the right of the white color in the Current Colors column and the line will change into an arrow that looks dimmed.

The arrow indicates to Illustrator that you want the white color to be different, but there currently is no color in the New column to change it to.

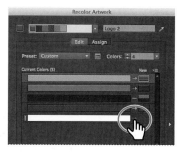

9 Click the Show Color Group Storage icon (▶) to show the color groups.

10 Click another color group in the Color Groups area on the right side of the panel, and then click to select the "Logo 2" color group again.

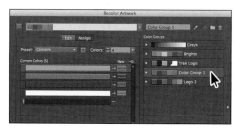
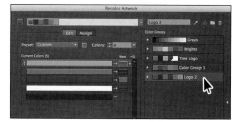

This is one of the easiest ways to reapply the color group colors, and it will fill in the missing color to the right of the white in the Current Colors column.

You might not like how it assigned the colors to your artwork, and that's what you'll edit next.

11 In the New column of the Recolor Artwork dialog box, drag the top blue color box in the column down on top of the brown color and release the mouse button.

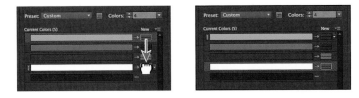

This is one way that you can reassign the "Logo 2" group colors to the colors in the logo. The colors in the New column show what you see in the artwork. If you click one of the colors in the New column, notice that the CMYK sliders at the bottom of the dialog box let you edit that one color.

12 Double-click the brown color box at the top of the New column. In the Color Picker dialog box, click the Color Swatches button (on the right side) and select the color named "Light Green." You may need to scroll in the list of color swatches. Click OK to return to the Recolor Artwork dialog box.

13 In the Recolor Artwork dialog box, click the Save Changes To Color Group button (⊞) to save the changes to the color group without closing the dialog box. Click OK.

The color changes that you made to the color group are saved in the Swatches panel.

14 Choose Select > Deselect, and then choose File > Save.

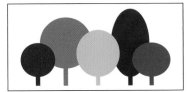

There are many kinds of color edits that can be made to selected artwork in the Recolor Artwork dialog box, including reducing the number of colors, applying other colors (like Pantone colors), and much more.

● **Note:** To learn more, search for "Working with color groups" in Illustrator Help.

Painting with patterns

In addition to process and spot colors, the Swatches panel can also contain pattern and gradient swatches. Illustrator provides sample swatches of each type in the default Swatches panel as separate libraries, and lets you create your own patterns and gradients. In this section, you will focus on creating, applying, and editing patterns.

● **Note:** To learn more about working with gradients, see Lesson 9, "Blending Colors and Shapes."

Applying existing patterns

A *pattern* is artwork saved in the Swatches panel that can be applied to the stroke or fill of an object. You can customize existing patterns and design patterns from scratch with any of the Illustrator tools. All patterns start with a single tile that is *tiled* (repeated) within a shape, starting at the ruler origin and continuing to the right. Next, you will apply an existing pattern to a shape.

1   Choose 1 from the Artboard Navigation menu in the lower-left corner of the Document window.

2   With the Selection tool (◤) selected, click to select the large light-brown shape in the sign and choose Object > Hide > Selection to temporarily hide it.

3   In the Swatches panel, click the Swatch Libraries Menu button (◪) at the bottom of the panel and choose Patterns > Basic Graphics > Basic Graphics_ Textures to open the pattern library.

4   Using the Selection tool, click to select the large white rectangle off the left edge of the first artboard. Make sure that the Fill box toward the bottom of the Tools panel is selected.

● **Note:** Selecting the Fill box is important. When you apply a pattern swatch, it applies to the stroke or the fill that is selected.

5   Select the "Sticks" pattern swatch in the Basic Graphics_Textures panel to fill the path with the pattern.

6   Close the Basic Graphics_Textures panel, and notice that the pattern swatch fills the shape and is added to the list in the Swatches panel. Click the Swatches panel icon to collapse the panel.

▶ **Tip:** You can type the word "sticks" in the Find field to sort the pattern swatches, or choose Small List View from the panel menu to see the names of the pattern swatches.

7   Choose Select > Deselect, and then choose File > Save.

● **Note:** You may also see the PANTONE+ Solid Coated panel grouped with the Basic Graphics_Textures panel and that's okay.

Creating your own pattern

In this section of the lesson, you will create your own custom pattern and add it to the Swatches panel.

1   With the Selection tool (◤), click to select the yellow leaf shape off the left edge of the artboard.

● **Note:** You don't need to have anything selected to start with a blank pattern.

2 Choose Object > Pattern > Make. Click OK in the dialog box that appears.

When you create a pattern, Illustrator enters Pattern Editing mode, which is similar to the group Isolation mode you've worked with in previous lessons. Pattern Editing mode allows you to create and edit patterns interactively, while previewing the changes to the pattern on the artboard. The Pattern Options panel (Window > Pattern Options) also opens, giving you all of the necessary options to create your pattern.

● **Note:** A pattern can be composed of shapes, symbols, or embedded raster images, among other objects. For instance, to create a flannel pattern for a shirt, you can create three overlapping rectangles or lines, each with varying appearance options.

3 With the Selection tool, click the center leaf to select it.

4 Press Command++ (Mac OS) or Ctrl++ (Windows) several times, to zoom in.

Notice the series of lighter-colored leaves around the center shape. This is the leaf shape repeated into a pattern and dimmed to let you focus on the original. The blue box around the leaf is the *pattern tile* (the area that repeats).

5 With the leaf shape selected, change the Fill color to the "Forest Green" swatch (in the "Tree Logo" color group) and the Stroke to None (⬜) in the Control panel, if necessary.

6 Change the Opacity to **80%** in the Control panel to make it partially transparent.

The first thing you'll do is explore some of the pattern options, and then you'll edit the artwork in the pattern some more.

7 In the Pattern Options panel, change the Name to **Leaves** and choose Hex By Column for the Tile Type.

The name appears in the Swatches panel as a tool tip and can be useful to distinguish multiple pattern swatches. The Tile Type determines how the pattern is tiled. You have three main Tile Type choices: the default grid pattern, a brick-style pattern, or the hex pattern. The Brick Offset options can be selected when you choose a brick Tile Type.

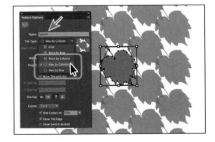

8 With the Selection tool selected, drag the leaf to the left a little. Notice that the blue tile moves with the artwork.

9 Click the Symbols panel (◩) icon to open the panel. Hover the pointer over the green leaves to see a tool tip name of "MediumLeaf." Drag the MediumLeaf symbol just to the right of the original leaf.

10 Drag the "SmallLeaf" symbol from the Symbols panel just below the two other symbols. Drag the two symbols so they look something like the following figure.

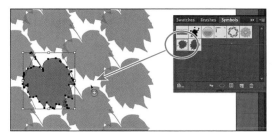

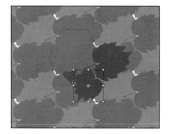

Drag the symbols into the pattern.

Arrange the leaves.

After adding the new content to the pattern, you can see that the pattern tile does not contain the new content.

11 Select the Size Tile To Art option in the Pattern Options panel.

The Size Tile To Art selection fits the tile area (the blue hex shape) to the bounds of the artwork, changing the spacing between the repeated objects. With Size Tile To Art deselected, you could manually change the width and the height of the pattern definition area in the Width and Height fields to include more content or to edit the spacing between. You can also edit the tile area manually with the Pattern Tile Tool button (⊞) in the upper-left corner of the Pattern Options panel.

● **Note:** In this step, you can see the leaves more clearly. At this point, try to arrange the leaves like you see in the figure.

12 Change the H Spacing to **−18 pt**, and change the V Spacing to **−18 pt**.

13 For Overlap, click the Bottom In Front button (▦) to see the change in the pattern.

The artwork in a pattern may begin to overlap, due to the size of the tile or the spacing values. By default, when objects overlap horizontally, the left object is on top; when objects overlap vertically, the top object is on top.

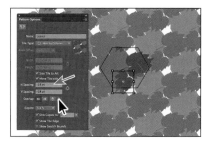

▶ **Tip:** The spacing values can be either positive or negative values, to move the tiles apart or to bring them closer together.

14 Change the H Spacing and V Spacing values back to **0** in.

The Pattern Options panel has a host of other pattern-editing options, including the ability to see more or less of the pattern, called Copies. To learn more about the Pattern Options panel, search for "Create and edit patterns" in Illustrator Help (Help > Illustrator Help).

Tip: If you want to create pattern variations, you can click Save A Copy in the bar along the top of the Document window when in Pattern Editing mode. This saves the current pattern in the Swatches panel as a copy and allows you to continue creating.

15 Select Show Swatch Bounds at the bottom of the Pattern Options panel to see the dotted area that will be saved in the swatch. Deselect Show Swatch Bounds.

16 Click Done in the bar along the top of the Document window. In the dialog box that appears, click OK.

17 Choose File > Save.

Applying your pattern

You can assign a pattern using a number of different methods. In this lesson, you will use the Swatches panel to apply the pattern. You can also apply the pattern using the Fill color in the Control panel.

1 Choose View > Fit Artboard In Window.

2 With the Selection tool (⬥), click the shape filled with the "Sticks" pattern swatch off the left edge of the artboard.

3 Select the swatch named "Leaves" from the Fill color in the Control panel.

4 Choose Select > Deselect, and then choose File > Save.

● **Note:** Your pattern may look different, and that's okay.

Editing your pattern

Next, you will edit the Leaves pattern swatch in Pattern Editing mode.

Tip: You can also select an object filled with a pattern swatch and, with the Fill box selected in the Swatches, Color, or Tools panel, choose Object > Pattern > Edit Pattern.

1 In the Swatches panel, double-click the Leaves pattern swatch to edit it.

2 In Pattern Editing mode, with the Selection tool (⬥) selected, choose Select > All to select all three green leaves.

3 In the Control panel, change the Fill color to the swatch named "Forest Green" (it's in the "Tree Logo" color group). Right now there are different green colors applied, so it won't look that different.

4 Choose Select > Deselect.

5 Click the smallest leaf, and change the Opacity to **30%** in the Control panel. Click the medium-sized leaf, and change the Opacity to **45%**, by typing in the value.

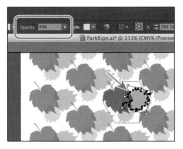

6 Click Done in the gray bar along the top of the Document window to exit Pattern Editing mode.

7 Click the shape off the left edge of the artboard with the Leaves pattern fill to select it. Double-click the Scale tool () in the Tools panel to scale the pattern, but not the shape. In the Scale dialog box, change the following options (if not already set):

- Uniform Scale: **90%**
- Scale Rectangle Corners: **Deselected** (the default setting)
- Scale Strokes & Effects: **Deselected** (the default setting)
- Transform Objects: **Deselected**
- Transform Patterns: **Selected**

▶ **Tip:** In the Scale dialog box, if you wanted to scale the pattern AND the shape, you could select Transform Objects and select Transform Patterns. You can also transform patterns in the Transform panel by choosing Transform Pattern Only, Transform Object Only, or Transform Both from the panel menu (▼≣) before applying a transformation.

8 Select Preview to see the change. Click OK, and leave the shape selected.

9 With the Selection tool selected and the Leaves pattern-filled shape still selected, Shift-click the dark-green rectangle behind the sign to select both shapes. Release the Shift key, and click once more on the dark-green shape to set it as the key object to align to. Click the Horizontal Align Center (■) button and the Vertical Align Center (■) button to align the leaf-filled shape to the green rectangle.

● **Note:** The Align options may not appear in the Control panel. If you don't see the Align options, click the word "Align" in the Control panel to open the Align panel. The number of options displayed in the Control panel depends on your screen resolution.

10 On the artboard, select and delete the original yellow leaf that you used to create the pattern.

11 Open the Layers panel (■), and make all layers visible by selecting the Visibility column to the left of the layer named "Sign Text." Click the Layers panel icon to collapse the panel group.

12 Choose Object > Show All.

13 Choose Select > Deselect, and then choose File > Save.

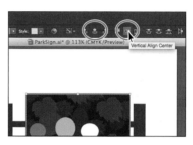

Working with Live Paint

● **Note:** To learn more about Live Paint and all that it can do, search for "Live Paint groups" in Illustrator Help (Help > Illustrator Help).

Live Paint lets you paint vector graphics intuitively, by automatically detecting and correcting gaps that might otherwise affect the application of fills and strokes. Paths divide the drawing surface into areas that can be colored, whether the area is bounded by a single path or by segments of multiple paths. Painting objects with Live Paint is like coloring in a coloring book or using watercolors to paint a sketch, and the underlying shapes are not edited.

Creating a Live Paint group

Next, you will paint a simpler version of the logo using the Live Paint Bucket tool.

1   Choose 5 Artboard 5 from the Artboard Navigation menu in the lower-left corner of the Document window.

2   With the Selection tool (▶) selected, choose Select > All On Active Artboard.

3   Choose View > Zoom Out, several times, until you see the tree shape off the right edge of the artboard.

   That shape is not selected, but you will add it to the rest of the shapes soon.

4   Select the Live Paint Bucket tool (🪣) from the Shape Builder tool (🔘) group in the Tools panel.

● **Note:** Positioning the pointer over a color group will show you the name of the color group in a tool tip.

5   Click the Swatches panel icon (▦) to show the panel. Select the first (dark) blue swatch in the "Logo 2" color group in the Swatches panel.

6   Position the pointer over the first tree shape (on the left), and click to convert the selected shapes to a Live Paint group.

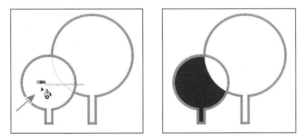

You can click any of the shapes to convert it to a Live Paint group, but the shape you click is filled with the dark-blue color. Clicking selected shapes with the Live Paint Bucket tool creates a Live Paint group that you can paint with that same tool. Once a Live Paint group is created, the paths are fully editable, but they are treated like a group. Colors are automatically reapplied to new regions created when you move or adjust a path's shape.

Painting with the Live Paint Bucket tool

After objects are converted to a Live Paint group, you can paint them using several methods, which is what you'll do next.

1   Position the pointer over the second tree from the left in the Live Paint group (not where the trees overlap).

    A red highlight appears around the shape that will be painted, and three color swatches appear above the pointer. The selected color (dark blue) is in the middle, and the two adjacent colors in the Swatches panel are on either side.

2   Press the left arrow key once to select the lighter-green swatch (shown in the three swatches above the pointer). As you press the arrow key to change colors, notice, in the Swatches panel, that the color is highlighted. You can press the up or down arrow key, along with right or left arrow keys, to select a new swatch to paint with. Click to apply the lighter-green color to the tree shape.

3   In the Swatches panel, click to select the swatch named "Dark Brown." Click to fill the overlapping (white) shape between the trees.

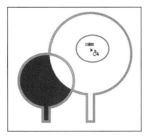 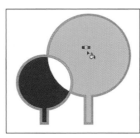  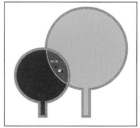

Position the pointer.   Click to apply the swatch.   Select the swatch.   Click to apply it.

4   Double-click the Live Paint Bucket tool (⊞) in the Tools panel. This opens the Live Paint Bucket Options dialog box. Select the Paint Strokes option, and then click OK.

Next, you'll remove the inner gray stroke from the shapes and retain the outer strokes.

5   Select None (⬚) from the Stroke color in the Control panel. Press the Escape key.

6   Position the tip (▶) of the pointer directly over the gray stroke, between the two tree shapes, as shown in the figure. When the pointer changes to a paintbrush (↘), click the stroke to remove the stroke color (by applying the None swatch).

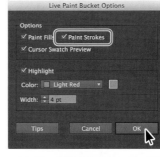

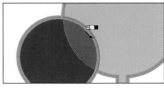

● **Note:** To learn more about the Live Paint Bucket Options dialog box, including working with Gap Options, search for "Paint with the Live Paint Bucket tool" in Illustrator Help (Help > Illustrator Help).

● **Note:** We exaggerated the red line in the figure so you could more easily see it.

7   Choose Select > Deselect, and then choose File > Save.

Modifying a Live Paint group

When you make a Live Paint group, each path remains editable. When you move or adjust a path, the colors that were previously applied don't just stay where they were, like they do in natural media paintings or with image-editing software. Instead, the colors are automatically reapplied to the new regions that are formed by the intersecting paths. Next, you will edit the paths by adding another shape.

1   Select the Selection tool (➤), and click to select the white tree shape off the right edge of the artboard. Drag it so that it overlaps the rightmost tree shape.

2   With the Selection tool, Shift-click the Live Paint group to select both objects.

3   Click the Merge Live Paint button in the Control panel to add the new white shape to the Live Paint group.

4   Select the Live Paint Bucket tool (🪣) in the Tools panel. In the Swatches panel (▦), click to select one of the brown colors in the "Logo 2" group. Click to paint the part of the new tree that is not overlapping the other tree.

5   Select another swatch (we chose white), and click to paint the part of the circle that overlaps the light-green tree.

● **Note:** If you find that the stroke is not going away, try selecting the None swatch again for the Stroke color, positioning the pointer over the stroke, and clicking again when you see the paintbrush icon.

6   Select None (▧) from the Stroke color in the Control panel. Press the Escape key to hide the panel. Position the pointer directly over the stroke, between the tree shapes. When the paintbrush (↘) appears, click the stroke to remove it.

7   Select the Selection tool, and with the Live Paint object selected, you will see the words "Live Paint" on the left end of the Control panel. Double-click the Live Paint object (the trees) to enter Isolation mode.

8   Drag the rightmost tree shape to the left to reposition it.

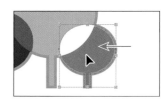

Notice how the color fill and stroke changes every time you release the mouse button.

▶ **Tip:** You could also edit the anchor points of the selected artwork using the Direct Selection tool (▷), for instance. The paths are still editable, and the colors are reapplied to the new regions that are formed by edited paths.

9   Choose Select > Deselect, and then press the Escape key to exit Isolation mode.

10 Choose View > Fit All In Window.

11 Choose File > Save, and then choose File > Close.

Review questions

1 Describe what a *global color* is.

2 How can you save a color?

3 How can you choose color harmonies for color inspiration?

4 Name two things that the Recolor Artwork dialog box allows you to do.

5 How do you add pattern swatches to the Swatches panel?

6 Explain what Live Paint allows you to do.

Review answers

1 A global color is a color swatch that, when you edit it, automatically updates all artwork to which it is applied. All spot colors are global; however, process colors can be either global or local.

2 You can save a color for painting other objects in your artwork by adding it to the Swatches panel by doing one of the following:

   - Drag the color from a Fill box, and drop it over the Swatches panel.

   - Click the New Swatch button (⬛) at the bottom of the Swatches panel.

   - Choose New Swatch from the Swatches panel menu (▾≡).

   - Choose Create New Swatch from the Color panel menu (▾≡).

3 You can choose color harmonies from the Color Guide panel. Color harmonies are used to generate a color scheme based on a single color.

4 You use the Recolor Artwork dialog box to change the colors used in selected artwork, create and edit color groups, or reassign or reduce the colors in your artwork, among other functions.

5 You can add pattern swatches to the Swatches panel either by creating content for the pattern or by deselecting all content and choosing Object > Pattern > Make. In Pattern Editing mode, you can edit the pattern and preview it. You can also drag artwork into the swatch list in the Swatches panel.

6 Live Paint lets you paint vector graphics intuitively, by automatically detecting and correcting gaps that might otherwise affect the application of fills and strokes. Paths divide the drawing surface into areas, any of which can be colored, regardless of whether the area is bounded by a single path or by segments of multiple paths.

7

ADDING TYPE TO A POSTER

Lesson overview

In this lesson, you'll learn how to do the following:

- Create and edit area and point type.

- Import text.

- Create columns of text.

- Change text attributes.

- Modify text with the Touch Type tool.

- Create and edit paragraph and character styles.

- Copy and apply text attributes by sampling type.

- Reshape text with a warp.

- Create type on a path and on shapes.

- Wrap type around an object.

- Create text outlines.

 This lesson takes approximately 75 minutes to complete.

Download the project files for this lesson from the Lesson & Update Files tab on your Account page at www.peachpit.com and store them on your computer in a convenient location, as described in the Getting Started section of this book.

Your Account page is also where you'll find any updates to the chapters or to the lesson files. Look on the Lesson & Update Files tab to access the most current content.

ZOO TALES

Bedtime Stories With Your Wildest Friends

The Animal Zoo welcomes children of all ages for an hour of bedtime stories Thursday evenings in June and July.

Hear classic tales featuring our favorite zoo residents. Our zoo keepers will also share fascinating stories about the secret lives of our zoo friends at night.

Feel free to come dressed in your pajamas and slippers, and don't forget your favorite stuffed animal!

Stories will include Good Night Zoo Animals; Once Upon a Time; Animals in the Wild; The Animal Zoo; Joseph the Giraffe; Zoo Animals Can't Dance; and many others.

This program is free and open to the public.

Special thanks to our generous Zoo Circle members and the Towne Public Library for supporting this program.

ANIMAL ZOO

Thursdays at 6:30 pm

Support the Animal Zoo by becoming a Zoo Circle Member today. Simply fill out the back of this card and return it along with your tax-deductible donation, and you will start enjoying all of the benefits of membership, including unlimited zoo admission, free parking, concession discounts, birthday party and program discounts, and invitations to exclusive member events, including the annual Zoo Gala. Plus you'll have the special joy of knowing you've helped the Animal Zoo continue providing amazing experiences to our community and a world-class home for our animals.

ZOO CIRCLE LEVELS

Lion Circle	$5,000 and higher
Polar Bear Circle	$2,500 - 4,999
Orangutan Circle	$1,000 - 2,499
Penguin Circle	$500 - 999
Meerkat Circle	$100 - 499

ZOO CIRCLE BECOME A MEMBER

Text as a design element plays a major role in your illustrations. Like other objects, type can be painted, scaled, rotated, and more. In this lesson, you'll discover how to create basic text and interesting text effects.

Getting started

You'll be adding type to a poster during this lesson, but before you begin, restore the default preferences for Adobe Illustrator CC. Then open the finished art file for this lesson to see the illustration.

● **Note:** If you have not already downloaded the project files for this lesson to your computer from your Account page, make sure to do so now. See "Getting Started" at the beginning of the book.

1 To ensure that the tools and panels function exactly as described in this lesson, delete or deactivate (by renaming) the Adobe Illustrator CC preferences file. See "Restoring default preferences" in the Getting Started section at the beginning of the book.

2 Start Adobe Illustrator CC.

3 Choose File > Open. Locate the file named L7_end.ai in the Lessons > Lesson07 folder. Click Open. You will most likely see a Missing Fonts dialog box since the file is using a specific Typekit font. Simply click Close in the Missing Fonts dialog box. You will learn all about Typekit fonts later in this lesson.

In this lesson, you will create the text for this poster. Leave it open for reference later in the lesson, if you like.

4 Choose File > Open. In the Open dialog box, navigate to the Lessons > Lesson07 folder. Open the L7_start.ai file.

This file already has non-text components in it. You will add all of the text elements to complete the poster and card.

5 Choose File > Save As. In the Save As dialog box, navigate to the Lesson07 folder and name the file **ZooPoster.ai**. Leave the Format option set to Adobe Illustrator (ai) (Mac OS) or Save As Type option set to Adobe Illustrator (*.AI) (Windows), and then click Save. In the Illustrator Options dialog box, leave the Illustrator options at their default settings, and then click OK.

6 Choose View > Smart Guides to turn off the Smart Guides. Turning off the Smart Guides will make it easier to create text without snapping to existing content.

7 Choose Window > Workspace > Reset Essentials.

● **Note:** If you don't see "Reset Essentials" in the Workspace menu, choose Window > Workspace > Essentials before choosing Window > Workspace > Reset Essentials.

Adding type to the poster

Type features are some of the most powerful tools in Illustrator. You can add a single line of type to your artwork, create columns and rows of text like you do in Adobe InDesign, flow text into a shape or along a path, and work with letterforms as graphic objects. In Illustrator, you can create text in three different ways: as point type, area type, and type on a path. You will learn about each as you proceed through this lesson.

Adding text at a point

Point type is a horizontal or vertical line of text that begins where you click and expands as you enter characters. Each line of text is independent—the line expands or shrinks as you edit it but doesn't wrap to the next line unless you add a paragraph return or a soft return. Entering text this way is useful for adding a headline or a few words to your artwork. Next, you will enter some text in the poster as point type.

1   Ensure that 1 Flyer is chosen in the Artboard Navigation menu in the lower-left corner of the Document window, and choose View > Fit Artboard In Window.

2   Select the Zoom tool (🔍) in the Tools panel, and click the upper-left corner of the artboard twice, slowly. Remember that where you click is centered in the Document window.

3   Choose Window > Layers to show the panel. Select the Text layer, if it's not already selected, to ensure that the content you create is on that layer. Click the Layers panel tab to collapse it.

4   Select the Type tool (**T**), and click in the white area in the upper-left corner of the artboard. The cursor appears on the artboard. Type **ZOO TALES** (in uppercase). By simply clicking with the Type tool, you create a point type object.

5   Select the Selection tool (▶) in the Tools panel, and notice the bounding box that appears around the text. Drag the right, middle bounding point (*NOT* the circle), to the right. Notice that the text stretches as you drag any bounding point.

Note: Point type that is scaled may not be a whole number (such as 12 pt).

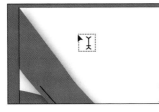
Position the pointer.

Type the text.

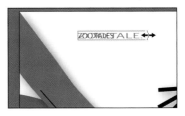
Drag the point.

6   Choose Edit > Undo Scale, and then choose View > Fit Artboard In Window.

Adding area type

Area type uses the boundaries of an object (like a rectangle) to control the flow of characters, either horizontally or vertically. When the text reaches a boundary, it automatically wraps to fit inside the defined area. Entering text in this way is useful when you want to create one or more paragraphs, such as for a poster or a brochure.

To create area type, you click with the Type tool (**T**) where you want the text and drag to create an area type object (also called a *text area*). You can also convert an existing shape or object to a type object by clicking the edge of an object (or inside the object) with the Type tool. When the cursor appears, you can type. An area type object has two extra boxes on the bounding box, called ports. Ports are used to thread (flow) text from one type area to another, which you will learn about later in this lesson.

Next, you will create an area type object and enter more text.

1   Choose View > Smart Guides to turn on the Smart Guides.

● **Note:** The Zoo Sign view is at the bottom of the View menu, and you may need to scroll.

2   Choose View > Zoo Sign to zoom in to the black shape at the bottom of the artboard that will become a zoo sign.

3   Select the Type tool (**T**). Position the cursor to the left of the striped orange-and-black tail, in the white area (see the red X in the figure). Click and drag down and to the right to create a text area with an approximate width and height of 1 inch.

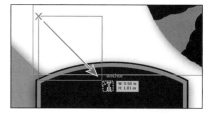

4   With the cursor in the new text area, type **Safari Zoo California**.

Notice how the text wraps horizontally to fit within the type area. By default, when you create area type by dragging with the Type tool, the type area will not resize to fit the text within (similar to how InDesign treats text frames, by default). If there is too much text, the text that doesn't fit will not be visible and will be considered overset.

5   Select the Selection tool (▶), and looking at the bottom, middle bounding point you will see the Autosize widget (↓) indicating that the type area is not set to autosize. Hover the pointer over the box at the end of the widget (the pointer will change [▶冊]), and double-click.

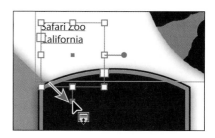

By double-clicking the widget, you turn Autosizing on. As the text is edited and re-edited, the frame shrinks and grows vertically to accommodate the changing amount of copy, and eliminates overset text without manually sizing and resizing frames.

Tip: If Autosizing is enabled for a selected type area, you can also drag one of the bottom bounding points on the type area down and Autosizing will be disabled for the type area.

6 Select the Type tool and insert the cursor after the word "California" press Enter or Return and type **San Diego**.

The type area will expand vertically to fit the new text.

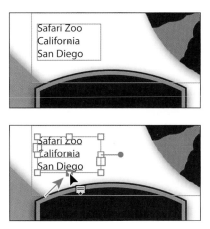

Tip: If you double-click text with the Selection (▶) or Direct Selection tool (▷), the Type tool becomes selected.

7 Select the Selection tool and hover the pointer over the bottom, middle point again and the cursor will change (▶▤).

This annotator indicates that the type area is set to auto size. If you were to double click, Autosizing would be turned off for the area type. The type area would remain the current size no matter how much text was added.

8 Select the Type tool and select all of the text, except for "Safari Zoo" and delete it.

Notice that the type area shrank vertically to fit around the text.

9 Select the Selection tool and drag from within the "Safari Zoo" text down and to the left of the black sign shape with the green stroke. You need to drag directly from the text, not from a blank area in the type area.

10 Choose Select > Deselect, and then choose File > Save.

Converting between area and point type

You can easily convert between area and point type objects. This method can be useful if you type a headline by clicking (creating point type), but later wish to resize and add more text without stretching it. This method is also useful if you paste a paragraph of text from InDesign into Illustrator, and it pastes as point type but would be better suited as an area type object so that you could flow the text within.

Next, you will convert a text object from point type to area type.

1 Choose View > Fit Artboard In Window.

2 Select the Type tool (**T**), and click to create a point type object in the white space to the right of the orange-and-black tail. Type **Thursdays at 6:30 pm** (without a period). You will move this text later, as well.

3 Select the Zoom tool (🔍), and click several times to zoom in to the text.

● **Note:** Converting an area type object that has overflow text (you will learn about overflow text later) will show a warning when converted to point type, indicating that the overset text will be deleted.

4 Select the Selection tool (▶), and notice the bounding box around the text. Drag the right-center bounding point to the left. Since it's point type, the text stretches. Choose Edit > Undo Scale to reset the text.

The text "6:30 pm" needs to wrap down below the text "Thursdays at…" An easy way to do that is to convert the point type to area type, which is what you'll do next. Of course, you could also insert a paragraph or soft return in the text, but later you may want to resize the type area.

5 Position the pointer over the annotator (—○) off the right edge of the type object. A hollow end on the annotator indicates point type. When the pointer changes (▶⊞), click once to see the message "Double-click to convert to Area Type." Double-click the annotator to convert the point type to area type. The annotator end should now be filled (—●), indicating that it is an area type object.

▶ **Tip:** With a text object selected, you can also choose Type > Convert To Point Type or Convert To Area Type, depending on what the selected text area is.

6 Drag the lower-right bounding point down and to the left until the text "6:30 pm" wraps to the second line.

7 Drag the text area down on top of the brown end of the yellow lion's tail.

Convert to area type.   Resize the type object.   Position the type object.

Importing a plain text file

You can import text into artwork from a file that was created in another application. Illustrator supports the following formats for importing text:

- Microsoft Word (doc)
- Microsoft Word DOCX (docx)
- Microsoft RTF (rtf)
- Plain text (txt) (ASCII) with ANSI, Unicode, Shift JIS, GB2312, Chinese Big 5, Cyrillic, GB18030, Greek, Turkish, Baltic, and Central European encoding.

One of the advantages of importing text from a file, rather than copying and pasting it, is that imported text retains its character and paragraph formatting (by default). For example, text from an RTF file retains its font and style specifications in Illustrator, unless you choose to remove formatting when you import the text.

1 Choose View > Fit Artboard In Window, and then choose Select > Deselect.

2 In the Layers panel (Window > Layers), click the visibility column (the eye icon [⊙]) of the Tails layer to temporarily hide some of the artwork.

3 Choose File > Place. In the Lessons > Lesson07 folder, select the L7_text.txt file, select Show Import Options, and click Place.

4 In the Text Import Options dialog box, you can set some options prior to importing text. Leave the default settings, and then click OK.

5 Position the loaded text pointer over the upper-left corner of the aqua guide box in the center of the artboard. When the word "anchor" appears, click and drag down and to the right. As you drag, notice that the width and height are constrained (always the same proportion). Drag until the pointer reaches the bottom of the aqua guide box, and then release the mouse button.

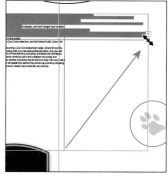

● **Note:** The figures are from the Windows OS, so the Platform option that you see may be different on Mac OS, and that's okay.

6 With the Selection tool (▶), drag the corner bounding point of the text area up and to the right so that it snaps to the right edge of the aqua guide box and drag up until an overset text icon (⊞) appears in the out port. Leave the text area selected.

Position the loaded text pointer.

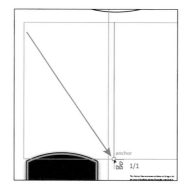
Drag to place the text.

Resize the area type object.

Placing Microsoft Word documents

When you place (File > Place) RTF (Rich Text Format) or Word documents (DOC or DOCX) in Illustrator, the Microsoft Word Options dialog box appears.

In this dialog box, you can select to keep the generated Table of Contents, footnotes and endnotes, and index text, and even choose to remove the formatting of the text before you place it (the styles and formatting are brought in from Word by default).

Working with overflow text and text reflow

Each area type object contains an *in port* and an *out port*. The ports enable you to link to other type objects and flow text between type objects. An empty out port

indicates that all the text is visible and that the object isn't linked. An arrow in a port indicates that the type object is linked to another type object. A red plus sign (⊞) in an out port indicates that the object contains additional text, which is called *overflow text*.

There are three main methods for remedying overflow text:

- Thread the text to another type object.
- Resize the type object.
- Adjust the text.

Threading text

To *thread*, or continue, text from one object to the next, you have to link the objects. Linked type objects can be of any shape; however, the text must be entered in an object or along a path, not as point type (by simply clicking to create text).

Next, you will thread text from one type object to another by linking the type objects together.

1   Choose View > Smart Guides to turn them off so that you can more easily move objects without snapping.

● **Note:** It may be difficult to click the out port because of the guides. You can always zoom in, remembering to zoom out again for the next steps.

2   With the Selection tool (➤), click the out port (larger box) in the lower-right corner of the type object that has the red plus sign in it (⊞). The pointer changes to a loaded text icon (▤) when you move it away.

● **Note:** If you double-click an out port, a new type object appears. If this happens, you can either drag the new object where you would like it to be positioned or choose Edit > Undo Link Threaded Text, and the loaded text icon reappears.

Next, you will flow the overflow text into an existing type object on the next artboard.

3 Click the Next Artboard button (▶) in the lower-left corner of the Document window to navigate to the postcard artboard.

4 Choose Select > All On Active Artboard to see the type object that's already there.

5 Position the pointer over the edge of the type object. When the pointer changes to (▶⊂ᵒ), click to thread the text areas and the thread (line) will appear to connect this text area.

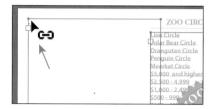

● **Note:** With the loaded text icon, you can also click the artboard instead of dragging to create a new type object.

With the second type object still selected, notice the line between the two objects (the figure at right probably shows more than you can see). This line is the thread that tells you that the two objects are connected. If you don't see this thread (line), choose View > Show Text Threads.

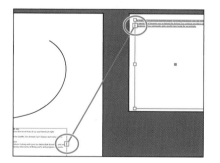

● **Note:** Even if there isn't enough text to fill them, you can still thread multiple type objects together.

Notice the out port (▶) of the type object on the larger artboard and the in port (▷) of the type object on the smaller artboard (both circled in the previous figure). The arrows in the ports indicate how the text is flowing from one to the other. If you delete the second type object, the text is pulled back into the original object as overflow text. Although not visible, the overflow text is not deleted.

▶ **Tip:** Another way to thread text between objects is to select an area type object, select the object (or objects) you want to link to, and then choose Type > Threaded Text > Create.

6 Choose Select > Deselect, and then choose File > Save.

Creating columns of text

You can easily create columns and rows of text by using the Type > Area Type Options command. This can be useful for a single type object with multiple columns (instead of separate threaded text areas) or for organizing text, like a table or simple chart, for instance. Next, you'll add a few columns to the existing type object on the larger artboard.

1   While still on the 2 Card artboard, with the Selection tool (➤), click to select the text area that starts with the orange text "Lion Circle…"

▶ **Tip:** To learn more about the large number of options in the Area Type Options dialog box, search for "Creating Text" in Illustrator Help (Help > Illustrator Help).

2   Choose Type > Area Type Options. In the Area Type Options dialog box, in the Columns section, change the Number to **2** and select Preview. Click OK. The text won't change in appearance, but you should see the column guides.

● **Note:** If the cursor is still in the type object, you don't have to select the type object with the Selection tool to access the Area Type Options dialog box.

Next, you'll drag the bottom of the type object up to see the columns at work.

3   Drag the bottom, middle bounding point up until the text flows into the second column, like you see in the figure. Try to balance the text in the columns (make them even).

4   Choose Select > Deselect.

5   Choose File > Save.

Formatting type

When it comes to text, you can format it using character and paragraph formatting, apply fill and stroke attributes to it, and change its transparency (how see-through it is). You can apply these changes to one character, a range of characters, or all characters in a type object that you select.

As you'll soon see, selecting the type object, rather than selecting the text inside, lets you apply global formatting options to all of the text in the object, including options from the Character and Paragraph panels, fill and stroke attributes, and transparency settings.

In this section, you'll discover how to change text attributes, such as size and font, and how to save that formatting as text styles.

Changing font family and font style

In this section, you'll apply a font to text. Aside from applying local fonts from your machine, Creative Cloud users can apply Typekit fonts that have been synced with their computer. Typekit is a subscription service offering access to a library of fonts for use in desktop applications such as InDesign or Microsoft Word, and on websites. A Typekit Portfolio plan is included with your Creative Cloud subscription, and free Creative Cloud members have access to a selection of fonts from Typekit for Web and desktop use. The fonts appear alongside other locally installed fonts in the Fonts list in Illustrator, as you'll soon see.

● **Note:** For questions about Typekit font licensing, visit: http://help.typekit.com/customer/portal/articles/1341590-typekit-font-licensing. For more information on working with Typekit fonts, visit: http://helpx.adobe.com/creative-cloud/help/add-fonts-typekit.html.

● **Note:** The Creative Cloud desktop application must be installed on your computer and you must have an Internet connection to initially sync fonts. The Creative Cloud desktop application is installed automatically when you install your first Creative Cloud application, like Illustrator.

First, you'll make sure that Typekit is set up to ensure that you can add fonts.

1 Launch the Creative Cloud for desktop application and sign in with your Adobe ID, if you aren't already (*this requires an Internet connection*). If you do not have the application installed, you can do so from here: https://creative.adobe.com/products/creative-cloud.

2 In the Creative Cloud desktop application, choose Assets > Fonts, and if you see "Turn Typekit On," click it to allow font syncing.

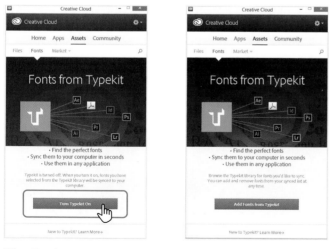

When Typekit is not on.   When Typekit is on.

If you have already selected fonts to sync in your Web browser at this point, they will automatically begin syncing to your computer. Now you can start using Typekit fonts.

3 Back in Illustrator, choose 1 Flyer from the Artboard Navigation menu in the lower-left corner of the Document window.

4 Press Command++ (Mac OS) or Ctrl++ (Windows) twice to zoom in to the text in the center of the artboard.

Note: If you miss the text, you will create point type. Choose Edit > Undo Type, if that's the case, and try again.

5 Select the Type tool (T) in the Tools panel, and with the pointer over the text, click to insert the cursor in the text. Choose Select > All, or press Command+A (Mac OS) or Ctrl+A (Windows), to select all the text in both threaded text objects.

▶ **Tip:** You will accidentally click with the Type tool and create a type object from time to time and want to get rid of the ones you aren't using. Illustrator has an easy way to clean up those objects: Object > Path > Clean Up.

Note: You may see the word "Character" instead of the Font menu listed in the Control panel. Click the word "Character" to reveal the Character panel, then click the Font menu.

6 Click the arrow to the right of the Font menu in the Control panel, and notice the fonts that appear in the menu. These fonts are those that are installed locally. Click the Add Fonts From Typekit button.

A browser will open and should open the typekit.com website and log you in using your Adobe ID. If you do not have an Internet connection, you can choose any other font in the font menu instead.

Note: If you are taken to the Typekit.com home page, you can simply click the Browse Fonts button.

7 Once on the Typekit.com website, click the Sans Serif button in the Classification options to sort the fonts, showing only available sans serif fonts.

8 Click the Desktop Use button if it's not already selected, to show all fonts that are available for use in desktop applications.

Note: If you don't see "+Use Fonts," you will most likely need to log in to the Typekit site using your Adobe ID.

9 Hover over the font "Adelle Sans" or another font and click "+Use Fonts."

Note: The fonts you see may not be the same and that's okay. If Adelle Sans is not available select another sans serif font.

10 In the pop-up that appears, click "Sync Selected Fonts." After the fonts have synced, click Close. You can close the browser and return to Illustrator.

▶ **Tip:** The fonts are synced to all computers where you've installed the Creative Cloud application and logged in. To view fonts, open the Creative Cloud desktop application and click the Assets > Fonts panel.

Once the fonts are synced to your computer (be patient, it may take a few minutes), a quick notification is usually displayed in your OS, indicating how many fonts have been added.

11 Back in Illustrator, click the arrow to the right of the Font menu in the Control panel, and click the Apply Typekit Filter button (🌠) to filter the font list (circled in the figure) and show only the Typekit font you just synced.

12 Click the arrow to the left of Adelle Sans in the menu, and choose Regular.

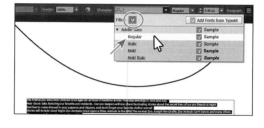

This sets the Font Family to Adelle Sans and the Font Style to Regular for all of the threaded text.

● **Note:** You may see other Typekit fonts (aside from the Adelle Sans font), and that's okay.

13 Scroll down the artboard so that you can see the text that starts with "Thursdays at..."

14 With the Type tool selected, click three times anywhere in the text to select the entire paragraph. Choose Type > Font to see a list of available fonts. Scroll down, and choose Adobe Garamond Pro > Bold Italic (or another font). If your font list is long, you may need to scroll quite far to find this font.

● **Note:** Be careful when selecting text. If you attempt to drag across the text to select it, you may wind up creating a new text object.

Next, you will use Font search to locate a font. This next method is the most dynamic method for selecting a font.

15 Insert the cursor in the text "Safari Zoo" to the far left of the "Thursdays at..." text, and choose Select > All.

16 With the text selected, click whatever font is listed in the Font menu in the Control panel to select the font name. Begin typing the letters **ga**.

Notice that a menu appears beneath where you are typing. Illustrator filters through the list and displays the font names that contain  "ga," regardless of where "ga" is in the font name and regardless of whether it's capitalized. The Typekit font filter is still turned on from before, so you will turn it off next.

▶ **Tip:** Once a font name is selected, you can also click the X on the right side of the Font Family field to remove the current font shown.

17 Click the Clear Filter button (▣) to see all of the available fonts again (see previous figure). Continue typing an "r" to make it **gar**, and the list is filtered further. In the menu that appears beneath where you are typing, click to select "Adobe Garamond Pro" and Adobe Garamond Pro Regular is applied to the selected text.

If you don't have Adobe Garamond Pro, feel free to choose something else. Your font list most likely won't be the same as you see in the figure and that's okay.

▶ **Tip:** You can click the Eyeglass icon (🔍) to the left of the Font Name field and choose to search the first word only. You can also open the Character panel (Window > Type > Character) and search for a font by typing the name.

When the menu of fonts appears, you could also use the arrow keys (Up and Down) to navigate the list of fonts. When the font you want is chosen, you can press Enter or Return to apply it. Font styles are specific to each font family. Although you may have the Adobe Garamond Pro font family on your system, you may not have the bold or italic styles of that family.

Changing font size

By default, typeface size is measured in points (a point equals 1/72 of an inch). You can specify any typeface size from 0.1 point to 1296 points, in 0.001-point increments.

1 With the "Safari Zoo" text and Type tool (**T**) still selected, choose 36 pt from the preset sizes in the Font Size menu in the Control panel.

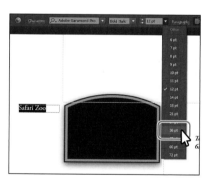

● **Note:** You may see the word "Character" instead of the Font Size field in the Control panel. Click the word "Character" to reveal the Character panel.

2 Select the 36 pt in the Font Size field in the Control panel and type **37**. Press Enter or Return.

The type area will resize to fit the text vertically, but the text may wrap horizontally. Remember, type objects don't resize by default when the text resizes unless you turn on Autosize (like we did earlier).

▶ **Tip:** You can dynamically change the font size of selected text using keyboard shortcuts. To increase the font size in increments of 2 points, press Command+Shift+> (Mac OS) or Ctrl+Shift+> (Windows). To reduce the font size, press Command+Shift+< (Mac OS) or Ctrl+Shift+< (Windows).

3   Select the Selection tool (↖), and drag the middle-right point of the text object to the right until "Safari" is on one line and "Zoo" is on the next.

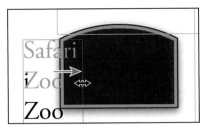

Make sure that the word "Zoo" is on its own line in the text object. You'll adjust the text later to make it look better. By dragging a bounding point, Autosize is turned off for the text area.

4   Choose View > Fit Artboard In Window.

5   With the Selection tool, click the "ZOO TALES" text at the top of the artboard.

6   Select the 12 pt font size in the Font Size field in the Control panel and type **74**. Press Enter or Return.

7   Drag the text object down, if need be, so that it's still on the artboard. Leave the text object selected.

Notice that the text object resizes since it's point type.

Changing font color

You can change the appearance of text by applying fills, strokes, and more. In this example, you will change the stroke and then the fill of selected text.

1   With the "ZOO TALES" text object still selected, click the Stroke color in the Control panel. When the Swatches panel appears, select White. The text stroke changes to white.

2   Change the Stroke weight of the text to **2 pt** in the Control panel.

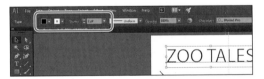

3   Select the Type tool (**T**) in the Tools panel, and click on the text in the threaded text frames in the middle of the artboard. Press Command+A (Mac OS) or Ctrl+A (Windows) to select all of the text.

● **Note:** The text that once fit in the two threaded text objects no longer fits. That's okay, since you'll get it all to fit shortly.

4   Click the Fill color in the Control panel. When the Swatches panel appears, select White. Change the Font Size by typing **15** in the Control panel and pressing Enter or Return.

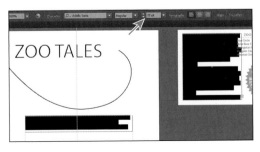

5   Choose Select > Deselect.

6   Select the Selection tool (➤). Shift-click the two text objects, at the bottom of the artboard, that contain the words "Safari Zoo" and "Thursdays at..."

7   Change the Fill color in the Control panel to White.

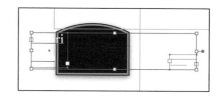

The text will be white on the white artboard, which will make it difficult to see. In the next section, you will turn on layers to make it easier to see the text.

Note: You will find that, if a text object contains text with different formatting, like a heading and body text, selecting the text object will make the formatting the same.

You can either select the text or the text object to change most of the formatting, including fill and stroke.

8   Choose Select > Deselect, and then choose Chose File > Save.

Changing additional text attributes

You can change many additional text attributes in the Character panel, which you can access by clicking the underlined word "Character" in the Control panel or by choosing Window > Type > Character. Below are the formatting options available in the Character panel when all options are showing.

1   Open the Character panel by choosing Window > Type > Character. Click the double arrow on the left side of the Character panel tab to show more options.

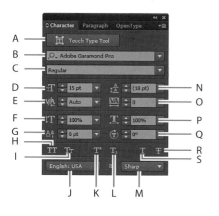

A. Touch Type tool	**K.** Superscript
B. Font Family	**L.** Subscript
C. Font Style	**M.** Text Anti-Aliasing
D. Font Size	**N.** Leading
E. Kerning	**O.** Tracking
F. Vertical Scale	**P.** Horizontal Scale
G. Baseline Shift	**Q.** Character Rotation
H. All Caps	
I. Small Caps	**R.** Strikethrough
J. Language	**S.** Underline

In this section, you will apply some of the many possible attributes to experiment with the different ways you can format text. You can close the Character panel.

2   Click the Layers panel icon (◆) to expand the panel. Click the visibility column to the left of the layer named Background and the layer named Tails. Click the Layers panel tab to collapse it.

3   Select the Type tool (**T**), and click in either of the threaded text objects that contain the placed text. Choose Select > All.

▶ **Tip:** You could also just work with the Character panel (Window > Type > Character).

4   Click the word "Character" in the Control panel, and click the down arrow to the left of the Leading (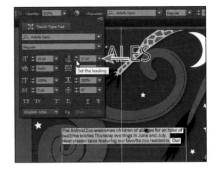) field to change the value to 17 pt. Press the Escape key to hide the panel.

Leading is the vertical space between lines. Notice the change in the vertical distance between the lines. Adjusting the leading can be useful for fitting text into a text area. Like other Character panel options, you can also type in a value for the Leading.

5   Insert the cursor in the text "Safari Zoo" in the lower-left corner of the artboard. With the cursor in the text, triple-click to select the entire paragraph.

6   With the text selected, click the Tracking icon () in the Character panel to select the value in the Tracking field, and type **–50**. Press Enter or Return.

Tracking changes the spacing between characters. A positive value pushes the letters apart horizontally; a negative value pulls the letters closer together.

● **Note:** If you choose to open the Character panel (Window > Type > Character), you may need to click the double arrow next to the word "Character" in the panel tab to reveal more options, like you learned earlier.

7   Choose Type > Change Case > UPPERCASE and the text may wrap oddly in the type object.

8   With the Selection tool (↖), drag the lower-right corner of the "SAFARI ZOO" text object to the right and up until the text fits again on two lines.

9   Double-click the text that begins with "Thursdays at…" to switch to the Type tool. With the cursor in the text, triple-click to select the entire paragraph.

10 Change the Font Size to **33 pt** in the Character panel. You'll need to either click the up arrow or type the value.

11 With the Selection tool, drag the lower-right corner of the "Thursdays at…" text object to the right and down until the text fits again on two lines.

12 With the text object still selected, click the Vertical Scale icon () in the Character panel to select the value and type **120**. Press Enter or Return to accept the value. Leave the Character panel open.

13 Choose View > Fit Artboard In Window.

14 Choose Select > Deselect.

Modifying text with the Touch Type tool

Using the Touch Type tool (🛱), you can modify the properties of a character, like size, scale, and rotation, using a mouse cursor or touch controls. This is a very visual (and more fun) way of applying the character formatting properties: baseline shift, horizontal and vertical scale, rotation, and kerning.

Next, you are going to use the Touch Type tool to alter the appearance of the "ZOO TALES" headline at the top of the artboard.

1 Select the Zoom tool (🔍), and click the headline "ZOO TALES" several times, to zoom in closely. Make sure you can still see all of the "ZOO TALES" text.

2 With the Selection tool (🔧), click to select the "ZOO TALES" text object. Select whatever font is listed in the Font menu in the Control panel, and type **Gar**. In the menu that appears beneath where you are typing, click to select Adobe Garamond Pro Bold (or choose another font).

3 Click the Touch Type Tool button at the top of the Character panel.

A message appears at the top of the Document window telling you to click on a character to select it.

4 Click the letter "Z" to select it. A box with a dot above it appears around the letter. The different points around the box allow you to adjust the character in different ways, as you'll see.

5 Choose View > Smart Guides to turn them on.

▶ **Tip:** You can also click and hold down the mouse button on the Type tool (**T**) in the Tools panel, and select the Touch Type tool (🛱) from the menu.

▶ Tip: By dragging
the upper-left corner
point of the box, you
can adjust the vertical
scale. By dragging the
lower-right corner of
the box, you can adjust
the horizontal scale.

6   Click and drag the upper-right corner of the box away from the center, to make
the letter larger. Stop dragging when you see roughly 190% for width (W:) and
height (H:) in the measurement label.

Notice that the movement is constrained—width and height change together
proportionally. You just adjusted the horizontal scale and the vertical scale for
the letter "Z" in the Character panel.

7   Look in the Character panel to see that the Horizontal Scale and Vertical Scale
values are *roughly* 190%.

Position the pointer.

Drag to resize the letter "Z."

Notice the scaling.

8   With the letter "Z" still selected, position the pointer in the center of the letter.
Click and drag the letter down until the Baseline value shows approximately
−24 pt in the gray measurement label.

You just edited the baseline shift of the letter in the Character panel.

9   Click the "O" to the right of the "Z," and drag the rotate handle (the circle above the
letter) counterclockwise until you see approximately 20° in the measurement label.

10 Click and drag the upper-right corner of the box around the selected "O," away
from the center, to make the letter larger. Stop dragging when you see roughly
125% for width (W:) and height (H:) in the measurement label.

Drag the letter "Z."

Rotate the letter "o."

Drag to resize the letter "o."

11 Drag the letter "O" from the center, to the left, until it looks something like the figure.

12 Click to select the second letter "O" in "ZOO," and change the following using the Touch Type tool:

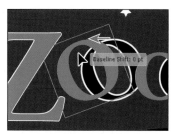

- Rotate the letter clockwise −35° (clockwise rotation shows a negative value).

- Click and drag (what was) the upper-right corner of the box, away from the center, until you see roughly 105% for width (W:) and height (H:) in the measurement label.

- Drag the letter from the center into the position you see in the figure.

▶ **Tip:** You can also nudge the selected letter with the arrow keys or press Shift+arrow key to move the letter in bigger increments.

Rotate the letter "o."

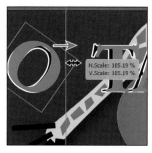

Resize the letter "o."

Drag the letter "o."

13 Click to select the letter "T" in "TALES," and change the following using the Touch Type tool:

- Click and drag the upper-right corner of the box, away from the center, until you see roughly 150% for width (W:) and height (H:) in the measurement label.

- Drag the letter "T" from the center down and to the left (a bit closer to the second "O" in "ZOO"), into the position you see in the figure.

- Click and drag the upper-left point up until you see a Vertical Scale of 185%.

● **Note:** There are limits to how far you can drag in any direction. Those limits are based on the kerning and baseline shift value limits.

Resize the letter "T."

Drag the letter "T" into position.

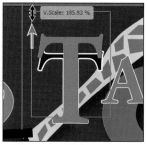

Change the Vertical Scale.

14 Click the letter "A" in "TALES." Drag the letter straight to the left to make it closer to the "T." See the figure for placement. Try not to drag up or down. The measurement label will show Baseline Shift: 0 pt.

Changing paragraph attributes

As with character attributes, you can set paragraph attributes, such as alignment or indenting, before you enter new type or to change the appearance of existing type. If you select several type paths and type containers, you can set attributes for them all at the same time. Most of this type of formatting is done in the Paragraph panel, which you can access by clicking the underlined word "Paragraph" in the Control panel or by choosing Window > Type > Paragraph.

Below are the formatting options available in the Paragraph panel.

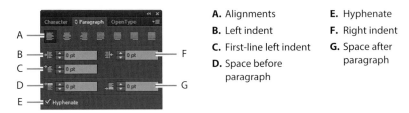

A. Alignments
B. Left indent
C. First-line left indent
D. Space before paragraph
E. Hyphenate
F. Right indent
G. Space after paragraph

Next, you'll add more space after all the paragraphs in the main text.

1 Choose View > Fit Artboard In Window.

2 Position the pointer over the Touch Type tool (⯐) in the Tools panel, click and hold down the mouse button, and select the Type tool (**T**). Insert the cursor in the text in middle of the artboard that begins with "The Animal Zoo welcomes..."

3 Click the word "Paragraph" in the Control panel to open the Paragraph panel.

4 Type **11 pt** in the Space After Paragraph text field (in the lower-right corner), and press Enter or Return.

Setting a spacing value after paragraphs, rather than pressing the Return key, is useful for maintaining consistency and ease of editing later.

5 With the Selection tool (), click the text "SAFARI ZOO" and then Shift-click the text "Thursdays at 6:30 pm" to select the two text objects only. Choose Window > Type > Paragraph to open the Paragraph panel. In the panel, click the Align Center button ().

● **Note:** You can also click the Paragraph panel tab in the Character panel group, if the Character panel is still open.

6 Close the Paragraph panel group.

7 Choose Select > Deselect, and then choose File > Save.

Working with glyphs

Glyphs are characters within a certain typeface that may be harder to find, like a bullet point or a registration symbol. In Illustrator, the Glyphs panel is used to insert type characters, like trademark symbols (™). The panel shows all of the characters (glyphs) available for a given font.

To learn more about working with glyphs in Illustrator, search for "Glyphs" in Illustrator Help (Help > Illustrator Help).

Resizing and reshaping type objects

You can create unique type object shapes by reshaping them using a variety of methods, including reshaping objects using the Direct Selection tool. In this next section, you'll reshape and resize type objects to better fit text in them.

1 Choose View > Fit All In Window.

At times, you may need to reflow the text between text objects. Next, you will learn how to resize, unlink, relink, and reshape type objects.

2 With the Selection tool (), click the text in the main type object on the larger artboard that is threaded to select it. Drag the right, middle point to the vertical guide in the center of the artboard.

Note: It may be difficult to double-click on the out port since you are zoomed out. You may wish to zoom in closer to the type area.

3   Double-click the out port (▶) in the lower-right corner of the text object (where the thread [blue line] is coming out).

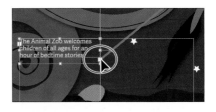

Because the two text objects were threaded, double-clicking the out port of the first text object (or the in port of the second type object) breaks the connection between them. Any text threaded between the type objects flows back into the first one. The other text object is still there, but it has no stroke or fill.

4   Using the Selection tool, drag the bottom, middle handle of the bounding box down until the text "…favorite stuffed animal!" is the last text in the object. The text object changes in size vertically.

5   With the Selection tool, click the out port (⊞) in the lower-right corner of the type object. The pointer changes to the loaded text icon (▤).

6   Position the loaded text icon (▤) to the right of the existing type object and down from its top edge (see the figure). Click, and a new type object is created that should roughly fit into the aqua guide box. Leave the new type object selected.

When type objects are threaded, you can move them anywhere and still maintain the connection between them. When type objects are resized, especially those in the beginning of the thread, text can reflow. Now you will link the new type object to the type object on the Card artboard.

Note: It may be difficult to click the out port since there is other artwork there. You can always move the type object, click the out port, and continue on to the next steps. You can move it back into position later.

7   With the Selection tool, click the out port (⊞) in the lower-right corner of the new type object. The pointer changes to the loaded text icon (▤).

8   Choose View > Outline to see the artwork edges.

9   On the 2 Card artboard, position the loaded text icon on the edge (boundary) of the existing type object (see the figure), and click when the pointer changes to this (▶⊕).

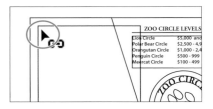

10 Choose View > Preview.

11 Using the Selection tool, on the 1 Flyer artboard, drag the bottom, middle handle of the right-hand type object up until the text "...for supporting this program." is the last text in the object. The text object changes in size vertically.

12 Select the Type tool (T) and position the pointer over the threaded text on the 2 Card artboard. When the cursor changes to (I), click three times to select the paragraph.

13 Change the Font Size to **10 pt** in the Control panel. Click the word "Character" in the Control panel and, in the Character panel, change the Leading to **15 pt**.

14 Select the Direct Selection tool (⟋). Click the upper-right corner of the type object to select the anchor point. Drag that point to the left to adjust the shape of the path to fit the orange shape. As you drag, press the Shift key. Release the mouse button and then the Shift key when finished.

● **Note:** You may need to adjust the shape of the type area or the size/leading of the text to fit the last paragraph in the type object, if you see the overset icon (⊞).

Change the Font size and leading.

Adjust the shape.

15 Choose File > Save.

Creating and applying text styles

Styles allow you to format text consistently and are helpful when text attributes need to be updated globally. Once a style is created, you only need to edit the saved style, and then all text formatted with that style is updated.

Illustrator provides two types of text styles:

- **Paragraph**—Retains character and paragraph attributes and applies them to an entire paragraph.

- **Character**—Retains character attributes and applies them to selected text.

Creating and applying a paragraph style

First, you will create a paragraph style for the body copy.

1 Choose 1 Flyer from the Artboard Navigation menu in the lower-left corner of the Document window (if it's not already chosen).

2 With the Type tool (**T**) selected, insert the cursor anywhere in the first paragraph in the first threaded type object that starts with "The Animal Zoo...".

   You do not need to select text to create a paragraph style, but you do have to place the text insertion point in the text that has the attributes you want to save.

3 Choose Window > Type > Paragraph Styles, and click the Create New Style button () at the bottom of the Paragraph Styles panel.

   This creates a new paragraph style in the panel, called "Paragraph Style 1." This style captures the character and paragraph formatting from the paragraph.

4 Double-click directly on the style name "Paragraph Style 1" in the list of styles. Change the name of the style to **Body**, and press Enter or Return to edit the name inline.

   By double-clicking the style to edit the name, you are also applying the new style to the paragraph (where the cursor is). This means that if you edit the Body paragraph style, this paragraph will update as well.

● **Note:** Make sure not to select the threaded text on the artboard 2 Card.

5 With the Type tool selected, click and drag from before the first word in the first paragraph that starts with the text "The Animal Zoo..." to after the last word "...for supporting this program." in the second "column" to select it.

6 Click the Body style in the Paragraph Styles panel.

   Notice that a plus sign (+) appears to the right of the Body style name. The plus sign indicates that the style has an override. An override is any formatting that doesn't match the attributes defined by the style, for example, if you changed the font size for the selected paragraph.

7   Press the Option (Mac OS) or Alt (Windows) key, and select the Body style again in the Paragraph Styles panel to overwrite existing attributes on the selected text.

The text attributes of the Body style are applied to the selected text, including the Space After value, so the text may no longer all fit in the two columns.

8   Choose Select > Deselect.

9   Select the Selection tool ( ), and click to select the type object on the right (the right column). Click and drag the bottom bounding point down until the text "supporting this program" is the last to appear in the column (if necessary).

10 Choose Select > Deselect.

Note: If you place a Microsoft Word document and choose to keep the formatting, the styles used in the Word document may be brought into the Illustrator document and may appear in the Paragraph Styles panel.

Editing a paragraph style

After creating a paragraph style, you can easily edit the style formatting. Then anywhere the style has been applied, the formatting will be updated automatically.

1   Double-click to the right of Body style name in the Paragraph Styles panel list to open the Paragraph Style Options dialog box.

2   Select the Indents And Spacing category on the left side of the dialog box.

3   Change the Space After to **8 pt**.

Since Preview is selected by default, you can move the dialog box out of the way to see the text change.

4   Click OK.

5   Choose File > Save.

There are many options for working with paragraph styles, most of which are found in the Paragraph Styles panel menu, including duplicating, deleting, and editing paragraph styles.

Tip: You can also choose Paragraph Style Options from the Paragraph Styles panel menu ( ).

Note: You may need to click and drag the bottom bounding point up until the text "supporting this program" is the last to appear in the column.

Creating and applying a character style

Character styles, unlike paragraph styles, can only be applied to selected text and can only contain character formatting. Next, you will create a character style from text styling within the columns of text.

1   Choose View > Zoom In, twice, to zoom in to the threaded text in the center.

2   Using the Type tool (**T**), in the first paragraph, select "The Animal Zoo."

3 Click the Fill color, and select the swatch named "gold" in the Control panel.

Note: If you chose a font other than Adelle Sans, and don't see Italic, try choosing another font style.

4 Click the word "Character" in the Control panel and choose Italic from the Font Style menu, and then click the Underline button (🔳) to underline the text.

Change the text color.   Edit other attributes.

5 In the Paragraph Styles panel group, click the Character Styles panel tab.

6 In the Character Styles panel, Option-click (Mac OS) or Alt-click (Windows) the Create New Style button (🔳) at the bottom of the Character Styles panel.

Option-clicking (Mac OS) or Alt-clicking (Windows) the Create New Style button in the Character or Paragraph Styles panel allows you to edit the style options before it is added to the panel.

7 Name the style **Emphasis**, and click OK.

The style records the attributes applied to your selected text.

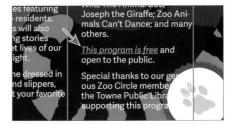

8 With the text still selected, Option-click (Mac OS) or Alt-click (Windows) the style named Emphasis in the Character Styles panel to assign the style to that text so that it will update if the style changes.

Note: You must select the entire phrase rather than just placing the cursor in the text.

9 In the next column (text object), select the text "This program is free" and Option-click (Mac OS) or Alt-click (Windows) the style named Emphasis in the Character Styles panel to apply it.

10 Choose Select > Deselect.

Editing a character style

After creating a character style, you can easily edit the style formatting, and, anywhere the style is applied, the formatting will be updated automatically.

1 Double-click to the right of the Emphasis style name in the Character Styles panel (not the style name itself). In the Character Style Options dialog box, make sure that Preview is selected. Click the Basic Character Formats category on the left side of the dialog box, and choose Regular from the Font Style menu. Click OK.

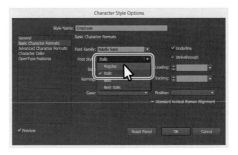

● **Note:** If the Font Family field is blank, choose Adelle Sans (or the font you chose), then you can select a font style.

2 Choose File > Save.

Sampling text formatting

Using the Eyedropper tool (🖊), you can quickly sample type attributes and copy them to text without creating a style.

1 Using the Type tool (T), select the text "dressed in your pajamas and slippers" in the first column of text.

2 Select the Eyedropper tool (🖊) in the Tools panel, and click in the first text "The Animal Zoo." A letter "T" appears above the Eyedropper pointer.

The attributes are immediately applied to your selected text, along with the Emphasis character style.

3 Choose Select > Deselect, and then select the style named [Normal Character Style] in the Character Styles panel. Close the Character Styles panel group.

● **Note:** Clicking [Normal Character Style] ensures that any new text you add to the document will not have the style named Emphasis applied.

4 Choose File > Save. Leave the file open.

Warping text

You can create some great design effects by warping text into different shapes using envelopes. You can make an envelope out of an object on your artboard, or you can use a preset warp shape or a mesh grid as an envelope. As you explore warping with envelopes, you'll also discover that you can use envelopes on any object except graphs, guides, or linked objects.

▶ **Tip:** There are several additional ways to warp content like text, including with a mesh and with an object you create. To learn more about these other methods, search for "Reshape using envelopes" in Illustrator Help (Help > Illustrator Help).

Reshaping text with a preset envelope warp

Illustrator comes with a series of preset warp shapes that you can warp text with. Next, you'll apply one of the preset warp shapes that Illustrator provides.

1 Choose View > Fit Artboard In Window. Select the Zoom tool (🔍) and click the "SAFARI ZOO" text in the lower-left corner of the artboard several times.

2 With the Type tool (**T**), select the word "ZOO" and change the Font Size to **66 pt** in the Control panel.

3 Adjust the type object size just large enough to show all of the text with the Selection tool (▸), if the word "ZOO" doesn't fit.

● **Note:** The same visual result can be achieved by choosing Object > Envelope Distort > Make With Warp. For more information about envelopes, see "Reshape using envelopes" in Illustrator Help (Help > Illustrator Help).

4 With the Type tool, select the word "ZOO" again, and click the word "Character" in the Control panel to open the Character panel. Change the Leading value to **52 pt**.

5 Select the Selection tool and make sure that the text object is selected. Click the Make Envelope button (🔲) in the Control panel (not the arrow to the right). In the Warp Options dialog box, select Preview. The text appears as an arc.

6 Choose Arc Upper from the Style menu. Drag the Bend slider to the right to see it bend up further. You can experiment with many combinations. Drag the Horizontal and Vertical Distortion sliders to see the effect on the text. When you are finished experimenting, drag the Distortion sliders to **0%**, make sure that the Bend is **20%**, and then click OK.

7 Drag the envelope object (warped text) into the approximate center of the black sign shape.

Editing the envelope warp

If you want to make any changes, you can edit the text and shape that make up the envelope warp object separately. Next, you will edit the text and then the warp shape.

1 With the envelope object still selected, click the Edit Contents button (□) in the Control panel. This is how you edit the text in the warped shape.

2 Make sure that Smart Guides are on (View > Smart Guides).

3 Using the Type tool (T), position the cursor over the warped text. Notice that another copy of the text appears in blue. The Smart Guides show you the original unwarped text in blue. Click the word "SAFARI" to insert the cursor, and then click twice to select the word "SAFARI."

▶ **Tip:** If you double-click with the Selection tool instead of with the Type tool, you enter Isolation mode. This is another way to edit the text within the envelope warp object. Press the Escape key to exit Isolation mode.

4 Type **ANIMAL**, and then press Shift+Enter or Shift+Return to add a soft return after the word and to break the word "ZOO" to the next line.

   Notice that the text automatically warps in the envelope shape.

You can also edit the preset shape, which is what you'll do next.

▶ **Tip:** To take the text out of the warped shape, select the text with the Selection tool and choose Object > Envelope Distort > Release. This gives you two objects: the type object and an arc upper shape.

5 Select the Selection tool (▶), and make sure that the envelope object is still selected. Click the Edit Envelope button (□) in the Control panel.

   Notice the options for the envelope warp object in the Control panel. You can choose another warp shape from the Style menu and then change the warp options, like Horizontal, Vertical, and Bend. These are the same options you saw in the Warp Options dialog box when you first created the envelope warp.

● **Note:** Changing the warp style will most likely move the warp object on the artboard.

6 Change the Bend to **28%** in the Control panel. Make sure that the H (horizontal) Distortion is **0** and the V (vertical) Distortion is **0**.

7 Choose View > Smart Guides to turn them off.

8 Select the Selection tool, and Shift-drag the lower-right-corner bounding point away from the center to make the object a bit larger. Make sure that the text stays within the black sign shape. See the next figure for placement help.

9 Shift-click the black sign shape to select both objects, and then release the Shift key. Click the black sign shape once more to make it the key object. Click the Horizontal Align Center button (🗎), and then click the Vertical Align Center button (🗎) to align the warped text to the black sign shape.

Working with type on a path

In addition to having text in point and type areas, you can also have type along a path. Text can flow along the edge of an open or closed path and can lead to some really creative ways to display text.

Creating type on a path

First, you'll insert some text on an open path.

1 Choose View > Fit Artboard In Window. You may wish to zoom in further to see the text you type.

2 With the Selection tool (▶), select the black curved path on top of the brown monkey tail.

   When creating a new type object, this resets the formatting to default.

3 With the Type tool (T), position the cursor over the middle of the path to see an insertion point with an intersecting wavy path (⭝) (see the figure). Click when this cursor appears.

   The text starts where you click the path. Also, the stroke attributes of the path change to None and a cursor appears.

4   Choose Window > Type > Paragraph Styles to open the panel. Option-click (Mac OS) or Alt-click (Windows) the [Normal Paragraph Style].

5   Type the text **Bedtime Stories With Your Wildest Friends**. Note that the new text follows the path.

6   With the Type tool, click three times on the new text to select it.

7   Select the Eyedropper tool (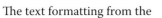) in the Tools panel, and click in the text that begins, "Thursdays at..." A letter "T" appears above the Eyedropper pointer (without the Caps Lock key selected).

The text formatting from the "Thursdays at..." text applies to the text on the path. This makes the text not fit on the path, so the overset icon (⊞) in the out port appears.

8   Click the word "Character" in the Control panel, and change the Vertical Scale to **100%** in the Character panel. Press the Escape key to hide the panel.

9   Click the Align Left button (▣) in the Control panel.

Next, you'll reposition the text on the path so that all of the text appears.

10 Select the Selection tool, and position the pointer over the line on the left edge of the text (just to the left of the "B"). When you see this cursor (▸ₚ), click and drag to the left—all the way to the left end of the path.

11 Choose Select > Deselect, and then choose File > Save.

Creating type on a closed path

Next, you will add text around a circle.

1   Select the Zoom tool (🔍) in the Tools panel, and click the yellow paw print three times to zoom in.

2   With the Selection tool (▸), Shift-click the threaded type object and the yellow paw print to select both and choose Object > Hide > Selection.

> **Note:** If the text is yellow and underlined it means that the character style is applied. Select the text and Option (Mac OS) or Alt (Windows) click the [Normal Character Style] in the Character Styles panel.

> **Note:** If you don't see the text align options in the Control panel, click the word "Paragraph" to reveal the Paragraph panel.

> **Tip:** With the path or the text on the path selected, you can choose Type > Type On A Path > Type On A Path Options to set more options.

3   Select the Type tool ($\mathbf{T}$), and position the pointer over the edge of the white circle. The Type cursor (⌶) changes to a Type cursor with a circle (⌶). This indicates that, if you click (don't click), text will be placed inside of the circle, creating a type object in the shape of a circle.

● **Note:** Instead of pressing the Option (Mac OS) or Alt (Windows) key to allow the Type tool to type on a path, you can select the Type On A Path tool (✑) by holding down the Type tool in the Tools panel.

4   While pressing the Option (Mac OS) or Alt (Windows) key, position the pointer over the left side of the circle. The insertion point with an intersecting wavy path (↲) appears. Click and type **ZOO CIRCLE**. The text flows on the circular path. Click three times on the text to select it.

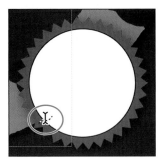

5   With the text still selected, in the Control panel, change the font size to **16 pt**, the Font Style to Bold (the Font Family should already be Adobe Garamond Pro), and the Fill color to the swatch named gold.

Next, you will adjust the position of the text.

● **Note:** Brackets appear at the beginning of the type, at the end of the path, and at the midpoint between the start and end brackets. All of these brackets can be adjusted to reposition the text in the path.

6   Select the Selection tool in the Tools panel. Position the pointer over the line on the left end of the text (to the left of the word "ZOO"). That line is called a bracket. When you see this cursor (▸₊), with an arrow pointing to the right, drag up around the circle in a clockwise fashion. See the figure for position.

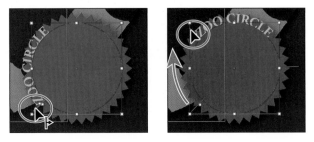

Editing type on a path options

When you create type on a path, you can set options to change the appearance of the text, including effects, alignment, and spacing. Next, you'll edit the type on a path options for the text on the circle.

● **Note:** To learn about the Type On A Path options, search for "Creating type on a path" in Illustrator Help (Help > Illustrator Help).

1   With the path type object selected with the Selection tool, choose Type > Type On A Path > Type On A Path Options. In the Type On A Path Options dialog box, select Preview and change the following options:

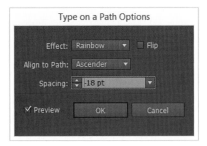

   • Choose **Skew** from the Effect menu, and then choose **Rainbow**.

- Align To Path: **Ascender**
- Spacing: **−18 pt**

2 Click OK.

3 With the Selection tool (⬆), position the
   pointer over the line on the left end of
   the text (to the left of the word "ZOO").
   When you see this cursor (⬆), drag down
   around the circle in a counterclockwise fashion.
   See the figure.

4 Choose Object > Show All and then choose
   Select > Deselect.

Wrapping text around an object

In Illustrator, you can easily wrap text around objects, like type objects, imported
images, and vector artwork, to avoid text running over those objects or to create
interesting design effects. Next, you will wrap text around the text on a path object.

1 With the Selection tool (⬆) selected, click directly on the "ZOO CIRCLE" text to
   select it. Choose Object > Arrange > Bring To Front.

2 Choose Object > Text Wrap > Make.
   Click OK if a dialog box appears. The
   text in the column wraps around the
   text on a path shape.

   If you move the object with the text
   wrap applied, the text responds
   and wraps differently.

Note: To wrap text
around an object, the
object that the text is
to wrap around must
be in the same layer as
the text and must be
located above the text
in the layer hierarchy.

3 Choose Object > Text Wrap > Text
   Wrap Options. In the Text Wrap
   Options dialog box, change Offset to 13
   pt and select Preview to see the change.

Note: Your text may
wrap differently, and
that's okay.

4 Click OK.

5 With the Selection tool (⬆) selected,
   drag the bottom, middle point of the
   threaded text box down to make sure
   that the text "…for supporting this
   program" is the last showing.

6 Choose View > Fit Artboard In Window,
   and then choose Select > Deselect.

Creating text outlines

Converting text to outlines means converting text into *vector* shapes that you can edit and manipulate as you would any other graphic object. Text outlines are useful for changing the look of large display type, but they are rarely useful for body text or other type at small sizes. The file recipient doesn't need to have your fonts installed to open and view the file correctly.

When you create outlines from text, you should consider that text as no longer editable. Also, bitmap fonts and outline-protected fonts cannot be converted to outlines, and outlining text that is less than 10 points in size is not recommended. When type is converted to outlines, the type loses its hints—instructions built into outline fonts to adjust their shape to display or print optimally at many sizes. You must also convert all type in a selection to outlines; you cannot convert a single letter within a type object.

Next, you will convert the main heading to outlines and position content.

● **Note:** To keep your original text, you can save a layer with the original text (and hide the layer).

1   With the Selection tool (▶) selected, click the heading text "Zoo Tales" at the top of the artboard to select it. Choose Type > Create Outlines. Drag it into position like you see in the figure (if it's not already there).

The text is no longer linked to a particular font. Instead, it is now artwork, much like any other vector art in your illustration.

2   With the Selection tool, drag the text "Thursdays at 6:30 pm" at the bottom of the artboard into position, like you see in the following figure.

3   Choose View > Guides > Hide Guides, and then choose Select > Deselect.

4   Choose File > Save, and then choose File > Close.

Review questions

1 Name two methods for creating a text area in Adobe Illustrator.

2 What does the Touch Type tool (⧉) let you do?

3 What is *overflow text*?

4 What is *text threading*?

5 What is the difference between a *character style* and a *paragraph style*?

6 What is the advantage of converting text to outlines?

Review answers

1 The following methods can be used for creating text areas:

   • With the Type tool (**T**), click the artboard and start typing when the cursor appears. A text area is created to accommodate the text.

   • With the Type tool, drag to create a text area. Type when a cursor appears.

   • With the Type tool, click a path or closed shape to convert it to text on a path, or click in a text area. Option-clicking (Mac OS) or Alt-clicking (Windows) when crossing over the stroke of a closed path creates text around the shape.

2 The Touch Type tool (⧉) allows you to visually edit certain character formatting options for individual characters in text. You can edit the character rotation, kerning, baseline shift, and horizontal and vertical scale of text.

3 Overflow text is text that does not fit within an area type object or path. A red plus sign (⊞) in an out port indicates that the object contains additional text.

4 Text threading allows you to flow text from one object to another by linking type objects. Linked type objects can be of any shape; however, the text must be entered in an area or along a path (not at a point).

5 A character style can be applied to selected text only. A paragraph style is applied to an entire paragraph. Paragraph styles are best for indents, margins, and line spacing.

6 Converting text to outlines eliminates the need to send the fonts along with the Illustrator file when sharing with others.

8 ORGANIZING YOUR ARTWORK WITH LAYERS

Lesson overview

In this lesson, you'll learn how to do the following:

- Work with the Layers panel.

- Create, rearrange, and lock layers and sublayers.

- Move objects between layers.

- Copy and paste objects and their layers from one file to another.

- Merge layers into a single layer.

- Locate objects in the Layers panel.

- Isolate content in a layer.

- Make a layer clipping mask.

- Apply an appearance attribute to objects and layers.

This lesson takes approximately 45 minutes to complete.

Download the project files for this lesson from the Lesson & Update Files tab on your Account page at www.peachpit.com and store them on your computer in a convenient location, as described in the Getting Started section of this book.

Your Account page is also where you'll find any updates to the chapters or to the lesson files. Look on the Lesson & Update Files tab to access the most current content.

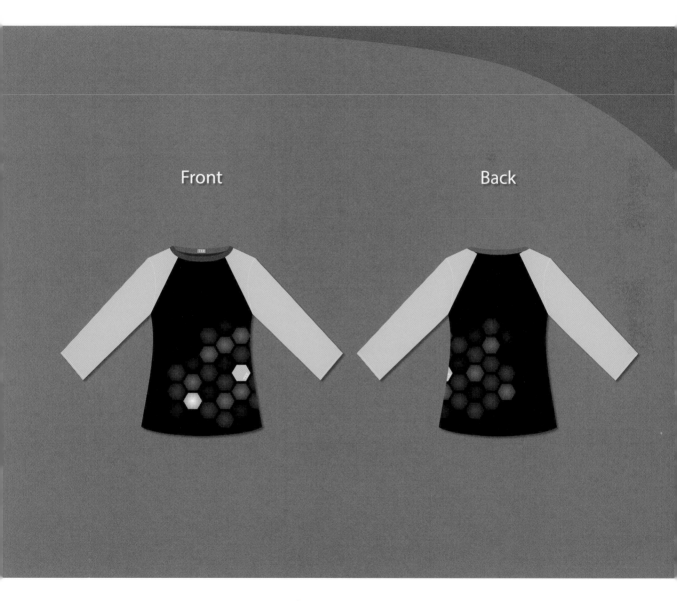

Front

Back

Layers let you organize your work into distinct
levels that can be edited and viewed individually or
together. Every Adobe Illustrator CC document has
at least one layer. Creating multiple layers in your
artwork lets you easily control how artwork is printed,
displayed, selected, and edited.

Getting started

In this lesson, you'll organize the artwork for several shirts as you explore the various ways to use the Layers panel.

● **Note:** If you have not already downloaded the project files for this lesson to your computer from your Account page, make sure to do so now. See the "Getting Started" section at the beginning of this book.

1 To ensure that the tools and panels function exactly as described in this lesson, delete or deactivate (by renaming) the Adobe Illustrator CC preferences file. See "Restoring default preferences" in the Getting Started section at the beginning of the book.

2 Start Adobe Illustrator CC.

3 Choose File > Open, and open the L8_end.ai file in the Lesson08 folder, located in the Lessons folder on your hard disk.

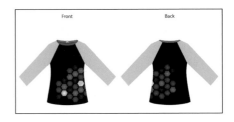

4 Choose View > Fit Artboard In Window.

5 Choose Window > Workspace > Reset Essentials.

● **Note:** If you don't see "Reset Essentials" in the Workspace menu, choose Window > Workspace > Essentials before choosing Window > Workspace > Reset Essentials.

Understanding layers

Layers are like invisible folders to help you hold and manage all of the items (some of which can be difficult to select or track) that make up your artwork. If you shuffle those folders, you change the stacking order of the items in your artwork. (You learned about stacking order in Lesson 2, "Techniques for Selecting Artwork.")

The structure of layers in your document can be as simple or as complex as you want. When you create a new Illustrator document, all of the content you create is organized in a single layer. However, you can create new layers and sublayers (like subfolders) to organize your artwork, as you'll learn about in this lesson.

1 Click the Layers panel icon (▣) on the right side of the workspace, or choose Window > Layers.

In addition to organizing content, the Layers panel offers an easy way to select, hide, lock, and change your artwork's appearance attributes.

In the next figure, the Layers panel you see will not look exactly the same, and that's okay. You can refer back to this figure as you progress through the lesson.

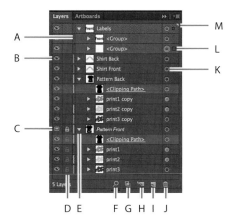

A. Layer color
B. Visibility column
C. Template layer icon
D. Edit column (lock/unlock)
E. Disclosure triangle (expand/collapse)
F. Locate Object
G. Make/Release Clipping Mask
H. Create New Sublayer
I. Create New Layer
J. Delete Selection
K. Target column
L. Selection column
M. Current layer indicator (small triangle)

To begin working, you'll open an existing art file that is incomplete.

2 Choose File > Open, and open the L8_start.ai file in the Lessons > Lesson08 folder on your hard disk.

The Missing Fonts dialog box will most likely appear, indicating that a font was used in the file that Illustrator can't find. The file uses a Typekit font that you most likely don't have synced with your machine, so you will fix the missing font before moving on.

3 In the Missing Fonts dialog box, a single font (CreteRound-Regular) will appear in the list. Ensure that Sync is selected in the Sync column and click Sync Fonts. The font should be synced with your machine, and you should see a success message in the Missing Fonts dialog box. Click Close.

This should sync the Typekit font to your machine and ensure that the font shows as intended in Illustrator. If you see a warning message in the Missing Fonts dialog box or cannot select Sync, you can click Find Fonts to replace the font with a local font. In the Find Font dialog box, make sure that "CreteRound Regular" is selected in the Fonts in Document section and choose System from the Replace With Font From menu. This shows all of the local fonts that are available to Illustrator. Select a font from the Fonts In System section and click Change All to replace the font. Click Done.

● **Note:** If the font is unable to sync, you may not have an Internet connection or you may need to launch the Creative Cloud desktop application, sign in with your Adobe ID, choose Assets > Fonts, and click Turn Typekit On. If you went through Lesson 7, "Adding Type to a Poster," you would have this already turned on. For more information, visit http://helpx.adobe.com/creative-cloud/help/add-fonts-typekit.html.

4   Choose File > Save As, name the file **Shirts.ai**, and select the Lesson08 folder. Leave the Format option set to Adobe Illustrator (ai) (Mac OS) or the Save As Type option set to Adobe Illustrator (*.AI) (Windows), and then click Save. In the Illustrator Options dialog box, leave the Illustrator options at their default settings, and then click OK.

5   Choose Select > Deselect (if available), and then choose View > Fit Artboard In Window.

Creating layers and sublayers

By default, every document begins with one layer, named "Layer 1." As you create artwork, you can rename and add layers and sublayers at any time. Placing objects on separate layers lets you more easily select and edit them. For example, by placing type on a separate layer, you can change the type all at once without affecting the rest of the artwork.

Next, you'll change the default layer name, and then create new layers using different methods. The idea for this project is to organize the "Shirt Front" and back content so you can more easily work with it later.

1   If the Layers panel isn't visible, click the Layers panel icon (⬖) on the right side of the workspace, or choose Window > Layers. Layer 1 (the default name for the first layer) is highlighted, indicating that it is active.

● **Note:** If you double-click just to the right or left of a layer name, the Layer Options dialog box will open. You can also change the layer name there.

2   In the Layers panel, double-click the layer name "Layer 1" to edit it inline. Type **Shirt Front**, and then press Enter or Return.

Instead of keeping all of the content on one single layer, you'll create several layers and sublayers to better organize the content and to make it easier to select content later.

▶ **Tip:** You can easily delete a layer by selecting the layer or sublayer and clicking the Delete Selection button (🗑) at the bottom of the Layers panel. This deletes the layer or sublayer and all content on it.

3   Click the Create New Layer button (▣) at the bottom of the Layers panel.

Layers and sublayers that aren't named are numbered in sequence. For example, the second layer is named Layer 2. When a layer or sublayer in the Layers panel contains other items, a disclosure triangle (▶) appears to the left of the layer or sublayer name. You can click the disclosure triangle to show or hide the contents. If no triangle appears, the layer has no content on it.

4 Double-click to the right or left of the layer name "Layer 2" to open the Layer Options dialog box. Change the name to **Shirt Back** and notice all of the other options available. Click OK.

By default, the new layer is added above the currently selected layer ("Shirt Front") in the Layers panel and becomes active. Notice that the new layer has a different layer color (a light red) to the left of the layer name. This will become more important later, as you select content.

Next, you will create a layer and name it in one step, using a modifier key.

5 Option-click (Mac OS) or Alt-click (Windows) the Create New Layer button (⬛) at the bottom of the Layers panel. In the Layer Options dialog box, change the name to **Pattern Front**, and then click OK.

6 Option-click (Mac OS) or Alt-click (Windows) the Create New Layer button (⬛) at the bottom of the Layers panel. In the Layer Options dialog box, change the name to **Labels**, and then click OK.

▶ **Tip:** Choosing New Layer from the Layers panel menu (▼≡) will also create a new layer and open the Layer Options dialog box.

7 Drag the "Pattern Front" layer to the Create New Layer button. This creates a copy of the layer and names it "Pattern Front copy." Double-click the layer name and change it to **Pattern Back**.

Next, you'll create a sublayer, which is a layer nested within a layer.

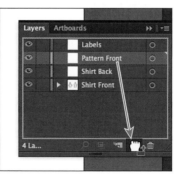

● **Note:** Depending on
your operating system,
the selection color of
objects (the bounding
box) may be different
colors, and that's okay.

8 Click the layer named "Shirt Front" once, and
then click the Create New Sublayer button
(⊞) at the bottom of the Layers panel to
create a new sublayer in the Shirt Front layer.

9 Drag the left edge of the Layers panel to the
left to make it wider so that you can more
easily read the layer names.

10 Double-click the new sublayer name (Layer 6,
in our case), change the name to **Front Collar**,
and then press Enter or Return.

The new sublayer appears directly beneath its main layer, "Shirt Front", and
is selected. Creating a new sublayer opens the selected layer to show existing
sublayers. Sublayers are used to organize content within a layer without
grouping or ungrouping content.

● **Note:** To create a new sublayer and name it in one step, Option-click (Mac OS) or Alt-click
(Windows) the Create New Sublayer button or choose New Sublayer from the Layers panel menu to
open the Layer Options dialog box.

11 Click the disclosure triangle (▶) to the left of
the "Shirt Front" layer to hide the content of
the layer.

Layers and color

By default, Illustrator assigns a unique
color to each layer in the Layers panel.
The color displays next to the layer name
in the panel. The same color displays
in the artwork bounding box, path,
anchor points, and center point of a
selected object.

You can use this color to quickly locate an
object's corresponding layer in the Layers panel, and you can change the layer color
to suit your needs.

—From Illustrator Help

Editing layers and objects

By rearranging the layers in the Layers panel, you can change the stacking order of objects in your artwork. On an artboard, objects in layers that are higher in the Layers panel list are in front of objects located on layers lower in the list, and each layer has its own stacking order as well. Layers are useful for a variety of reasons, including the ability to move objects between layers and sublayers to organize and more easily select your artwork.

Locating layers

When working in artwork, there may be times when you select content on the artboard and then want to locate that same content in the Layers panel. This can help you to determine how content is organized.

1   With the Selection tool (➤), click to select the yellow/green sleeves on the shirt below the word "Front." Click the Locate Object button (🔍) at the bottom of the Layers panel to reveal the group of objects within the Layers panel.

Clicking the Locate Object button will open the layer so that the layer content can be seen, and the Layers panel will scroll, if necessary, to reveal the selected content. With an Illustrator file that has a lot of layered content, this can be helpful. In the Layers panel, you will see the selection indicator to the far right of the <Group> object (it's the small colored box to the far right in the figure that the arrow is pointing to), as well as the two <Path> objects in the group.

2   Double-click the <Group> text and rename it **Front Sleeves**.

By default, when content is grouped, a group object is created that contains the grouped content. Look on the left end of the Control panel to see the word "Group" in the Selection Indicator. Renaming a group doesn't change the fact that it is still a group.

3 Choose Select > Deselect.

4 Click the disclosure triangle (▼) for the main "Shirt Front" layer to hide the contents of the layer. The "Shirt Front" layer is the only layer with a disclosure triangle because it's currently the only layer with content on it.

Moving layers and content between layers

Now you'll move the artwork to the different layers, to which you'll later add content from another Illustrator file.

1 Choose View > Outline Mode.

2 In the artwork, using the Selection tool (▶), drag a marquee selection across the artwork for the "Back" shirt content, to select it (see the figure for what to select).

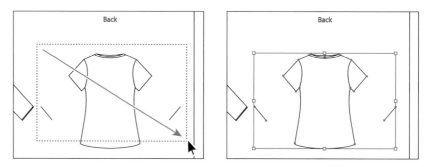

In the Layers panel, notice that the "Shirt Front" layer name has the selected-art indicator (color square). Also notice that the color of the bounding box, paths, and anchor points of the selected artwork matches the color of the layer. If you want to move selected artwork from one layer to another, you can either drag the selected-art indicator to the right of each sublayer or drag the selected-art indicator to the right of the layer name.

3 Drag the selected-art indicator (the blue box) from the right of the "Shirt Front" layer name straight up to the right of the target icon (◉) on the "Shirt Back" layer.

This action moves all of the selected artwork to the "Shirt Back" layer. The color of the bounding box, paths, and anchor points in the artwork changes to the color of the "Shirt Back" layer, which is red.

4 Choose Select > Deselect.

5 Choose View > Preview.

6   Click the disclosure triangle (▶) to the left of the "Shirt Front" layer to show the layer content. Drag the bottom of the Layers panel down to see more layers. Click the <Group> layer that contains the "Front" type shapes, and then press the Shift key and click the "Back" <Group> object to select both layers without selecting the artwork on the artboard. Drag either <Group> object to the "Labels" layer at the top of the list. When the Labels layer is highlighted, release the mouse button.

This is another way to move artwork between layers. Any content that is dragged to another layer is automatically at the top of the layer stack.

7   Click the disclosure triangle (▼) to the left of the "Shirt Front" layer to hide the layer contents.

▶ **Tip:** Keeping layers and sublayers closed can make it easier to navigate content in the Layers panel.

8   Shift-click the "Shirt Front" and "Shirt Back" layers to select them. Drag either of them up, below the Labels layer in the Layers panel. When a line appears below the Labels layer, release the mouse button.

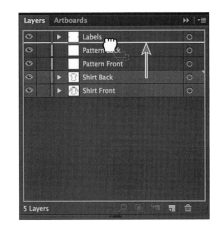

● **Note:** Be careful not to drag the layer into one of the other layers. If the Side panel layer disappears, you can choose Edit > Undo Reorder Layers and then try again.

9   With the Selection tool, click the white shirt shape for the shirt labeled "Front" on the artboard. Choose Edit > Cut.

10 Select the "Pattern Front" layer in the Layers panel, and choose Edit > Paste In Front.

The cut artwork is pasted onto the layer named "Pattern Front."

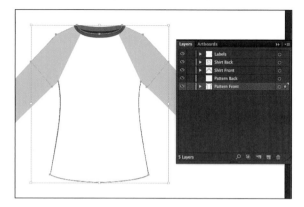

● **Note:** The white shirt shape appears *behind* the yellow sleeves because it's pasted onto the "Pattern Front" layer. The yellow sleeves are on the "Shirt Front" layer which is higher in the layer order.

11 Click to select the other white shirt shape under the "Back" label on the artboard.

12 Choose Edit > Cut, select the "Pattern Back" layer, and choose Edit > Paste In Front.

13 Choose Select > Deselect.

Duplicating layer content

In previous lessons, you've worked with the Edit > Copy and Edit > Cut commands. You can also use the Layers panel as another method for duplicating layers and other content. Next, you'll duplicate content between layers.

1 Click the disclosure triangle (▶) to the left of the "Shirt Front" layer to show the layer content.

2 Press the Option (Mac OS) or Alt (Windows) key, and click the "Front Sleeves" sublayer to select the content on the artboard.

3 While still pressing the Option (Mac OS) or Alt (Windows) key, drag the Front Sleeves row up onto the "Shirt Back" layer. When the layer is highlighted and a plus sign (+) appears to the right of the pointer, release the mouse button, and then release the key. Leave the artwork selected on the artboard.

This copies the content onto the "Shirt Back" layer.

Notice that the new copied artwork has a red color on the bounding box, paths, and anchor points, indicating that it's on the "Shirt Back" layer now. Dragging with the modifier key copies the selected content. This is the same as selecting the content on the artboard and choosing Edit > Copy, selecting the "Shirt Back" layer in the Layers panel, and then choosing Edit > Paste In Place.

▶ **Tip:** You can also Option-drag (Mac OS) or Alt-drag (Windows) the selected-art indicator to duplicate content. You can also select the Front Sleeves row in the Layers panel and choose Duplicate "Front Sleeves" from the Layers panel menu to create a copy on the same content.

4 Click the disclosure triangle to the left of the "Shirt Front" layer to hide the contents, and click the disclosure triangle to the left of the "Shirt Back" layer to see its contents.

5 With the yellow/green sleeves artwork still selected, Shift-click the middle of the white shirt shape on the right side of the artboard to select both objects. Release the Shift key. Click again on the white shirt shape to make it the key object. Click the Horizontal Align Center button (🖳) in the Control panel to align the objects to each other.

6 Choose Object > Arrange > Send To Back. In the Layers panel, notice that the stacking order of the sublayers is now different, reflecting how the artwork is arranged on the artboard.

7 Choose Select > Deselect.

Merging layers

To streamline your artwork, you can merge layers, sublayers, content, or groups to combine the contents into one layer or sublayer. Note that items will be merged into the layer or group that you selected last. Next, you will merge content into a new layer, and then merge a few sublayers into one.

▶ **Tip:** You can also Command-click (Mac OS) or Ctrl-click (Windows) layers or sublayers in the Layers panel to select multiple, nonsequential layers.

1 In the content for the "Shirt Back" layer in the Layers panel, click the top <Path> object in the Layers panel to highlight it, and then Shift-click the bottom <Path> object in the layer to select four <Path> objects.

   ● **Note:** Layers can merge only with other layers that are on the same hierarchical level in the Layers panel. Likewise, sublayers can only merge with other sublayers that are in the same layer and on the same hierarchical level. Objects can't be merged with other objects.

2 Click the Layers panel menu icon (), and choose Collect In New Layer to create a new layer and put the <Path> objects in it.

   The objects in the new layer retain their original stacking order.

3 Double-click the thumbnail to the left of or directly to the right of the new layer name. In the Layer Options dialog box, change the name to **Shirt Back Stitching** and choose Light Red from the Color menu. Click OK.

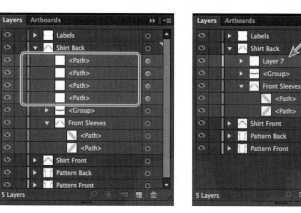

Select the objects.   Collect the objects in a new layer.   Rename the layer.

▶ **Tip:** Choose Merge Selected from the Layers panel menu to merge selected content into a single layer. The last layer you select determines the name and color of the merged layer.

Changing the layer color to match the main layer isn't necessary. The Layer Options dialog box has a lot of the options you've already worked with, including naming layers, Preview or Outline mode, locking layers, and showing and hiding layers. You can also deselect the Print option in the Layer Options dialog box, and any content on that layer will not print.

Next, you'll do the same thing to the stitching artwork on the "Shirt Front" layer.

4 Click the disclosure triangle to the left of the "Shirt Back" layer to hide its contents, and click the disclosure triangle to the left of the "Shirt Front" layer to show the contents.

5   Command-click (Mac OS) or Ctrl-click (Windows) the four <Path> objects on the "Shirt Front" layer, like you see in the figure, to select them all (they have shaded circles to the far right of their names).

6   Choose Collect In New Layer from the Layers panel menu () to create a new layer and put the <Path> objects in it.

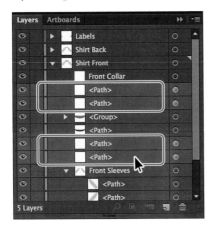

7   Double-click the layer name and change the name to **Shirt Front Stitching**. Press Enter or Return to accept the name.

8   In the "Shirt Front" layer, drag the <Path> object up into the <Group> object above it.

The <Path> object is now a part of the group (<Group>), but it appears on top of the other objects in the group.

9   Click the disclosure triangle to the left of the <Group> object to show the contents. Drag the top <Path> object to just below the bottom <Path> object in the group. When a line appears, release the mouse button. Click the disclosure triangle to the left of the <Group> object to hide the contents of the group.

This changes the stacking order of the artwork in your project and is the same as choosing Object > Arrange > Send To Back.

► **Tip:** If you want to merge layers or groups, you could also select the layers or content to merge in the Layers panel, and then choose Merge Selected from the Layers panel menu (▤). In the case of the two groups you selected, it simply creates a single group that contains the artwork from the original two groups. If you were to merge selected sublayers, a single sublayer would be created.

10 Click the top <Group> object to select it in the "Shirt Front" layer. Command-click (Mac OS) or Ctrl-click (Windows) the other <Group> beneath it in the layer to select both (see the figure for what to select). Drag the selected <Group> objects onto the "Front Collar" sublayer to move them.

11 Choose File > Save.

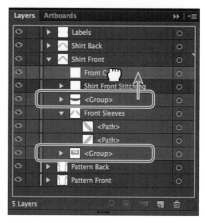

● **Note:** You cannot merge selected content that is not either a layer, sublayer, or group. For instance, if you were to select a <Path> object and a sublayer or group in the Layers panel, the Merge Selected command would be available, but it wouldn't work.

Pasting layers

To complete the shirts, you'll copy and paste the remaining pieces of artwork from another file. You can paste a layered file into another file and even keep the layers intact. In this section, you'll also learn a few new things, including how to apply appearance attributes to layers and reordering layers.

1   Choose Window > Workspace > Reset Essentials.

2   Choose File > Open, and open the Pattern.ai file, located in the Lesson08 folder in the Lessons folder on your hard disk.

3   Click the Layers panel icon (▨) to show the panel. To see how the objects in each layer are organized, Option-click (Mac OS) or Alt-click (Windows) the eye icon (◉) for each layer in the Layers panel to show one layer and hide the others. You can also click the disclosure triangles (▶) to the left of each layer

name to expand and collapse the layers for further inspection. When you're finished, make sure that all the layers are showing and that they are collapsed.

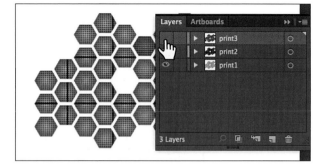

4 Choose Select > All, and then choose Edit > Copy to select and copy the content to the clipboard.

5 Choose File > Close to close the Pattern.ai file without saving any changes. If a warning dialog box appears, click No (Windows) or Don't Save (Mac OS).

6 In the Shirts.ai file, choose Paste Remembers Layers from the Layers panel menu (▤). A check mark next to the option indicates that it's selected.

When Paste Remembers Layers is selected, artwork is pasted into the layer(s) from which it was copied, regardless of which layer is active in the Layers panel. If the option is not selected, all objects are pasted into the active layer and the layers from the original file are not pasted in.

● **Note:** If the target document has a layer of the same name, Illustrator combines the pasted content into a layer of the same name.

7 Choose Edit > Paste, to paste the pattern content into the center of the artboard.

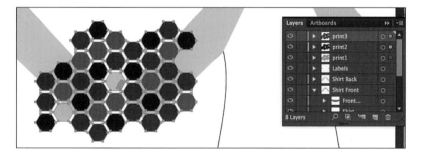

The Paste Remembers Layers option causes the Pattern.ai layers to be pasted as three separate layers at the top of the Layers panel (print3, print2, print1).

Now you'll move the newly pasted layers into the "Pattern Front" layer, and then change the ordering of the layers.

8 Drag the bottom of the Layers panel down so that you can see the new layers and the "Pattern Front" layer.

9   In the Layers panel, select the print3 layer (if it's not already selected) and Shift-click the print1 layer name. Drag any of the three selected layers down on top of the "Pattern Front" layer to move it to the new layer.

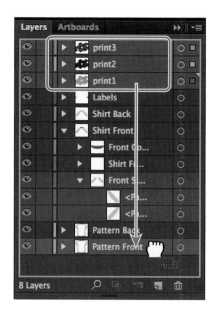

The three pasted layers become sublayers of the "Pattern Front" layer. Notice that they keep their individual layer colors.

10 Choose Select > Deselect, and then choose File > Save.

Changing layer order

As you've seen, you can easily drag layers, sublayers, groups, and other content in the Layers panel to reorganize the layer ordering. There are also several Layers panel options for commands like reversing layer ordering and more.

1   Click the print3 layer and Shift-click the print1 layer names to select all three layers again.

2   Choose Reverse Order from the Layers panel menu (▼≡) to reverse the layer ordering.

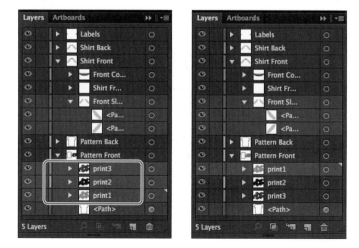

3   Choose Select > Deselect (if available), and then click the disclosure triangle for the "Pattern Front" and "Shirt Front" layers, if need be, to hide their contents.

Viewing layers

The Layers panel lets you hide layers, sublayers, or individual objects from view. When a layer is hidden, the content on the layer is also locked and cannot be selected or printed. You can also use the Layers panel to display layers or objects individually, in either Preview or Outline mode.

1   Select the Zoom tool (🔍) and click three times on the gray collar (top part of the shirt) for the Front shirt to zoom in.

2   Choose View > Outline. This displays the artwork so that only its outlines (or paths) are visible and you can see the "TEE" text that is hidden.

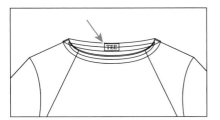

3   Choose View > Preview.

Sometimes, you may want to view part of the artwork in outline mode, while retaining the strokes and fills for the rest of the artwork. This can be useful if you need to see all artwork in a given layer, sublayer, or group.

4   In the Layers panel, click the disclosure triangle for the "Shirt Front" layer to reveal the layer content. Command-click (Mac OS) or Ctrl-click (Windows) the eye icon (👁) to the left of the "Front Collar" layer name to show the content for that layer in Outline mode.

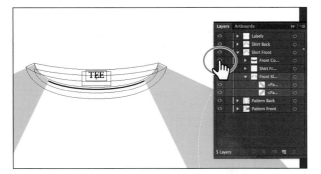

▶ **Tip:** To view layer artwork in Outline mode, you can also double-click either the layer thumbnail or just to the right of the layer name to open the Layer Options dialog box. You can then deselect Preview and click OK.

Displaying a layer in Outline mode is also useful for selecting the anchor points or center points on objects.

5   Attempt to click the "TEE" text and you will most likely select the group of content that is on top of it.

6 Click the Locate Object (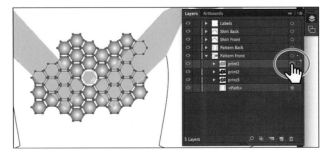) button at the bottom of the Layers panel to see where the selected group is in the Layers panel. Drag the left edge of the Layers panel to the left so you can see more of the layer names.

7 Choose Object > Arrange > Send To Back to send the group to the bottom of the "Front Collar" layer.

8 Command-click (Mac OS) or Ctrl-click (Windows) the eye icon (👁) to the left of the "Front Collar" layer name to show the content for that layer in Preview mode again.

9 Choose View > Fit Artboard In Window.

Note: This will hide and show all other layers, even sublayers on the "Shirt Back" layer.

10 Option-click (Mac OS) or Alt-click (Windows) the eye icon (👁) to the left of the "Shirt Back" layer to hide the other layers.

Hiding all layers except those that you want to work with can be very useful.

11 Choose Show All Layers from the Layers panel menu (▾≡).

12 Click the disclosure triangle to the left of each of the layers to ensure that they are all closed.

Applying appearance attributes to layers

Note: To learn more about working with appearance attributes, see Lesson 11, "Exploring Creative Uses of Effects and Graphic Styles."

You can apply appearance attributes, such as styles, effects, and transparency, to layers, groups, and objects, using the Layers panel. When an appearance attribute is applied to a layer, any object on that layer takes on that attribute. If an appearance attribute is applied only to a specific object on a layer, it affects only that object, not the entire layer.

You will apply an effect to an object on one layer, and then you'll copy that effect to another layer to change all objects on that layer.

1 Click the disclosure triangle to the left of the "Pattern Front" layer name to show its contents, and then click the target icon (◎) to the right of the print1 layer in the target column.

Note: Clicking the target icon also selects the object(s) on the artboard. You could simply select the content on the artboard to apply an effect.

Clicking the target icon indicates that you want to apply an effect, style, or transparency change to that layer, sublayer, group, or object. In other words, the layer, sublayer, group, or object is *targeted*. The content is also selected in the Document window. When the target button appears as a double-ring icon (either ⊚ or ⊚), the item is targeted; a single-ring icon indicates that the item is not targeted.

2   Click the Opacity link in the Control panel to show the Transparency panel. Choose Overlay from the Blending Mode menu, which shows as Normal by default.

For the print1 layer, the target icon (⊚) is now shaded, indicating that the layer has at least one appearance attribute (a blending mode) applied to it.

3   Click the target icon (⊚) to the right of the print2 layer in the target column. Click the Opacity link in the Control panel to show the Transparency panel. Choose Luminosity from the Blending Mode menu, which shows as Normal by default. Change the Opacity to **20**.

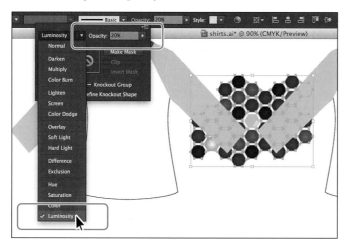

4   Choose Select > Deselect.

Creating a clipping mask

The Layers panel lets you create clipping masks to control whether artwork on a layer (or in a group) is hidden or revealed. A *clipping mask* is an object or group of objects that masks (with its shape) artwork below it in the same layer or sublayer, so that only artwork within the shape is visible. In Lesson 14, "Using Illustrator CC with Other Adobe Applications," you will learn about creating clipping masks that are independent of the Layers panel.

Now you'll create a clipping mask for the pattern for each shirt. As you create the clipping mask, you'll learn about working with Isolation mode so that you can focus on specific parts of the artwork.

1   Click the disclosure triangle to the left of all main layers to hide their content.

2   Select the layer named "Pattern Front" and choose Enter Isolation Mode from the Layers panel menu ( ).

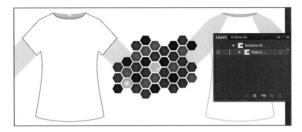

When a layer is in Isolation mode, objects on that layer are dimmed and locked, much like when you enter Isolation mode for a group, so that you can easily edit them without affecting other layers. The Layers panel now shows a layer called Isolation Mode and a layer that contains the "Pattern Front" layer content.

3   In the Layers panel, click the disclosure triangle for the "Pattern Front" layer to reveal the layer contents. Click the selection column to the right of the "Pattern Front" layer to select all of the contents on the layer. Shift-click the selection column to the right of the <Path> object (the shirt shape) to deselect it.

4   With the Selection tool selected, drag any of the selected shapes on the artboard to the left and onto the shirt shape until it's positioned roughly as in the figure.

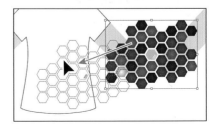

In the Layers panel, a masking object must be above the objects it masks. You can create a clipping mask for an entire layer, a sublayer, or a group of objects. Because you want to mask the content in the "Pattern Front" layer, the clipping object needs to be at the top of the "Pattern Front" layer, which is what you did in the previous section.

5   Choose Object > Arrange > Send To Back.

The white shirt shape will now be on top of the pattern artwork on the "Pattern Front" layer.

6   Select the "Pattern Front" layer to highlight it in the Layers panel. Click the Make/Release Clipping Mask button (⊡) at the bottom of the Layers panel.

Note: Deselecting the artwork on the artboard is not necessary to complete the next steps, but it can be helpful for viewing the artwork.

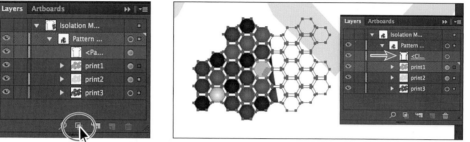

The name of the <Path> sublayer is underlined to indicate that it is the masking shape and it has been renamed to "Clipping Path." On the artboard, the <Path> sublayer has hidden the parts of the pattern content that extended outside of the shape.

Tip: To release the clipping mask, you can select the "Pattern Front" layer again and click the same Make/Release Clipping Mask button (⊡).

7   Click the selection column for the Clipping Path layer to select the shirt path. Change the Fill color to Black in the Control panel.

8   Press the Escape key to exit Isolation mode.

Note: You can also double-click in a blank area of the artboard to exit Isolation mode.

Next, you will practice creating a clipping mask by performing the same steps on the Back shirt.

9   Click the print1 layer and Shift-click the print3 layer to select all three layers.

10 Option-drag (Mac OS) or Alt-drag (Windows) any of the layers to the "Pattern Back" layer to copy them there.

11 Select the "Pattern Back" layer and choose Enter Isolation Mode from the Layers panel menu ().

12 Drag a selection marquee across the pattern objects to select them all. Begin dragging to the right, and as you drag, press the Shift key to constrain the movement. Drag them into position like you see in the figure.

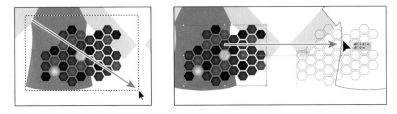

13 Choose Object > Arrange > Send To Back to put the pattern content behind the white shirt.

14 Select the "Pattern Back" layer to highlight it in the Layers panel. Click the Make/Release Clipping Mask button ( ) at the bottom of the Layers panel.

15 Click the selection column for the "Clipping Path" layer to select the shirt path. Change the Fill color to Black in the Control panel.

16 Double-click in a blank area of the artboard to exit Isolation mode.

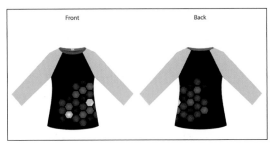

● **Note:** For a complete list of shortcuts that you can use with the Layers panel, see "Keyboard shortcuts" in Illustrator Help (Help > Illustrator Help).

Now that the artwork is complete, you may want to combine all the layers into a single layer, and then delete the empty layers. This is called flattening artwork. Delivering finished artwork in a single-layer file can prevent accidents, such as hiding layers or omitting parts of the artwork during printing. To flatten specific layers without deleting hidden layers, you can select the layers you want to flatten, and then choose Merge Selected from the Layers panel menu.

17 Choose File > Save, and then choose File > Close.

Review questions

1 Name at least two benefits of using layers when creating artwork.

2 How do you hide layers? How do you show individual layers?

3 Describe how to reorder layers in a file.

4 What is the purpose of changing the color for a layer?

5 What happens if you paste a layered file into another file? Why is the "Paste Remembers Layers" option useful?

6 How do you create a layer clipping mask?

7 How do you apply an effect to a layer? How can you edit that effect?

Review answers

1 The benefits of using layers when creating artwork include: organizing content, selecting content more easily, protecting artwork that you don't want to change, hiding artwork that you aren't working with so that it's not distracting, and controlling what prints.

2 To hide a layer, click to deselect the eye icon (👁) to the left of the layer name in the Layers panel. Select the blank, leftmost column (the Visibility column) to show a layer.

3 You reorder layers by selecting a layer name in the Layers panel and dragging the layer to its new location. The order of layers in the Layers panel controls the document's layer order—topmost in the panel is frontmost in the artwork.

4 The color for a layer controls how selected anchor points and direction lines are displayed on a layer and helps you identify the different layers in your document.

5 The paste commands paste layered files or objects copied from different layers into the active layer by default. The "Paste Remembers Layers" option keeps the original layers intact when the objects are pasted.

6 Create a clipping mask on a layer by selecting the layer and clicking the Make/Release Clipping Mask button (▣) in the Layers panel. The topmost object in the layer becomes the clipping mask.

7 Click the target icon for the layer to which you want to apply an effect. Then, choose an effect from the Effect menu or by clicking the Add New Effect button (𝑓𝑥) in the Appearance panel. To edit the effect, make sure that the layer is selected, and then click the name of the effect in the Appearance panel. The effect's dialog box opens, and you can change the values.

9 BLENDING COLORS AND SHAPES

Lesson overview

In this lesson, you'll learn how to do the following:

- Create and save a gradient fill.

- Apply and edit a gradient on a stroke.

- Apply and edit a radial gradient.

- Add colors to a gradient.

- Adjust the direction of a gradient.

- Adjust the opacity of color in a gradient.

- Blend the shapes of objects in intermediate steps.

- Create smooth color blends between objects.

- Modify a blend and its path, shape, and color.

This lesson takes approximately 60 minutes to complete.

Download the project files for this lesson from the Lesson & Update Files tab on your Account page at www.peachpit.com and store them on your computer in a convenient location, as described in the Getting Started section of this book.

Your Account page is also where you'll find any updates to the chapters or to the lesson files. Look on the Lesson & Update Files tab to access the most current content.

For the adventure of a lifetime

SAIL WITH A WHALE >

Gradient fills are graduated blends of two or more colors. Using the Gradient tool and/or the Gradient panel, you can create or modify a gradient fill or a gradient stroke. With the Blend tool, you can blend the shapes and colors of objects together into a new, blended object or a series of intermediate shapes.

Getting started

You'll explore various ways to create your own color gradients and to blend colors and shapes together using the Gradient tool, the Gradient panel, and the Blend tool.

Before you begin, you'll restore the default preferences for Adobe Illustrator CC. Then you'll open the finished art file for this lesson to see what you'll create.

● **Note:** If you have not already downloaded the project files for this lesson to your computer from your Account page, make sure to do so now. See the "Getting Started" section at the beginning of this book.

1   To ensure that the tools and panels function exactly as described in this lesson, delete or deactivate (by renaming) the Adobe Illustrator CC preferences file. See "Restoring default preferences" in the Getting Started section at the beginning of the book.

2   Start Adobe Illustrator CC.

3   Choose File > Open, and open the L9_end.ai file in the Lessons > Lesson09 folder on your hard disk.

4   Choose View > Zoom Out to make the finished artwork smaller, if you want to leave it on your screen as you work.
(Use the Hand tool [🖑] to move the artwork where you want it in the window.)
If you don't want to leave the document open, choose File > Close.

To begin working, you'll open an existing art file.

5   Choose File > Open, and open the L9_start.ai file in the Lesson09 folder, located in the Lessons folder on your hard disk.

● **Note:** In Mac OS, when opening lesson files, you may need to click the round, green button in the upper-left corner of the Document window to maximize the window's size.

6   Choose View > Fit Artboard In Window.

7   Choose File > Save As, name the file **Sailing.ai**, and select the Lesson09 folder in the Save As menu. Leave the Format option set to Adobe Illustrator (ai) (Mac OS) or Save As Type option set to Adobe Illustrator (*.AI) (Windows), and then click Save. In the Illustrator Options dialog box, leave the Illustrator options at their default settings, and then click OK.

8   Choose Reset Essentials from the workspace switcher in the Application bar.

● **Note:** If you don't see "Reset Essentials" in the workspace switcher menu, choose Window > Workspace > Essentials before choosing Window > Workspace > Reset Essentials.

Working with gradients

A *gradient fill* is a graduated blend of two or more colors, and it always includes a starting and an ending color. You can create different types of gradient fills in Illustrator, including *linear*, in which the beginning color blends into the ending color along a line, and *radial*, in which the beginning color radiates outward, from the center point to the ending color. You can use the gradients provided with Adobe Illustrator CC or create your own gradients and save them as swatches for later use.

You can use the Gradient panel (Window > Gradient) or the Gradient tool (⬛) to apply, create, and modify gradients. In the Gradient panel, the Gradient Fill or Stroke box displays the current gradient colors and gradient type applied to the fill or stroke of an object.

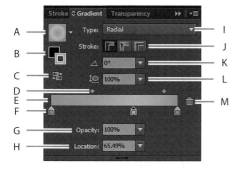

A. Gradient	**G.** Opacity
B. Fill box/ Stroke box	**H.** Location
C. Reverse Gradient	**I.** Gradient type
D. Gradient midpoint	**J.** Stroke gradient type
E. Gradient slider	**K.** Angle
F. Color stop	**L.** Aspect ratio
	M. Delete Stop

● **Note:** The Gradient panel you see will not match the figure, and that's okay.

In the Gradient panel, the leftmost gradient stop (labeled F—also called a *color stop*) under the gradient slider marks the starting color; the right gradient stop marks the ending color. A *gradient color stop* is the point at which a gradient changes from one color to the next. You can add more color stops by clicking below the gradient slider. Double-clicking a color stop opens a panel where you can choose a color from swatches, color sliders, or the eyedropper.

Creating and applying a linear gradient to a fill

With the simplest, two-color linear gradient, the starting color (leftmost color stop) blends into the ending color (rightmost color stop) along a line. To begin the lesson, you'll create a gradient fill for the background shape.

1   Using the Selection tool (▶), click to select the large yellow rectangle in the background.

   The background is painted with a yellow fill color and no stroke, as shown in the Fill and Stroke boxes toward the bottom of the Tools panel or in the Swatches panel.

2 Change the Fill color to the gradient swatch named "White, Black" in the Control panel.

The default black-and-white gradient is applied to the fill of the selected background shape.

3 Open the Gradient panel (Window > Gradient) and make sure that the Fill box is selected (circled in the figure). Double-click the white, leftmost gradient stop to select the starting color of the gradient. Click the Swatches button (▦) in the panel that appears. Click to select the light-gray swatch named "Sky 1."

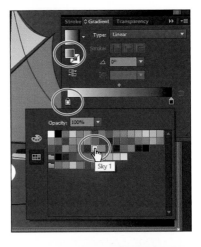

4 Press the Escape key, or click in a blank area of the Gradient panel to close the Swatches panel.

▶ **Tip:** To move between text fields, press the Tab key. Press Enter or Return to apply the last value typed.

5 Double-click the black color stop on the right side of the gradient slider to edit the color (circled in the figure). In the panel that appears, click the Color button (▦) to open the Color panel. Click the menu icon (▦) and choose CMYK from the menu, if CMYK values aren't showing. Change the values to C=**40**, M=**4**, Y=**10**, and K=**0**. After entering the last value, click in a blank area of the Gradient panel to return to the Gradient panel.

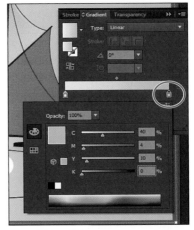

Next, you'll save the gradient in the Swatches panel.

▶ **Tip:** You can also save a gradient by selecting an object with a gradient fill or stroke, clicking the Fill box or Stroke box in the Tools panel (whichever the gradient is applied to), and then clicking the New Swatch button (▦) at the bottom of the Swatches panel.

6 Click the Gradient menu arrow (▾) to the left of the word "Type:" and then click the Add To Swatches button (▦) at the bottom of the panel that appears.

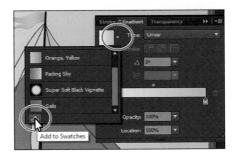

The Gradient menu lists all the default and saved gradients that you can apply.

7   Click the Swatches panel icon () on the right
    side of the workspace to open the Swatches
    panel. In the Swatches panel, double-click the
    "New Gradient Swatch 1" thumbnail to open
    the Swatch Options dialog box.

8   In the Swatch Options dialog box, type **Sky** in
    the Swatch Name field, and then click OK.

The Swatches panel lets you sort colors based on type. So if you want to only show
gradient swatches in the panel, for instance, you can temporarily sort the swatches
in the panel.

9   Click the Show Swatch Kinds Menu
    button () at the bottom of the Swatches
    panel and choose Show Gradient Swatches
    from the menu to display only gradient
    swatches in the Swatches panel.

10 With the rectangle still selected on the
    artboard, apply some of the different gradients
    to the shape fill by clicking them in the
    Swatches panel.

11 Click the gradient named Sky (the one you just saved) in the Swatches panel to
    make sure it is applied before continuing to the next step.

12 Click the Show Swatch Kinds Menu button () at the bottom of the Swatches
    panel, and choose Show All Swatches from the menu.

13 Choose File > Save, and leave the rectangle selected.

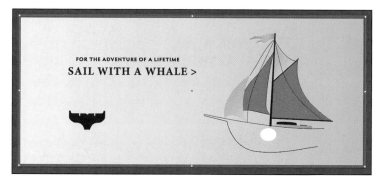

Adjusting the direction and angle of a gradient fill

Once you have painted an object with a gradient, you can adjust the direction, the origin, and the beginning and end points of the gradient using the Gradient tool.

Now you'll adjust the gradient fill in the background shape.

1   Select the Gradient tool (■) in the Tools panel.

The Gradient tool works only on selected objects that are filled with a gradient. Notice the horizontal gradient annotator (bar) that appears in the middle of the rectangle. The bar indicates the direction of the gradient. The larger circle on the left shows the starting point of the gradient (the first color stop), and the smaller square on the right is the ending point (the last color stop).

▶ **Tip:** You can hide the gradient annotator (bar) by choosing View > Hide Gradient Annotator. To show it again, choose View > Show Gradient Annotator.

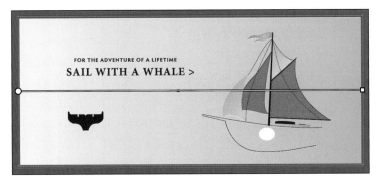

● **Note:** If you move the pointer to different areas of the gradient slider, the appearance of the pointer may change. This indicates that different functionality has been activated.

2   Position the pointer over the bar in the gradient annotator.

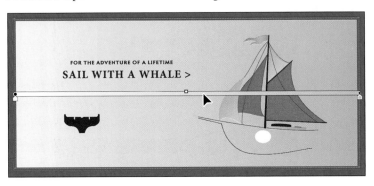

The bar turns into the gradient slider, much like the one found in the Gradient panel. You can use the gradient slider to edit the gradient without opening the Gradient panel.

3   With the Gradient tool, Shift-click the top of the rectangle and drag down to the bottom of the rectangle to change the position and direction of the starting and ending colors of the gradient. Release the mouse button, and then release the key.

Holding down the Shift key constrains the gradient to 45-degree angles.

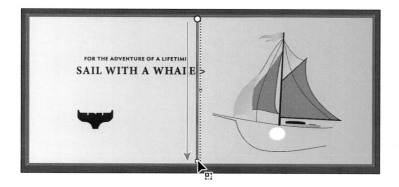

4   With the Gradient tool, Shift-click below the bottom of the rectangle and drag up to just past the top of the rectangle to change the position and direction of the starting and ending colors of the gradient. Release the mouse button, and then release the key.

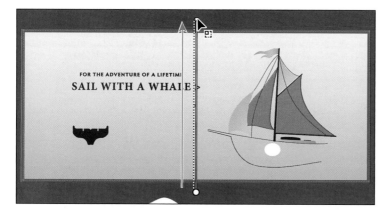

5   With the Gradient tool, position the pointer just off the small white square at the top of the gradient annotator. A rotation icon (⟳) appears. Drag to the right to rotate the gradient in the rectangle, and then release the mouse button.

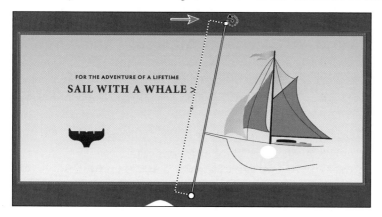

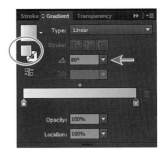

6   Double-click the Gradient tool in the Tools panel to show the Gradient panel. Ensure that the Fill box is selected in the panel (circled in the figure), and then change the rotation angle in the Angle field to **80** and press Enter or Return.

7   Choose Object > Lock > Selection to lock the rectangle, and then choose File > Save.

Applying and editing a gradient on a stroke

You can also apply a gradient blend to the stroke of an object. Unlike a gradient applied to the fill of an object, you cannot use the Gradient tool to edit a gradient on the stroke of an object. A gradient on a stroke, however, has more options available in the Gradient panel than a gradient fill. Next, you will add a series of colors to a stroke gradient to create a frame for the artwork.

First, you will apply a gradient to the stroke to the background rectangle with the red stroke applied, to make it look like the wood frame of a painting.

1   Select the Selection tool (▶) in the Tools panel and click the red stroke on the edge of the artboard to select that rectangle. Choose **18 pt** from the Stroke weight menu in the Control panel.

2   Click the Stroke box at the bottom of the Tools panel and click the Gradient box below the Fill box to apply the last used gradient (the light gray to blue for the rectangle fill).

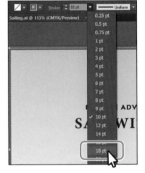

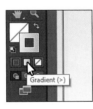

3   Click the word Transform in the Control panel. Make sure that the Constrain Width And Height Proportions is turned off (not selected). Change the Width to **14.75 in** and the Height to **6.25 in**.

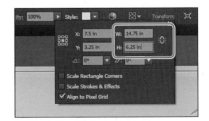

This will ensure that the stroke fits within the bounds of the artboard. Normally, we would simply align the stroke to the inside in the Stroke panel, but you can't do that with a gradient applied to a stroke.

4 Select the Zoom tool (🔍) in the Tools panel, and drag a marquee across the upper-right corner of the selected rectangle to zoom in to it.

5 In the Gradient panel, click the Stroke box (if not already selected) circled in the figure below to edit the gradient applied to the stroke. Leave the Type as Linear, and click the Apply Gradient Across Stroke button (▣) to change the gradient type.

You can apply a gradient to a stroke in three ways: within a stroke (default) (▣), along a stroke (▣), and across a stroke (▣).

6 Double-click the blue color stop on the right, and click the Swatches button (▦) to show the swatches. Click to select the swatch named "Border 2." Click outside the panel to accept the selection.

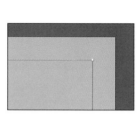  

Zoom in to the corner.   Edit the stroke gradient type.   Adjust the color stop color.

7 Double-click the leftmost color stop, and with the Swatches button (▦) selected, click to select the swatch named "Border 3." Press the Escape key to hide the swatches and return to the Gradient panel.

8 Position the pointer below the color ramp and between the two color stops, to add another color stop. When the pointer with a plus sign (▶₊) appears, click to add another color stop like you see in the figure.

9 Double-click that new color stop and, with the swatches selected (▦), click the swatch named "Border 1." Press the Escape key to hide the swatches and return to the Gradient panel.

Edit the leftmost color stop.   Add a new color stop.   Change the color of the color stop.

10 With the color stop still selected, change the Location to **80%**.

11 Pressing the Option (Mac OS) or Alt (Windows) key, drag the selected color stop to the left, closer to the leftmost color stop, release the mouse button when you see roughly 25% in the Location value, and then release the modifier key. This is an easy way to duplicate a color in a gradient.

▶ **Tip:** You can delete a color in the color ramp by selecting a color stop and clicking the Delete Stop button (▣) or by dragging the color stop downward and out of the Gradient panel. Remember that the gradient must contain at least two colors!

12 Pressing the Option (Mac OS) or Alt (Windows) key, drag the rightmost (Border 3) color stop to the left. Release the mouse button, and then release the modifier key when it is positioned at roughly 35%, as you see in the figure below.

Edit the color stop location.   Duplicate a color stop.   Duplicate the rightmost color stop.

13 Choose Select > Deselect, and then choose File > Save.

Creating and applying a radial gradient

As previously noted, with a *radial gradient*, the starting color (leftmost color stop) of the gradient defines the center point of the fill, which radiates outward to the ending color (rightmost color stop).

Next, you will create and apply a radial gradient fill to the windows of the ship (called portholes).

1 Choose View > Fit Artboard In Window.

2 With the Zoom tool (🔍) selected, drag a marquee across the white ellipse below the red sails on the ship to zoom in very closely.

3 Select the Selection tool (▶) in the Tools panel and click the white ellipse.

4 In the Control panel, change the Fill color to the White, Black gradient. Press the Escape key to hide the Swatches panel.

5 Click the Gradient panel icon (▣) to show the Gradient panel (if necessary). In the Gradient panel, make sure the Fill box is selected. Choose Radial from the

Type menu to convert the linear gradient in the shape to a radial gradient. Keep the ellipse selected and the Gradient panel showing.

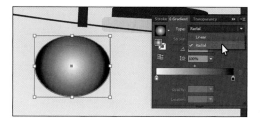

Editing the radial gradient colors

Next, you will use the Gradient tool to adjust the colors in the radial gradient.

1   In the Gradient panel, with the ellipse still selected, click the Reverse Gradient button to swap the white and black colors in the gradient.

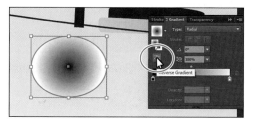

2   Select the Gradient tool (■) in the Tools panel.

3   Position the pointer over the gradient annotator (bar) in the artwork to reveal the gradient slider. Double-click the black color stop in the center of the circle to edit the color. In the panel that appears, click the Color button (⬤), if it's not already selected. Choose CMYK from the panel menu (if necessary) and change the color values to C=**22**, M=**0**, Y=**3**, K=**0**. Press the Escape key to hide the panel.

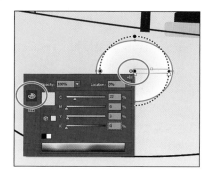

● **Note:** When you double-click the color stop, you can see the Location in the panel that appears. As you build this radial gradient, you can copy the values you see in the figures to closely match the positions of the color stops.

● **Note:** For the next steps, we zoomed in a little further into the artwork to more easily see the color stops in the gradient.

Notice that the gradient annotator starts from the center of the ellipse and points to the right. The dashed circle around it indicates that it is a radial gradient. You can set additional options for radial gradients, as you'll soon see.

4 Position the pointer beneath the gradient slider, a little to the left of the white color stop at the right end of the color ramp. When the pointer with a plus sign (k_+) appears, click to add another color to the gradient (circled in the figure).

5 Double-click the new color stop. In the panel that appears, click the Swatches button (⊞) and select the swatch named "Window 1." Change the Location to **87%**. Press the Escape key to close the panel.

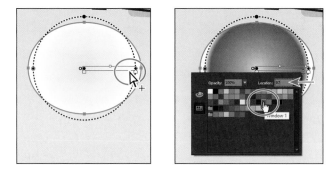

6 Pressing the Option (Mac OS) or Alt (Windows) key, drag the color stop you just created to the left (see the following figure for how far). Release the mouse button, and then release the modifier key.

7 Double-click the new color stop, and change the Location value to **80%** in the panel that appears. Press Enter or Return to change the value and hide the panel.

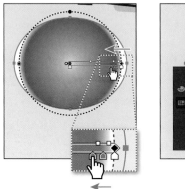

Once the colors are set in the gradient, you can always delete, add more, or even change the order of colors.

8 Double-click the leftmost light-blue color stop, and change the Location value to **70%** in the panel that appears. Press Enter or Return to change the value and hide the panel.

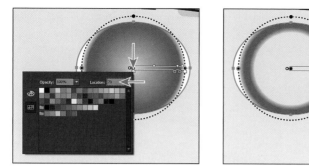

9 Choose File > Save.

Adjusting the radial gradient

Next, you will change the aspect ratio of the radial gradient, adjust the position, and change the radius and the origin of the radial gradient.

1 With the Gradient tool (▨) selected, position the pointer over the gradient annotator. Click and drag the black diamond shape (◆) on the right, to the right, stopping just before the right edge of the ellipse shape, and release the mouse button.

Note: You may not see the dotted circle as you drag the end of the gradient annotator. That's okay. It appears if you position the pointer over the gradient annotator bar first, before dragging the right end point.

Make sure that you still see some white on the edges of the gradient. If you don't, you can drag the diamond shape back to the left a bit. This lengthens the gradient slightly.

2 In the Gradient panel, ensure that the Fill box is selected, and then change the Aspect Ratio (▣) to **80%** by selecting it from the menu.

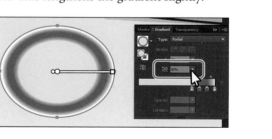

Note: The aspect ratio is a value between 0.5% and 32,767%. As the aspect ratio gets smaller, the ellipse flattens and widens.

The aspect ratio changes a radial gradient into an elliptical gradient and makes the gradient better match the shape of the artwork. Another way to edit the aspect ratio is to do so visually. If you position the pointer over the gradient on the selected artwork with the Gradient tool selected, and then position the pointer over the top black circle that appears on the dotted path, the pointer changes to ▸○. You can then drag to change the aspect ratio of the gradient.

Next, you will drag the gradient slider to reposition the gradient in the ellipse.

3   With the Gradient tool, click and drag the
    gradient slider up a little bit to move the
    gradient in the ellipse. See the figure for
    approximately where to drag to.

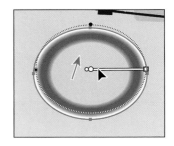

4   With the Gradient tool, click the small white dot to the left of the leftmost color
    stop and drag to the left.

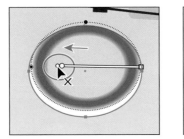 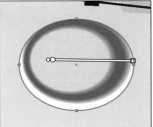

This dot repositions the center of the gradient (the leftmost color stop), without
moving the entire gradient bar, and changes the radius of the gradient.

5   Choose Edit > Undo Gradient, to put the gradient back to the center.

6   Select the Selection tool (►)
    and double-click the Scale
    tool (⬚) in the Tools panel.
    Change the Uniform Scale
    value to **60%**, and click OK.

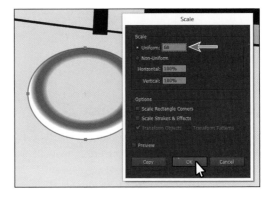

    If you transform a shape
    with a gradient applied,
    such as scale or rotate the
    shape (among other types
    of transformations), the
    gradient transforms as well.

7   Select the Selection tool in the Tools
    panel and Option-drag (Mac OS)
    or Alt-drag (Windows) the window to
    the right to create a copy. Position it
    to the right of the original, like you see in
    the figure.

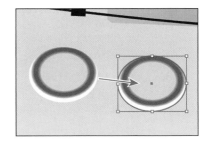

8   Choose Select > Deselect, and then
    choose File > Save.

Applying gradients to multiple objects

You can apply a gradient to multiple objects by selecting all the objects, applying a gradient color, and then dragging across the objects with the Gradient tool.

Now you'll apply a linear gradient fill to the sails and edit the colors in it.

1   Choose View > Fit Artboard In Window.

2   With the Selection tool (▶) selected, click to select the leftmost red sail shape. Shift-click the other red sail to the right to select both shapes.

3   In the Control panel, choose the gradient named Sails from the Fill color. Press the Escape key to hide the Swatches panel, if necessary.

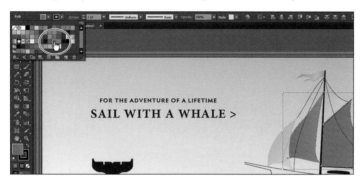

When you apply a gradient to the fill or stroke of multiple selected objects, they are applied independently.

Now you'll adjust the gradient on the shapes so that the gradient blends across all of them as one object.

4   Make sure that the Fill box at the bottom of the Tools panel or in the Swatches panel is selected.

5   Select the Gradient tool (▭) in the Tools panel.

    Notice that there is a gradient annotator (a bar) on each of the sails. This shows that by applying a gradient to multiple selected objects, the gradients are applied to each object independently.

6   Drag from the center of the leftmost sail shape to the rightmost edge of the sail on the right, as shown in the figure, to apply the gradient uniformly as a single gradient across both shapes.

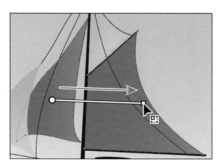

7   Choose Select > Deselect, and then choose File > Save.

Adding transparency to gradients

By specifying varying opacity values for the different color stops in your gradient, you can create gradients that fade in or out and that show or hide underlying images. Next, you will apply a gradient that fades to transparent.

1   Open the Layers panel and select the Ship layer, if it isn't already selected.

Note: The Transform panel group may open after clicking OK in the Rectangle dialog box. You can close the panel group if it does.

2   Select the Rectangle tool (▪) in the Tools panel and click anywhere in the Document window. In the Rectangle dialog box, change the Width to **15 in** and the Height to **2 in**. Click OK to create a rectangle.

Since the units for the document are set to inches, you don't need to enter the "in."

3   Click the Gradient panel icon (▪) to open the panel. Ensure that the Fill box is selected, click the Gradient menu arrow (▼), and then select "White, Black."

Note: Depending on your screen resolution, you may need to click the word "Align" in the Control panel to access the Align panel.

4   Select the Selection tool (▶) and choose Align To Artboard from the Align To menu in the Control panel (if necessary). Click the Horizontal Align Center button (▪) and the Vertical Align Bottom button (▪) to align the rectangle to the center and bottom of the artboard.

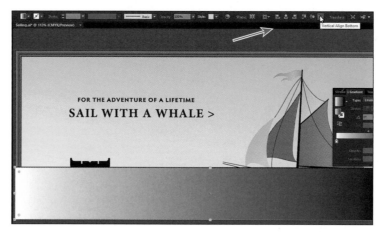

5   Click the Stroke color in the Control panel, and change the color to None (☐) (if necessary).

6 Change the Angle to **–90°** by choosing it from the menu in the Gradient panel.

7 Double-click the white color stop in the Gradient panel. In the panel that appears, make sure that the Swatches button (▦) is selected and select the color swatch named Water. Press the Escape key once to hide the swatches.

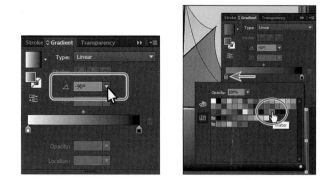

8 With the leftmost color stop still selected in the Gradient panel, change the Opacity to **0%**.

9 Double-click the rightmost color stop (the black color). In the panel that appears, with the Swatches button (▦) selected, select the color swatch named Water. Press the Escape key once to hide the swatches.

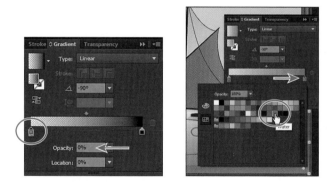

10 With the rightmost color stop still selected in the Gradient panel, change the Opacity to **50%**.

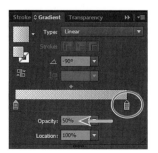

11 Drag the gradient midpoint (the diamond shape) to the right until you see a value of approximately 60% in the Location field. Click the Gradient panel tab to collapse the Gradient panel group.

12 Choose Object > Lock > Selection.

13 Select the wood frame and choose Object > Arrange > Bring To Front.

14 Choose Select > Deselect, and then choose File > Save.

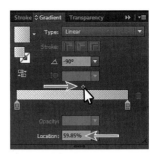

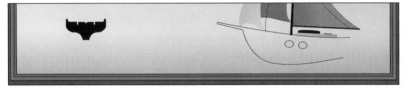

Working with blended objects

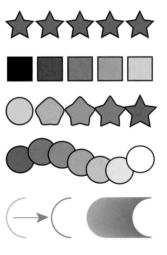

Blend between two of the same shape.

Blend between the same shape and different colors.

Blend between two different shapes with different fill colors.

Blend along a path.

Smooth color blend between two stroked lines (original lines on left, blend on right).

You can blend two distinct objects to create and distribute shapes evenly between two objects. The two shapes you blend can be the same or different. You can also blend between two open paths to create a smooth transition of color between objects, or you can combine blends of colors and objects to create color transitions in the shape of a particular object.

When you create a blend, the blended objects are treated as one object, called a *Blend object*. If you move one of the original objects or edit the anchor points of the original object, the blend changes accordingly. You can also expand the blend to divide it into distinct objects.

Creating a blend with specified steps

Next, you'll use the Blend tool (🔲) to blend two shapes that will eventually make up the water beneath the ship.

1   Open the Layers panel and click the eye icon to the left of the Ship layer to hide the layer content.

2   Scroll down in the Document window so that you can see shapes off the bottom of the artboard. You will create a blend between the large and small circles.

3   Select the Blend tool (⬛) in the Tools panel and position the pointer over the larger shape on the left. Click when the pointer displays an asterisk (⬛*). Then, hover over the small shape on the right until the pointer displays a plus sign (⬛+), indicating that you can add an object to the blend. Click to create a blend between these two objects.

▶ **Tip:** You can add more than two objects to a blend.

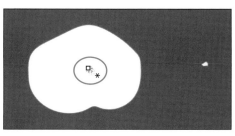 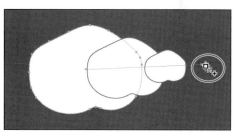

● **Note:** If you wanted to end the current path and blend other objects, you would first click the Blend tool in the Tools panel, and then click the other objects, one at a time, to blend them.

4   With the blended object still selected, choose Object > Blend > Blend Options. In the Blend Options dialog box, choose Specified Steps from the Spacing menu and change the Specified Steps to **15**, and then click OK.

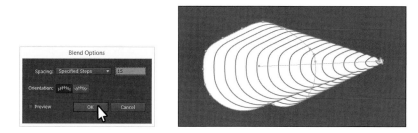

▶ **Tip:** To edit the blend options for an object, you can also select the blend object, and then double-click the Blend tool. You can also double-click the Blend tool (⬛) in the Tools panel to set tool options before you create the blend object.

5   Select the Selection tool (▶) in the Tools panel and double-click anywhere on the blend object to enter Isolation mode.

This temporarily ungroups the blended objects and lets you edit each original shape, as well as the spine (path).

6 Choose View > Outline.

In Outline mode, you can see the outlines of the two original shapes and a straight path between them. These three objects are what a blend object is composed of, by default. It can be easier to edit the path between the original objects in Outline mode.

7 Click to select the edge of the smaller shape.

You may want to zoom in (Command++ [Mac OS] or Ctrl++ [Windows]) to make it easier to select.

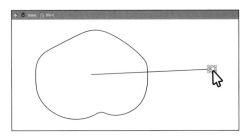

8 Choose View > Preview.

9 Drag the smaller shape roughly into the center of the larger shape and you will see the blend change.

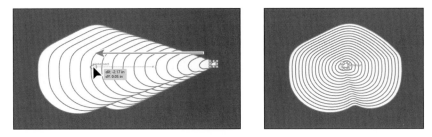

10 Choose Select > Deselect and press the Escape key to exit Isolation mode.

Modifying a blend

Now you'll create another blend and edit the shape of the straight path, called the *spine*, which the objects blend along. You will create a blend between two copies of the blended object you just created. Blending between two objects that are also blended objects can produce unexpected results. That's why you will expand the blended object first (and understand what that means).

1 With the Selection tool ( ) selected, click to select the blend object. You will see the word "Blend" on the left end of the Control panel in the Selection Indicator.

2 Choose Object > Blend > Expand.

Expanding a blended object divides the blend into distinct objects, which you can edit individually like any object. The objects are grouped together by default. You can no longer edit the blended object as a single object because it has become a group of individual shapes.

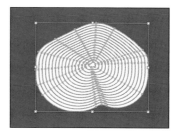

▶ **Tip:** To release, or remove, a blend from the original objects, select the blend and choose Object > Blend > Release.

3 Choose View > Fit Artboard In Window, and then press Command+– (Mac OS) or Ctrl+– (Windows) *twice* to zoom out.

4 Drag the expanded group off the left edge of the artboard, like you see in the figure. Option-drag (Mac OS) or Alt-drag (Windows) the group off the right edge of the artboard, keeping it roughly horizontally aligned with the original.

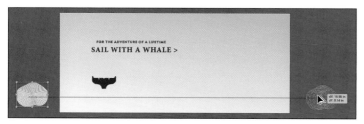

5 Double-click the Blend tool (⬚) in the Tools panel to open the Blend Options dialog box. Change the specified steps to **16**. Click OK.

6 With the Blend tool selected, position the pointer over the group off the left edge of the artboard. Click when the pointer displays an asterisk (⬚ₓ). Then, hover over the group off the right edge of the artboard until the pointer displays a plus sign (⬚₊), indicating that you can add an object to the blend. Click to blend the objects. There is now a blend between these two objects.

7 Choose View > Outline.

8 Choose Select > Deselect.

9 Select the Direct Selection tool (◮) in the Tools panel and click the path between the groups to select it.

10 Choose Object > Path > Add Anchor Points *twice* to add three anchor points to the path.

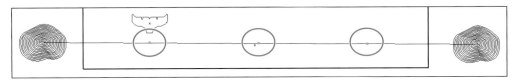

● **Note:** You are editing the spine. However you edit the spine, the blend objects will follow.

11 Select the Pen tool (✐) in the Tools panel. Press the Option (Mac) or Alt (Windows) key and position the pointer on the line segment between the first two anchor points. When the pointer changes in appearance, drag up a little to curve the path. Go to the next segment between the anchor points, holding down the same modifier key, and drag down. Don't create a path that is too curvy, otherwise the waves will be too tall and won't cover the background (plus, they might make the sailors on the ship seasick).

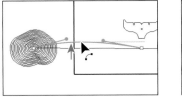 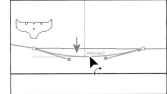

12 Drag the next segment up with the modifier key held, and so on. The idea is to create a path that curves up and down to create the effect of waves in the water. See the figure for the final effect.

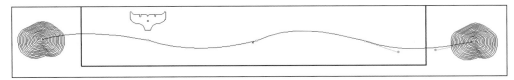

13 Choose View > Preview to see the change, and then choose Select > Deselect.

▶ **Tip:** A quick way to reshape the spine of a blend is to blend the shapes along another path. You can draw another path, select the blend as well, and then choose Object > Blend > Replace Spine.

Finishing the blend

Next, you'll reposition one of the groups in the blend object, and then copy the blend object several times to create the waves in the water.

1   Select the Selection tool (▶), and click the blend object and choose Object > Arrange > Bring To Front to bring it in front of the whale tail. You may need to move the blend object to see more of the tail (we did).

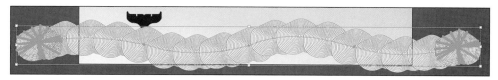

2   Option-drag (Mac OS) or Alt-drag (Windows) the blend object up and to the right a bit. Release the mouse button and then the key to create a copy.

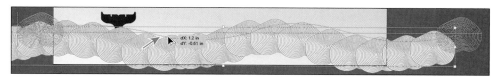

3   Choose Object > Arrange > Send To Back to send it behind the original blend object and the whale tail.

4   Option-drag (Mac OS) or Alt-drag (Windows) the selected blend object down and to the left a bit. Release the mouse button and then the key when it looks something like the figure.

5   Choose Object > Arrange > Bring To Front to bring it in front of the original blend object.

6   Double-click anywhere on the selected blend object to enter Isolation mode. Click the right group and drag it to the right and up a little bit, just beyond the farthest point of the other blend objects.

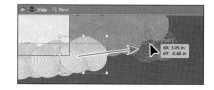

▶ **Tip:** You can reverse a blend by choosing Object > Blend > Reverse Front To Back.

The blend object keeps the same number of steps (16) no matter where you position the two groups in the blend. The 14 copies between the original groups are just spread farther or brought closer, depending on the position of the original groups.

7   Press the Escape key to exit Isolation mode.

Make sure that the blend objects are covering the background. If you need to reposition them, go ahead.

8 Choose Select > Deselect, and then choose File > Save.

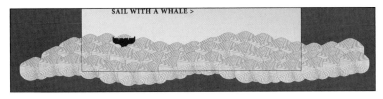

Creating and editing a smooth color blend

You can choose several options for blending the shapes and colors of objects to create a new object. When you choose the Smooth Color blend option in the Blend Options dialog box, Illustrator combines the shapes and colors of the objects into many intermediate steps, creating a smooth, graduated blend between the original objects. If objects are filled or stroked with different colors, the steps are calculated to provide the optimum number of steps for a smooth color transition. If the objects contain identical colors, or if they contain gradients or patterns, the number of steps is based on the longest distance between the bounding box edges of the two objects.

Now you'll combine two shapes into a smooth color blend to make the ship.

1 Open the Layers panel and click the edit column to the left of the Ship layer to show the layer content. Click any disclosure triangles for layers that are displaying their contents to collapse them. Click the eye icon to the left of the Water layer to hide the contents.

2 Select the Zoom tool and click a few times to zoom in to the windows on the ship.

You will now blend the two paths that will become the ship. Both paths have a stroke color and no fill. Objects that have strokes blend differently than those that have no stroke.

3 Select the Blend tool (⬚) in the Tools panel, and position the pointer over the top line until it displays an asterisk (⬚∗), and then click. Position the pointer over the bottom line, and click when a plus sign appears next to the pointer (⬚₊). Leave the blend object selected.

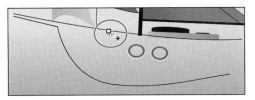
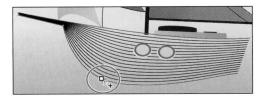

The blend you created is using the last settings from the Blend Options dialog box (Specified Steps: 16).

Next, you'll change the blend settings for the ship so that it blends as smooth color, rather than in specified steps.

4   Double-click the Blend tool in the Tools panel. In the Blend Options dialog box, choose Smooth Color from the Spacing menu to set up the blend options, which will remain set until you change them. Select Preview, and then click OK.

5   Choose Select > Deselect.

When you make a smooth color blend between objects, Illustrator automatically calculates the number of intermediate steps necessary to create the transition between the objects. Once you've applied a smooth color blend to objects, you can edit it.

Next, you will edit the paths that make up the blend.

● **Note:** Creating smooth color blends between paths can be difficult in certain situations. For instance, if the lines intersect or the lines are too curved, unexpected results can occur.

6   Using the Selection tool ( ), double-click the color blend (the ship) to enter Isolation mode. Click on the top path to select it, and change the Stroke color in the Control panel to any color you want. Notice how the colors are blended.

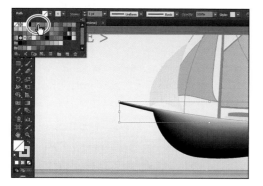

7   Choose Edit > Undo Apply Swatch until the original stroke color is showing.

8   Double-click away from the blend to exit Isolation mode and deselect the ship.

9   Open the Layers panel and click the edit column to the left of the Water layer to show the contents.

10 Choose Object > Unlock All.

11 Click the bottom blend object that is a part of the waves in the water. In the Layers panel, drag the color box in the selection column straight up to the Ship layer to move the wave to the Ship layer and arrange it on top of the ship. Leave the blend object selected.

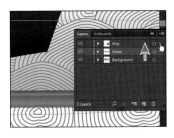

● **Note:** You may wish to edit the bottom blend object by double-clicking it to enter Isolation mode, then dragging the group on the right up or down or editing the spine (path) of the blend to cover the bottom of the ship. With the blend object still selected from the previous step, we selected the Direct Selection tool and clicked on the anchor point closest to the ship, then positioned the pointer over the path and dragged (up in our case) until the blend covered the bottom of the ship. This will give you a bit of practice in editing a blend object.

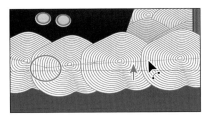

12 With the bottom blend object (the water) still selected, choose Object > Arrange > Send Backward a few times to send the wave blend object behind the wood border and the gradient rectangle (with the transparent green color) (if necessary). Make sure it's still in front of the ship.

13 Choose View > Fit Artboard In Window, and then choose Select > Deselect.

14 Choose File > Save, and then choose File > Close.

Review questions

1 What is a *gradient*?

2 How do you adjust the blend between colors in a gradient?

3 Name two ways you can add colors to a gradient.

4 How can you adjust the direction of a gradient?

5 What is the difference between a gradient and a blend?

Review answers

1 A gradient is a graduated blend of two or more colors or of tints of the same color. Gradients can be applied to the stroke or fill of an object.

2 To adjust the blend between colors in a gradient, with the Gradient tool (◧) selected and with the pointer over the gradient annotator or in the Gradient panel, you can drag the diamond icons or the color stops of the gradient slider.

3 To add colors to a gradient, in the Gradient panel, click beneath the gradient slider to add a gradient stop to the gradient. Then, double-click the color stop to edit the color, using the panel that appears to mix a new color or to apply an existing color swatch. You can select the Gradient tool in the Tools panel, position the pointer over the gradient-filled object, and then click beneath the gradient slider that appears in the artwork to add a color stop.

4 Drag with the Gradient tool to adjust the direction of a gradient. Dragging a long distance changes colors gradually; dragging a short distance makes the color change more abrupt. You can also rotate the gradient using the Gradient tool and change the radius, aspect ratio, starting point, and more.

5 The difference between a gradient and a blend is the way that colors combine together—colors blend together within a gradient and between objects in a blend.

10 USING BRUSHES TO CREATE A POSTER

Lesson overview

In this lesson, you'll learn how to do the following:

- Use four brush types: Calligraphic, Art, Bristle, and Pattern.

- Apply brushes to paths.

- Paint and edit paths with the Paintbrush tool.

- Create an Art brush from a raster image.

- Change brush color and adjust brush settings.

- Create new brushes from Adobe Illustrator artwork.

- Work with the Blob Brush tool and the Eraser tool.

This lesson takes approximately 60 minutes to complete.

Download the project files for this lesson from the Lesson & Update Files tab on your Account page at www.peachpit.com and store them on your computer in a convenient location, as described in the Getting Started section of this book.

Your Account page is also where you'll find any updates to the chapters or to the lesson files. Look on the Lesson & Update Files tab to access the most current content.

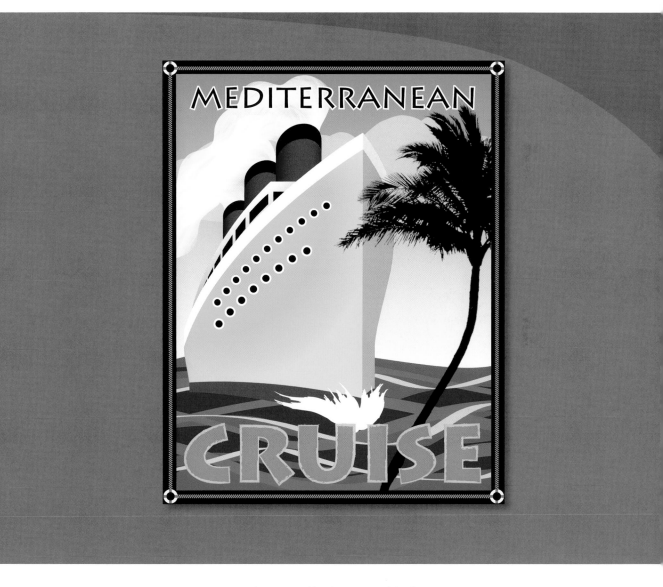

The variety of brush types in Adobe Illustrator CC lets you create a myriad of effects simply by painting or drawing using the Paintbrush tool or the drawing tools. You can work with the Blob Brush tool, choose from the Art, Calligraphic, Pattern, Bristle, or Scatter brushes, or create new brushes based on your artwork.

Getting started

In this lesson, you will learn how to work with the different brush types in the Brushes panel and how to change brush options and create your own brushes. Before you begin, you'll restore the default preferences for Adobe Illustrator CC. Then you'll open the finished art file for the lesson to see the finished artwork.

● **Note:** If you have not already downloaded the project files for this lesson to your computer from your Account page, make sure to do so now. See "Getting Started" at the beginning of the book.

1   To ensure that the tools and panels function exactly as described in this lesson, delete or deactivate (by renaming) the Adobe Illustrator CC preferences file. See "Restoring default preferences" in the Getting Started section at the beginning of the book.

2   Start Adobe Illustrator CC.

3   Choose File > Open, and open the L10_end.ai file in the Lesson10 folder, located in the Lessons folder on your hard disk.

4   If you want, choose View > Zoom Out to make the finished artwork smaller, and then adjust the window size and leave the artwork on your screen as you work. (Use the Hand tool [✋] to move the artwork to where you want it in the Document window.) If you don't want to leave the artwork open, choose File > Close.

To begin working, you'll open an existing art file.

● **Note:** In Mac OS, when opening lesson files, you may need to click the round, green button in the upper-left corner of the Document window to maximize the window's size.

5   Choose File > Open, to open the L10_start.ai file in the Lesson10 folder in the Lessons folder on your hard disk.

6   Choose View > Fit Artboard In Window.

7   Choose File > Save As. In the Save As dialog box, name the file **CruisePoster.ai** and select the Lesson10 folder. Leave the Format option set to Adobe Illustrator (ai) (Mac OS) or Save As Type option set to Adobe Illustrator (*.AI) (Windows), and then click Save. In the Illustrator Options dialog box, leave the Illustrator options at their default settings, and then click OK.

8   Choose Reset Essentials from the workspace switcher in the Application bar to reset the workspace.

● **Note:** If you don't see "Reset Essentials" in the workspace switcher menu, choose Window > Workspace > Essentials before choosing Window > Workspace > Reset Essentials.

Working with brushes

Using brushes you can decorate paths with patterns, figures, brush strokes, textures, or angled strokes. You can modify the brushes provided with Illustrator and create your own brushes.

You can apply brush strokes to existing paths, or you can use the Paintbrush tool to draw a path and apply a brush stroke simultaneously. You can change the color, size, and other features of a brush, and you can edit paths after brushes are applied (including adding a fill).

Types of brushes

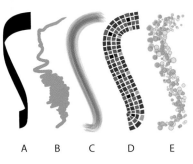

A. Calligraphic brush
B. Art brush
C. Bristle brush
D. Pattern brush
E. Scatter brush

There are five types of brushes that appear in the Brushes panel (Window > Brushes): Calligraphic, Art, Bristle, Pattern, and Scatter. In this lesson, you will discover how to work with all of these except for the Scatter brush.

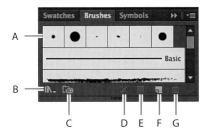

A. Brushes
B. Brush Libraries Menu
C. Libraries Panel
D. Remove Brush Stroke
E. Options Of Selected Object
F. New Brush
G. Delete Brush

Using Calligraphic brushes

Calligraphic brushes resemble strokes drawn with the angled point of a calligraphic pen. Calligraphic brushes are defined by an elliptical shape whose center follows the path. You can use these brushes to create the appearance of hand-drawn strokes made with a flat, angled pen tip.

Calligraphic brush examples

Applying a Calligraphic brush to artwork

The first type of brush you'll apply to artwork is a Calligraphic brush. To get started, you'll filter the type of brushes shown in the Brushes panel so that it only shows Calligraphic brushes.

1   Click the Brushes panel icon (▦) on the right side of the workspace to show the Brushes panel. Click the Brushes panel menu icon (▾≣), and choose List View.

2 Click the Brushes panel menu icon (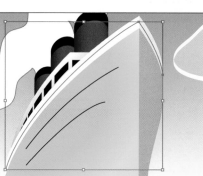) again, and deselect Show Art Brushes, Show Bristle Brushes, and Show Pattern Brushes, leaving only the Calligraphic brushes visible in the Brushes panel.

3 Select the Selection tool (▶) in the Tools panel, and Shift-click both of the two curved purple paths above the orange/yellow shape of a ship to select both of them.

4 Click the "5 pt. Flat" brush in the Brushes panel to apply it to the purple paths.

5 Change the Stroke weight to **6 pt**, and change the Stroke color to White in the Control panel. Press the Escape key to hide the Swatches panel, if necessary.

6 Choose Select > Deselect.

7 With the Selection tool, click the smaller of the white paths (the path on the right) that you just applied the brush to. Change the Stroke color to a light gray in the Control panel (we chose the color with the tool tip values C=0, M=0, Y=0, K=10).

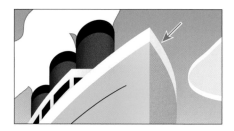

8 Choose Select > Deselect, and then choose File > Save.

Drawing with the Paintbrush tool

As mentioned earlier, the Paintbrush tool allows you to apply a brush as you paint. Painting with the Paintbrush tool creates vector paths that you can edit with the Paintbrush tool or other drawing tools. Next, you'll use the Paintbrush tool to paint waves in the water with a calligraphic brush from a default brush library.

Your waves may not look identical to what you see in the lesson, and that's okay—*just have some fun.*

1 With the Selection tool (▶), click the darker blue water shape below the ship.

2 Choose Select > Deselect.

The water shape is on a sublayer behind the ship. Selecting the water shape selects that sublayer in the Layers panel, which means that all of the waves you draw will also be on the same sublayer as the water shape.

3 Select the Paintbrush tool (✎) in the Tools panel.

4 Click the Brush Libraries Menu button (📖) at the bottom of the Brushes panel, and choose Artistic > Artistic_Calligraphic. A brush library panel with various borders appears.

Illustrator comes with a host of brush libraries that you can use in your artwork. Each of the brush types discussed previously has a series of libraries to choose from.

5 Click the Artistic_Calligraphic panel menu icon (▤), and choose List View. Click the brush named "50 pt. Flat" to add it to the Brushes panel. Close the Artistic_Calligraphic brush library.

Selecting a brush from a brush library, like the Artistic_Calligraphic library, adds that brush to the Brushes panel for the active document only.

6 Change the Fill color to None (☐), the Stroke color to the swatch named "Dark Blue," and the Stroke weight to **1 pt** (if necessary), in the Control panel.

Notice that the Paintbrush pointer has an asterisk next to it (✎₊), indicating that you are about to draw a new path.

7 Position the pointer off the left side of the artboard, just below the ship. Paint a long, curving path from left to right, stopping about halfway across the water (see the figure). Try creating three more paths, painting from left to right, going all the way across the water. You can see the figure for ideas on how we painted.

● **Note:** This Calligraphic brush creates random angles on the paths, so yours may not look like what you see in the figures, and that's okay.

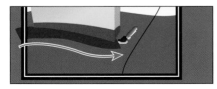

Paint the first path.

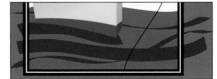

Paint the remaining paths.

8 Choose Select > Deselect (if necessary), and then choose File > Save.

Editing paths with the Paintbrush tool

Now you'll use the Paintbrush tool to edit a selected path.

Tip: You can also edit paths drawn with the Paintbrush tool using the Smooth tool (✎) and the Path Eraser tool (✎), located under the Pencil tool (✎) in the Tools panel.

1   Select the Selection tool (▶) in the Tools panel, and click to select the first path you drew on the water (the one that is just below the bottom of the ship).

2   Select the Paintbrush tool (✐) in the Tools panel. Position the pointer near the right end of the selected path. An asterisk will not appear next to the pointer when it's positioned over a selected path. Drag to the right to extend the path all the way to the right edge of the artboard. The selected path is edited from the point where you began drawing.

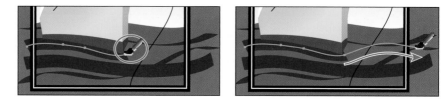

3   Press and hold the Command (Mac OS) or Ctrl (Windows) key to toggle to the Selection tool, and click to select another curved path you drew with the Paintbrush tool. After clicking, release the key to return to the Paintbrush tool.

4   With the Paintbrush tool, move the pointer over some part of the selected path. When the asterisk disappears next to the pointer, drag to the right to redraw the path.

5   Choose Select > Deselect (if necessary), and then choose File > Save.

Next, you will edit the Paintbrush tool options.

6   Double-click the Paintbrush tool (✐) in the Tools panel to display the Paintbrush Tool Options dialog box and make the following changes:

   - Fidelity: drag the slider all the way to Smooth (to the right)

   - Keep Selected: **Selected**

7   Click OK.

   The Paintbrush Tool Options dialog box changes the way the Paintbrush tool functions. For the Fidelity option, the closer to Smooth you drag the slider, the smoother the path will be with fewer points. Also, because you selected Keep Selected, the paths remain selected after you finish drawing them.

8   Change the Stroke color to the swatch named "Medium Blue," and change the Stroke weight to **0.5 pt** in the Control panel.

9   With the Paintbrush tool selected, paint three or four more paths from either left to right or right to left across the water shape below the ship.

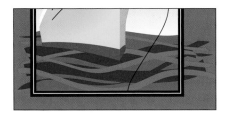

Notice that, after painting each path, the path is still selected, so you could edit it if you needed to. We already deselected in the figure.

10 Double-click the Paintbrush tool in the Tools panel. In the Paintbrush Tool Options dialog box, deselect the Keep Selected option, and then click OK.

Now the paths will not remain selected after you finish drawing them, and you can draw overlapping paths without altering previously drawn paths.

● **Note:** When the Keep Selected option is deselected, you can edit a path by selecting it with the Selection tool (▸) or by selecting a segment or point on the path with the Direct Selection tool (▸), and then redrawing part of the path with the Paintbrush tool.

11 Choose Select > Deselect, and then choose File > Save.

Editing a brush

To change the options for a brush, you can double-click the brush in the Brushes panel. When you edit a brush, you can also choose whether to change artwork to which the brush has been applied. Next, you'll change the appearance of the 50 pt. Flat brush you've been painting with.

1   In the Brushes panel, double-click the brush thumbnail for the brush named "50 pt. Flat" to open the Calligraphic Brush Options dialog box. In the dialog box, make the following changes:

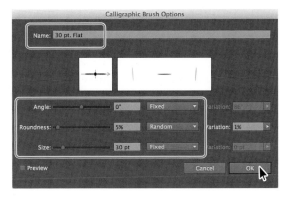

▸ **Tip:** The Preview window in the dialog box (below the Name field) shows the changes that you make to the brush.

● **Note:** The edits you make will change the brush for this document only.

- Name: **30 pt. Flat**

- Angle: **0°**

- Choose **Fixed** from the menu to the right of Angle. (When Random is chosen, a random variation of brush angles is created every time you draw.)

- Roundness: **5%** (the default setting)

- Size: **30 pt**

2   Click OK.

3   In the dialog box that appears, click Leave Strokes so as not to apply the brush change to the existing waves that have the brush applied.

4   Change the Stroke color to the swatch named "Light Blue," and change the Stroke weight to **1 pt** in the Control panel.

5   Click the 30 pt. Flat brush in the Brushes panel to ensure that you will paint with it applied. With the Paintbrush tool (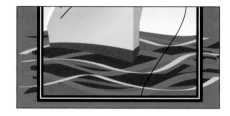) selected, paint three paths across the water to create more waves, overlapping the existing waves. Use the figure as a guide, if you like.

6   Choose Select > Deselect, if necessary, and then choose File > Save.

The artwork should be deselected already and, if it is, the Deselect command will be dimmed (you can't select it).

Removing a brush stroke

You can easily remove a brush stroke applied to artwork where you don't want it. Now you'll remove the brush stroke on the cloud.

1   Select the Selection tool (▶), and click the blue cloud with the white stroke in the sky.

2   Click the Remove Brush Stroke button (◪) at the bottom of the Brushes panel.

Removing a brush stroke doesn't remove the stroke color and weight; it just removes the brush applied.

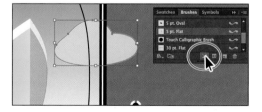

3   Change the Stroke weight to **0 pt** in the Control panel.

4   Choose Select > Deselect, and then choose File > Save.

Using Art brushes

Art brushes stretch artwork or an embedded raster image evenly along the length of a path. As with other brushes, you can edit the brush options to affect how the brush is applied to artwork.

Applying an existing Art brush

Next, you will apply an existing Art brush to waves at the front of the boat.

Art brush examples

1   In the Brushes panel, click the Brushes panel menu icon (), and deselect Show Calligraphic Brushes. Then select Show Art Brushes from the same panel menu to make the art brushes visible in the Brushes panel.

2   Click the Brush Libraries Menu button () at the bottom of the Brushes panel, and choose Artistic > Artistic_Paintbrush.

3   Click the Artistic_Paintbrush panel menu icon (), and choose List View. Click the brush named "Brush 3" in the list to add the brush to the Brushes panel for this document. Close the Artistic_Paintbrush panel group.

4   Select the Paintbrush tool () in the Tools panel.

5   Change the Stroke color to White and the Stroke weight to **1 pt**, and make sure that the Fill color is None () in the Control panel.

6   Click the Layers panel icon () on the right side of the workspace to open the Layers panel. Click the Spray/Tree layer so that the new artwork is on that layer. Click the Layers panel icon to collapse the panel.

7   Position the Paintbrush pointer () at the bottom-front of the ship, in the red area (marked with an X in the figure). Drag to the left along the bottom of the red strip on the ship, just along the water line. See the figure for how we painted it, and don't worry about being exact. You can always choose Edit > Undo Art Stroke and repaint the path.

▶ **Tip:** With the Paintbrush pointer selected, press the Caps Lock key to see a precise cursor (**X**). In certain situations, this can help to paint with more precision.

8 Paint a path from the same starting point (the red X in previous figure), but drag to the right this time. Then paint a "U" shape around the starting point (from left to right) to cover any red showing. The figure shows both paths. (See the figure—start at the X in the figure for the "U" shape.)

9 Try adding a few more painted paths, always starting from the same point as the end of the original path you painted.

10 Choose File > Save.

Creating an Art brush using a raster image

● **Note:** To learn about guidelines for creating brushes, see "Create or modify brushes" in Illustrator Help (Help > Illustrator Help).

In this section, you'll place a raster image, embedding it, to use in a new Art brush. When you create a new brush (for any of the brush types), it appears in the Brushes panel of the current document only.

1 Choose File > Place. In the Place dialog box, navigate to the Lesson10 folder and select the image named tree.psd. Make sure to deselect the Link option. Click Place.

2 Position the pointer off of the artboard on the right. Click to place the image.

Next, you will make an Art brush from the selected artwork. You can make an Art brush from vector artwork or from *embedded* raster images, but that artwork must not contain gradients, blends, other brush strokes, mesh objects, graphs, linked files, masks, or text that has not been converted to outlines.

● **Note:** When dealing with embedded images and brushes, there is a direct impact on the performance of the document in Illustrator. There is a fixed limit to the size of the embedded image that can be used for a brush. You may see a dialog box telling you that the image needs to be resampled before you can make a brush from it.

3   Select the Selection tool (▶), and click the New Brush button (▣) at the bottom of the Brushes panel. This begins the process of creating a new brush from the selected raster artwork.

4   In the New Brush dialog box, select Art Brush, and then click OK.

5   In the Art Brush Options dialog box that appears, change the Name to **Palm Tree**. Click OK.

6   Delete the image you placed off the right side of the artboard, since you don't need it anymore.

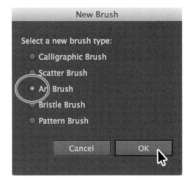

7   With the Selection tool selected, click to select the curved black line to the right of the ship.

8   Click the brush named "Palm Tree" in the Brushes panel to apply it.

Notice that the original tree image is stretched along the shape. This is the default behavior of an Art brush.

Editing an Art brush

Next, you'll edit the Palm Tree Art brush and update the appearance of the palm tree on the artboard.

▶ Tip: To learn more about the Art Brush Options dialog box, see "Art brush options" in Illustrator Help (Help > Illustrator Help).

1 With the curved path still selected on the artboard, double-click the brush thumbnail to the left of the text "Palm tree" or to the right of the name in the Brushes panel to open the Art Brush Options dialog box.

2 In the Art Brush Options dialog box, select Preview to see the changes as you make them and move the dialog box so you can see the curvy line with the brush applied. Make the following changes:

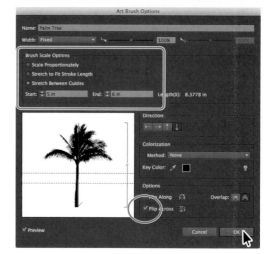

- Stretch Between Guides: **Selected**

- Start: **5 in**

- End: **6 in**

- Flip Across: **Selected**

3 Click OK.

4 In the dialog box that appears, click Apply To Strokes to apply the change to the curvy line that has the Palm Tree brush applied.

5 Click the word "Opacity" in the Control panel, and choose Multiply from the Blend Mode menu. Press Enter or Return to close the Transparency panel.

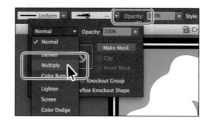

6 Choose Select > Deselect, and then choose File > Save.

Using Bristle brushes

Bristle brushes allow you to create strokes with the appearance of a natural brush with bristles. Painting with a Bristle brush, using the Paintbrush tool, creates vector paths with the Bristle brush applied, as you'll see in this section. You'll start by adjusting options for a brush to change how it appears in the artwork, and then paint with the Paintbrush tool and Bristle brush to create smoke.

Bristle brush examples

Changing Bristle brush options

As you've seen, you can change the appearance of a brush by adjusting its settings in the Brush Options dialog box, either before or after brushes have been applied to artwork. In the case of Bristle brushes, it's usually best to adjust the brush settings prior to painting, since it can take some time to update the brush strokes.

1 In the Brushes panel, click the panel menu icon (![icon]), choose Show Bristle Brushes, and then deselect Show Art Brushes.

2 Double-click the thumbnail for the default Mop brush or double-click directly to the right of the brush name to open the Bristle Brush Options dialog box for that brush. In the Bristle Brush Options dialog box, make the following changes:

- Shape: **Round Fan** (the default setting)

- Size: **7 mm** (The brush size is the diameter of the brush.)

- Bristle Length: **150%** (the default setting) (The bristle length starts from the point where the bristles meet the handle of the bristle tip.)

- Bristle Density: **20%** (The bristle density is the number of bristles in a specified area of the brush neck.)

- Bristle Thickness: **75%** (the default setting) (The bristle thickness can vary from fine to coarse [between 1% and 100%].)

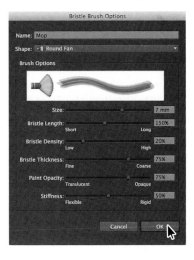

- Paint Opacity: **75%** (the default setting) (This option lets you set the opacity of the paint being used.)

- Stiffness: **50%** (the default setting) (Stiffness refers to the rigidness of the bristles).

3 Click OK.

Note: To learn more about the Bristle Brush Options dialog box and its settings, see "Using the Bristle brush" in Illustrator Help (Help > Illustrator Help).

Tip: Illustrator comes with a series of default Bristle brushes. Click the Brush Libraries Menu button (![icon]) at the bottom of the Brushes panel, and choose Bristle Brush > Bristle Brush Library.

Painting with a Bristle brush

Now you'll use the Mop brush to draw some smoke above the ship. Painting with a Bristle brush can create a very organic, fluid path. In order to constrain the painting, you will paint inside a shape. This will mask (hide) part of the painting to be in the shape of smoke.

1 Select the Zoom tool (🔍) in the Tools panel, and click a few times, slowly, on the smoke shape above the ship (not the cloud), to zoom in on it.

2 Select the Selection tool (▸) in the Tools panel, and click to select the smoke shape. This selects the layer that the shape is on so that any artwork you paint will be on the same layer.

● **Note:** To learn more about the drawing modes, see Lesson 3, "Using Shapes to Create Artwork for a Postcard."

3 Click the Draw Inside button (▣) at the bottom of the Tools panel.

● **Note:** If the Tools panel appears as one column, click the Drawing Modes button (▣) at the bottom of the Tools panel, and then choose Draw Inside from the menu that appears.

4 With the smoke shape still selected, change the Fill color to None (▱) in the Control panel (press the Escape key to hide the Swatches panel). Leave the stroke as is.

5 Choose Select > Deselect to deselect the smoke shape.

The dotted lines on the corners of the shape indicate that any paths you paint will be masked by the smoke shape.

6 Select the Paintbrush tool (✏) in the Tools panel. Choose the Mop brush from the Brush Definition menu in the Control panel, if it's not already chosen.

7 Make sure that the Fill color is None (▱) and the Stroke color is White in the Control panel. Press the Escape key to hide the Swatches panel. Make sure that the Stroke weight is **1 pt** in the Control panel.

▶ **Tip:** If you want to edit paths as you draw, you can select the Keep Selected option in the Paintbrush Tool Options for the Paintbrush tool or you can select paths with the Selection tool. You don't need to completely fill the shape.

8 Position the pointer at the top of the largest smokestack. (See the next figure for the red X.) Drag up and then down and to the left, to loosely follow the edge of the smoke shape. Release the mouse button when you reach the end of the smoke shape.

When you release the mouse button, notice that the path you just painted is masked by the smoke shape.

▶ **Tip:** If you don't like what you just painted, you can choose Edit > Undo Bristle Stroke.

9 Use the Paintbrush tool to paint more paths inside the smoke shape, using the Mop brush. Try drawing from each of the smokestacks, following the smoke shape. The idea is to fill up the smoke shape with the paths you paint.

● **Note:** In the first part of the figure, we dimmed the shape paths so you could more easily see the smoke paths.

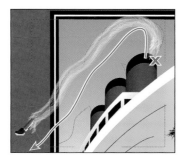
Paint the first path.

Note the result after painting more.

10 Choose View > Outline to see all of the paths you just created when painting.

11 Choose Select > Object > Bristle Brush Strokes to select all of the paths created with the Paintbrush tool using the Mop brush.

12 Choose Object > Group, and then choose View > Preview.

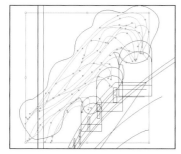
View the artwork in Outline mode.

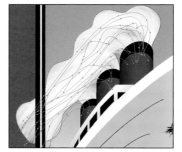
Note the result in Preview mode.

13 Click the Draw Normal button (🔲) at the bottom of the Tools panel.

14 Select the Selection tool in the Tools panel. Choose Select > Deselect.

15 Double-click the edge of the smoke shape to enter Isolation mode. Click the same smoke shape to select it. Change the Stroke color to None (◻) in the Control panel.

● **Note:** If the Tools panel appears as one column, click the Drawing Modes button at the bottom of the Tools panel, and then choose Draw Normal from the menu that appears.

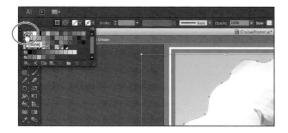

▶ **Tip:** You can also double-click away from the artwork to exit Isolation mode.

16 Press the Escape key several times to hide the panel and to exit Isolation mode.

17 Click the Layers panel icon ( ) on the right side of the workspace to open the Layers panel. Click the eye icon ( ) to the left of the Spray/Tree layer name to hide the artwork on that layer. Click the Layers panel icon to collapse the panel.

18 Choose Select > Deselect, and then choose File > Save.

When saving, you may see a warning dialog box indicating that the document contains multiple Bristle brush paths with transparency. As mentioned earlier, painting with a Bristle brush creates a series of individual vector paths with the brush applied. This can lead to issues with printing or saving to EPS/PDF or legacy versions of Illustrator documents. In order to reduce the complexity and number of the Bristle Brush paths, you can rasterize paths with a Bristle brush applied. Select the path(s) with the Bristle brush applied, and choose Object > Rasterize.

The Bristle brush and graphic tablets

When you use Bristle brush with a graphic tablet, Illustrator interactively tracks the movements of the stylus over the tablet. It interprets all aspects of its orientation and pressure input at any point along a drawing path. Illustrator provides the output that is modeled on the stylus's x-axis position, y-axis position, pressure, tilt, bearing, and rotation.

—From Illustrator Help

Using Pattern brushes

Pattern brushes paint a pattern made up of separate sections, or *tiles*. When you apply a Pattern brush to artwork, different tiles of the pattern are applied to different sections of the path, depending on where the section falls on the path—the end, middle, or corner. There are hundreds of interesting Pattern brushes that you can choose from when creating your own projects, from grass to cityscapes. Next, you'll apply an existing Pattern brush to a path to create windows on the ship.

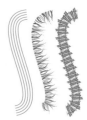

Pattern brush examples

1 Choose View > Fit Artboard In Window.

2 In the Brushes panel, click the panel menu icon (), choose Show Pattern Brushes, and then deselect Show Bristle Brushes. The Windows brush that appears in the Brushes panel is a brush that we created and saved with the file.

Next, you will apply a Pattern brush and then edit its properties.

3 With the Selection tool (▶) selected, Shift-click the two black paths on the orange shape of the ship to select them both.

4 Choose the Windows pattern brush from the Brush Definition menu in the Control panel to apply the Pattern brush.

Next, you will edit the brush properties for the selected paths.

5 Choose Select > Deselect.

6 Click the bottommost path with the Windows brush applied to select it.

▶ **Tip:** Just like other brush types, there is a series of default Pattern brush libraries that come with Illustrator. To access them, click the Brush Libraries Menu button (🔳) and choose a library from one of the menus (the Decorative menu, for example).

7 Click the Options Of Selected Object button (▣) at the bottom of the Brushes panel to edit the brush options for only the selected path on the artboard.

This opens the Stroke Options (Pattern Brush) dialog box.

8 Select Preview in the Stroke Options (Pattern Brush) dialog box. Change the Scale to **110%** either by dragging the Scale slider or by typing in the value. Click OK.

▶ **Tip:** To change the size of the windows, you can also change the stroke weight of the lines on the artboard, with the brush applied.

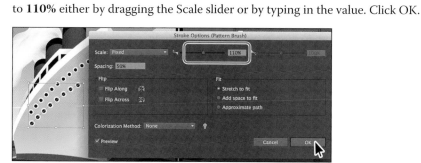

When you edit the brush options of the selected object, you only see some of the brush options. The Stroke Options (Pattern Brush) dialog box is used to edit the properties of the brushed path without updating the corresponding brush.

9 Choose Select > Deselect, and then choose File > Save.

Creating a Pattern brush

You can create a Pattern brush in several ways. For a simple pattern applied to a straight line, for instance, you can select the content that you're using for the pattern and click the New Brush button (⬚) at the bottom of the Brushes panel.

To create a more complex pattern to apply to objects with curves and corners, you can select artwork in the Document window to be used in a pattern brush, create swatches in the Swatches panel from the artwork that you are using in the Pattern brush, and even have Illustrator auto-generate the Pattern brush corners. In Illustrator, only the side tile needs to be defined. Illustrator automatically generates four different types of corners based on the art used for the side tile. These four auto-generated options fit the corners perfectly.

Next, you'll create a Pattern brush for the border around the poster.

1   Choose View > Pattern objects. This should show you a zoomed-in view of the life preserver and the rope off the right edge of the artboard.

2   With the Selection tool (▶) selected, click to select the rope group.

3   Click the Brushes panel icon (▨) to expand the panel, if necessary, click the panel menu icon (▾≡), and choose Thumbnail View. In the Brushes panel, click the New Brush button (⬚) to create a pattern out of the rope.

4   In the New Brush dialog box, select Pattern Brush. Click OK.

Notice that Pattern brushes in Thumbnail view are segmented in the Brushes panel. Each segment corresponds to a pattern tile. The side tile is repeated in the Brushes panel thumbnail preview.

A new Pattern brush can be made regardless of whether artwork is selected. If you create a Pattern brush without artwork selected, it is assumed that you will add artwork by dragging it into the Brushes panel later or by selecting the artwork from a pattern swatch you create as you edit the brush. You will see the latter method later in this section.

● **Note:** Some brushes have no corner tiles because they are designed for curved paths.

5   In the Pattern Brush Options dialog box, name the brush **Border**.

Pattern brushes can have up to five tiles—the side, start, and end tiles, plus an outer-corner tile and an inner-corner tile to paint sharp corners on a path.

You can see all five tiles as buttons below the Spacing option in the dialog box. The tile buttons let you apply different artwork to different parts of the path. You can click a tile button for the tile you want to define, and then you select an auto-generated selection (if available) or a pattern swatch from the menu that appears.

6 Under the Spacing option, click the Side Tile box (the second tile from the left). The artwork that was originally selected is in the menu that appears, along with None and any pattern swatches found in the Swatches panel. Choose Pompadour from the menu.

In the Preview area below the tiles, you will see how the new artwork affects a path.

7 Click the Side Tile box again, and choose the Original option.

8 Click the Outer Corner Tile box to reveal the menu.

The outer-corner tile has been generated automatically by Illustrator, based on the original rope artwork. In the menu, you can choose from four types of corners that are generated automatically:

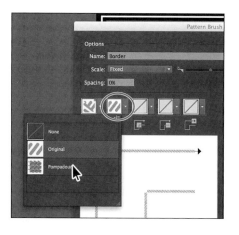

► **Tip:** Position the pointer over the tile squares in the Pattern Brush Options dialog box to see a tool tip indicating which tile it is.

► **Tip:** Selected artwork becomes the side tile, by default, when creating a Pattern brush.

► **Tip:** To save a brush and reuse it in another file, you can create a brush library with the brushes you want to use. For more information, see "Work with brush libraries" in Illustrator Help.

- **Auto-Centered.** The side tile is stretched around the corner and centered on it.

- **Auto-Between.** Copies of the side tile extend all the way into the corner, with one copy on each side. Folding elimination is used to stretch them into shape.

- **Auto-Sliced.** The side tile is sliced diagonally, and the pieces come together, similar to a miter joint in a wooden picture frame.

- **Auto-Overlap.** Copies of the tiles overlap at the corner.

9 Choose Auto-Between from the menu. This generates the outer corner of any path that the Pattern brush will be applied to from the rope.

10 Click OK. The Border brush appears in the Brushes panel.

Applying a Pattern brush

In this section, you'll apply the Border Pattern brush to a rectangular border around the artwork. As you've seen, when you use drawing tools to apply brushes to artwork, you first draw the path with the drawing tool, and then select the brush in the Brushes panel to apply the brush to the path.

1 Choose View > Fit Artboard In Window.

2 With the Selection tool (▶) selected, click the white stroke of the rectangle on the border.

3 In the Tools panel, click the Fill box and make sure that None (⊘) is selected. Then click the Stroke box and select None (⊘).

4 With the rectangle selected, click the Border brush in the Brushes panel.

5 Choose Select > Deselect.

The rectangle is painted with the Border brush, with the side tile on the sides and the outer-corner tile on each corner.

Editing the Pattern brush

▶ **Tip:** For more information on creating pattern swatches, see "About patterns" in Illustrator Help.

Now you'll edit the Border brush using a pattern swatch that you create.

1 Click the Swatches panel icon (▦) to expand the Swatches panel, or choose Window > Swatches.

2 Choose View > Pattern objects to zoom in to the life preserver off the right edge of the artboard.

3 With the Selection tool (▶), drag the life preserver into the Swatches panel. The new pattern swatch appears in the Swatches panel.

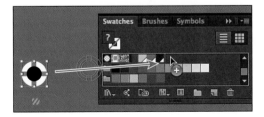

After you create a pattern brush, you can delete the pattern swatches from the Swatches panel, if you don't plan to use them for additional artwork.

4 Choose Select > Deselect.

5 In the Swatches panel, double-click the pattern swatch that you just created. In the Pattern Options dialog box, name the swatch **Corner** and choose 1 x 1 from the Copies menu.

6 Click Done in the gray bar, along the top of the Document window, to finish editing the pattern.

7 Choose View > Fit Artboard In Window.

8 In the Brushes panel, double-click the Border Pattern brush to open the Pattern Brush Options dialog box.

9 Click the Outer Corner Tile box, and choose the Corner pattern swatch from the menu that appears (you'll need to scroll). Change the Scale to **70%**, and click OK. The figure shows choosing the outer-corner tile.

10 In the dialog box that appears, click Apply To Strokes to update the border on the artboard.

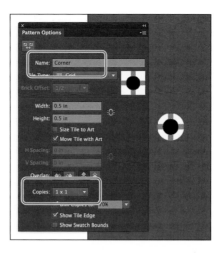

▶ **Tip:** You can also change the pattern tiles in a Pattern brush by pressing the Option (Mac OS) or Alt (Windows) key and dragging artwork from the artboard onto the tile of the Pattern brush you wish to change in the Brushes panel.

11 With the Selection tool selected, click to select one of the paths that contains a row of windows. Click the Border brush in the Brushes panel to apply it.

Notice that the life preservers are not applied to the path. The path is painted with the side tile from the Border brush. Because the path does not include sharp corners, outer-corner and inner-corner tiles are not applied to the path.

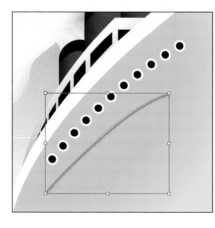

● **Note:** Earlier in the lesson, you learned how to remove a brush from an object by clicking the Remove Brush Stroke button (▨) in the Brushes panel. In this case, you chose Edit > Undo Apply Pattern Brush instead, because clicking the Remove Brush Stroke button would strip the previous formatting from the path, leaving it with a default fill and stroke.

12 Choose Edit > Undo Apply Pattern Brush to remove the brush from the path.

13 Choose Select > Deselect, and then choose File > Save.

Working with the Blob Brush tool

You can use the Blob Brush tool (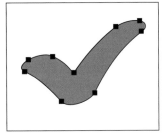) to paint filled shapes that intersect and merge with other shapes of the same color. With the Blob Brush tool, you can draw with Paintbrush tool artistry. Unlike the Paintbrush tool, which lets you create open paths, the Blob Brush tool lets you create a closed shape with a fill only (no stroke) that you can then easily edit with the Eraser or Blob Brush tool. Shapes that have a stroke cannot be edited with the Blob Brush tool.

Path created with the
Paintbrush tool.

Shape created with the
Blob Brush tool.

Drawing with the Blob Brush tool

Next, you'll use the Blob Brush tool to create part of a cloud.

1   Click the Layers panel icon (▣) on the right side of the workspace to expand the Layers panel. Click the eye icon (◉) to the left of the Ship layer to hide the contents of the layer. Click the Background layer to select it.

2   Change the Fill color to the swatch named "Light Blue," and change the Stroke color to None (◻) in the Control panel.

When drawing with the Blob Brush tool, if a fill and stroke are set before drawing, the stroke becomes the fill of the shape made by the Blob Brush tool. If only a fill is set before drawing, it becomes the fill of the shape created.

3   Click and hold down on the Paintbrush tool () in the Tools panel and select the Blob Brush tool. Double-click the Blob Brush tool in the Tools panel. In the Blob Brush Tool Options dialog box, select the Keep Selected option and change the Size to **70 pt** in the Default Brush Options area. Click OK.

4   Position the pointer to the left of the little blue cloud in the sky. Drag to create a cloud shape that doesn't touch the little cloud to the right of it (see the figure).

▶ **Tip:** You can also change the Blob Brush size by pressing the right bracket key ( ]) or left bracket key ([ ) several times to increase or decrease the size of brush.

When you draw with the Blob Brush tool, you create filled, closed shapes. Those shapes can contain any type of fill, including gradients, solid colors, patterns, and more. Notice that the Blob Brush pointer has a circle around it before you begin painting. That circle indicates the size of the brush (70 pt, which you set in the previous step).

Merging paths with the Blob Brush tool

In addition to drawing new shapes with the Blob Brush tool, you can use it to intersect and merge shapes of the same color. Objects merged with the Blob Brush tool need to have the same appearance attributes, have no stroke, be on the same layer or group, and be adjacent to each other in the stacking order.

● **Note:** To learn more about Blob Brush tool guidelines, search for "Painting with fills and strokes" in Illustrator Help (Help > Illustrator Help). On that Help page, go to the section titled "Draw and merge paths with the Blob Brush tool."

Next, you will merge the cloud you just created with the little cloud to the right of it to create one big cloud.

1 Choose Select > Deselect.

● **Note:** In the figure, the cloud you drew has a blue outline. You may not see that, and that's okay.

2 With the Blob Brush tool (🖌) selected, drag from inside the cloud shape you created to the inside of the little cloud to the right, connecting the two shapes.

● **Note:** If you find that the shapes are not merging, it may be that they have different strokes and fills. You can select both the cloud you created and the small cloud with the Selection tool (▶), and ensure that the Fill color is the light blue swatch and the stroke is None, in the Control panel. Then you can select the Blob Brush tool and try dragging from one cloud to the other.

3 Continue drawing with the Blob Brush tool to make the two clouds look more like a single cloud.

If you find that new shapes are being made instead of the existing cloud shape being edited, undo what you've created. Then, with the Selection tool (▶), reselect and deselect the cloud shape and continue.

4 Choose Select > Deselect, and then choose File > Save.

Editing with the Eraser tool

As you draw and merge shapes with the Blob Brush tool, you may draw too much and want to edit what you've done. You can use the Eraser tool (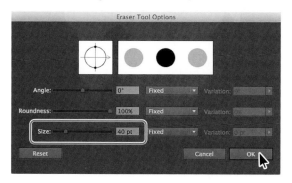) in combination with the Blob Brush tool to mold the shape and to correct any changes you don't like.

▶ **Tip:** As you draw with the Blob Brush and Eraser tools, it is recommended that you use shorter strokes and release the mouse button often. You can undo the edits that you make, but if you draw in one long stroke without releasing the mouse button, an undo removes the entire stroke.

1 With the Selection tool (▶), click to select the cloud shape.

   Selecting the shape(s) before erasing limits the Eraser tool to erasing only the selected shape(s).

2 Double-click the Eraser tool ( ) in the Tools panel. In the Eraser Tool Options dialog box, change the Size to **40 pt**, and click OK.

3 Position the pointer over the edge of the cloud shape and, with the Eraser tool, drag along the bottom of the cloud shape to remove some of it. Try switching between the Blob Brush tool and the Eraser tool to edit the cloud.

   The Blob Brush and Eraser tools both have pointers that include a circle, indicating the diameter of the brush.

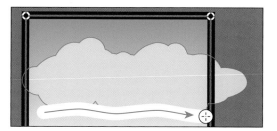

4 Choose Select > Deselect.

5   Click the Layers panel icon () on the right side of the workspace to expand
    the Layers panel, if necessary. Click the visibility columns to the left of all of
    the sublayers to ensure that they are all showing. Click to select the main layer
    named "Mask" at the top of the Layers panel. Click the Make/Release Clipping
    Mask button ( ) at the bottom of the Layers panel.

By clicking the Make/Release Clipping Mask button, you are taking an existing
rectangle shape and using it to mask content. To learn more about masking, see
Lesson 14, "Using Illustrator CC with Other Adobe Applications."

6   Click the Layers panel tab to collapse the panel group.

7   Choose Object > Show All to show some poster text.

8   Choose Select > Deselect.

9   Choose File > Save, and close all open files.

Review questions

1 What is the difference between applying a brush to artwork using the Paintbrush tool (✒) and applying a brush to artwork using one of the drawing tools?

2 Describe how artwork in an Art brush is applied to content.

3 Describe how to edit paths with the Paintbrush tool as you draw. How does the Keep Selected option affect the Paintbrush tool?

4 What must be done to a raster image in order for it to be used in certain brushes?

5 For which brush types must you have artwork selected on the artboard before you can create a brush?

6 What does the Blob Brush tool (✒) allow you to create?

Review answers

1 When painting with the Paintbrush tool (✒), if a brush is chosen in the Brushes panel and you draw on the artboard, the brush is applied directly to the paths as you draw. To apply brushes using a drawing tool, you select the tool and draw in the artwork. Then you select the path in the artwork and choose a brush in the Brushes panel. The brush is applied to the selected path.

2 An Art brush is made from artwork (vector or embedded raster). When you apply an Art brush to the stroke of an object, the artwork in the Art brush, by default, is stretched along the selected object stroke.

3 To edit a path with the Paintbrush tool, drag over a selected path to redraw it. The Keep Selected option keeps the last path selected as you draw with the Paintbrush tool. Leave the Keep Selected option selected when you want to easily edit the previous path as you draw. Deselect the Keep Selected option when you want to draw layered paths with the paintbrush without altering previous paths. When Keep Selected is deselected, you can use the Selection tool (▶) to select a path and then edit it.

4 In order to be used in certain brushes (Art, Pattern, and Scatter), a raster image must be embedded.

5 For Art and Scatter brushes, you need to have artwork selected in order to create a brush using the New Brush button (▣) in the Brushes panel.

6 Use the Blob Brush tool (✒) to edit filled shapes that you can intersect and merge with other shapes of the same color or to create artwork from scratch.

11 EXPLORING CREATIVE USES OF EFFECTS AND GRAPHIC STYLES

Lesson overview

In this lesson, you'll learn how to do the following:

- Work with the Appearance panel.

- Edit and apply appearance attributes.

- Copy, disable and enable, and remove appearance attributes.

- Reorder appearance attributes.

- Apply and edit an effect.

- Apply a variety of effects.

- Save and apply an appearance as a graphic style.

- Apply a graphic style to a layer.

- Scale strokes and effects.

This lesson takes approximately 60 minutes to complete.

Download the project files for this lesson from the Lesson & Update Files tab on your Account page at www.peachpit.com and store them on your computer in a convenient location, as described in the Getting Started section of this book.

Your Account page is also where you'll find any updates to the chapters or to the lesson files. Look on the Lesson & Update Files tab to access the most current content.

You can change the look of an object without changing its structure simply by applying attributes, such as fills, strokes, and effects, from the Appearance panel. And because the effects themselves are live, they can be modified or removed at any time. This allows you to save the appearance attributes as graphic styles and apply them to another object.

Getting started

In this lesson, you'll change the appearance of artwork using the Appearance panel, various effects, and graphic styles. Before you begin, you'll need to restore the default preferences for Adobe Illustrator. Then you'll open a file containing the finished artwork to see what you'll create.

● **Note:** If you have not already downloaded the project files for this lesson to your computer from your Account page, make sure to do so now. See "Getting Started" at the beginning of the book.

1 To ensure that the tools and panels function exactly as described in this lesson, delete or deactivate (by renaming) the Adobe Illustrator CC preferences file. See "Restoring default preferences" in the Getting Started section at the beginning of the book.

2 Start Adobe Illustrator CC.

● **Note:** On Windows, if you see a message that refers to a "compatible GPU," click OK.

3 Choose File > Open, and open the L11_end.ai file in the Lesson11 folder, located in the Lessons folder on your hard disk.

This file displays a completed illustration of a flyer for a music event.

● **Note:** You will need an Internet connection to sync the font.

4 In the Missing Fonts dialog box that most likely will appear, click Sync Fonts to sync all of the missing fonts from the FranklinGothicURW-Hea family to your computer. After it is synced and you see the message stating that there are no more missing fonts, click Close.

If you can't get the fonts to sync (a "Syncing Typekit fonts…" message doesn't go away), you can go to the Creative Cloud desktop application and choose Assets > Fonts to see what the issue may be (refer to the section "Changing font family and font style" in Lesson 7, "Adding type to a Poster," for more information on how to resolve it).

You can also just click Close in the Missing Fonts dialog box and ignore the missing fonts as you proceed. A third method is to click the Find Fonts button in the Missing Fonts dialog box and replace the fonts with a local font on your machine. You can also go to Help (Help > Illustrator Help) and search for "Find missing fonts."

5   Choose View > Zoom Out to make the finished artwork smaller. Adjust the window size, and leave it on your screen as you work. (Use the Hand tool [✋] to move the artwork where you want it in the window.) If you don't want to leave the image open, choose File > Close.

To begin working, you'll open an existing art file.

6   Choose File > Open, and open the L11_start.ai file in the Lesson11 folder, located in the Lessons folder on your hard disk.

● **Note:** For more help on resolving the missing font, refer to the previous steps.

The L11_start.ai file uses the same FranklinGothicURW-Hea font as the L11_end.ai file. If you synced the font once, you don't need to do it again. If you didn't open the L11_end.ai file, then the Missing Fonts dialog box will most likely will appear for this step. Click Sync Fonts to sync all of the missing fonts from the FranklinGothicURW-Hea family to your computer. After it is synced and you see the message stating that there are no more missing fonts, click Close.

● **Note:** In Mac OS, when opening lesson files, you may need to click the round, green button in the upper-left corner of the Document window to maximize the window's size.

7   Choose File > Save As, name the file **JazzFestival.ai**, and select the Lesson11 folder. Leave the Format option set to Adobe Illustrator (ai) (Mac OS) or Save As Type option set to Adobe Illustrator (*.AI) (Windows), and then click Save. In the Illustrator Options dialog box, leave the Illustrator options at their default settings, and then click OK.

8   Choose Reset Essentials from the workspace switcher in the Application bar to reset the workspace.

● **Note:** If you don't see "Reset Essentials" in the workspace switcher menu, choose Window > Workspace > Essentials before choosing Window > Workspace > Reset Essentials.

Using the Appearance panel

An *appearance attribute* is an aesthetic property—such as a fill, stroke, transparency, or effect—that affects the look of an object but does not affect its basic structure. Up to this point, you've been changing these appearance attributes in the Control panel, Swatches panel, and more. These attributes and more (effects, opacity, and more) can also be found in the Appearance panel for selected artwork.

1 Click the Appearance panel icon (▣) on the right side of the workspace to see the Appearance panel.

● **Note:** Depending on your operating system, the selection color of objects (the bounding box) may be different colors, and that's okay.

2 Select the Selection tool (▶), and click to select the largest of the shapes that make up the trumpet. The Appearance panel shows what the object is (a Path) and the appearance attributes applied to it (Stroke, Fill, and Opacity, as well as a Drop Shadow effect).

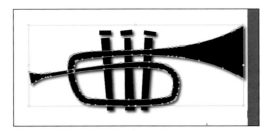

The different options available in the Appearance panel are described below:

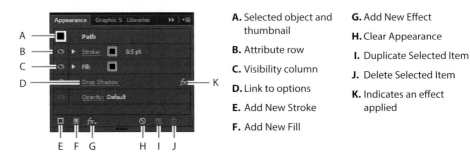

A. Selected object and thumbnail

B. Attribute row

C. Visibility column

D. Link to options

E. Add New Stroke

F. Add New Fill

G. Add New Effect

H. Clear Appearance

I. Duplicate Selected Item

J. Delete Selected Item

K. Indicates an effect applied

The Appearance panel (Window > Appearance) can be used to view and adjust the appearance attributes for a selected object, group, or layer. Fills and strokes are listed in stacking order; top to bottom in the panel correlates to front to back in the artwork. Effects applied to artwork are listed from top to bottom in the order in which they are applied to the artwork. An advantage of using appearance attributes is that they can be changed or removed at any time without affecting the underlying artwork or any other attributes applied to the object in the Appearance panel.

Editing appearance attributes

You'll start by changing the basic appearance of artwork using the Appearance panel.

1 With the trumpet shape still selected (see steps in previous section), choose Select > Same > Fill Color to select the rest of the black trumpet shapes.

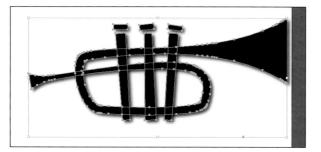

Notice that the content of the Appearance panel doesn't really change. The same appearance properties are listed. If you were to select multiple objects that had different fills, for instance, the Appearance panel would show "Mixed Appearance," indicating that the selected artwork has some appearance attributes that are different.

2 In the Appearance panel, click the black Fill color box in the Fill attribute row until the Swatches panel appears. Click the swatch named "Trumpet" to apply it to the Fill. Press the Escape key to hide the Swatches panel.

● **Note:** You may need to click the Fill box twice to open the Swatches panel.

You will find that you can change appearance attributes, like Fill color, in the Appearance panel or elsewhere in the workspace.

3 Click the words "0.5 pt" in the Stroke row. The Stroke Weight option appears. Change the Stroke weight to **0** to remove it.

4 Click the underlined word "Stroke" to reveal the Stroke panel.

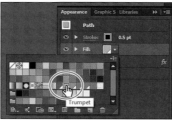

Clicking underlined words in the Appearance panel, as in the Control panel, shows more formatting options—usually in a panel like the Swatches or Stroke panels. Appearance attributes, like Fill or Stroke, can have other options, like Opacity or an effect applied to only that attribute. These additional options are listed as a subset under the attribute row and can be shown or hidden by clicking the disclosure triangle (▶) on the left end of the attribute row.

5 Press the Escape key to hide the Stroke panel.

6 Click the disclosure triangle (▶) to the left of the word "Fill" in the Appearance panel to reveal the Opacity option (if necessary). Click the word "Opacity" to reveal the Transparency panel. Change the Opacity value to **100%**. Press the Escape key to hide the Transparency panel and to return to the Appearance panel.

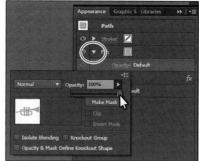

7 Click the visibility column (👁) to the left of the Drop Shadow attribute name in the Appearance panel.

Appearance attributes can be deleted or temporarily hidden so that they no longer are applied.

8 With the Drop Shadow row selected (click to the right of the link "Drop Shadow" if it isn't selected), click the Delete Selected Item button (🗑) at the bottom of the panel to completely remove the shadow, rather than just turning off the visibility.

Hide the drop shadow.   Delete the drop shadow.

▶ **Tip:** You may want to drag the bottom of the Appearance panel group up to make it shorter (we did).

9 With the trumpet shapes still selected, choose Object > Group and leave the new group selected for the next section.

In the Appearance panel, the word "Group" appears at the top. With the group selected, you can now apply appearance attributes to the group and they will appear in the panel. The word "Contents" also appears below the word "Group." If you were to double-click the word "Contents" in the Appearance panel, you would see the appearance attributes of the individual items in the group.

▶ **Tip:** You can view all hidden attributes by choosing Show All Hidden Attributes from the Appearance panel menu.

Adding another stroke and fill

Artwork in Illustrator can have more than one stroke and fill applied to it to add interesting design elements. You'll now add another fill to an object using the Appearance panel.

1   With the trumpet group still selected, click the Add New Fill button (■) at the bottom of the Appearance panel. The first part of the figure shows what the panel looks like after clicking the Add New Fill button.

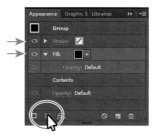

● **Note:** The figure has the Fill row toggled open revealing the content. Yours may not look like that, and that's okay.

New Stroke and Fill rows are added to the Appearance panel and applied to the group as a whole. The fill and stroke attributes tend to be applied on top of the fill and stroke attributes applied to the individual objects in the group.

2   Click the black Fill color box in the Fill attribute row until the Swatches panel appears. Click the pattern swatch named "Paper" to apply it to the Fill. Press the Escape key to hide the Swatches panel.

3   Click the disclosure triangle (▶) to the left of the word "Fill," if necessary. Click the word Opacity (under the Fill row) to show the Transparency panel and choose Multiply from the Blending Mode menu.

In the Appearance panel, appearance attributes with a disclosure triangle have options like Opacity that affect only that appearance attribute.

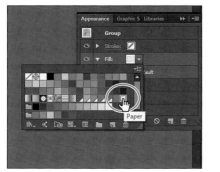

Change the fill.

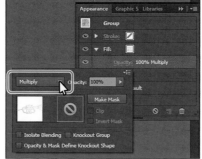

Edit the blending mode of the fill.

▶ **Tip:** Other ways to close panels that appear when clicking an underlined word, like "Stroke," include pressing the Escape key or clicking the Stroke attribute row.

4   Choose Select > Deselect, and then choose File > Save.

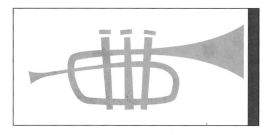

Now you'll add another stroke to text using the Appearance panel. This can be a great way to achieve interesting design effects with just one object.

5   In the Layers panel (Window > Layers), click the visibility column to the left of the Text layer to show its contents.

6   Select the Type tool (**T**) in the Tools panel and click twice on the black "JAZZ" text to select it.

In the Appearance panel, notice the Stroke (None) and the Fill (black). Also notice that you cannot add another stroke or fill to the text since the Add New Stroke and Add New Fill buttons are dimmed at the bottom of the panel.

7   Select the Selection tool and notice "Type" at the top of the Appearance panel.

With the type object selected (and not the text), you can now add multiple fills and strokes to text.

● **Note:** We dragged the bottom of the Appearance panel down to see more of the appearance attributes.

8   Click the Add New Fill button (▣) at the bottom of the Appearance panel.

A new fill row and stroke row are added above the word "Characters" in the Appearance panel.

9 With the new Fill attribute row selected, click the Fill color box and select the blue/green gradient swatch named "Jazz." This new fill will cover the existing black text fill. Press the Escape key to hide the swatches.

10 Click the Add New Fill button (⬛) at the bottom of the Appearance panel once more to add another fill.

A duplicate of the existing Fill row appears above.

11 Click the bottom Fill attribute row to select it. Click the Fill color box and select the pattern swatch named "Paper." Press the Escape key to hide the swatches.

Notice that the paper swatch doesn't show in the artwork. That's because it is beneath the Fill attribute row with the gradient applied. Like we mentioned earlier, the ordering of the attribute rows is important, much like the ordering of layers is important. The top appearance row shows on top of the appearance attributes beneath it.

▶ **Tip:** Depending on which attribute row is selected in the Attributes panel, the options in panels, like the Control panel, Gradient panel, and others, will affect the attribute selected.

Reordering appearance attributes

The ordering of the appearance attribute rows can greatly change how your artwork looks. In the Appearance panel, fills and strokes are listed in stacking order—top to bottom in the panel correlates to front to back in the artwork. You can reorder attribute rows in a way similar to dragging layers in the Layers panel to rearrange the stacking order. Now you'll change the appearance of the artwork by reordering attributes in the Appearance panel.

1   Click the disclosure triangle (▼) to the left of all of the appearance rows in the Appearance panel to hide their properties.

2   Drag the bottom Fill attribute row (with the Paper pattern swatch applied) up above the original Fill attribute row with the blue/green gradient.

▶ **Tip:** You can also apply blending modes and opacity changes to each Fill row to achieve different results.

Moving the new Fill attribute above the original Fill attribute changes the look of the artwork. The pattern fill is now covering the gradient fill.

3   Click the disclosure triangle to the left of the Fill attribute row with the Paper pattern fill. Click the word Opacity to show the Transparency panel and choose Multiply from the Blending Mode menu.

4   Choose Select > Deselect, and then choose File > Save.

Now that you've begun to explore the options in the Appearance panel, you'll begin adding effects to the artwork and use the Appearance panel for those as well.

Using live effects

Effects alter the appearance of an object without changing the underlying artwork. Applying an effect adds the effect to the object's appearance attribute, which you can edit, move, delete, or duplicate, at any time, in the Appearance panel.

● **Note:** When you apply a raster effect, the original vector data is rasterized using the document's raster effects settings, which determine the resolution of the resulting image. To learn about document raster effects settings, search for "Document raster effects settings" in Illustrator Help.

Artwork with a Drop Shadow effect applied.

There are two types of effects in Illustrator: *vector effects* and *raster effects*. In Illustrator, click the Effect menu item to see the different types of effects available.

- **Vector (Illustrator) effects:** The top half of the Effect menu contains vector effects. You can apply these effects only to vector objects or to the fill or stroke of a bitmap object in the Appearance panel. The following vector effects can be applied to both vector and bitmap objects: 3D effects, SVG filters, Warp effects, Transform effects, Drop Shadow, Feather, Inner Glow, and Outer Glow.
- **Raster (Photoshop) effects:** The bottom half of the Effect menu contains raster effects. You can apply them to either vector or bitmap objects.

In this section, you will first explore how to apply and edit effects. You will then explore a few of the more widely used effects in Illustrator to get an idea for the range of effects available.

Applying an effect

Effects are applied using the Effect menu or the Appearance panel and can be applied to objects, groups, or layers. You are first going to learn how to apply an effect using the Effect menu, and then you will apply an effect using the Appearance panel.

1   With the Selection tool (▶) selected, click the trumpet group on the artboard.

2   Choose Effect > Stylize > Drop Shadow from the Illustrator Effects section of the menu that appears.

3   In the Drop Shadow dialog box, change the following options:

    - Mode: **Multiply** (the default setting)

    - Opacity: **100%**

    - X Offset: **.03 in**

    - Y Offset: **.03 in**

    - Blur: **.04 in**

    - Darkness: **Selected, 50%**

4   Select Preview to see the drop shadow applied to the artwork. Click OK.

    Later in the lesson, you'll apply an effect using a different method.

5   Choose File > Save, and leave the trumpet group selected.

Editing an effect

Effects are live, so they can be edited after they are applied to an object. You can edit the effect in the Appearance panel by selecting the object with the effect applied, and then either clicking the name of the effect or double-clicking the attribute row in the Appearance panel. This displays the dialog box for that effect. Changes you make to the effect update in the artwork. In this section, you will edit the Drop Shadow effect applied to the trumpet group.

1   With the grouped trumpet shapes still selected and the Appearance panel showing, click the orange text "Drop Shadow" in the Appearance panel.

2   In the Drop Shadow dialog box, change Opacity to **75%**. Select Preview to see the change, and then click OK.

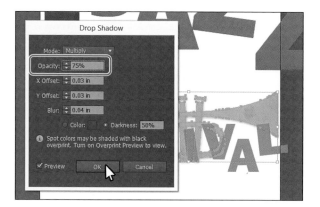

3   Choose Object > Ungroup to ungroup the trumpet shapes.

Notice that the drop shadow is no longer applied to the trumpet group. When an effect is applied to a group, it affects the group as a whole. If the objects are no longer grouped together, the effect is no longer applied.

4   Choose Edit > Undo Ungroup to regroup the artwork and apply the drop shadow again.

Styling text with a Warp effect

Text can have all sorts of effects applied, including a Warp, like you saw in Lesson 7, "Adding Type to a Poster." Next, you will use a Warp effect to warp the date text. The difference between the Warp you applied in Lesson 7 and this Warp effect is that this Warp effect can be turned on and off, edited, or removed easily.

1   With the Selection tool (▶) selected, select the text "May 10-17."

2   Choose Effect > Warp > Flag.

3   In the Warp Options dialog box, to create an arcing effect, set Bend to **20%**. Select Preview to preview the changes. Try choosing other styles from the Style menu, and then return to Flag. Try adjusting the Horizontal and Vertical Distortion sliders to see the effect. Make sure that the Distortion values are returned to **0**, and then click OK.

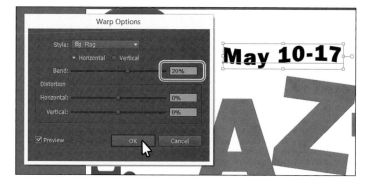

▶ **Tip:** In the Appearance panel, you can drag an attribute row, such as Drop Shadow, to the Delete Selected Item button (🗑) to delete it, or select the attribute row and click the Delete Selected Item button.

4　With the warped text object still selected, click the visibility icon () to the left of the "Warp: Flag" row in the Appearance panel to turn off visibility for the effect. Notice that the text is no longer warped on the artboard (see the figure below).

5　Select the Type tool (T) in the Tools panel, and select the text "10-17" on the artboard and change it to **10-18**.

6　Select all of the text "May 10-18" and change the Fill color to White in the Control panel.

If the Appearance panel is still open and the cursor is in the text, notice that the effect isn't listed in the panel. That's because the effect was applied to the type area, not to the text within.

7　Select the Selection tool (▶) in the Tools panel. Click the visibility column to the left of the "Warp: Flag" row in the Appearance panel, to turn on visibility for the effect so that the text is once again warped.

Since the text is white on a white background (for now), you won't be able to see the warp.

8　Choose Select > Deselect, and then choose File > Save.

Editing shapes with a Pathfinder effect

Pathfinder effects are similar to working with Pathfinder commands in the Pathfinder panel, except that they are applied as effects and do not change the underlying artwork. To learn more about the Pathfinder commands, see the "Working with the Pathfinder panel" section in Lesson 3, "Using Shapes to Create Artwork for a Postcard."

Applying the Offset Path effect

Next, you will offset the stroke for the "JAZZ" text. This process allows you to create the appearance of multiple stacked shapes.

1 With the Selection tool (➤) selected, click the "JAZZ" text object to select it.

2 Click the Stroke color in the Appearance panel, and make sure that the White swatch is selected in the Swatches panel. Press Enter or Return to close the Swatches panel, and return to the Appearance panel.

3 Make sure that the Stroke weight is **1 pt**.

4 With the Stroke attribute row selected in the Appearance panel, choose Effect > Path > Offset Path.

5 In the Offset Path dialog box, change the Offset to **−0.04 in**, select Preview, and then click OK.

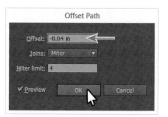

6 In the Appearance panel, click the disclosure triangle to the left of the words "Stroke: 1 pt" to toggle it open (if it's not already open). Notice that the "Offset Path" effect is a subset of Stroke. This indicates that the Offset Path effect is applied to only that Stroke.

7   Choose Select > Deselect, and then choose File > Save.

Applying a raster effect

As described earlier in the lesson, raster effects generate pixels rather than vector data. Raster effects include SVG Filters, all of the effects in the bottom portion of the Effect menu, and the Drop Shadow, Inner Glow, Outer Glow, and Feather commands in the Effect > Stylize submenu. You can apply them to either vector or bitmap objects.

Next, you will apply a raster (Photoshop) effect to the "FESTIVAL" text.

1   With the Selection tool (➤), click to select the "FESTIVAL" text.

2   Choose Effect > Texture > Texturizer.

When you choose most of the raster (Photoshop) effects (not all), the Filter Gallery dialog box opens. Similar to working with filters in Adobe Photoshop, where you can also access a Filter Gallery, in the Illustrator Filter Gallery, you can try out different raster effects to see how they affect your artwork.

3   With the Filter Gallery dialog box open, choose Fit In View from the view menu in the lower-left corner of the dialog box. That should fit the artwork in the preview area, so you can see how the effect alters the artwork.

The Filter Gallery dialog box, which is resizable, contains a preview area (labeled A); effect thumbnails that you can click to apply (labeled B); settings for the currently selected effect (labeled C); and the list of effects applied (labeled D). If you want to apply a different effect, expand a category in the middle panel of the dialog box, click a thumbnail, or choose an effect name from the menu in the upper-right corner of the dialog box.

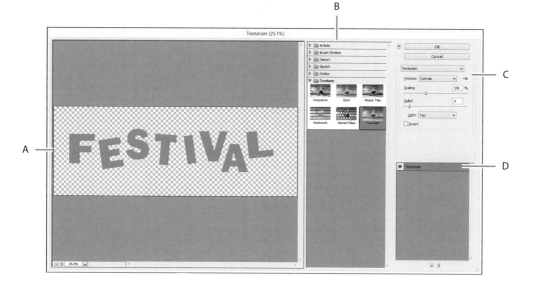

4 Change the Texturizer settings in the upper-right corner of the dialog box as follows (if necessary):

- Texture: **Canvas** (the default setting)
- Scaling: **110**
- Relief: **5**
- Light: **Top** (the default setting)

5 Click the eye icon (⊙) to the left of the name Texturizer to see the artwork without the effect applied. Click the same icon area again to preview the effect on the artwork. Click OK to apply the raster effect.

● **Note:** The Filter Gallery only lets you apply one effect at a time. If you want to apply multiple Photoshop effects, you can click OK to apply the current effect, and then choose another from the Effect menu.

Working with 3D effects

Using Illustrator 3D effects, you can create three-dimensional (3D) objects from your two-dimensional (2D) artwork. You can control the appearance of 3D objects with lighting, shading, rotation, and other attributes, such as mapping artwork to each surface of the three-dimensional object (mapping is allowed with Extrude & Bevel or Revolve). There are three 3D effects that you can apply to artwork: Extrude & Bevel, Revolve, and Rotate. Below are visual examples of each type of 3D effect:

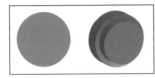

Extrude & Bevel 3D effect.

Revolve 3D effect.

Rotate 3D effect.

Applying a 3D Rotate effect

The Rotate effect is a simple way to rotate artwork in 3D. Next, you are going to rotate the JAZZ text.

1 With the Selection tool (➤), click to select the JAZZ text object.

2 Choose Effect > 3D > Rotate.

3 In the 3D Rotate Options dialog box, set the following options:

   • X axis: **10°**
   • Y axis: **−20°**
   • Z axis: **10°**
   • Perspective: **0°** (the default setting)
   • Surface: **No Shading** (the default setting)

   ● **Note:** 3D objects may display anti-aliasing artifacts onscreen, but these artifacts generally won't print or appear in artwork optimized for the Web.

4 Select Preview to see the effect applied (if it's not selected).

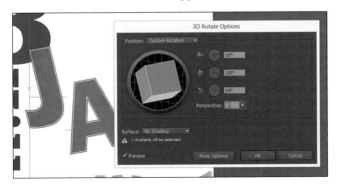

Notice the warning near the bottom of the 3D Rotate Options dialog box that states, "Gradients will be rasterized." This means that the gradient used in the JAZZ text fill will be rasterized (that is, displayed and printed as a bitmap graphic). The resolution (PPI) of the rasterized portion of the artwork is based on the settings in the Document Raster Effects Settings dialog box (Effect > Document Raster Effects Settings).

5 Click and drag the left edge of the face of the track cube (it's blue in color) to the right (see the figure). Notice the text rotate as you drag.

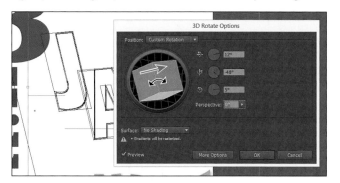

● **Note:** Depending on the speed of the computer you are working on and the amount of RAM available, it may take some time to process changes made. If that's the case, you can deselect Preview, change the options, and then select Preview at the end.

For unconstrained rotation, you can drag a track cube face. The front of the object is represented by the track cube's blue face, the object's top and bottom faces are light gray, the sides are medium gray, and the back face is dark gray.

6 Choose "Off-Axis Front" from the Position menu and click OK.

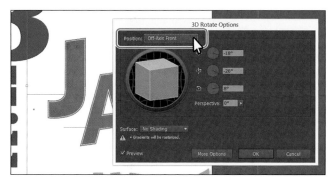

7 With the Selection tool, drag the text up to position it, like you see in the figure.

8 Choose Select > Deselect, and then choose File > Save.

● **Note:** Notice that every time you release the mouse button, Illustrator needs to process the change and redraw the 3D text. You will not see the 3D text as you drag; instead, you will see the text without the effect.

Using graphic styles

A *graphic style* is a saved set of appearance attributes that you can reuse. By applying graphic styles, you can quickly and globally change the appearance of objects and text.

The Graphic Styles panel (Window > Graphic Styles) lets you create, name, save, apply, and remove effects and attributes for objects, layers, and groups. You can also break the link between an object and an applied graphic style to edit that object's attributes without affecting other objects that use the same graphic style.

For example, if you have a map that uses a shape to represent a city, you can create a graphic style that paints the shape green and adds a drop shadow. You can then use that graphic style to paint all the city shapes on the map. If you decide to use a different color, you can change the fill color of the graphic style to blue. All the objects that use that graphic style are then updated to blue.

Applying an existing graphic style

You can apply graphic styles to your artwork from graphic style libraries that come with Illustrator. Now you'll add a graphic style to some of the text in the design.

1   Click the Graphic Styles panel tab. Click the Graphic Styles Libraries Menu button ([icon]) at the bottom of the panel, and choose Vonster Pattern Styles.

▶ **Tip:** Use the arrows at the bottom of the Vonster Pattern Styles library panel to load the previous or next Graphic Styles library in the panel.

2   With the Selection tool (▸), select the number 3 shape in the upper-left corner of the artboard. Make sure that the "JAZZ" text isn't selected.

3   Click the "Alyssa 1" graphic style in the Vonster Pattern Styles panel. Close the Vonster Pattern Styles panel.

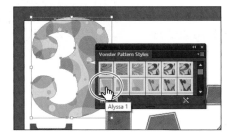

Clicking that style applies the appearance attributes to the selected "3" artwork and adds the graphic style to the Graphic Styles panel for the active document.

With the number 3 still selected, look in the Appearance panel to see the stroke and multiple fills applied to the selected artwork. Also notice "Path: Alyssa 1" at the top of the panel. This indicates that the graphic style named "Alyssa 1" is applied.

4   Click the Graphics Style panel tab to show the panel again. Click the JAZZ text, and then right-click and hold down the mouse button on the Alyssa 1 graphic style thumbnail in the Graphic Styles panel to preview the graphic style on the artwork. When you're finished previewing, release the mouse button.

Previewing a graphic style is a great way to see how it will affect the selected object, without actually applying it.

5   Choose File > Save.

● **Note:** You may see a warning icon appear on the left end of the Control panel. That's okay. This is a helpful indicator that the topmost fill/stroke is not active in the Appearance panel.

Creating and applying a graphic style

Now you'll create a new graphic style and apply that graphic style to artwork.

1   Click the number 3 again, and click the Appearance panel tab to show the panel. Click the Add New Fill button (▣) at the bottom of the Appearance panel.

● **Note:** You can drag the bottom of the Appearance panel down to see more of the attributes.

There should now be a total of three fills applied to the number 3. Also notice that the "Alyssa 1" is gone from the "Path" toward the top of the panel. This means that the graphic style is no longer applied to the artwork. The number 3 will not update if the Alyssa 1 graphic style is edited.

2   Make the following changes to the Fill attribute rows, using the figure as a guide:

- **Top Fill attribute row:** Click the Fill color and select the pattern swatch named "Lines." Press the Escape key to hide the swatches.

- **Middle Fill attribute row:** Click the Fill color and select the pattern swatch named "Paper." Click the disclosure triangle to the left of the same Fill row, and click the Opacity link below the Paper fill row to show the Transparency panel. Choose Luminosity from the Blending Mode menu. Press the Escape key to hide the Transparency panel.

- **Bottom Fill attribute row:** Click the Fill color and select the orange swatch named "Festival." Press the Escape key to hide the swatches.

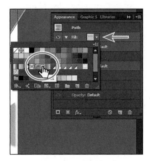
Top Fill attribute row.

Middle Fill attribute row.

Bottom Fill attribute row.

The number 3 should now have a series of textures and an orange color applied to the fill. Remember that the order of the attribute rows in the Appearance panel is very important. This is especially important when you change the Opacity blending modes and want to blend the appearance attributes to achieve certain visual effects. Blending modes affect attribute rows below the attribute row that the blend mode is applied to in the Appearance panel.

3   Leave the number 3 shape selected.

4   Click the Graphic Styles panel tab to show the Graphic Styles panel. Click the New Graphic Style button (🔳) at the bottom of the panel.

The appearance attributes from the number 3 are saved as a graphic style.

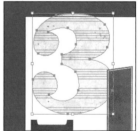

▶ **Tip:** To create a graphic style, you can also click to select the object that you are using to make the graphic style. In the Appearance panel, drag the appearance thumbnail at the top of the listing into the Graphic Styles panel. The panels can't be in the same panel group.

5   In the Graphic Styles panel, double-click the new graphic style thumbnail. In the Graphic Style Options dialog box, name the new style **Number**. Click OK.

6 Click the Appearance panel tab and, at the top of the Appearance panel, you will see "Path: Number."

This indicates that a graphic style named Number is applied to the selected artwork (a path). You could now apply the Number graphic style to other artwork.

7 Open the Layers panel (Window > Layers) and click the visibility column for the Background layer to show the black shape behind the other content on the artboard. Click the lock icon in the edit column to unlock the Background layer as well.

8 With the Selection tool, click the black rectangle in the background. In the Graphic Styles panel, click the graphic style named "Number" to apply the styling.

9 Choose Select > Deselect, and then choose File > Save.

Applying a graphic style to text

When you apply a graphic style to type, the fill color of the text overrides the fill color of the graphic style by default. If you deselect Override Character Color from the Graphic Styles panel menu (▤), the fill color (if there is one) in the graphic style will override the color of the text. If you choose Use Text For Preview from the Graphic Styles panel menu (▤), you can then right-click and hold down the mouse button on a graphic style to preview the graphic style on the text.

Updating a graphic style

Once you create a graphic style, you can still edit the object that the style is applied to. You can also update a graphic style, and all artwork with that style applied will update its appearance as well.

1 With the Selection tool (▶) selected, click the number 3 to select it.

   Look in the Graphic Styles panel; you will see that the "Number" graphic style thumbnail is highlighted (has a border around it), indicating that it is applied.

2 Click the Appearance panel tab. Notice the text "Path: Number" at the top of the panel, indicating that the Number graphic style is applied. This is another way to tell if a graphic style is applied to selected artwork.

3 Click the Fill color for the bottom appearance row (the one with the orange color). Select the purple swatch named "Hills." Press the Escape key to hide the swatches.

   Notice that the "Path: Number" text at the top of the Appearance panel is now just "Path," telling you that the graphic style is no longer applied to the selected artwork.

4 Click the Graphic Styles panel tab to see that the Number graphic style no longer has a highlight (border) around it, which means that the graphic style is no longer applied.

5 Press the Option (Mac OS) or Alt (Windows) key, and drag the selected number 3 shape on top of the Number graphic style thumbnail in the Graphic Styles panel. Release the mouse button, and then release the modifier key when the thumbnail is highlighted. The number 3 and the background rectangle now look the same, since the Number graphic style has been applied to both objects.

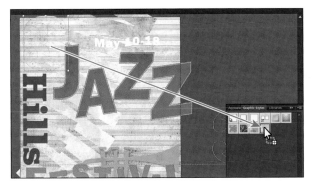

6　Choose Select > Deselect.

7　Click the Appearance panel tab. You will see "No Selection: Number" at the top of the panel (you may need to scroll up).

When you apply appearance settings, graphic styles, and more to artwork, the next shape you draw will have the appearance settings listed in the Appearance panel.

8　Click to select the rectangle in the background that has the Number graphic style applied.

Next, you will remove all formatting from the rectangle and then add a black fill again.

9　Click the Clear Appearance button (... ⊘) at the bottom of the Appearance panel.

▶ **Tip:** If you were to click the Clear Appearance button with nothing selected, you would set the default appearance for new artwork to no fill and no stroke.

With artwork selected, the Clear Appearance button removes all appearance attributes applied to selected artwork, including any stroke or fill.

● **Note:** The figure shows the result after clicking the Clear Appearance button.

10 Click the Fill color for the Fill appearance row and select the Black swatch.

11 Choose Select > Deselect, and then choose File > Save.

Applying a graphic style to a layer

When a graphic style is applied to a layer, everything added to that layer has that same style applied to it. Now you'll apply a Drop Shadow graphic style that comes with Illustrator to the Text layer; this will apply the style to all of the contents of that layer at once.

● **Note:** If you apply a graphic style to artwork and then apply a graphic style to the layer (or sublayer) that it's on, the graphic style formatting is added to the appearance of the artwork—it's cumulative. This can change the artwork in ways you didn't expect, since applying a graphic style to the layer will be added to the formatting of the artwork.

1 In Layers panel, click the target icon (◉) for the Text layer.

This selects the layer content and targets the layer for any appearance attributes.

▶ **Tip:** In the Layers panel, you can drag a target icon to the Trash button (🗑) at the bottom of the Layers panel to remove the appearance attributes.

2 Click the Graphic Styles panel icon (▦), and then click the Drop Shadow graphic style thumbnail to apply the style to the layer and all its contents.

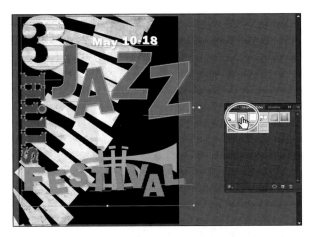

The target icon in the Layers panel for the Text layer is now shaded.

3 Click the Appearance panel tab and you should see, with all of the artwork on the Text layer still selected, the words "Layer: Drop Shadow."

This is telling you that the layer target icon is selected in the Layers panel and that the Drop Shadow graphic style is applied to that layer.

▶ **Tip:** In the Graphic Styles panel, graphic style thumbnails that show a small box with a red slash (▱) indicate that the graphic style does not contain a stroke or fill. It may just be a drop shadow or outer glow, for instance.

4 Choose Select > Deselect, and then choose File > Save.

Applying multiple graphic styles

You can apply a graphic style to an object that already has a graphic style applied. This can be useful if you want to add properties to an object from another graphic style. After you apply a graphic style to selected artwork, you can then Option-click (Mac OS) or Alt-click (Windows) another graphic style thumbnail to add the graphic style formatting to the existing formatting, rather than replacing it.

Scaling strokes and effects

In Illustrator, when scaling (resizing) content, any strokes and effects that are applied do not change. For instance, suppose you scale a circle with a 2-pt. stroke from small to the size of the artboard. The shape may change size, but the stroke will remain 2 pt. by default. That can change the appearance of scaled artwork in a way that you didn't intend, so you'll need to watch out for that when transforming artwork.

1   Click the trumpet group to select it.

Next, you will make the trumpet group larger, but you will also scale the drop shadow effect applied to it proportionally.

● **Note:** If you choose Window > Transform to open the Transform panel, you may need to choose Show Options from the panel menu.

2   Click X, Y, W, or H link in the Control panel to reveal the Transform panel (Window > Transform). Select Scale Strokes & Effects at the bottom of the Transform panel. Click the Constrain Width And Height Proportions button (🔗). Change the Width (W) to **12.7 in**. Press the Tab key to tab to the next field. The Height should change proportionally with the Width.

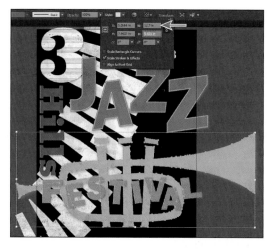

If you were to open the Drop Shadow options in the Appearance panel for the trumpet group, you would see that the values have adjusted according to the sizing. If "Scale Strokes & Effects" weren't selected, the drop shadow values would be the same before and after the transformation.

3   Choose Select > Deselect.

4   Choose File > Save, and then choose File > Close.

Review questions

1 How do you add a second stroke to artwork?

2 What's the difference between applying a graphic style to a *layer* versus applying it to *selected artwork*?

3 Name two ways to apply an effect to an object.

4 When you apply a Photoshop (raster) effect to vector artwork, what happens to the artwork?

5 Where can you access the options for effects applied to an object?

Review answers

1 To add a second stroke to an object, click the Add New Stroke button (■) in the Appearance panel or choose Add New Stroke from the Appearance panel menu. A stroke is added to the top of the appearance list. It has the same color and stroke weight as the original.

2 When a style is applied to a single object, other objects on that layer are not affected. For example, if a triangle object has a Roughen effect applied to its path and you move it to another layer, it retains the Roughen effect.

After a graphic style is applied to a layer, everything you add to the layer has that style applied to it. For example, if you create a circle on Layer 1 and then move that circle to Layer 2, which has a Drop Shadow effect applied, the circle adopts that effect.

3 You can apply an effect to an object by selecting the object and then choosing the effect from the Effect menu. You can also apply an effect by selecting the object, clicking the Add New Effect button (*fx.*) at the bottom of the Appearance panel, and then choosing the effect from the menu that appears.

4 Applying a Photoshop effect to artwork generates pixels rather than vector data. Photoshop effects include SVG Filters, all of the effects in the bottom portion of the Effect menu, and the Drop Shadow, Inner Glow, Outer Glow, and Feather commands in the Effect > Stylize submenu. You can apply them to either vector or bitmap objects.

5 You can edit effects applied to selected artwork by clicking the effect link in the Appearance panel to access the effect options.

12 CREATING A PRODUCT MOCKUP IN PERSPECTIVE

Lesson overview

In this lesson, you'll learn how to do the following:

- Understand perspective drawing.

- Use grid presets.

- Adjust the perspective grid.

- Draw and transform content in perspective.

- Edit grid planes and content.

- Bring content into perspective.

- Create text and bring it into perspective.

- Bring symbols into perspective.

- Edit symbols in perspective.

 This lesson takes approximately 60 minutes to complete.

Download the project files for this lesson from the Lesson & Update Files tab on your Account page at www.peachpit.com and store them on your computer in a convenient location, as described in the Getting Started section of this book.

Your Account page is also where you'll find any updates to the chapters or to the lesson files. Look on the Lesson & Update Files tab to access the most current content.

In Adobe Illustrator CC, you can easily draw or render artwork in perspective using the perspective grid. The perspective grid allows you to approximately represent a scene, on a flat surface, as the human eye naturally perceives it.

Getting started

In this lesson, you'll explore working with the perspective grid by adding content to and editing content on the grid. Before you begin, you'll restore the default preferences for Adobe Illustrator. Then, you'll open the finished art file for this lesson to see what you'll create.

● **Note:** If you have not already downloaded the project files for this lesson to your computer from your Account page, make sure to do so now. See the "Getting Started" section at the beginning of this book.

1   To ensure that the tools and panels function exactly as described in this lesson, delete or deactivate (by renaming) the Adobe Illustrator CC preferences file. See "Restoring default preferences" in the Getting Started section at the beginning of the book.

2   Start Adobe Illustrator CC.

3   Choose File > Open, and open the L12_end.ai file in the Lessons > Lesson12 folder on your hard disk.

    You are going to create some product boxes for a makeup ad.

4   Choose View > Fit Artboard In Window and leave the file open for reference, or choose File > Close.

5   Choose File > Open. Navigate to the Lessons > Lesson12 folder on your hard disk. Open the L12_start.ai file.

6   Choose View > Fit Artboard In Window.

● **Note:** In Mac OS, when opening lesson files, you may need to click the round, green button in the upper-left corner of the Document window to maximize the window's size.

7   Choose File > Save As. In the Save As dialog box, navigate to the Lesson12 folder and name the file **MakeupAd.ai**. Leave the Format option set to Adobe Illustrator (ai) (Mac OS) or Save As Type option set to Adobe Illustrator (*.AI) (Windows), and then click Save. In the Illustrator Options dialog box, leave the Illustrator options at their default settings, and then click OK.

8   Choose Reset Essentials from the workspace switcher in the Application bar.

    ● **Note:** If you don't see "Reset Essentials" in the menu, choose Window > Workspace > Essentials before choosing Window > Workspace > Reset Essentials.

Understanding the perspective grid

In Illustrator, using the Perspective Grid tool (⊞) and the Perspective Selection tool (▶⊙), you can easily draw or render artwork in perspective. You can define the perspective grid in one-point, two-point, or three-point perspective, define a scale, move the grid planes, and draw objects directly in perspective. You can even attach flat art onto the grid planes by dragging with the Perspective Selection tool.

1 Click the Layers panel icon (◪) to show the Layers panel. In the Layers panel, select the Perspective layer. Click the Layers panel icon to collapse the panel again.

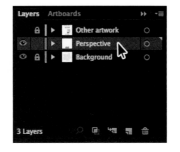

2 Select the Perspective Grid tool (⊞) in the Tools panel.

The default two-point perspective grid (which is non-printing) appears on the artboard and can be used to draw and snap content in perspective. The two-point grid (for short) is composed of several *planes* or surfaces, by default—left (blue), right (orange), and a ground plane (green).

The figure below shows the default perspective grid by itself, with all of its options showing. It may be helpful to refer back to this figure as you progress through the lesson.

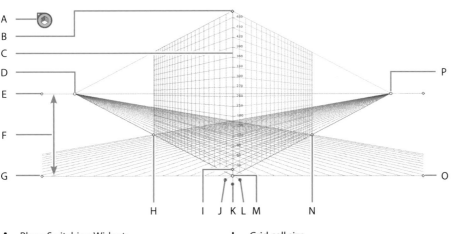

A. Plane Switching Widget
B. Vertical grid extent
C. Perspective Grid ruler
(not showing, by default)
D. Left vanishing point
E. Horizon level
F. Horizon height
G. Left ground level point
H. Extent of grid

I. Grid cell size
J. Right grid plane control
K. Horizontal grid plane control
L. Left grid plane control
M. Origin
N. Extent of grid
O. Right ground level point
P. Right vanishing point

Working with the perspective grid

In order to begin working with content in perspective, it is helpful to see and set up the perspective grid the way you want.

Using a preset grid

● **Note:** A one-point perspective can be very useful for roads, railway tracks, or buildings viewed so that the front is directly facing the viewer. Two-point perspective is useful for drawing a cube, such as a building, or for two roads going off into the distance, and it typically has two vanishing points. Three-point perspective is usually used for buildings seen from above or below.

To begin the lesson, you'll work with the perspective grid, starting with an Illustrator preset. The perspective grid, by default, is set up as a two-point perspective. You can easily change the grid to a one-point, two-point, or three-point grid using presets, which is what you'll do next.

1   Choose View > Perspective Grid > Three Point Perspective > [3P-Normal View]. Notice that the grid changes to a three-point perspective.

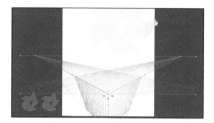

In addition to showing vanishing points for each wall, there is now a point showing those walls receding into the ground or high in space.

2   Choose View > Perspective Grid > Two Point Perspective > [2P-Normal View]. Notice that the grid changes back to the default two-point perspective.

Adjusting the perspective grid

To create artwork in the perspective you want, you can adjust the grid using the Perspective Grid tool (▦) or using the View > Perspective Grid > Define Grid command. You can make changes to the grid if you have content on it, although it will be easier to establish what your grid looks like before you add content. In this section, you'll make a few adjustments to the grid. First, you'll move the grid where you're going to draw some boxes. You can also draw content in the default grid position and move that content later.

1   Make sure that the Smart Guides are on (View > Smart Guides).

2   With the Perspective Grid tool (▦) selected, position the pointer over the left ground-level point (circled in the figure). When the pointer changes (▶₊), drag it to the left and up to move the whole perspective grid. Match the position in the figure as closely as you can, but it does not have to match exactly.

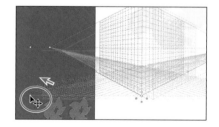

The left and right ground-level points allow you to drag the perspective grid to different parts of the artboard or to a different artboard altogether.

Next, you'll change the height of the grid.

3 With the Perspective Grid tool, position the pointer over the Vertical Grid Extent point (indicated by the red X in the figure). When the pointer changes (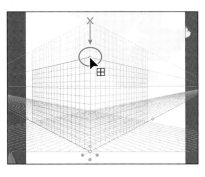), drag it down to *roughly* match the figure to shorten the vertical extent.

Dragging the vertical extent down is a way to minimize the grid if you are drawing objects that are less precise, as you will see later in the lesson.

▶ **Tip:** The location of the ground level in relation to the horizon line will determine how far above or below eye level the object will be viewed.

4 Position the pointer over the right end of the horizon line, and the pointer shows a vertical arrow (↕). Click and drag up a bit until you see approximately 270 pt in the gray measurement label next to the pointer. The closer you are zoomed in to the grid, the finer the increments that you can adjust it with.

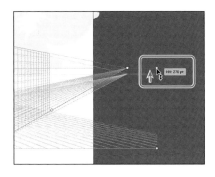

Next, you will adjust the planes so that you can draw a product box that shows one side more than the other. This requires that you move a vanishing point.

5 Press Command+− (Mac OS) or Ctrl+− (Windows), twice, to zoom out.

6 Choose View > Perspective Grid > Lock Station Point.

This locks the left and right vanishing points so that they move together.

7 With the Perspective Grid tool, position the pointer over the right vanishing point (circled in the figure). When the pointer includes a horizontal arrow (↔), drag to the right until the measurement label shows an X value of approximately 15 in.

This changes both planes on the grid, and the product box you create will have a more visible right face.

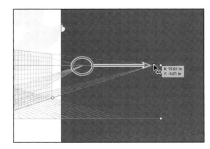

▶ **Tip:** If you had artwork on the grid, it would move with the grid.

Setting the grid up for your drawing is an important step in creating the artwork with the perspective you desire. Next, you will access some of the perspective grid options you have already adjusted, and more, using the Define Perspective Grid dialog box.

8 Choose View > Fit Artboard In Window.

9 Choose View > Perspective Grid > Define Grid.

▶ **Tip:** After setting the Define Perspective Grid settings, you can save them as a preset to access later. In the Define Perspective Grid dialog box, change the settings, and then click the Save Preset button (⬆️).

10 In the Define Perspective Grid dialog box, change the following options:

- Units: **Inches**

- Gridline Every: **0.3 in**

Changing the Gridline Every option adjusts the grid cell size and can help you be more precise when drawing and editing on the grid, since content snaps to the lines of the grid by default. Notice that you can also change the Scale of the grid, which you might want to do if real-world measurements are involved. You can also edit settings, like Horizon Height and Viewing Angle, on the artboard, using the Perspective Grid tool. Leave the Grid Color & Opacity settings at their defaults.

● **Note:** If the rest of the values in the Define Perspective Grid dialog box don't match the figure, that's okay. Don't attempt to match the values since it can change your grid in unexpected ways.

When you have finished making changes, click OK. The grid will change in appearance slightly. The grid should now look pretty close to this (but doesn't have to match *exactly*):

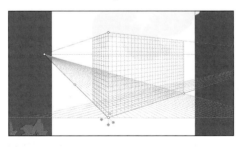

● **Note:** To learn more about the options in the Define Perspective Grid dialog box, search for "Perspective drawing" in Illustrator Help (Help > Illustrator Help).

11 Choose View > Perspective Grid > Lock Grid.

This command restricts the grid movement and other grid-editing features of the Perspective Grid tool. You can only change the visibility and the grid plane position, which you will work with later in this lesson.

● **Note:** When you select a tool other than the Perspective Grid tool (⬛), you cannot edit the perspective grid. Also, if the perspective grid is locked you cannot edit most of the grid settings with the Perspective Grid tool. You can edit a locked grid by choosing View > Perspective Grid > Define Grid.

12 Choose File > Save.

Drawing objects in perspective

To draw objects in perspective, you can use the line group tools or the rectangle group tools (except for the Flare tool) while the grid is visible. Before you begin drawing using any of these tools, you need to select a grid plane to attach the content to, using the Plane Switching Widget or keyboard shortcuts.

When the perspective grid is showing, a Plane Switching Widget appears in the upper-left corner of the Document window by default. The grid plane that is selected in the Plane Switching Widget is the active grid plane of the perspective grid to which you'll add content. In the widget, you can select the planes, as well as see their keyboard shortcut when you hover over each part of the widget.

A. Left Grid(1)
B. Horizontal Grid(2)
C. Right Grid(3)
D. No Active Grid(4)

1 Select the Rectangle tool (■) in the Tools panel.

2 Select Left Grid(1), in the Plane Switching Widget (if it's not already selected).

3 Position the pointer at the origin of the perspective grid (where the two planes meet at the bottom). Notice that the cursor has an arrow pointing to the left (◄┤), indicating that you are about to draw on the left grid plane. Drag up and to the left, until the gray measurement label shows an approximate width of 2.4 in and a height of approximately 3 in. As you drag, the pointer should be snapping to the gridlines.

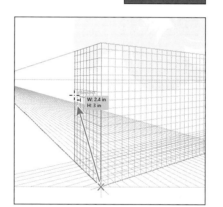

Zooming in brings into view more gridlines that are closer to the vanishing point. That's why, depending on the zoom level, your grid may not match the figures exactly, and that's okay.

> **Tip:** When drawing in perspective, you will find that you can still use the usual keyboard shortcuts for drawing objects, such as Shift-drag to constrain.

> **Tip:** You can turn off grid snapping by choosing View > Perspective Grid > Snap To Grid. Snapping is enabled by default.

4 With the rectangle selected, change the Fill color in the Control panel to the orange/red swatch named "Box Left." Press the Escape key to hide the Swatches panel.

5 Change the Stroke color to None (▱), in the Control panel.

There are many ways to add content to the perspective grid. Next, you'll create another rectangle a different way.

6   Press Command++ (Mac OS) or Ctrl++ (Windows), twice, to zoom in to the grid.

7   With the Rectangle tool still selected, click Right Grid(3) in the Plane Switching Widget to draw in perspective on the right grid plane.

8   Position the pointer over the upper-right corner of the rectangle you drew. When the word "anchor" appears, click. In the Rectangle dialog box, the width and height of the last rectangle you drew are showing. Click OK.

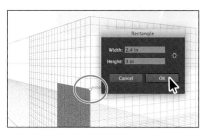

Notice that the pointer now has an arrow pointing to the right (⊢►), indicating that content you create will appear on the right grid plane.

● **Note:** To learn more about working with graphic styles, see Lesson 11, "Exploring Creative Uses of Effects and Graphic Styles."

9   Click the Graphic Styles panel (▦) to show the panel. With the new rectangle still selected, click the graphic style named "Box Right" to apply it.

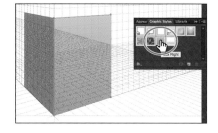

A *graphic style* is something you can use to save formatting from content you create and then apply it elsewhere. It's a great way to apply a gradient to another object so that it looks the same as the first one.

10 With the Rectangle tool still selected, click Horizontal Grid(2) in the Plane Switching Widget to draw in perspective on the ground (horizontal) plane.

11 Position the pointer over the upper-left corner point of the first rectangle you drew (on the left plane). When the word "anchor" appears, along with a large, hollow anchor point, click and drag to the upper-right corner point of the second rectangle you created. When a large, hollow anchor point appears on the second anchor point, release the mouse button.

▶ **Tip:** You can also show and hide the perspective grid by pressing Shift+Command+I (Mac OS) or Shift+Ctrl+I (Windows) to toggle back and forth.

12 With the rectangle selected, change the Fill color in the Control panel to the orange/red swatch named "Box Top."

13 Choose View > Perspective Grid > Hide Grid to hide the perspective grid and to see your artwork.

Selecting and transforming objects in perspective

You can select objects in perspective using selection tools, like the Selection tool (▶) and using the Perspective Selection tool (▶⬡). The Perspective Selection tool uses the active plane settings to select the objects. If you use the Selection tool to drag an object that was drawn in perspective, it maintains its original perspective, but it doesn't change to match the perspective grid.

Next, you will move and resize several of the rectangles you drew.

1 Choose View > Fit Artboard In Window.

2 Choose View > Perspective Grid > Show Grid.

3 Position the pointer over the Perspective Grid tool (⊞), click and hold down the mouse button, and then select the Perspective Selection tool (▶⬡). Click the rectangle with the gradient fill on the right grid plane to select it. Notice that the right grid plane, Right Grid(3), is now selected in the Plane Switching Widget.

4 With the Perspective Selection tool selected, drag the upper-right point of the rectangle up and to the left. When the measurement label shows a width of about 2.1 in and a height of 3.3 in, release the mouse button. Make sure that the rectangle is snapping to the gridlines.

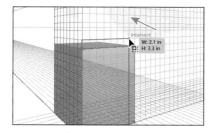

> **Tip:** Zooming in to the grid may make it easier when resizing content.

Notice that the rectangle that you resized is behind the rectangle that is the top of the box. Content on the perspective grid has the same stacking order as content you draw off of the perspective grid.

5 Choose Object > Arrange > Bring To Front.

6 With the Perspective Selection tool, click to select the first rectangle you created (on the left plane). Click the word "Transform" in the Control panel, and then click the bottom, middle point of the reference point locator (▦) in the Control panel. With the Constrain Width And Height Proportions option deselected (⬚), change the Height to **3.3 in** (or the same height as the shape on the right grid plane if your height is different).

> ● **Note:** Depending on the resolution of your screen, you may see the Transform options in the Control panel.

7   Select the Zoom tool (🔍) in the Tools panel, and click several times on the top of the box to zoom in.

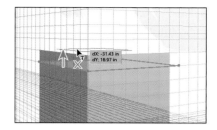

8   Select the Perspective Selection tool. Click to select the orange/red rectangle that is the top of the box. Drag the rectangle up from its center slightly above the other two rectangles.

Note: Select the top of the box (the rectangle) on its left side, since the right side of the box is arranged on top of it.

Dragging artwork on the horizontal grid up or down with the Perspective Selection tool makes it smaller and larger. Dragging it up moves the artwork "farther away" in perspective, and dragging it down moves it "closer" in perspective.

▶ **Tip:** You can also move objects from one plane to another using a keyboard command. With the objects selected, begin dragging them with the Perspective Selection tool, without releasing the mouse button yet. Press the number 1, 2, or 3 key (depending on which grid you intend to attach the objects to) to switch to the grid plane of your choice. These keyboard commands only work from the main keyboard and not from the extended numeric keypad.

9   Press Command++ (Mac OS) or Ctrl++ (Windows), twice, to zoom in to the grid.

10 Drag the leftmost point of the top rectangle so that it snaps to the upper-left corner of the rectangle on the left plane. Drag the rightmost point of the top rectangle so that it snaps to the upper-right corner of the rectangle on the right plane.

Snap the left anchor point.

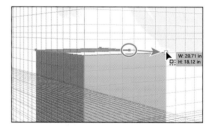

Snap the right anchor point.

11 Choose Select > Deselect, and then choose File > Save.

Duplicating content in perspective

You can easily duplicate content on the grid using copy and paste or other methods. Next, you will duplicate an object in perspective, as well as move an object perpendicular to an existing object.

1 Choose View > Fit Artboard In Window.

2 Choose View > Perspective Grid > Unlock Grid, so you can edit the grid again.

3 Position the pointer over the Perspective Selection tool (▶🗗), click and hold down the mouse button, and then select the Perspective Grid tool (▦). Position the pointer over the right grid extent widget, indicated by the red X in the figure below. When the pointer changes (▶▦), drag to the left until it reaches the right edge of the rectangle.

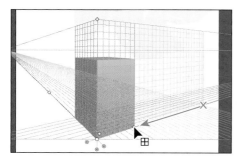

Changing the extent of the grid plane allows you to see more or less of the gridlines.

Next, you will begin to create another product box to the left of the box you've already created. To do this, you will copy content.

4 Select the Perspective Selection tool (▶🗗) in the Tools panel. Click to select the gradient-filled rectangle on the right grid plane. Begin dragging the rectangle to the left. As you drag, press Option+Shift (Mac OS) or Alt+Shift (Windows). Stop dragging when the measurement labels shows a dX value of –1.4 in. Release the mouse button, and then release the keys.

▶ **Tip:** You can also use the Transform Again command (Object > Transform > Transform Again) or the keyboard shortcut Command+D (Mac OS) or Ctrl+D (Windows).

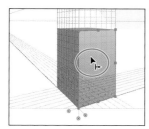 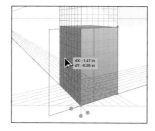

The Shift key constrains the movement to 45 degrees on the grid, and the Option (Mac OS) or Alt (Windows) key copies the object.

5 Drag the upper-right point of the new rectangle up and to the left to make the rectangle narrower and taller. Stop dragging when the measurement label shows an approximate width of 0.62 in and a height of 5.8 in.

▶ **Tip:** For more precision, you can also zoom in on the artwork or change the size of the selected rectangle by changing the W and H values in the Control panel or in the Transform panel (Window > Transform).

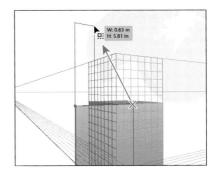

Moving objects in a perpendicular direction

With the new rectangle in place, you are going to move the rectangle in a direction perpendicular to the current location. This technique is useful when creating parallel objects, such as the legs of a chair.

● **Note:** The keyboard shortcut 5, which is for perpendicular movement (and the keyboard shortcuts 1, 2, 3, and 4 for plane switching) while drawing or moving objects, works only from the main keyboard and not from the extended numeric keypad.

1 With the rectangle still selected, hold down the number 5 key and drag the rectangle to the right a bit. When the measurement label shows a dX value of approximately 0.25 in, release the mouse, and then release the 5 key.

This action moves the object parallel to its current location. You could also press the Option key (Mac OS) or Alt key (Windows), while dragging, to copy the object that you are dragging.

2 Press the Escape key to hide the perspective grid.

● **Note:** If the new rectangle is now behind the other shapes, choose Object > Arrange > Bring To Front.

3 Choose Select > Deselect, and then choose File > Save.

Moving planes and objects together

As you saw in the beginning of this lesson, it's usually best to adjust the grid before there is artwork on it. But Illustrator allows you to move objects perpendicularly, similar to what you just did, by moving the grid planes instead. This can be better for more precise perpendicular movement.

Next, you will move a grid plane and artwork together.

1 Press Command+Shift+I (Mac OS) or Ctrl+Shift+I (Windows) to show the perspective grid again.

2 Select the Zoom tool (🔍), and click the lower-left corner of the right face of the larger box twice, slowly, to zoom in to the grid.

3 Select the Perspective Selection tool (▶▣). Position the pointer over the right grid plane control (circled in the figure). When the pointer changes (▶↔), drag to the right until D: 0.5 in appears in the measurement label, and then release the mouse button.

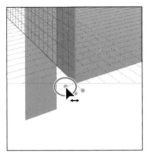
Position the pointer.

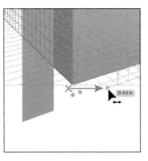
Drag the right grid plane.

Notice how the plane moved but the artwork stayed in place. Next, you will put the right grid plane back where it was.

4 Double-click the same right grid plane control you just dragged (circled in the figure). In the Right Vanishing Plane dialog box, change the Location to **0 in**, make sure that Do Not Move is selected, and click OK.

Edit the grid plane control.

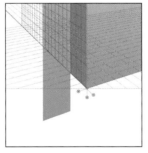
Notice the result.

▶ **Tip:** If you move a plane using the grid plane control, you can also choose Edit > Undo Perspective Grid Edit to put the plane back to its original location.

In the Right Vanishing Plane dialog box, the Do Not Move option allows you to move the grid plane and not the objects on it. The Copy All Objects option allows you to move the grid plane and to bring a copy of the objects on the grid plane with it. The Location option in the Right Vanishing Plane dialog box starts at the station point, which is 0. The station point is indicated by the very small green diamond on the perspective grid, above the horizontal grid control.

5   With the Perspective Selection tool still selected, double-click the left grid plane control (an arrow is pointing to it in the figure). In the Left Vanishing Plane dialog box, change the Location to −**1.4 in**, select Copy All Objects, and click OK.

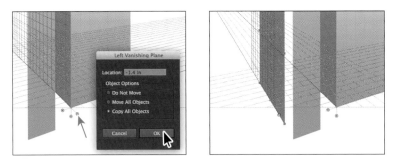

▶ **Tip:** If you select an object or objects on the grid plane first and then drag the grid plane control while holding down the Shift key, only the selected objects move with the grid plane.

This moves the left plane to the left (positive values move the plane to the right) and copies the rectangle, moving the copy as well. There are also a lot of keyboard commands associated with moving grid planes. You can hold down the Option (Mac OS) or Alt key (Windows) and drag a grid plane control to move the grid plane and copy the content. Dragging a grid plane control while pressing the Shift key moves the objects with the grid plane without copying them.

Next, you'll resize the new rectangle so that it can become the left side of the tall box. For the following step, reference the figure as you progress.

6   Drag the lower-right point of the new rectangle, snapping it to the lower-left corner of the tall rectangle.

7   Choose View > Fit Artboard In Window.

8   Drag the upper-right corner point of the new rectangle up, snapping it to the upper-left corner of the tall rectangle.

9   Drag the left, middle point of the rectangle to the right until a width of approximately 0.65 in shows in the measurement label.

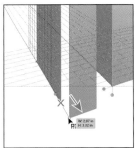
Drag the lower-right point.

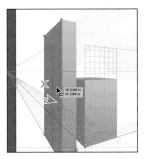
Drag the upper-right point.   Change the width.

10   Choose Select > Deselect, and then choose File > Save.

Bringing content into perspective

If you have already created content that is not in perspective, Illustrator provides an option to bring objects into perspective on an active plane in the perspective grid. You will now add a flower logo to both boxes.

1 With the Perspective Selection tool () selected, select Right Grid(3) in the Plane Switching Widget to make sure that the flower will be added to the right grid plane.

▶ **Tip:** You can also select the active plane by pressing keyboard shortcuts: 1=Left Grid, 2=Horizontal Grid, 3=Right Grid, and 4=No Active Grid.

2 With the Perspective Selection tool, drag one of the red flowers off of the lower-left corner of the artboard onto the right side of the larger box.

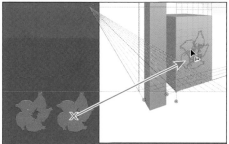

● **Note:** Instead of dragging an object onto the plane using the Perspective Selection tool, you can also select the object with the Perspective Selection tool, choose the plane using the Plane Switching Widget, and then choose Object > Perspective > Attach To Active Plane. This adds the content to the active plane, but it doesn't change its appearance.

The artwork is added to the grid that is selected in the Plane Switching Widget and is behind the rectangles in the stacking order.

3 Choose Object > Arrange > Bring To Front.

4 Choose View > Zoom In, a few times, to zoom in to the boxes.

Next, you will scale the flower artwork, making it smaller.

5 With the Perspective Selection tool, press Shift+Option (Mac OS) or Shift+Alt (Windows) and drag the upper-right corner of the flower shape toward the center until an approximate width of 1.5 in shows in the measurement label. You won't have to drag very far.

6 Choose Select > Deselect, and then choose File > Save.

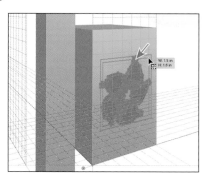

Drawing with no active grid

There will be times when you need to draw or add content that is not meant to be in perspective. In a case like that, you can select No Active Grid in the Plane Switching Widget to draw without regard to the grid. You will now add a rectangle to the background of the ad.

1 Choose View > Fit Artboard In Window.

2 Click the Layers panel icon () to show the Layers panel. In the Layers panel, select the Background layer. Click the lock icon (🔒) to the left of the Background name in the panel to unlock the content of the Background layer. Leave the panel showing.

3 Select the Rectangle tool (⬛) in the Tools panel. Click No Active Grid(4) in the Plane Switching Widget.

Note: You can close the Transform panel group that opens by default after drawing a rectangle.

4 Starting from the upper-left corner of the artboard, drag down to the lower-right corner of the artboard to create a rectangle the size of the artboard, as shown in the figure below.

5 Click the Graphic Styles panel icon (▦) to show the panel. With the new rectangle still selected, position the pointer over the graphic style thumbnail with the yellow tool tip that shows "Background" and click to apply the style.

6 Choose Object > Arrange > Send To Back.

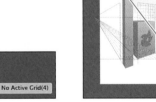

Select No Active Grid.　　Create the rectangle.

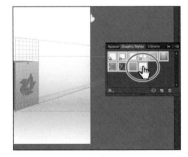

Apply the graphic style.

7 In the Layers panel, click the edit column to the left of the Background name in the panel to lock the content of the Background layer.

8 Select the Perspective layer so that any content you add will be added to the Perspective layer. Click the Layers panel tab to hide the panel.

9 Choose Select > Deselect (if necessary).

Adding and editing text in perspective

You cannot add text directly to a perspective plane when the grid is visible. However, you can bring text into perspective after creating it off of the perspective grid. Next, you will add some text, and then edit it in perspective.

1   Select the Type tool (**T**) in the Tools panel. Click in a blank area on the artboard and type **La Nouvelle**, press Enter or Return, and then type **Femme**.

2   Select the text with the Type tool, change the Font to Trajan Pro 3 (or another font if you don't have that one), ensure that the Font Style is Regular, and change the Font Size to **20 pt** in the Control panel.

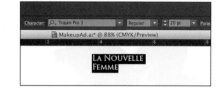

Note: If you don't see the Font Formatting options in the Control panel, click the word "Character" in the Control panel to reveal the Character panel.

3   Click the Align Center button (⊞) in the Control panel to align the text to center.

Note: If you don't see the Align options, click the word "Paragraph" in the Control panel to reveal the Paragraph panel.

4   Select the Perspective Selection tool (▶□) in the Tools panel. Press the number 3 key on the keyboard to select the Right Grid(3) in the Plane Switching Widget. Drag the text below the red flower on the right side of the larger box.

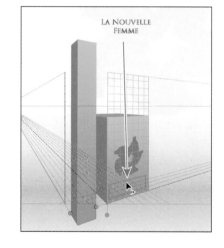

5   With the text object still selected, double-click the text with the Perspective Selection tool to enter Isolation mode. The Type tool is selected automatically.

▶ **Tip:** You can also enter Isolation mode to edit text by clicking the Edit Text button (⊞) in the Control panel. To exit Isolation mode, you can also click twice on the gray arrow that appears below the document tab at the top of the Document window.

6   Double-click the word "Femme," and change the Font Size to **24 pt** in the Control panel. Click the word "Character" in the Control panel, and change the Leading value to **22 pt**. Press the Escape key to hide the Character panel.

7   Select all of the text, and change the Fill color to White in the Control panel.

8   Select the Selection tool (▶) and double-click the artboard to exit Isolation mode.

Note: We zoomed in to more easily edit the text.

Moving a plane to match an object

When you want to draw or bring objects in perspective at the same depth or height as an existing object, such as the tall box, you can bring the corresponding grid to the desired height or depth. Next, you will move the right grid plane to the same depth as the right side of the tall box and add more text to it.

1 With the Selection tool (), click to select the white text "LA NOUVELLE FEMME" that is off the upper-left corner of the artboard.

2 Choose Object > Transform > Rotate. In the Rotate dialog box, change the Angle value to **90°** and select Preview. Click OK.

You will find that, most of the time, it's best to rotate content *before* bringing it into perspective.

● **Note:** The gridlines on the right grid plane will most likely not cover the right side of the tall box. That's okay. Imagine that those gridlines go on forever in the same plane.

3 Select the Perspective Selection tool () in the Tools panel. Click to select the right face of the tall box. Choose Object > Perspective > Move Plane To Match Object. Now anything you add to the right grid plane will be at the same depth as the right side of the tall box.

4 With the Perspective Selection tool selected, click to drag the rotated text object into the lower-left corner of the right side of the tall box. See the figure for placement help.

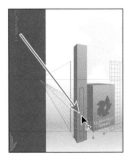

The plane before you move it.   The plane after moving it.   Drag the text.

5 Choose Object > Arrange > Bring To Front to bring the text on top of the box.

To finish the tall box, you will add a red flower to it.

6 With the Perspective Selection tool selected, make sure that the Right Grid(3) in the Plane Switching Widget is selected.

7 Drag the last remaining red flower off the lower-left corner of the artboard onto the right side of the tall box, just above the text.

8 Choose Object > Arrange > Bring To Front to bring the flower on top of the box.

9 Choose View > Zoom In, a few times, to zoom in.

10 With the Perspective Selection tool, press Shift+Option (Mac OS) or Shift+Alt (Windows) and drag the upper-right corner of the flower shape toward the center until an approximate width of 0.5 in shows in the measurement label. Drag to position the flower like you see in the figure.

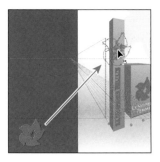
Drag the flower into perspective.

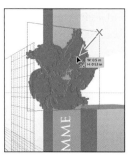
Resize the flower.

Notice the result.

11 With the Perspective Selection tool (⏵⬤), click to select the white text "LA NOUVELLE FEMME" and choose Object > Arrange > Bring To Front to bring it in front of the flower.

12 Choose View > Fit Artboard In Window.

13 Choose Select > Deselect, and then choose File > Save.

Automatic plane positioning

Using the automatic plane positioning options, you can select to move the active plane temporarily when you mouse over the anchor point or gridline intersection point by pressing the Shift key.

The automatic plane positioning options are available in the Perspective Grid Options dialog box. To display this dialog box, double-click the Perspective Grid tool (⊞) or the Perspective Selection tool (⏵⬤) in the Tools panel.

—From Illustrator Help

Adding symbols to the perspective grid

● **Note:** Symbols that you wish to bring into perspective cannot contain such things as raster images, envelopes, or gradient meshes.

Adding symbols to a perspective plane when the grid is visible is a great way to add repeating items, such as windows. Like text, you can bring symbols into perspective. Next, you will add a symbol to one of the boxes.

1   With the Perspective Selection tool (▶⊡) selected, click to select the left side of the tall box. This ensures that the correct grid plane is selected in the Plane Switching Widget, since selecting content that is attached to the grid also selects the grid plane that it is on.

● **Note:** To learn more about symbols, see Lesson 13, "Using Symbols to Create a Map."

2   Click the Symbols panel icon (⊡) on the right side of the workspace to expand the Symbols panel. Drag the symbol named "Orange Flower" from the Symbols panel to the left of the tall box. Notice that the flower isn't in perspective yet.

3   With the Perspective Selection tool, drag the selected symbol to the bottom of the left side of the tall box to attach it to the left grid plane.

4   Select the Zoom tool (🔍) in the Tools panel, and click several times on the symbol instance of the flower to zoom in.

5   Select the Perspective Selection tool. Press the Shift key, and drag the middle, top point down until the symbol instance fits within the side of the tall box.

6   Choose Select > Deselect.

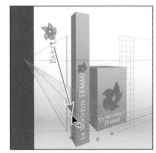

● **Note:** To edit a symbol that is on the perspective grid, you can also select the symbol, and then click the Edit Symbol button (⊡) in the Control panel or double-click the symbol instance on the artboard. With either of these methods, a dialog box appears, telling you that you are about to edit the symbol definition.

Editing symbols in perspective

After bringing symbols into perspective, you may need to edit them. Just know that functionalities, such as replacing a symbol or breaking a link to a symbol instance, do not work on symbols in perspective. Next, you will make a change to the flower symbol.

1   Choose View > Fit Artboard In Window.

2   Double-click the Orange Flower thumbnail in the Symbols panel. This enters Symbol Editing mode and hides the rest of the artwork on the artboard.

3 Choose View > Outline, so it's easier to see the white text.

4 Press Command++ (Mac OS) or Ctrl++ (Windows) twice to zoom in to the grid.

5 Select the Type tool (**T**) in the Tools panel. Position the cursor over the text "PARFUM," and double-click the text to select it. Type **Pencil**.

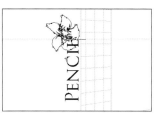

6 Choose View > Preview, and then press the Escape key twice to exit Isolation mode.

7 Choose View > Fit Artboard In Window.

Notice that the symbol instance on the left side of the tall box has updated.

8 Choose Select > Deselect (if necessary), and then choose File > Save.

Grouping content in perspective

Grouping content on the grid allows you to combine several objects into a group so that the objects are treated as a single unit, much like groups that are not in perspective. Next, you are going to group content, and then apply a drop shadow.

1 Select the Perspective Selection tool (▶⊡), and position the pointer off of the lower-right corner of the shorter box. Drag a marquee selection across the right side, left side, and top of the shorter box.

2 Choose Object > Group.

By grouping content that is on the perspective grid, you release it from the grid.

3 Click the Graphic Styles panel (▣) to show the panel. Click the graphic style named Drop Shadow to apply the styling to the new group.

4 Choose Object > Arrange > Send To Back, and then choose Select > Deselect.

5 With the Perspective Selection tool, Shift-click the left and right sides of the tall box, and then choose Object > Group.

6 With the group still selected, click the graphic style named Drop Shadow in the Graphic Styles panel to apply it.

● **Note:** When content is ungrouped, the selected object is released from the associated perspective plane and is available as normal artwork, but it doesn't affect the appearance of the artwork. Another way to release content from the grid is to choose Object > Perspective > Release With Perspective.

● **Note:** Grouping content that is on different grid planes will not allow you to move the content as a single unit in perspective.

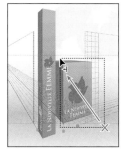

Group the content.

Apply the graphic style.

Apply the style again.

Releasing content from perspective

There will be times when you want to use objects that are currently in perspective elsewhere or you want to detach an object from a grid plane. Illustrator allows you to release an object from the associated perspective plane, but it still appears to be in perspective (its appearance doesn't change).

The ad needs a smaller version of the larger box near the bottom of the ad. You will copy and paste the perspective content to release it with perspective.

1 With the Perspective Selection tool ( ) selected, click the shorter box content to select it.

2 Choose Edit > Copy, and then choose Edit > Paste.

3 Choose Object > Transform > Scale. In the Scale dialog box, change the following options:

- Uniform: **20%**
- Scale Strokes & Effects: **Selected**

Click OK.

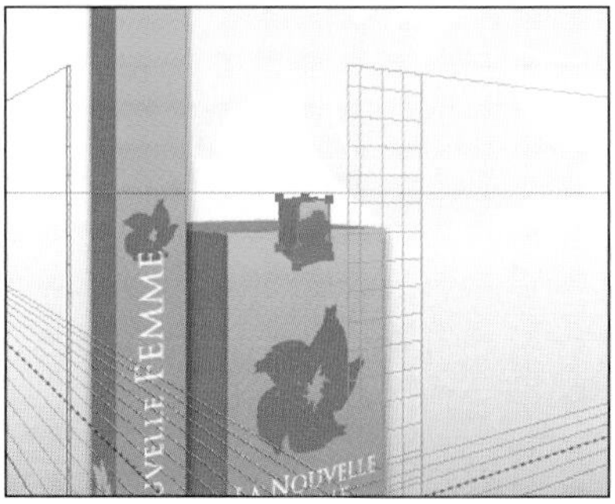

4 Click the Layers panel icon ( ) to expand the Layers panel. In the Layers panel, click the visibility column to the far left of the layer named "Other artwork." Click the Layers panel icon to collapse the panel again.

You may find that the artwork from the "Other artwork" layer that just appeared is covering part of the content on the perspective grid. You may want to reposition the content from the "Other artwork" layer after unlocking that same layer in the Layers panel.

5 Select the Selection tool ( ), and drag the small grouped box down to the left of the text "Order online today at our website."

6 Choose Select > Deselect.

7 Press Command+Shift+I (Mac OS) or Ctrl+Shift+I (Windows) to hide the perspective grid.

8 Choose File > Save.

9 Choose File > Close.

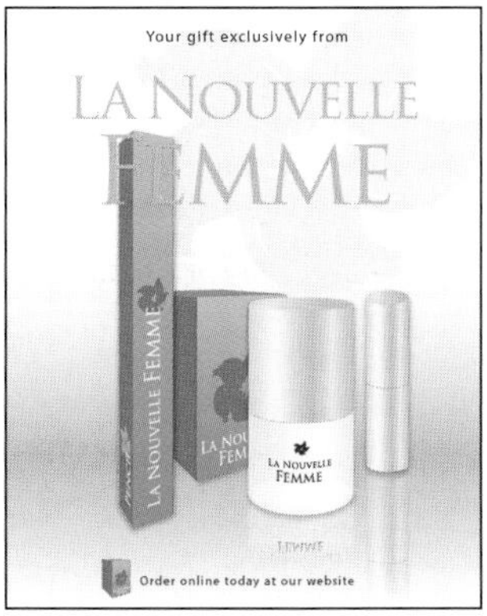

Review questions

1 There are three preset grids. Briefly describe what each could be used for.

2 How can you show or hide the perspective grid?

3 Before drawing content on a grid plane, what must be done to ensure that the object is on the correct grid plane?

4 What does double-clicking a grid plane control allow you to do?

5 How do you move an object perpendicular to the grid?

Review answers

1 The three preset grids are: one-point perspective, two-point perspective, and three-point perspective. A one-point perspective can be very useful for roads, railway tracks, or buildings viewed so that the front is directly facing the viewer. Two-point perspective is useful for drawing a cube, such as a building, or for two roads going off into the distance, and it typically has two vanishing points. Three-point perspective is usually used for buildings seen from above or below. In addition to vanishing points for each wall, there is a vanishing point in three-point perspective showing those walls receding into the ground or high in space.

2 You can show the perspective grid by selecting the Perspective Grid tool (▦) in the Tools panel, by choosing View > Perspective Grid > Show Grid, or by pressing Command+Shift+I (Mac OS) or Ctrl+Shift+I (Windows). To hide the grid, choose View > Perspective Grid > Hide Grid, press Command+Shift+I (Mac OS) or Ctrl+Shift+I (Windows), or press the Escape key with the Perspective Selection or Perspective Grid tools selected.

3 The correct grid plane must be selected by choosing it in the Plane Switching Widget. You can select it by using the following keyboard commands: Left Grid(1), Horizontal Grid(2), Right Grid(3), or No Active Grid(4); or by selecting content on the grid you want to choose with the Perspective Selection tool (▶▣).

4 Double-clicking a grid plane control allows you to move the plane. You can specify whether to move the content associated with the plane and whether to copy the content as the plane moves.

5 To move an object perpendicular to the grid, with the Perspective Selection tool, hold down the number 5 key and drag the object perpendicular to the plane.

13 USING SYMBOLS TO CREATE A MAP

Lesson overview

In this lesson, you'll learn how to do the following:

- Work with existing symbols.

- Create a symbol.

- Modify and redefine a symbol.

- Use the Symbolism tools.

- Store and retrieve artwork in the Symbols panel.

 This lesson takes approximately 45 minutes to complete.

Download the project files for this lesson from the Lesson & Update Files tab on your Account page at www.peachpit.com and store them on your computer in a convenient location, as described in the Getting Started section of this book.

Your Account page is also where you'll find any updates to the chapters or to the lesson files. Look on the Lesson & Update Files tab to access the most current content.

The Symbols panel lets you apply multiple objects by painting them on the page. Symbols used in combination with the Symbolism tools offer options that make creating repetitive shapes, such as blades of grass, easy and fun.

Getting started

In this lesson, you'll add symbols to a map. Before you begin, restore the default preferences for Adobe Illustrator CC. Then, open the file containing the finished artwork to see what you are going to create.

● **Note:** On Windows, if you see a message about compatible GPU, click OK.

1 To ensure that the tools and panels function exactly as described in this lesson, delete or deactivate (by renaming) the Adobe Illustrator CC preferences file. See "Restoring default preferences" in the Getting Started section at the beginning of the book.

2 Start Adobe Illustrator CC.

● **Note:** If you have not already downloaded the project files for this lesson to your computer from your Account page, make sure to do so now. See the "Getting Started" section at the beginning of this book.

3 Choose File > Open, and open the L13_end.ai file in the Lesson13 folder in the Lessons folder on your hard disk.

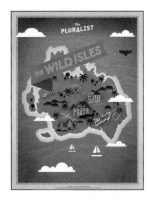

If you want to view the finished map as you work, choose View > Zoom Out and adjust the window size. Use the Hand tool (✋) to move the artwork where you want it in the Document window. If you don't want to leave the finished map open, choose File > Close.

To begin working, you'll open an existing art file that is incomplete.

● **Note:** In Mac OS, when opening lesson files, you may need to click the round, green button in the upper-left corner of the Document window to maximize the window's size.

4 Choose File > Open, to open the L13_start.ai file in the Lesson13 folder, located in the Lessons folder on your hard disk.

5 Choose File > Save As. In the Save As dialog box, name the file **Map.ai** and navigate to the Lesson13 folder. Leave the Format option set to Adobe Illustrator (ai) (Mac OS) or the Save As Type option set to Adobe Illustrator (*.AI) (Windows), and click Save. In the Illustrator Options dialog box, leave the Illustrator options at their default settings, and then click OK.

6 Choose Window > Workspace > Reset Essentials.

● **Note:** If you don't see "Reset Essentials" in the menu, choose Window > Workspace > Essentials before choosing Window > Workspace > Reset Essentials.

7 Double-click the Hand tool to fit the artboard in the window.

Working with symbols

A *symbol* is a reusable art object that is stored in the Symbols panel (Window > Symbols). For example, if you create a symbol from a fish you drew, you can then quickly add multiple instances of that fish symbol to your artwork, which saves you from having to draw each fish again. All instances of the fish symbol are linked to the associated symbol in the Symbols panel, so you can easily alter them using Symbolism tools.

When you edit the original symbol, all instances of the fish that are linked to it are updated. You can turn that fish from blue to green instantly! Not only do symbols save time, but they also greatly reduce file size.

- Click the Symbols panel icon (⬛) on the right side of the workspace. Take a minute to familiarize yourself with the parts of the Symbols panel.

● **Note:** The figure shows the Symbols panel with the Map.ai file displaying in the Document window.

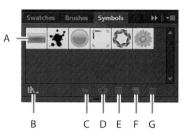

A. Symbols
B. Symbol Libraries Menu
C. Place Symbol Instance
D. Break Link To Symbol
E. Symbol Options
F. New Symbol
G. Delete Symbol

Illustrator comes with a series of symbol libraries, which range from tiki icons to hair to Web icons. You can access those symbol libraries in the Symbols panel or by choosing Window > Symbol Libraries and easily incorporate them into your own artwork.

Using existing Illustrator symbol libraries

You will start by adding a symbol from an existing symbol library to the map.

1   Choose View > Smart Guides to deselect (turn off) the Smart Guides.

2   Click the Layers panel icon (⬛) on the right side of the workspace to expand the Layers panel. Click the Symbols layer to make sure it is selected. Make sure that all of the layers are collapsed by clicking the disclosure triangles to the left of the layer names (if necessary).

When adding symbols to a document, the layer that is selected when they are added is the same layer they become a part of. In this project, some of the artwork, such as the text and the mountains, will be on top of the symbols you add since they are on the Text layer, which is above the Symbols layer.

3   Click the Symbols panel icon () on the right side of the workspace to show the panel.

4   In the Symbols panel, click the Symbol Libraries Menu button () at the bottom of the panel and choose Tiki.

The Tiki library opens as a free-floating panel. This library is external to the file that you are working on, but you can import any of the symbols into the document and use them in the artwork.

Tip: If you want to see the symbol names along with the symbol pictures, click the Symbols panel menu icon (), and then choose Small List View or Large List View.

5   Position the pointer over the symbols in the Tiki panel to see their names as tool tips. Click the symbol named "Tiki Hut" to add it to the Symbols panel for the document. Close the Tiki panel.

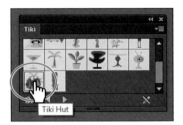

Every document has a default set of symbols in the Symbols panel. When you add symbols to the panel, as you just did, they are saved with the active document only.

Tip: You can also copy a symbol instance on the artboard and paste as many as you need. This is the same as dragging a symbol instance out of the Symbols panel onto the artboard.

6   Using the Selection tool (), drag the Tiki Hut symbol from the Symbols panel onto the artboard below the "PEAKS" text, like you see in the figure. Drag another onto the artboard to the right of the "JUNGLE" text (see the figure for where to drag it), and leave it selected.

Each time you drag a symbol onto the artboard, an instance of the Tiki Hut symbol is created. Next, you will resize one of the symbol instances on the page.

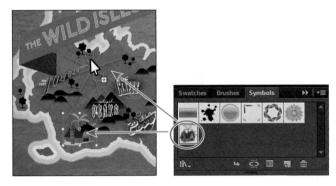

● **Note:** The pointer that you see when dragging a symbol from the Symbols panel into the Document window may look different, and that's okay.

7 Option+Shift-drag (Mac OS) or Alt+Shift-drag (Windows) the top-middle bounding point of the selected Tiki Hut symbol instance toward the center to make it a little smaller, while constraining its proportions. Release the mouse button, and then release the modifier keys.

● **Note:** Although you can transform symbol instances in many ways, specific properties of instances cannot be edited. For example, the fill color is locked because it is controlled by the original symbol in the Symbols panel.

With the symbol instance still selected on the artboard, notice that, in the Control panel, you see the word "Symbol" and symbol-related options.

Editing a symbol

In this next section, you will edit the Tiki Hut symbol and all instances on the artboard will be updated. There are several ways to edit a symbol, and in this section we will focus on one.

1 With the Selection tool (▶), double-click the Tiki Hut symbol instance you resized. A warning dialog box appears, stating that you are about to edit the original symbol and that all instances will update. Click OK to continue.

▶ **Tip:** Another way to edit a symbol is to select the symbol instance on the artboard, and then click the Edit Symbol button in the Control panel.

This takes you into Symbol Editing mode, so you can't edit any other objects on the page. The Tiki Hut symbol instance you double-clicked may change in size. That's because you are looking at the original symbol, not at the resized symbol instance on the page. You can now edit the shapes that make up the symbol.

2 Select the Zoom tool (🔍), and draw a marquee around the symbol content to zoom in.

3 Select the Selection tool and click to select the cream-colored shape under the house. Change the Fill color to Black in the Control panel.

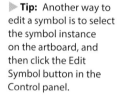

4 Double-click away from the symbol content, or click the Exit Symbol Editing Mode button (◀) in the upper-left corner of the artboard until you exit Symbol Editing mode so that you can edit the rest of the content.

5 Choose View > Fit Artboard In Window, and notice that both Tiki Hut instances on the artboard have been changed.

6 Click one of the Tiki Hut symbol instances and choose Select > Same > Symbol Instance.

This is a great way to select all instances of a symbol in the document.

7 Choose Object > Group to group them together.

Next, you'll put the group you just created on the Text layer so that it's above all other artwork.

8 In the Layers panel, drag the selected art indicator to the right of the Symbols layer name (the little colored box) up to the Text layer.

9 Click the Edit column to the left of the Text layer name to lock the layer content.

10 Choose Select > Deselect (if available), and then choose File > Save, and leave the document open.

Creating symbols

Illustrator also lets you create your own symbols. You can make symbols from objects, including paths, compound paths, text, embedded (not linked) raster images, mesh objects, and groups of objects. Symbols can even include active objects, such as brush strokes, blends, effects, or other symbol instances. Now you will create your own symbol from existing artwork.

1 With the Selection tool (➤) selected, click the sailboat group of artwork off the right edge of the artboard to select it.

2 Click the New Symbol button (▣) at the bottom of the Symbols panel to make a symbol from the selected artwork.

▶ **Tip:** You can also drag the selected content into a blank area of the Symbols panel to create a symbol.

3 In the Symbol Options dialog box, change the name to **Sailboat** and choose Graphic as the Type. Click OK to create the symbol.

In the Symbol Options dialog box, you will see a note that explains that there is no difference between a Movie Clip and a Graphic Type in Illustrator, and so if you do not plan on exporting this content to Adobe Flash, you don't need to worry about choosing a Type.

▶ **Tip:** By default, the selected artwork becomes an instance of the new symbol. If you don't want the artwork to become an instance of the symbol, press the Shift key as you create the new symbol.

● **Note:** To learn about Align To Pixel Grid and artwork for use on the Web or for screen display, see Lesson 15, "Preparing Content for the Web."

After creating the Sailboat symbol, the sailboat artwork off the right edge of the artboard is converted to an instance of the Sailboat symbol. You can leave it there or delete it—it's up to you (we deleted it). The symbol also appears in the Symbols panel.

4 Drag the Sailboat symbol from the Symbols panel onto the artboard twice and position both instances like you see in the figure.

5 Try resizing one of the Sailboat symbol instances on the artboard like you did earlier (the figure shows the result after we resized one).

6 Choose Select > Deselect, and then choose File > Save.

▶ **Tip:** You can drag the symbol thumbnails in the Symbols panel to change their ordering. Reordering symbols in the Symbols panel has no effect on the artwork. It can simply be a way to organize your symbols.

Symbol Options

In the Symbol Options dialog box, you will encounter several options that are related to working with Adobe Flash. These options are briefly described below.

* Select Movie Clip for type. Movie Clip is the default symbol type in Flash and in Illustrator.

* Specify a location on the Registration grid where you want to set the symbol's anchor point. The location of the anchor point affects the position of the symbol within the screen coordinates.

* Select Enable Guides For 9-Slice Scaling if you want to utilize 9-Slice scaling in Illustrator or Flash.

—From Illustrator Help

Duplicating symbols

Often you will want to add a series of symbol instances to your artwork. After all, one of the reasons why we use symbols is for storing and updating frequently used content like trees or clouds. In this section, you'll create, add, and duplicate a symbol that happens to be a cloud.

1   Using the Selection tool (⬆), click and drag the top white cloud group off the right edge of the artboard into a blank area of the Symbols panel to create a new symbol. In the Symbol Options dialog box, change the name to **Cloud1** and choose Graphic as the Type. Click OK to create the symbol.

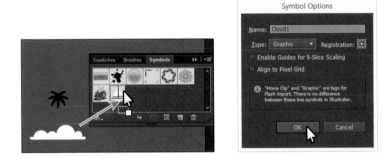

2   Drag an instance of the Cloud1 symbol from the Symbols panel to the left of "The PLURALIST" text. See the figure for placement.

Next, you will learn how to add more instances of a symbol that's already on the artboard, using a modifier key.

3   Press the Option key (Mac OS) or Alt key (Windows) and drag the Cloud1 symbol instance on the artboard to create a copy of the instance. Drag it to the right of "The PLURALIST" text. When the new instance is in position (see the figure), release the mouse button, and then release the modifier key.

4 Create four more copies by pressing the Option (Mac OS) or Alt (Windows) key and dragging either of the Cloud1 symbol instances. Drag them around the map. You can see where we dragged them in the figure.

5 Resize a few of the Cloud1 symbol instances, making some smaller and some a bit larger, so they look a bit different from each other.

6 Click the Cloud1 symbol instance to the left of "The PLURALIST" text. Click the word "Transform" (or the X, Y, W, or H links) in the Control panel, and choose Flip Horizontal from the Transform panel menu ().

Note: The figure shows the cloud before choosing Flip Horizontal.

7 Choose File > Save.

Replacing symbols

Next, you will create a symbol from some other shapes, and then replace a few of the Cloud1 symbol instances with the new symbol.

1 With the Selection tool (▶), select the blue cloud group off the right edge of the artboard.

2 Click the New Symbol button (⬛) at the bottom of the Symbols panel. In the Symbol Options dialog box, change the name to **Cloud2** and the Type to Graphic. Click OK.

3   With the Selection tool, select the
    Cloud1 symbol instance to the left
    of "The PLURALIST" text. In the
    Control panel, click the arrow to the
    right of the Replace Instance With
    Symbol field to open a panel showing
    the symbols in the Symbols panel.
    Click the Cloud2 symbol in the panel.

    Notice that the "Flip Horizontal" is still applied to the Cloud2 symbol instance.

4   Click another Cloud1 symbol instance on the artboard and replace it with the
    Cloud2 symbol using the same method.

Next, you'll edit the Cloud2 symbol using a different method.

5   Double-click the Cloud2 symbol thumbnail in the Symbols panel to edit
    the symbol.

    A temporary instance of the symbol appears in the center of the Document
    window. Editing a symbol by double-clicking the symbol in the Symbols panel
    hides all artboard content except the symbol. This is just another way to edit
    a symbol.

6   Press Command++ (Mac OS) or Ctrl++ (Windows) several times to zoom in.

7   Select the Direct Selection tool ($\mathbb{k}$) in the Tools panel and click one of the
    blue shapes.

8   Choose Select > Same > Fill Color to select all of the blue shapes.

● **Note:** The color of
the path selection you
see may be different
than what shows in the
figure and that's okay.

9   Change the Fill color in the Control panel to White.

10 Double-click away from the symbol content to exit Symbol Editing mode so that
    you can edit the rest of the content.

11 Choose View > Fit Artboard In Window.

Symbol layers

When you edit a symbol using any of the methods described, open the Layers panel and you will see that the symbol has its own layering.

Similar to working with groups in Isolation mode, you see the layers associated with that symbol only, not the document's layers. In the Layers panel, you can rename, add, delete, show/hide, and reorder content for a symbol.

Breaking a link to a symbol

At times, you need to edit specific instances on the artboard—but not all instances. Because you can only make changes, like scaling, opacity, and flipping, to a symbol *instance*, you may need to break the link between a symbol and an instance. This breaks the instance into the original objects or group, if the symbol content was originally grouped, on the artboard.

Next, you will break the link to one of the cloud symbol instances.

1   With the Selection tool (▶) selected, click to select the Cloud2 symbol instance to the left of "The PLURALIST" text on the artboard. In the Control panel, click the Break Link button.

This object is now a series of paths, as indicated by the words "Mixed Objects" on the left side of the Control panel and can be directly edited. You should be able to see the anchor points of the shapes. This content will no longer update if the Cloud2 symbol is edited.

▶ **Tip:** You can also break the link to a symbol instance by selecting the symbol instance on the artboard, and then clicking the Break Link To Symbol button (⊞) at the bottom of the Symbols panel.

2   Select the Zoom tool (🔍), and drag a marquee across the selected cloud content on the artboard to zoom in.

3   Choose Select > Deselect.

4   Select the Direct Selection tool (▷) in the Tools panel, and click the largest circle shape in the cloud.

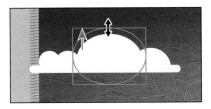

5 Select the Selection tool and Shift-drag the top, middle bounding point up to make the circle a bit larger.

6 Choose Select > Deselect, and then choose File > Save.

Editing symbol options

Using the Symbols panel, you can easily rename or change other options for a symbol, which then updates all the symbol instances in the artwork. Next, you will rename the Tiki Hut symbol.

1 Choose View > Fit Artboard In Window.

2 In the Symbols panel, click the Tiki Hut symbol to select it. Click the Symbol Options button (▤) at the bottom of the Symbols panel.

3 In the Symbol Options dialog box, change the name to **Wild Isles Hut** and the Type to Graphic. Click OK.

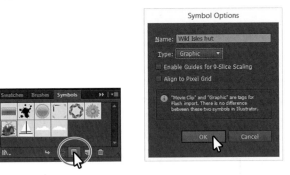

Working with the Symbolism tools

The Symbol Sprayer tool (⬚) in the Tools panel allows you to spray symbols on the artboard, creating symbol sets. A symbol set is a group of symbol instances that you create with the Symbol Sprayer tool. This can be really useful if, for instance, you were to create grass from individual blades of grass. Spraying the blades of grass speeds up this process greatly and makes it much easier to edit individual instances of grass or the sprayed grass as a group. You can create mixed sets of symbol instances by using the Symbol Sprayer tool with one symbol, and then using it again with another symbol.

Spraying symbol instances

Next, you will save a tree as a symbol, and then use the Symbol Sprayer tool (⬚) to apply those trees to your illustration.

1 With the Selection tool ( ), click to select the dark tree off the right edge of the artboard.

2 Drag the tree into the Symbols panel. In the Symbol Options dialog box, change the name to **Tree** and the Type to Graphic. Click OK.

3 Choose Select > Deselect.

4 Double-click the Symbol Sprayer tool ( ) in the Tools panel. In the Symbolism Tools Options dialog box, change the following options (if they aren't already set):

   • Diameter: **1 in**

   • Intensity: **1**

   • Symbol Set Density: **2**

5 Click OK.

● **Note:** A higher intensity value increases the rate of change—the Symbol Sprayer tool sprays more and faster. The higher the symbol set density value, the more tightly packed the symbols are as you spray them. If you were to spray grass, for instance, you would want the intensity and density set high.

6 Make sure the Tree symbol is selected in the Symbols panel. Click and drag in the map area from left to right and from right to left with the Symbol Sprayer, much like using an airbrush or a can of spray paint, to create a series of trees. You can release the mouse button at any time, and then click and drag to keep adding trees. Your trees don't have to match the figure, and if you add too many, you'll learn how to delete them next. When finished, leave the symbols selected.

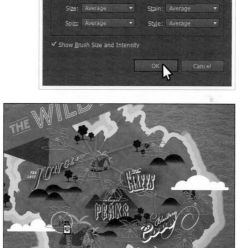

▶ **Tip:** Make sure to keep moving the pointer. If you don't like the results, you can choose Edit > Undo Spraying and try again.

Notice the bounding box around the selected Tree symbol instances, identifying them as a symbol set. As you spray, the instances are grouped together as a single object. If a symbol set is selected when you begin to spray with the Symbol Sprayer tool, the symbol instances that you are spraying are added to the selected symbol set. You can easily delete an entire symbol set by selecting it and then pressing the Delete key.

7　Position the Symbol Sprayer pointer over the trees you just created. Click and release a few times to add trees one at a time.

The symbol instances are added to the existing symbol set, since the set was still selected.

8　Double-click the Tree symbol thumbnail in the Symbols panel to edit the symbol.

9　Choose Select > All and double-click the Scale tool (⌖) in the Tools panel. In the Scale dialog box, change the Uniform Scale to **80%**. Click OK.

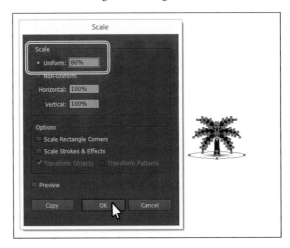

10　Select the Selection tool, and double-click away from the artwork to exit Symbol Editing mode. All of the Tree symbol instances in the symbol set have updated.

11　Choose File > Save.

Editing symbols with the Symbolism tools

There are a series of Symbolism tools that allow you to edit the size, color, rotation, and more of the instances within a symbol set. In the next steps, you will edit the trees in the Tree symbol set using one of the Symbolism tools in the Tools panel.

1　Click one of the Tree symbol instances on the artboard (on the map) to select the entire symbol set. Select the Symbol Sprayer tool (⬚) and position the pointer over one of the Tree symbol instances. Press the Option (Mac OS) or Alt (Windows) key, and click to delete one of the trees in the symbol set.

At this point, you could release the modifier key and click to add another Tree symbol instance if you wanted.

2   Select the Symbol Sizer tool (⊚) from the Symbol Sprayer tool (⬚) group in the Tools panel.

3   Double-click the Symbol Sizer tool, and change the Intensity to **5** in the Symbolism Tools Options dialog box. Click OK.

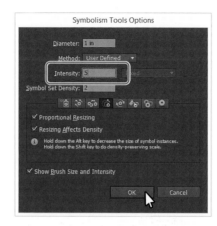

4   Position the pointer over some of the trees, and click the mouse button to increase the size of some of the trees. In another area of trees, press the Option (Mac OS) or Alt (Windows) key while you are using the Symbol Sizer tool to *reduce* the size of the selected symbol instance. Make some of the trees smaller than the rest, varying the sizes.

5   Choose Select > Deselect, and then choose File > Save.

▶ **Tip:** If the Symbol Sizer tool is sizing too quickly, double-click the Symbol Sizer tool in the Tools panel and try lowering the Intensity and Density values in the Symbolism Tools Options dialog box.

▶ **Tip:** You can copy and paste symbol sets and use the Symbolism tools to make the duplicate sets look different.

● **Note:** If the clouds appear behind some of the trees, you can arrange the sublayers in the Layers panel to bring the clouds to the front of the trees.

Symbolism tools

There are lots of Symbolism tools to experiment with, including the Symbol Styler tool (⊚), which allows you to apply graphic styles to symbol instances in the symbol set. To learn more about the different types of Symbolism tools available, search for "symbolism tool gallery" in Illustrator Help (Help > Illustrator Help).

Storing and retrieving artwork in the Symbols panel

Saving frequently used logos or other artwork as symbols lets you access them quickly. Unfortunately, symbols you create in one document are not accessible by default in another document. You can, however, take symbols that you've created and save them as a new symbol library that you can share with other documents or users. Here are the steps for saving your symbols:

1   In the Symbols panel, click the Symbol Libraries Menu button () at the bottom, and then choose Save Symbols.

2   In the Save Symbols As Library dialog box, choose a location, such as your Desktop, where you will place the symbol library file. Name the library file and click Save.

3   You can then open another document and click the Symbol Libraries Menu button () and choose Other Library at the bottom of the menu. Navigate to the folder where you saved the library, select it, and then click Open.

Working with Creative Cloud Design Libraries

With Creative Cloud Libraries, you can organize creative assets, such as colors, type styles, brushes and graphics, and automatically sync them to Creative Cloud, allowing you to access them whenever and wherever you need them from a single, convenient panel within Illustrator. Libraries make it easy to maintain design consistency across projects, and not have to dig around in files and folders to find the assets you need.

Design Libraries are found in the Libraries panel within Illustrator CC (Window > Libraries). You can create your own libraries that always stay in sync, so you always have the most current and correct visual assets. This makes it easy to maintain design consistency across projects, and not have to dig around in files and folders to find the assets you need.

To learn more about working with Design Libraries, search for "Creative Cloud Libraries" in Illustrator Help (Help > Illustrator Help).

Review questions

1 What are three benefits of using symbols?

2 How do you update an existing symbol?

3 Name something that cannot be used as a symbol.

4 Name the Symbolism tool that is used for sizing symbol instances in a symbol set.

5 If you are using a Symbolism tool on an area that has two different symbols applied, which one is affected?

6 How can you access symbols from other documents?

Review answers

1 Three benefits of using symbols are:

- You can edit one symbol, and all instances are updated.

- You can map artwork to 3D objects (we didn't discuss this in the lesson).

- Using symbols reduces file size.

2 To update an existing symbol, double-click the symbol icon in the Symbols panel, double-click an instance of the symbol on the artboard, or select the instance on the artboard, and then click the Edit Symbol button in the Control panel. Then you can make edits in Isolation mode.

3 A linked image cannot be used as a symbol.

4 The Symbol Sizer tool (⊘) allows you to resize symbol instances in a symbol set.

5 If you are using a Symbolism tool over an area that has two different symbol instances, the symbol active in the Symbols panel is the only instance affected.

6 You can access symbols from saved documents either by clicking the Symbol Libraries Menu button (▦) at the bottom of the Symbols panel and by choosing Other Library from the menu that appears; by choosing Open Symbol Library > Other Library from the Symbols panel menu; or by choosing Window > Symbol Libraries > Other Library.

14 USING ILLUSTRATOR CC WITH OTHER ADOBE APPLICATIONS

Lesson overview

In this lesson, you'll learn how to do the following:

- Place linked and embedded graphics in an Illustrator file.

- Place multiple images at once.

- Apply color edits to images.

- Create and edit clipping masks.

- Use text to mask an image

- Make and edit an opacity mask.

- Sample color in a placed image.

- Work with the Links panel.

- Embed and unembed images.

- Replace a placed image with another and update the document.

- Package a document.

 This lesson takes approximately 60 minutes to complete.

Download the project files for this lesson from the Lesson & Update Files tab on your Account page at www.peachpit.com and store them on your computer in a convenient location, as described in the Getting Started section of this book.

Your Account page is also where you'll find any updates to the chapters or to the lesson files. Look on the Lesson & Update Files tab to access the most current content.

You can easily add an image created in an image-editing program to an Adobe Illustrator file. This is an effective method for incorporating images into your vector artwork or for trying out Illustrator special effects on bitmap images.

Getting started

Before you begin, you'll need to restore the default preferences for Adobe Illustrator CC. Then you'll open the finished art file for this lesson to see what you'll create.

● **Note:** If you have not already downloaded the project files for this lesson to your computer from your Account page, make sure to do so now. See the "Getting Started" section at the beginning of this book.

1   To ensure that the tools and panels function exactly as described in this lesson, delete or deactivate (by renaming) the Adobe Illustrator CC preferences file. See "Restoring default preferences" in the Getting Started section at the beginning of the book.

2   Start Adobe Illustrator CC.

3   Choose File > Open. Locate the file named L14_end.ai in the Lesson14 folder in the Lessons folder that you copied onto your hard disk. This is a small poster for a vacation destination, and you will add and edit graphics in this lesson.

4   Choose View > Fit Artboard In Window and leave it open for reference, or choose File > Close.

● **Note:** The fonts in the L14_end.ai file have been converted to outlines (Type > Create Outlines) to avoid having missing fonts.

5   Choose File > Open. In the Lessons > Lesson14 folder, select the file named L14_start.ai. Click Open. This is a small poster for a travel company, and you will add and edit graphics in this lesson.

● **Note:** You need an Internet connection to sync the fonts. The syncing process may take a few minutes.

6   The Missing Fonts dialog box may appear. Click Sync Fonts to sync all of the missing fonts to your computer. After they are synced and you see the message stating that there are no more missing fonts, click Close.

If you can't get the fonts to sync (a "Syncing Typekit fonts…" message doesn't go away), you can go to the Creative Cloud desktop application and choose Assets > Fonts to see what the issue may be (refer to the section

"Changing font family and font style" in Lesson 7, "Adding type to a Poster," for more information on how to resolve it). You can also just click Close in the Missing Fonts dialog box and ignore the missing fonts as you proceed. A third method is to click the Find Fonts button in the Missing Fonts dialog box and replace the fonts with a local font on your machine. You can also go to Help (Help > Illustrator Help) and search for "Find missing fonts."

7   Choose File > Save As. In the Save As dialog box, navigate to the Lesson14 folder and open it. Name the file **GreenIsle.ai**. Leave the Format option set to Adobe Illustrator (ai) (Mac OS) or Save As Type option set to Adobe Illustrator (*.AI) (Windows), and then click Save. In the Illustrator Options dialog box, leave the Illustrator options at their default settings. Click OK.

8   Choose View > Fit Artboard In Window.

9   Choose Window > Workspace > Reset Essentials to reset the Essentials workspace.

Working with Adobe Bridge

Adobe Bridge CC is an application available with your Adobe Creative Cloud subscription. Bridge provides you with centralized access to all the media assets you need for your creative projects. Bridge simplifies your workflow and keeps you organized. You can batch edit with ease, add watermarks, and even set centralized color preferences. You can access Adobe Bridge from within Illustrator by choosing File > Browse In Bridge.

Combining artwork

You can combine Illustrator artwork with images from other graphics applications in a variety of ways for a wide range of creative results. Sharing artwork among applications lets you combine continuous-tone paintings and photographs with vector art. Illustrator lets you create certain types of raster images, and Adobe Photoshop excels at many additional image-editing tasks. The images edited or created in Photoshop can then be inserted into Illustrator.

This lesson steps you through the process of creating a composite image, including combining bitmap images with vector art and working between applications. You will add photographic images created in Photoshop to a small poster created in Illustrator. Then you'll adjust the color of an image, mask an image, and sample color from an image to use in the Illustrator artwork. You'll update a placed image, and then package the file.

● **Note:** To learn more about working with vector and raster images, see the "Introducing Adobe Illustrator" section in Lesson 1, "Getting to Know the Work Area."

Placing image files

You can bring raster artwork from Photoshop or other applications into Illustrator using the Open command, the Place command, the Paste command, and drag-and-drop operations. Illustrator supports most Adobe Photoshop data, including layer comps, layers, editable text, and paths. This means that you can transfer files between Photoshop and Illustrator without losing the ability to edit the artwork.

● **Note:** Illustrator includes support for DeviceN rasters. For instance, if you create a Duotone image in Photoshop and place it in Illustrator, it separates properly and prints the spot colors.

When placing files using the File > Place command, no matter what type of image file it is (JPG, GIF, PSD, etc.), it can either be embedded or linked. *Embedding* files stores a copy of the image in the Illustrator file, and the Illustrator file size increases to reflect the addition of the placed file. *Linked* files remain separate external files, and a link to the external file is placed in the Illustrator file. A linked file does not add significantly to the size of the Illustrator file. Linking to files can be a great way to ensure that image updates are reflected in the Illustrator file. The linked file must always accompany the Illustrator file, or the link will break and the placed file will not appear in the Illustrator artwork.

Placing an image

First, you will place a JPEG (.jpg) image into your document.

1   Click the Layers panel icon (⬛) to open the Layers panel. In the Layers panel, select the Pictures layer.

When you place an image, it is added to the selected layer. The layer already includes several shapes you see off the left edge of the artboard.

2   Choose File > Place.

3   Navigate to the Lessons > Lesson14 > images folder, and select the Kayak.jpg file. Make sure that Link is selected in the Place dialog box. Click Place.

The pointer should now show the loaded graphics cursor. You can see "1/1" next to the pointer, indicating how many images are being placed, and a thumbnail so you can see what image you are placing.

4   Position the loaded graphics cursor near the upper-left corner of the artboard, and click to place the image. Leave the image selected.

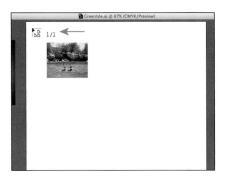

Position the graphics cursor.

Click to place the image.

> **Tip:** The X on a selected image indicates that the image is linked (with edges showing, View > Show Edges).

The image appears on the artboard, with the upper-left corner of the image where you clicked. The image is 100% of its original size. You could also have dragged with the loaded graphics cursor to size the image as you placed it. Notice in the Control panel that, with the image selected, you see the words "Linked File," indicating that the image is linked to its source file, together with other information about the image. By default, placed image files are linked to their source file. So, if the source file is edited (outside of Illustrator), the placed image in Illustrator is updated. Deselecting the Link option while placing embeds the image file in the Illustrator file.

Scaling a placed image

You can duplicate and transform placed images just as you do other objects in an Illustrator file. Unlike vector artwork, you need to consider the resolution of the raster image content in your document, since raster images without enough resolution may look pixelated when printed. Working in Illustrator, if you make an image smaller, the resolution of the image increases. If you make an image larger, the resolution decreases. Next, you will move, resize, and rotate the Kayak.jpg image.

● **Note:** Transformations performed on a linked image in Illustrator, and any resulting resolution changes, do not change the original image. The changes apply only to the image within Illustrator.

> **Tip:** To transform a placed image, you can also open the Transform panel (Window > Transform) and change settings there.

1 Holding down the Shift key, use the Selection tool to drag the lower-right bounding point toward the center of the image until the measurement label shows a width of approximately 5 in. Release the mouse button, and then release the key.

After resizing the image, notice that the PPI (Pixels Per Inch) value in the Control panel is approximately 150. PPI refers to the resolution of the image. Other transformations like rotation can also be applied to images using the various methods you learned in Lesson 4, "Transforming Artwork."

▶ **Tip:** Much like other artwork, you can also Option+Shift-drag (Mac OS) or Alt+Shift-drag (Windows) a bounding point around an image to resize from the center, while maintaining the image proportions.

2 Click the "Linked File" link on the left end of the Control panel to see the Links panel. With the Kayak.jpg file selected in the Links panel, click the Show Link Info arrow in the lower-left corner of the panel to see information about the image. You can see the percentage that the image was scaled as well as rotation information, size, and much more.

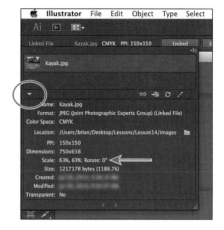

3 Choose Select > Deselect, and then choose File > Save.

Placing a Photoshop image with Show Import Options

When you place image files in Illustrator, you have the ability to change image options when the file is imported (when available). For instance, if you place a Photoshop file (.psd), you can choose to flatten the image or even to preserve the layers in the file.

Next, you will place a Photoshop file, set import options, and embed it in the Illustrator file.

1 In the Layers panel, click the eye icon (⬛) for the Pictures layer to hide the contents, and then select the Background layer.

2 Choose File > Place.

● **Note:** You may not see a preview for the Photoshop file, even though the figure shows one, and that's okay.

3 In the Place dialog box, navigate to the Lessons > Lesson14 > images folder and select the Lilypads.psd file. In the Place dialog box, set the following options:

- Link: **Deselected** (Deselecting the Link option embeds an image file in the Illustrator file. Embedding the Photoshop file allows for more options when it is placed, as you'll see.)

- Show Import Options: **Selected**

4 Click Place.

The Photoshop Import Options dialog box appears because you selected Show Import Options in the Place dialog box.

● **Note:** Even though you select Show Import Options in the Place dialog box, the Import Options dialog box will not appear if the image doesn't have any options to change.

5 In the Photoshop Import Options dialog box, set the following options:

- Layer Comp: **All**
  (A layer comp is a snapshot of a state of the Layers panel that you create in Photoshop. In Photoshop, you can create, manage, and view multiple versions of a layout in a single Photoshop file.)

- Show Preview: **Selected**
  (Preview displays a preview of the selected layer comp.)

- Convert Layers To Objects: **Selected** (This option and the next one are only available because you deselected the Link option and chose to embed the Photoshop image.)

- Import Hidden Layers: **Selected** (to import layers hidden in Photoshop)

6 Click OK.

● **Note:** A color mode warning may appear in the Photoshop Import Options dialog box. This indicates that the image you are placing may not be the same color mode as the Illustrator document. For this image (and going forward), if a color warning dialog box appears, click OK to dismiss it.

▶ **Tip:** To learn more about layer comps, see "Importing artwork from Photoshop" in Illustrator Help (Help > Illustrator Help).

Note: The word "intersect" may be hidden by the top edge of the Document window.

7 Position the loaded graphics cursor in the upper-left corner of the artboard. When the green word "intersect" appears (that's a part of the Smart Guides), click to place the image.

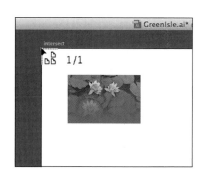

Rather than flatten the file, you have converted the Lilypads.psd Photoshop layers to layers that you can show and hide in Illustrator. When placing a Photoshop file in particular, if you had left the Link option selected (to link to the original PSD file), the only option in the Options section of the Photoshop Import Options dialog box would have been to flatten the content.

8 In the Layers panel, click the Locate Object button (⌖) to reveal the image content in the Layers panel. You may want to drag the left edge of the Layers panel to see more of the layer names.

Notice the sublayers of Lilypads.psd. These sublayers were Photoshop layers in Photoshop and appear in the Layers panel in Illustrator because you chose not to flatten the image when you placed it. Also notice that, with the image still selected on the page, the Control panel shows the word "Group" on the left side and includes an underlined link to "Multiple Images." When you place a Photoshop file with layers and you choose to convert the layers to objects in the Photoshop Import Options dialog box, Illustrator treats the layers as separate sublayers in a group. This particular image had a layer mask in Photoshop applied to Layer 0, which is why the image appears to fade.

9 Click the eye icon (👁) to the left of the "Color Fill 1" sublayer to hide it.

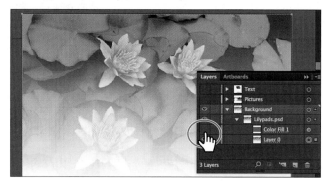

10 Choose Select > Deselect, and then choose File > Save.

Placing multiple images

In Illustrator you can also place multiple files in a single action. Next, you'll place two images at once and then position them.

1   In the Layers panel, click the disclosure triangle (▼) to the left of the Background layer to collapse the layer contents. Click the visibility column of the Pictures and the Text layers to show the contents for each, and then ensure that the Background layer is selected.

2   Choose File > Place.

3   In the Place dialog box, select the Water.jpg file in the images folder inside the Lesson14 folder. Command-click (Mac OS) or Ctrl-click (Windows) the image named Text.psd to select both image files. Deselect the Show Import Options option and make sure that the Link option is not selected. Click Place.

▶ **Tip:** You could also select a range of files in the Place dialog box by pressing the Shift key.

● **Note:** The Place dialog box may show the images in a different view, like a List view, and that's okay.

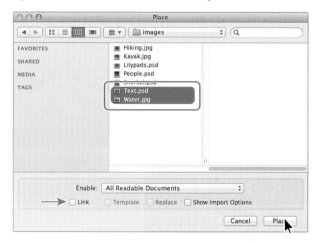

4   Position the loaded graphics cursor on the left side of the artboard. Press the Right or Left Arrow key (or Up and Down Arrow keys) a few times to see that you can cycle between the image thumbnails. Whichever thumbnail is showing when you click in the Document window is placed. Make sure that you see the water image thumbnail, and click the left edge of the artboard, about halfway down, to place the image.

● **Note:** The figure shows after clicking to place the Water.jpg image.

▶ **Tip:** To discard an asset that is loaded and ready to be placed, use the arrow keys to navigate to the asset, and then press the Escape key.

5   Press and hold the spacebar and drag to the left so that you see more area off the right side of the artboard.

6   Position the loaded graphics off the right side of the artboard. Click and drag down and to the right, stopping when the image is roughly as big as you see in the figure. Leave the image selected.

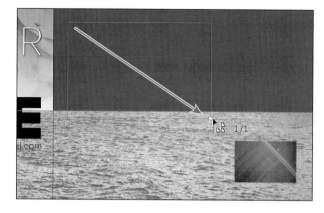

You can either click to place an image at 100% or click and drag to place an image and size it as you place it in the Document window. By dragging when you place an image, you are resizing the image. Resizing an image in Illustrator will most likely result in a different resolution than the original. Once again, you can look at the PPI (Pixels Per Inch) value in the Control panel to see the resolution of the image. The original PPI of the Text.psd image was 150 PPI.

7   With the Text.psd image selected, drag the selected art indicator (the colored box) in the Layers panel up to the Text layer to move the image to the Text layer.

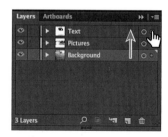

8   Choose View > Fit Artboard In Window.

Applying color edits to an image

In Illustrator, you can convert images to a different color mode (such as RGB, CMYK, or grayscale) or adjust individual color values. You can also saturate (darken) or desaturate (lighten) colors or invert colors (create a color negative).

In order to edit colors in the image, the image needs to be embedded in the Illustrator file. If the file is linked, you can edit the image in Photoshop and then update it in Illustrator.

1   In the Layers panel, click the eye icons (⬛) in the visibility column for the Pictures and Text layers to hide their contents.

2   With the Selection tool (▶), click to select the Lilypads.psd image at the top of the artboard. Choose Edit > Edit Colors > Adjust Color Balance.

3   In the Adjust Colors dialog box, drag the sliders or enter values for the CMYK percentages to change the colors in the image. You can press Tab to move between the text fields. We used the following values to create more of a red cast:

- C= **5**
- M= **−25**
- Y= **10**
- K= **0**

Feel free to experiment a little. Select Preview so that you can see the color changes. Click OK.

● **Note:** If you later decide to adjust the colors of the same image by choosing Edit > Edit Colors > Adjust Color Balance, the color values will be set to 0 (zero).

● **Note:** To see the results, you may need to select and deselect Preview as you change options in the Adjust Colors dialog box.

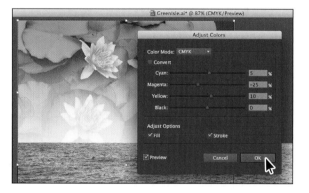

4   Choose Select > Deselect, and then choose File > Save.

5   In the Layers panel, click the visibility column for the Pictures and Text layers to show their contents. Click the eye icon (👁) in the visibility column for the Background layer to hide its contents.

Masking images

Clipping paths, or *masks*, crop an image so that only a portion of the image appears through the shape of the mask. Only vector objects can be clipping paths; however, any artwork can be masked. You can also import masks created in Photoshop files. The clipping path and the masked object are referred to as the *clipping set*.

Applying a simple mask to an image

In this short section, you'll create a simple clipping mask for the Kayak.jpg image.

1   With the Selection tool (▶), click the Kayak.jpg image to select it (the first image you placed). Click the Mask button in the Control panel.

● **Note:** You can also apply a clipping mask by choosing Object > Clipping Mask > Make.

Clicking the Mask button applies a clipping mask to the image in the shape and size of the image.

▶ **Tip:** Another way to create a mask is to use the Draw Inside mode. This mode allows you to draw inside the selected object. The Draw Inside mode can eliminate the need to perform multiple tasks, such as drawing and altering stacking order or drawing, selecting, and creating a clipping mask. To learn more about the drawing modes, see Lesson 3, "Using Shapes to Create Artwork for a Postcard."

● **Note:** You may need to drag the left edge of the Layers panel to the left to see more of the names, like we did for the figure.

2 In the Layers panel, click the Locate Object button (🔍) at the bottom of the panel.

Notice the <Clipping Path> and <linked File> sublayers that are contained within the <Clip Group> sublayer. The <Clipping Path> object is the clipping path that was created, and the <Clip Group> is a set that contains the mask and the object that is masked (the linked image).

Next, you will edit this simple mask.

Editing a clipping path (mask)

In order to edit a clipping path, you need to be able to select it. Illustrator offers several ways to do this.

1 With the kayak image still selected on the artboard, click the Edit Contents button (◉) in the Control panel and, in the Layers panel, notice that the <Linked File> sublayer (in the <Clip Group>) is showing the selected-art indicator (small color box) to the far right of the sublayer name.

▶ **Tip:** You can also double-click a clip group (object masked with a clipping path) to enter Isolation mode. You can then either click the masked object (the image in this case) to select it or click the edge of the clipping path to select the clipping path. After you are finished editing, you can then exit Isolation mode using a variety of methods we discussed in previous lessons (like pressing the Escape key).

2 Click the Edit Clipping Path button (▣) in the Control panel, and notice that the <Clipping Path> is showing the selected-art indicator in the Layers panel.

When an object is masked, you can edit the mask, the object that is masked, or both. Use these two buttons to select which to edit. When you first click to select an object that is masked, you will edit both the mask and the masked object.

3   With the Edit Clipping Path button (⊡) selected in the Control panel, choose View > Outline.

4   Use the Selection tool (▶) to drag the top, middle bounding point of the selected mask down until the measurement label shows a height of approximately 3.25 in.

▶ **Tip:** You can also edit a clipping path with transformation options, like rotate, skew, etc., or by using the Direct Selection tool (▷).

5   Choose View > Preview.

6   Click the word Transform (or X, Y, W, or H) in the Control panel (or open the Transform panel [Window > Transform]) and ensure that the center of the Reference Point is selected. Make sure that the Constrain Width And Height Proportions is off, and change the Width to **3.5 in**. If you see that the Height is not 3.25 in, go ahead and make it so.

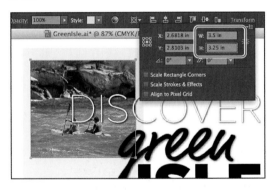

7   In the Control panel, click the Edit Contents button (◈) to edit the Kayak.jpg image, not the mask. With the Selection tool, be careful to drag from within the bounds of the mask, down a little bit, and release the mouse button. Notice that you are moving the image and not the mask.

With the Edit Contents button (◈) selected, you can apply many transformations to the image, including scaling, moving, rotating, and more.

▶ **Tip:** You can also press the arrow keys on the keyboard to reposition the image.

8 Choose Select > Deselect, and then click the image again to select the entire clip group. Drag the image onto the light gray rectangle and position it like you see in the figure.

9 Choose Select > Deselect, and then choose File > Save.

Masking an object with text

In this section, you'll create a mask in the shape of text for another image you place. In order to create a mask from text, the text needs to be on top of the image, as you'll see.

1 With the Selection tool ( ) selected, drag the leaf image (Text.psd) from off the right side of the artboard on top of the "ISLE" text.

2 Choose Object > Arrange > Send To Back. You should see the "ISLE" text now. Make sure that the image is positioned roughly like you see in the figure.

● **Note:** If the Text.psd image is not as wide as the "ISLE" text, make sure you resize the image, holding down the Shift key to constrain the proportions.

▶ **Tip:** You can also choose Object > Clipping Mask > Make.

3 With the image still selected, Shift-click the "ISLE" text to select them both. Right-click over the selected content and choose Make Clipping Mask from the context menu.

You can edit the Text.psd image and the clipping mask separately, just as you did previously with the masked Kayak.jpg image.

▶ **Tip:** You can use shapes or compound paths as a clipping mask, if you like. Just create the artwork, ensure that it's on top of the content to be masked, and then choose Object > Clipping Mask > Make.

4 With the text still selected, open the Graphic Styles panel (Window > Graphic Styles) and select the Text Shadow graphic style to apply a drop shadow.

5 Choose Select > Deselect, and then choose File > Save.

Masking an object with multiple shapes

You can easily create a mask from either a single shape or multiple shapes. In order to create a clipping mask with multiple shapes, the shapes first need to be converted to a compound path. This can be done by selecting the shapes that will be used as the mask and choosing Object > Compound Path > Make.

Creating an opacity mask

An *opacity mask* is different from a *clipping mask*, because it allows you to mask an object and alter the transparency of artwork. You can make and edit an opacity mask using the Transparency panel.

In this section, you'll create an opacity mask for the Water.jpg image so that it fades into the blue color of the background shape.

1 In the Layers panel, click the disclosure triangles for all layers (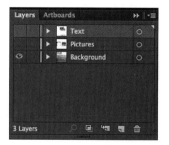) to collapse the contents, if necessary. Click the visibility column to the left of the Background layer to see its contents. Click the eye icon (◉) to the left of the Pictures and Text layers to hide their contents.

2 With the Selection tool selected, click the water image on the artboard. Choose Align To Artboard from the Align To menu, if necessary, in the Control panel. Click the Horizontal Align Center button (▤) and then the Vertical Align Center button (▦) in the Control panel to align the image to the artboard.

3   Select the Rectangle tool () in the Tools panel, and click in the approximate center of the artboard. In the Rectangle dialog box, change the Width to **9 in** and the Height to **8 in**. Click OK. This will become the mask.

4   Press the letter "D" to set the default stroke (black, 1pt) and fill (white) for the new rectangle.

5   Select the Selection tool (▶), and with the rectangle selected, click the Horizontal Align Center button (🔲) and then the Vertical Align Bottom button (🔲) in the Control panel to align the rectangle to the bottom, center of the artboard.

> **Note:** The object that is to become the opacity mask (the masking object) needs to be the top selected object in the artboard. If it is a single object, like a rectangle, it does not need to be a compound path. If the opacity mask is to be made from multiple objects, they need to be grouped.

> **Note:** If you wanted to create a mask that was the same dimensions as the image, instead of drawing a shape, you could have simply clicked the Make Mask button in the Transparency panel.

6   Press the Shift key, and click the Water.jpg image to select it as well.

7   Click the Transparency panel icon (⬤) on the right side of the workspace to expand the Transparency panel. Click the Make Mask button and leave the artwork selected.

After clicking the Make Mask button, the button now shows as "Release." If you were to click the button again, the image would no longer be masked.

Click the Make Mask button.   Notice the result.

Editing an opacity mask

Next, you'll adjust the opacity mask that you just created.

1. In the Transparency panel, Shift-click the mask thumbnail (as indicated by the white rectangle on the black background) to disable the mask.

   Notice that a red X appears on the mask in the Transparency panel and that the entire Water.jpg image reappears in the Document window.

▶ **Tip:** To disable and enable an opacity mask, you can also choose Disable Opacity Mask or Enable Opacity Mask from the Transparency panel menu.

2. In the Transparency panel, Shift-click the mask thumbnail to enable the mask again.

3. Click to select the mask thumbnail on the right side of the Transparency panel.

   Clicking the opacity mask in the Transparency panel selects the mask (the rectangle path) on the artboard. If the mask isn't selected, click to select it with the Selection tool (▶). With the mask selected, you can't edit other artwork on the artboard. Also, notice that the document tab shows (<Opacity Mask>/Opacity Mask), indicating that you are now editing the mask.

▶ **Tip:** To show the mask by itself (in grayscale if the original mask had color in it) on the artboard, you can also Option-click (Mac OS) or Alt-click (Windows) the mask thumbnail in the Transparency panel.

4. Click the Layers panel icon (◆) on the right side of the workspace to reveal the Layers panel.

   In the Layers panel, notice that the layer <Opacity Mask> appears, indicating that the mask—rather than the artwork that is being masked—is selected.

5. With the mask selected in the Transparency panel and on the artboard, in the Control panel, click the Fill color and select a white-to-black linear gradient, called "White, Black."

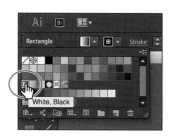

You will now see that where there is white in the mask, the Water.jpg image is showing, and where there is black, it is hidden. The gradient mask gradually reveals the image.

6 Make sure that the Fill box (toward the bottom of the Tools panel or in the Swatches panel) is selected.

7 Select the Gradient tool () in the Tools panel. Holding down the Shift key, position the pointer close to the bottom of the Water.jpg image. Click and drag up to just below the top of the mask shape, as shown in the figure. Release the mouse button, and then release the Shift key.

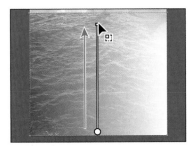

Drag to edit the opacity mask.   Notice the result.

8 Click the Transparency panel icon (⬛), and notice how the mask has changed appearance in the Transparency panel.

Next, you'll move the image but not the opacity mask. With the image thumbnail selected in the Transparency panel, both the image and the mask are linked together by default, so that if you move the image, the mask moves as well.

● **Note:** You have access to the link icon only when the image thumbnail, not the mask thumbnail, is selected in the Transparency panel.

9 In the Transparency panel, click the image thumbnail so that you are no longer editing the mask. Click the link icon (⬛) between the image thumbnail and the mask thumbnail. This allows you to move just the image or the mask, but not both.

● **Note:** The position of the Water.jpg does not have to match the figure exactly.

10 With the Selection tool, begin dragging the Water.jpg image down. As you drag, press and hold the Shift key to constrain the movement vertically. After you drag a little, release the mouse button, and then release the Shift key to see where it is positioned.

11 In the Transparency panel, click the broken link icon () between the image thumbnail and the mask thumbnail to link the two together again.

12 Choose Object > Arrange > Send To Back to send the Water.jpg image behind the Lilypads.psd image. It won't look like anything has changed on the artboard, but later you will attempt to select the Lilypads.psd image and it will need to be on top of the Water.jpg image.

13 Choose Select > Deselect, and then choose File > Save.

Sampling colors in placed images

You can *sample*, or *copy*, the colors in placed images to apply the colors to other objects in the artwork. Sampling colors enables you to easily make colors consistent in a file that combines images and Illustrator artwork.

1 In the Layers panel, make sure that all of the layers are collapsed, and then click the visibility column to the left of the Text and Pictures layers to show the layer contents on the artboard.

2 With the Selection tool (▶) selected, click the "green" text.

3 Make sure that the Fill box (toward the bottom of the Tools panel) is selected.

4 Select the Eyedropper tool (✐) in the Tools panel, and Shift-click a green area in the one of the lily pads to sample and apply a green color to the text. You can try sampling the color of different images and content, if you want. The color you sample is applied to the selected text.

● **Note:** Using the Shift key with the Eyedropper tool allows you to apply only the sampled color to the selected object. If you don't use the Shift key, you apply all appearance attributes to the selected object.

5 Choose Select > Deselect.

Working with image links

When you place images in Illustrator and either link to them or embed them, you can see a listing of these images in the Links panel. You use the Links panel to see and manage all linked or embedded artwork. The Links panel displays a small thumbnail of the artwork and uses icons to indicate the artwork's status. From the Links panel, you can view the images that have been linked to and embedded, replace a placed image, update a linked image that has been edited outside of Illustrator, or edit a linked image in the original application, such as Photoshop.

Finding link information

When you place an image, it can be helpful to see where the original image is located, what transformations have been applied to the image (such as rotation and scale), and more information. Next, you will explore the Links panel to discover image information.

1 Choose Window > Links to open the Links panel.

Looking in the Links panel, you will see a listing of all of the images you've placed. Images with a name to the right of the image thumbnail are linked, and those images without a name are embedded. You can also tell if an image has been embedded by the embedded icon (▣).

Note: You can also double-click the image in the Layers panel list to see the image information.

2 Scroll in the panel, if necessary, and select the Kayak.jpg image (which shows the name to the right of the thumbnail). Click the toggle arrow in the lower-left corner of the Layers panel to reveal the link information at the bottom of the panel.

You will see information, such as the name, original location of the image, the file format, resolution, modification and creation dates, transformation information, and more.

Tip: Another way to access the Links panel for a linked image is to click the orange text "Linked File" in the Control panel to open the Links panel. If you select a linked image or the image content of a Clip Group, you will see the text "Linked File."

3 Click the Go To Link button (🔗) below the list of images. The Kayak.jpg image will be selected and centered in the Document window. The word "Linked File" will appear in the Selection Indicator of the Control panel (on the left end).

4 In the Control panel, click the file name Kayak.jpg to reveal a menu of options.

The menu of options that appears mirrors those options found in the Links panel. If you were to select an embedded image, you would instead see the link named Embedded in the Control panel. Clicking that orange link would show the same menu options but some of them would be inaccessible.

5 Press the Escape key to hide the menu and leave the Kayak.jpg image selected.

Embedding and unembedding images

As was mentioned previously, if you choose not to link to an image when placing it, the image is embedded in the Illustrator file. That means that the image data is stored within the Illustrator document. You can choose to embed an image later, after placing and linking to it, if you choose. Also, you might want to use embedded images outside of Illustrator or to edit them in an image-editing application like Photoshop. Illustrator allows you to unembed images, which saves the embedded artwork to your file system as a PSD or TIFF file (you can choose) and automatically links it to the Illustrator file. Next, you will embed an image in the document.

Note: Neither 1-bit images nor images that are either locked or hidden can be unembedded.

1 With the Kayak.jpg image still selected, click the Embed button in the Control panel to embed the image.

The link to the original image file is removed, and the image data is embedded in the Illustrator document. Visually, you can tell the image is embedded because it no longer has the X going through the middle of it (with the image selected and edges showing [View > Show Edges]) and an embed icon (▣) appears in the Layers panel to the far right of the name.

Note: Certain file formats, like PSD, show an Import Options dialog box when you embed the image, allowing you to select placement options.

With an image embedded, you may realize that you need to make an edit to that image in a program like Adobe Photoshop. You can just as easily unembed an image, which is what you'll do next to the Kayak.jpg image.

2 With the Kayak.jpg image still selected on the artboard, click the Unembed button in the Control panel. You can also choose Unembed from the Links panel menu (▾☰).

3 In the Unembed dialog box, navigate to the Lessons > Lesson14 > images folder (if you are not already there). Choose File Format (Mac OS) or TIFF (*.TIF) from the Save As Type (Windows) menu and click Save.

Note: The embedded Kayak.jpg image data is unembedded from the file and saved as a TIFF file in the images folder. The kayak image on the artboard is now linked to the TIFF file.

Replacing a linked image

You can easily replace a linked or embedded image with another image to update the artwork. The replacement image is positioned exactly where the original image was, so no adjustment should be necessary if the new image is of the same dimensions. If you scaled the image that you are replacing, you may need to resize the replacement image to match the original. Next, you will replace several images.

1 With the Selection tool (▶) selected, drag the gradient-filled rectangle off the left edge of the artboard on top of the Kayak.tif image, centering it on the image using Smart Guides.

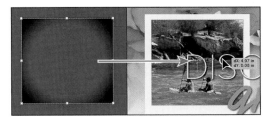

2 Choose Object > Arrange > Bring To Front.

3 In the Layers panel, click the edit column to the left of the Background layer to lock the layer content on the artboard.

4 Drag across the Kayak.tif image and the light-gray rectangle beneath it to select the artwork. Choose Object > Group.

5 Drag the new group up so that its top aligns with the top of the artboard.

6 Option-drag (Mac OS) or Alt-drag (Windows) the group down to create a copy (see the figure below for approximately where to drag it).

7 Repeat this two more times so that you have four image groups on the artboard and they are positioned roughly like you see in the following figure.

In the Links panel, you will see a series of Kayak.tif images listed in the panel. Next, you will replace the images and then rotate the pictures.

8 Click the second group from the top on the artboard. In the Links panel, with one of the Kayak.tif images selected, click the Relink button (⬚) below the list of images.

9   In the Place dialog box, navigate to the Lessons > Lesson14 > images folder and select People.psd. Make sure that the Link option is selected. Click Place to replace the kayak image with the People.psd image.

▶ **Tip:** The new image is masked in the same shape. If you need to edit either the image or the clipping path, you could click the Edit Contents button (⬚) or the Edit Clipping Path button (⬚) in the Control panel.

When you replace an image, any color adjustments made to the original image are not applied to the replacement. However, masks applied to the original image are preserved. Any layer modes and transparency adjustments that you've made to other layers also may affect the image's appearance.

10 Click the third group from the top on the artboard. In the Links panel, with one of the Kayak.tif selected, click the Relink button (⬚) below the list of images.

11 In the Place dialog box, navigate to the Lessons > Lesson14 > images folder and select Hiking.jpg. Make sure that the Link option is selected. Click Place to replace the kayak image with the new image.

12 Click the bottom group. In the Links panel, with one of the Kayak.tif images selected, click the Relink button (⬚) below the list of images.

13 In the Place dialog box, navigate to the Lessons > Lesson14 > images folder and select Snorkel.psd. Make sure that the Link option is selected. Click Place to replace the kayak image with the Snorkel.psd image.

14 Choose Select > Deselect. Click the top image group with the Kayak.tif image. Position the pointer just off the upper-right corner and when you see the rotate arrows (↖), click and drag to the left until you see approximately 10° in the measurement label.

Note: The figure shows rotating the final image group.

15 Click the group with the People.psd image just below the top group and rotate the group to the right, until you see approximately −5° in the measurement label. Rotate the Hiking.jpg group to the left until you see approximately 10° in the measurement label. Rotate the Snorkel.psd image group to the right until you see approximately −10° in the measurement label.

16 Choose File > Save.

Packaging a file

When you *package* a file, you create a folder that contains a copy of the Illustrator document, any necessary fonts, copies of the linked graphics, and a report that contains information about the packaged files. This is an easy way to hand off all necessary files for an Illustrator project. Next, you will package the poster files.

1 Choose File > Package. In the Package dialog box, set the following options:

Note: If the file needs to be saved, a dialog box will appear to notify you.

- Click the folder icon (📁) and navigate to the Lesson14 folder, if you are not already there. Click Choose (Mac OS) or Select Folder (Windows) to return to the Package dialog box.
- Folder name: **GreenIsle** (remove "_Folder" from the name)
- Options: Leave at default settings.

2 Click Package.

Note: The Create Report option, when selected, will create a package report (summary) in the form of a .txt (text) file, which by default is placed in the package folder.

The Copy Links option *copies* all of the linked files to the new folder it creates. The Collect Links In Separate Folder option creates a folder called Links and copies the links into there. The Relink Linked Files To Document option updates the links within the Illustrator document to link to the new copies.

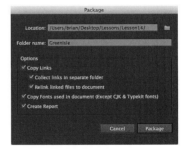

3 In the next dialog box that discusses font-licensing restrictions, click OK. Clicking Back would allow you to deselect Copy Fonts Used In Document (Except CJK & Typekit fonts).

4 In the final dialog box to appear, click Show Package to see the package folder.

In the package folder should be a folder called Links that contains all of the linked images. The GreenIsle Report (.txt file) contains information about the document contents.

5 Return to Illustrator, and choose File > Close.

Review questions

1 Describe the difference between *linking* and *embedding* in Illustrator.

2 What kinds of objects can be used as masks?

3 How do you create an opacity mask for a placed image?

4 What color modifications can you apply to a selected object using effects?

5 Describe how to replace a placed image with another image in a document.

6 Describe what *packaging* does.

Review answers

1 A *linked file* is a separate, external file connected to the Illustrator file by a link. A linked file does not add significantly to the size of the Illustrator file. The linked file must accompany the Illustrator file to preserve the link and to ensure that the placed file appears when you open the Illustrator file. An *embedded file* is included in the Illustrator file. The Illustrator file size reflects the addition of the embedded file. Because the embedded file is part of the Illustrator file, no link can be broken. You can update linked and embedded files using the Relink button (▨) in the Links panel.

2 A mask can be a simple or compound path. You can use type as a mask. You can import opacity masks with placed Photoshop files. You can also create layer clipping masks with any shape that is the topmost object of a group or layer.

3 You create an opacity mask by placing the object to be used as a mask on top of the object to be masked. Then you select the mask and the objects to be masked, and either click the Make Mask button in the Transparency panel or choose Make Opacity Mask from the Transparency panel menu.

4 You can use effects to change the color mode (RGB, CMYK, or grayscale) or to adjust individual colors in a selected object. You can also saturate or desaturate colors or invert colors in a selected object. You can apply color modifications to placed images, as well as to artwork created in Illustrator.

5 To replace a placed image with a different image, select the image in the Links panel. Then click the Relink button (▨) and locate and select the replacement image. Click Place.

6 *Packaging* is used to gather all of the necessary pieces for an Illustrator document. Packaging creates a copy of the Illustrator file, the linked images, and the necessary fonts (if desired), and gathers them all into a folder.

15 PREPARING CONTENT FOR THE WEB

Lesson overview

In this lesson, you'll learn how to do the following:

- Align content to the pixel grid.

- Work with the Slice and Slice Selection tools.

- Use the Save For Web command.

- Generate, export, and copy/paste CSS (Cascading Style Sheet) code.

- Save artwork as SVG.

 This lesson takes approximately 30 minutes to complete.

Download the project files for this lesson from the Lesson & Update Files tab on your Account page at www.peachpit.com and store them on your computer in a convenient location, as described in the Getting Started section of this book.

Your Account page is also where you'll find any updates to the chapters or to the lesson files. Look on the Lesson & Update Files tab to access the most current content.

Welcome to Venice

Experience true Venetian charm in this elegant, 3-bedroom apartment in a beautifully renovated 18th century building. Conveniently located within an easy walk from St. Mark's Square (*Piazza San Marco*), the apartment is tucked away on a quiet street to ensure that your stay is peaceful and relaxing.

Spend your days exploring this ancient city. Take a romantic gondola ride. Shop for fresh produce in the Rialto market. Visit St. Mark's basilica and the Doge's Palace. Tour the Grand Canal. View art by the Venetian masters. And don't forget to taste the gelato! Every two years, you can also experience the excitement of the Venice biennale, one of the most prestigious contemporary art exhibitions in the world.

You can optimize your Illustrator CC content for use on the Web and in screen presentations using various methods. For example, you can slice artwork and save it for the Web, export CSS and image files, and generate SVG (Scalable Vector Graphics) in the form of an .SVG file or SVG code.

Getting started

You'll be working in multiple art files during this lesson, but before you begin, restore the default preferences for Adobe Illustrator CC.

Note: If you have not already downloaded the project files for this lesson to your computer from your Account page, make sure to do so now. See the "Getting Started" section at the beginning of this book.

1 To ensure that the tools and panels function exactly as described in this lesson, delete or deactivate (by renaming) the Adobe Illustrator CC preferences file. See "Restoring default preferences" in the Getting Started section at the beginning of the book.

2 Double-click the Adobe Illustrator CC icon to start Adobe Illustrator.

3 Choose Window > Workspace > Reset Essentials to ensure that the workspace is set to the default settings.

Note: If you don't see "Reset Essentials" in the Workspace menu, choose Window > Workspace > Essentials before choosing Window > Workspace > Reset Essentials.

4 Choose File > Open. In the Open dialog box, navigate to the Lessons > Lesson15 folder. Select the L15_start.ai file and click Open.

This lesson contains a fictitious business name, address, and website address made up for the purposes of the project.

5 The Missing Fonts dialog box may appear. Click Sync Fonts to sync all of the missing fonts to your computer (your list may not match the figure). After they are synced and you see the message stating that there are no more missing fonts, click Close.

If you can't get the fonts to sync (a "Syncing Typekit fonts…" message doesn't go away), you can go to the Creative Cloud desktop application and choose Assets > Fonts to see what the issue may be (refer to the section "Changing font family and font style" in Lesson 7, "Adding type to a Poster," for more information on how to resolve it).

You can also just click Close in the Missing Fonts dialog box and ignore the missing fonts as you proceed. A third method is to click the Find Fonts button in the Missing Fonts dialog box and replace the fonts with a local font on your machine. You can also go to Help (Help > Illustrator Help) and search for "Find missing fonts."

6 Choose View > Fit Artboard In Window.

This fits the active artboard into the Document window so that you can see the entire artboard.

7   Choose File > Save As. In the Save As dialog box, navigate to the Lessons > Lesson15 folder and name the file **WebDesign.ai**. Leave the Format option set to Adobe Illustrator (ai) (Mac OS) or the Save As Type option set to Adobe Illustrator (*.AI) (Windows), and then click Save. In the Illustrator Options dialog box, leave the Illustrator options at their default settings, and then click OK.

Saving content for the Web

Using Illustrator CC, you can save your artwork for the Web using a variety of methods and formats. If you need Web images for use in a website or an onscreen presentation, you can use the File > Save For Web command. Images can be saved in several file formats, such as GIF, JPEG, and PNG. These three formats are optimized for use on the Web and are compatible with most browsers, yet each has different capabilities.

▶ **Tip:** To learn more about working with Web graphics, search for "File formats for exporting artwork" in Illustrator Help (Help > Illustrator Help).

If you are building a website or wish to hand off content to a developer, you can transform the visual designs in Illustrator to CSS styles using the CSS Properties panel (Window > CSS Properties) or File > Export command. Illustrator allows you to easily export CSS or copy and paste CSS from Illustrator into your HTML editor. You can also export Scalable Vector Graphics (SVG) using a variety of methods.

In the first part of the section on creating Web content, you will focus on the pixel grid and on slicing content for export using the Save For Web command. Then you will translate your design into CSS for use in a website.

Aligning content to the pixel grid

Before you save content for the Web, it's important to understand the pixel grid in Illustrator. It's critical that raster images look sharp, especially standard Web graphics at 72 pixels per inch (PPI) resolution. To enable Web designers to create pixel-accurate designs, you can align artwork to the pixel grid. The *pixel grid* is a grid of 72 squares per inch, vertically and horizontally, that is viewable when you zoom to 600% or higher with Pixel Preview mode enabled (View > Pixel Preview).

▶ **Tip:** To learn about working with text and anti-aliasing, see the PDF named "TextAntiAliasing.pdf" in the Lessons > Lesson_extras folder.

When the pixel-aligned property is enabled for an object, all the horizontal and vertical segments in the object get aligned to the pixel grid, which makes strokes appear especially crisp. When you create a new document, you can set the Align New Objects To Pixel Grid option at the document level by choosing Web from the Profile menu in the New Document dialog box. This makes all artwork (that can be aligned to the pixel grid) align to it automatically. You can also align content to the pixel grid after the content has been created, as you will do in this section.

1 Choose File > New. In the New Document dialog box, choose Web from the Profile menu. Click the triangle to the left of the Advanced content, toward the bottom of the dialog box.

In the Advanced settings, you can see that the Color Mode is RGB for all artwork you create, the Raster Effects are Screen (72 ppi), and Align New Objects To Pixel Grid is selected.

2 Click Cancel.

3 In the WebDesign.ai file, choose File > Document Color Mode and you will see that "RGB Color" is selected.

After you create a document, you can change the document color mode. This sets the default color mode for all new colors you create and the existing swatches. RGB is the correct color mode to use when creating content for the Web or for onscreen presentations.

4 Select the Zoom tool (🔍), and drag a marquee around the Bella Casa logo in the upper-left corner of the artboard, to zoom in very closely.

5 Choose View > Pixel Preview to preview a rasterized version of the design.

The artwork in Preview mode.   The artwork in Pixel Preview mode.

Tip: You can turn off the pixel grid by choosing Illustrator > Preferences > Guides & Grid (Mac OS) or Edit > Preferences > Guides & Grid (Windows) and deselecting Show Pixel Grid (Above 600% Zoom).

6 Choose 600% from the View menu in the lower-left corner of the Document window (in the Status bar).

By zooming in to at least 600%, and with Pixel Preview turned on, you can see a pixel grid appear, as in the figure. The pixel grid divides the artboard into 1 pt. (1/72-inch) increments.

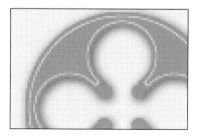

7 Choose View > Fit Artboard In Window.

8 Select the Zoom tool (🔍), and drag a marquee around the "Make Your Reservation Now" button at the bottom of the artboard to zoom in very closely. Click several times on the lower-left corner of the button until you see 800% in the View menu in the lower-left corner of the Document window.

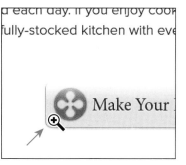

For the next steps, you need to see the pixel grid (zoom level of 600% or greater) and the stroke of the button.

9 Select the Selection tool (▶), and click to select the gray button shape (the rounded rectangle).

10 Choose View > Hide Edges so you can see the edge of the button more easily. Notice how the left edge of the button looks a little "fuzzy."

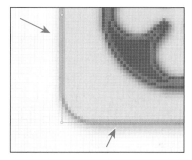

11 Click the word "Transform" (or X, Y, W, or H) in the Control panel, and select Align To Pixel Grid at the bottom of the Transform panel.

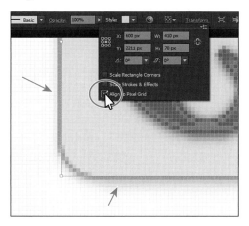

Objects that are pixel-aligned, but do not have any straight vertical or horizontal segments, are not modified to align to the pixel grid. For example, because a rotated rectangle does not have straight vertical or horizontal segments, it is not nudged to produce crisp paths when the pixel-aligned property is set for it.

12 Choose View > Fit Artboard In Window.

13 Choose View > Show Edges.

14 Choose Select > Object > Not Aligned To Pixel Grid to select all artwork in the document that is eligible to be, but is not currently, aligned to the pixel grid.

15 Click the word "Transform" (or X, Y, W, or H) in the Control panel, and select Align To Pixel Grid. Leave the Transform panel showing.

16 Click the Transform panel menu icon (▾≣).

Notice that Align New Objects To Pixel Grid is selected. This option sets all new artwork to be aligned to the pixel grid automatically. If this document were created using a Print profile, it would not be selected, but you could turn it on here. Bringing non-aligned objects into documents with the Align New Objects To Pixel Grid option enabled does not automatically pixel-align those objects. To make such objects pixel-aligned, select the object and then select the Align To Pixel Grid option from the Transform panel. You cannot pixel-align objects such as rasters, raster effects, and text objects because such objects do not have real paths.

17 Press the Escape key to hide the Transform panel.

18 Choose Select > Deselect (if available), and then choose File > Save.

Slicing content

If you create artwork on an artboard and choose File > Save For Web, Illustrator creates a single image file the size of the artboard. One way around that would be to create multiple artboards for artwork, each containing a piece of the Web page, like a button, and save each artboard as a separate image file.

● **Note:** To learn more about creating slices, search for "Create slices" in Adobe Illustrator Help (Help > Illustrator Help).

You can also design your artwork on an artboard and slice the content. In Illustrator, you can create *slices* to define the boundaries of different Web elements in your artwork. For example, if you design an entire Web page on an artboard and you want to save a particular vector shape as a button for your website, that artwork can be optimized in GIF or PNG format, while the rest of the image is optimized as a JPEG file. You can isolate the button image by creating a slice. When you save the artwork as a Web page using the Save For Web command, you can choose to save each slice as an independent file with its own format and settings.

Next, you will create a new layer that will contain the slices, and then you will create slices for different parts of the artwork.

1　Click the Layers panel icon () to open the
Layers panel. Click to select the Text layer.
Option-click (Mac OS) or Alt-click (Windows)
the Create New Layer button (⬛) at the
bottom of the Layers panel. In the Layer
Options dialog box that appears, change the
name of the layer to **Slices** and click OK.
Make sure that the new layer named Slices is
selected and is at the top of the layer stack.

● **Note:** To learn
more about creating
layers, see the section
"Creating layers" in
Lesson 8, "Organizing
Your Artwork
with Layers."

● **Note:** The new layer you create may have a different layer color, and that's okay.

When you create slices, they are treated as objects and are listed in the
Layers panel and can be selected, deleted, resized, and more. It helps to keep
them on their own layer so that you can more easily manage them, but this
isn't necessary.

2　Select the Zoom tool (🔍), and drag a marquee around the Bella Casa logo in
the upper-left corner of the artboard. The "Bella Casa" text in the logo has been
converted to outlines (paths).

3　Select the Slice tool (✏) in the Tools panel. Click and drag a slice around the
circle, "Bella Casa" text shapes, and the "Luxury Venetian Holiday Rental" text,
stopping the bottom of the slice below the bottom curve of the "e" in "Bella." See
the figure for help. Don't worry about it fitting perfectly right now; you will edit
it later.

When you create a slice, Illustrator divides the surrounding artwork into
automatic slices to maintain the layout of the page. Auto slices account for the
areas of your artwork that you did not define as a slice. Illustrator regenerates
auto slices every time you add or edit your own slices. Also, notice the number
(3, in our case) in the upper-left corner of the slice you created. Illustrator
numbers slices from left to right and from top to bottom, beginning in the
upper-left corner of the artwork.

Next, you will create a slice based on selected content.

4　Press the Spacebar and drag down in the Document window using the Hand tool
(✋), until you can see the nav bar above the logo (at the top of the artboard).

5 Choose Select > Deselect.

6 Select the Selection tool (▶), and Shift-click the "CHECK AVAILABILITY" text and the button shape beneath it.

7 Select the Slices layer in the Layers panel to place the new slice on that layer.

8 Choose Object > Slice > Create From Selection.

▶ **Tip:** Use the Object > Slice > Make command when you want the slice dimensions to match the boundary of an element in your artwork. Using the Make command, if you move or modify the element, the slice area automatically adjusts to encompass the new artwork.

Illustrator can create slices based on guides you create or on content that you select in the Document window. When using the Create From Selection command, effects such as drop shadows will be included in the slice area.

9 Choose Select > Deselect, and then choose File > Save.

Selecting and editing slices

Editing user created slices is necessary, for instance, when sliced content changes or when what is included in the slice needs to change.

1 If necessary, scroll down the artboard so that you can see the Bella Casa logo in the upper-left corner of the artboard again.

2 Select the Slice Selection tool (▶✏) from the Slice tool group in the Tools panel by clicking and holding down on the Slice tool (✏).

3 Click in the center of the first slice you created over the Bella Casa logo. The selected slice is highlighted, and four corner bounding points appear.

The Slice Selection tool allows you to edit slices you've created using different methods. You can also select a user slice with the Selection (▶) or Direct Selection (▷) tools by clicking the stroke (edge) of the slice or from within the Layers panel.

4 Position the pointer over the lower-right corner of the selected slice. When a double arrow appears, click and drag toward the center of the logo until it fits tighter around the logo content. Make sure to include all of the logo content within the slice area.

When adjusting slices manually, you should contain all appearance attributes, like drop shadows, in the slice area. This can be difficult if the shadow is very blurry. Using the Object > Slice > Create From Selection command creates a slice that surrounds all appearance properties, like effects, if those effects are applied directly to the artwork and not to the layer the artwork is on (with multiple objects on the same layer). Using the Slice Selection tool, you can click and drag a slice, copy and paste it, delete it, and much more.

5   Choose Select > Deselect, and then choose View > Lock Slices so that you cannot select them.

6   Choose File > Save.

Using the Save For Web command

After slicing your artwork, if necessary, you can then optimize that artwork for use on the Web. You can use the File > Save For Web command to select optimization options and to preview optimized artwork. The key to the effective use of images on a website is finding the balance of resolution, size, and color to achieve optimal quality.

1   Choose View > Fit Artboard In Window, and then choose View > Hide Slices.

While working on your artwork, you don't have to have the slices showing. This allows you to concentrate on selecting artwork without selecting slices. You can also hide the layer that the slices are on if you created a layer for them in the Layers panel.

2   Select the Selection tool (↖), and Shift-click the orange bar behind the top navigation, the white semi-transparent rectangle behind the Bella Casa logo, and the large image behind the Bella Casa logo.

3   Choose Object > Hide > Selection.

When you save sliced content using the Save For Web command, all content that is showing in a slice will be flattened into a raster image. If you want to have transparency in the selected artwork (part of the image will be see-through), you need to first hide what you don't want to save. The areas where you see the artboard in a slice can be transparent, depending on the type of image you choose.

4   Choose Select > Deselect, if necessary.

5   Choose View > Show Slices, and ensure that the artwork and drop shadows are contained within the slices (you may want to zoom in). If not, you can resize either slice using the Slice Selection tool.

6   Choose File > Save For Web.

● **Note:** To resize the slices, you need to make sure that they are unlocked. Choose View > Lock Slices. (If a check mark appears to the left of the menu item, they are locked.)

7   In the Save For Web dialog box, click the 2-Up tab at the top of the dialog box to select that display option, if it's not already selected.

This shows a split window with the original artwork on the left and the optimized artwork on the right (usually). You can tell which is the original artwork because it shows "Original: 'WebDesign.ai'" along with a file size below one of the preview areas. The optimized preview shows a file type like "GIF" and a file size below the preview area.

8   With the Slice Select tool (✄) selected (by default), click in the optimized area on the right. Click to select the slice that covers the Bella Casa logo at the top of the artboard, if it isn't selected already. A red arrow is pointing to it in the figure.

You can tell when a slice is selected because the artwork isn't dimmed and it has a light-brown border around it.

9   In the Preset area on the right side of the dialog box, choose PNG-24 from the Optimized File Format menu (below Name).

You can choose from four file formats, including GIF, JPEG, PNG-8, and PNG-24, as well as set the options for each in the Preset area. The available options change depending on the file format you select. If your image contains multiple slices that you are going to save, be sure to select each separately in the preview area and optimize all the slices.

10 Choose Selected Slices from the Export menu, if necessary.

Any slices that you select in the Save For Web dialog box will be exported. You can select multiple slices, after you've assigned optimization settings to them, by Shift-clicking the desired slices. By choosing All User Slices from the Export menu, all slices that you created will be exported.

11 Click the Preview button in the lower-left corner of the dialog box to launch the default Web browser on your computer and to preview the sliced content. After previewing the content, close the browser and return to Illustrator.

● **Note:** If nothing happens after clicking the Preview button, try clicking again. You may also need to click the Select Browser Menu button (🖳) to the right of the Preview button and choose Edit List to add a new browser.

12 In the Save For Web dialog box, click Save. In the Save Optimized As dialog box, navigate to the Lessons > Lesson15 folder and open it. Change the name to **Logo**, and click Save.

In your Lesson15 folder is a new images folder that Illustrator created. In that folder, you can see the single image that is labeled according to the name entered in the Save Optimized As dialog box, with the slice number appended to the end.

13 Choose View > Hide Slices.

14 Choose Object > Show All.

15 Choose Select > Deselect, and then choose File > Save.

Creating CSS code

As was mentioned earlier, you can transform the visual designs in Illustrator to CSS styles using the CSS Properties panel (Window > CSS Properties) or the File > Export command. This is a great way to move the styling from your Web design in Illustrator straight to your HTML editor or to hand it off to a Web developer.

● **Note:** Exporting or copying CSS from Illustrator CC does not create HTML for a Web page. It is intended to create CSS that is applied to HTML you create elsewhere, such as in Adobe Dreamweaver®.

Cascading Style Sheets are a collection of formatting rules, much like paragraph and character styles in Illustrator, that control the appearance of content in a Web page. Unlike paragraph and character styles in Illustrator, CSS can control the look and feel of text, as well as the formatting and positioning of page elements found in HTML.

```
1   html {
2       font-family: sans-serif;
3       -webkit-text-size-adjust: 100%;
4       -ms-text-size-adjust: 100%;
5   }
6   body {
7       margin: 0;
8   }
9   a:focus {
10      outline: thin dotted;
11  }
12  a:active, a:hover {
13      outline: 0;
14  }
15  h1 {
16      font-size: 2em;
17      margin: 0 0 0.2em 0;
18  }
```

An example of CSS code.

● **Note:** To learn more about CSS, visit the "Understanding Cascading Style Sheets" section of Adobe Dreamweaver Help (http://helpx.adobe.com/dreamweaver/using/cascading-style-sheets.html). You can also check out the CSS video series on Adobe Dreamweaver Developer Center: http://www.adobe.com/devnet/dreamweaver/articles/understanding_css_basics.html.

The great thing about generating CSS from your Illustrator artwork is that it allows for flexible Web workflows. You can export all of the styling from a document, or you can just copy the styling code for a single object or a series of objects and paste it into an external Web editor, like Adobe Dreamweaver. But creating CSS styling and using it effectively requires a bit of setup in your Illustrator CC document, and that's what you'll learn about first.

Setting up your design for generating CSS

If you intend to export or copy and paste CSS from Illustrator CC, slicing is not a necessary part of that process, but setting up the Illustrator CC file properly before creating CSS allows you to name the CSS styles that are generated. In this next section, you'll look at the CSS Properties panel and see how you can set up the content for style export using *named* or *unnamed* content.

1 Choose Window > Workspace > Reset Essentials.

● **Note:** The CSS Properties panel shown here is an example and will not reflect exactly what you see in your panel.

2 Choose Window > CSS Properties to open the CSS Properties panel.

Using the CSS Properties panel, you can do the following:

- Preview CSS code for selected objects.

- Copy CSS code for selected objects.

- Export generated styling for selected objects to a CSS file (along with any images used).

- Change options for the CSS code exported.

- Export the CSS for all objects to a CSS file.

3 With the Selection tool (▶) selected, click to select the orange rectangle behind the navigation at the top of the artboard (see the figure).

Take a look in the CSS Properties panel, and you will see that a message appears in the preview area. Instead of CSS code (which is what the preview area typically shows), the message states that the object needs to be named in the Layers panel or you need to allow Illustrator to create styling from "unnamed objects."

4 Open the Layers panel and click the Locate Object button () at the bottom of the panel, to easily find the selected object in the panel. Double-click directly on the name of the selected <Path> object, and change the name to **navbar** (lowercase). Press Enter or Return to make the change.

● **Note:** You may need to drag the left edge of the Layers panel to the left to see the entire name of the object.

5 Look in the CSS Properties panel again, and you should see a style named .navbar.

● **Note:** You may wish to drag the bottom edge of the CSS Properties panel down like we did, to see the entire style.

When content is unnamed in the Layers panel, a CSS style is not created for it, by default. If you name the object in the Layers panel, the CSS is generated and the name of the style created matches the object name in the Layers panel. Illustrator creates styles called *classes* for most content.

● **Note:** If you see a style named ".navbar_1_" it's usually because there is an extra space after the name "navbar" in the Layers panel.

▶ **Tip:** You can tell a style is a class in CSS because the name has a period (.) before it.

▶ **Tip:** If you are using HTML5 markup in your HTML editor, any objects in the Layers panel that you name according to the standard HTML5 markup tags, like "header," "footer," "section," or "aside," for instance, will not become a class style when the CSS code is generated. Rather, the style will be named according to the HTML5 markup tag.

For objects in the design (not including text objects, as you will see), the name you give them in the Layers panel should match the class name in the HTML that is created in a separate HTML editor, like Dreamweaver. But, you can also forgo naming the objects in the Layers panel and simply create generic styles that you can then export or paste into an HTML editor and name there. You will see how to do that next.

6 With the Selection tool, click to select the transparent white rectangle behind the Bella Casa logo. In the CSS Properties panel, a style will not appear since the object is unnamed in the Layers panel (it just has the generic <Path> name).

7 Click the Export Options button (▦) at the bottom of the CSS Properties panel.

The CSS Export Options dialog box that appears contains export options that you can set, such as which units to use, which properties to include in the styles, and other options, like which Vendor pre-fixes to include.

8 Select Generate CSS For Unnamed Objects, and click OK.

9 Look in the CSS Properties panel again. With the white rectangle still selected, a style called .st0 appears in the preview area of the CSS Properties panel.

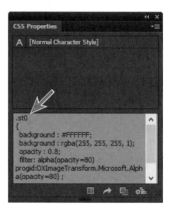

.st0 is short for "style 0" and is a generic name for the formatting that is generated. Every object that you don't name in the Layers panel will now be named .st1, .st2, and so on, after turning on Generate CSS For Unnamed Objects. This type of style naming can be useful if, for instance, you are creating the Web page yourself and you are going to paste or export the CSS from Illustrator and name it in your HTML editor, or if you simply needed some of the CSS formatting for a style you already have in your HTML editor.

10 Choose Select > Deselect, and then choose File > Save.

Working with character styles and CSS code

Illustrator will create CSS styles based on text formatting, as well. Formatting, such as font family, font size, leading (called *line-height* in CSS), color, kerning and tracking (collectively called *letter-spacing* in CSS), and more, can be captured in the CSS code. Any character styles that are applied to text in your design are listed in the CSS Properties panel as a CSS style and have the same name as the character style. Text that has formatting applied, without a character style applied, will have a generic CSS style name when Illustrator generates the style.

● **Note:** Currently, paragraph styles are not taken into account when naming styles in the CSS code that is generated.

Next, you will create and then apply a character style to text.

1. In the CSS Properties panel, notice the style named [Normal Character Style], toward the top of the panel.

   In the CSS Properties panel, only character styles that are applied to text appear. The Normal Character Style is applied to text by default, so it appears in the panel. If you create character styles but don't apply them to text, they will not appear in the CSS Properties panel.

2. Choose Window > Type > Character Styles to open the Character Styles panel.

3. Select the Type tool (**T**) in the Tools panel. Select the heading text "Welcome to Venice." You may want to zoom in on it.

4. Option-click (Mac OS) or Alt-click (Windows) the Create New Style button at the bottom of the Character Styles panel. In the Character Style Options dialog box, change the Style Name to **Head1**. Click OK.

5. Option-click (Mac OS) or Alt-click (Windows) the Head1 style in the Character Styles panel to apply it to the selected text. The text should now have the Head1 style applied.

In the CSS Properties panel, the character style named Head1 should appear in the list. This indicates that it is applied to text in the design.

6   Select the Selection tool (▶), and with the "Welcome to Venice" text object still selected, you will see CSS code in the preview area of the CSS Properties panel.

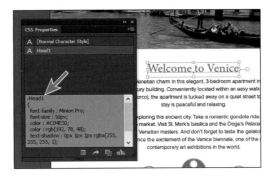

Selecting a text object will show all of the generated CSS code for the styling used in the entire text area. With just the text selected, the CSS is not shown in the CSS Properties panel.

You can also use the character styles listed in the CSS Properties panel as a way to apply the styles to text, which is what you'll do next.

7   Select the Type tool and scroll down to the artboard so you can see the "About Bella Casa" text toward the bottom. Select the black text "About Bella Casa."

8   Click the Head1 style name in the CSS Properties list to apply the formatting to the selected text.

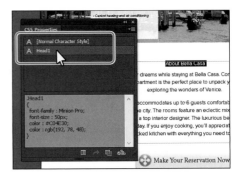

This applies the Head1 character style, but it may not apply all of the formatting. If you look in the Character Styles panel, you may see a plus sign (+) next to the Head1 style name, indicating local formatting that is overriding the Head1 style formatting.

9   If necessary, click once more on the Head1 style name in the CSS Properties panel to remove the local formatting. The text should now look like the "Welcome to Venice" text.

● **Note:** The text may no longer fit in the type object. You may need to resize it to fit the text.

10 Select the Selection tool, and make sure that the type object that contains the "About Bella Casa" heading is selected. Look in the CSS Properties panel, and you will see a series of CSS styles listed. These are the styles applied to all of the text in the type area.

● **Note:** Selecting a type area gives you the ability to see all of the CSS code generated from the styling. It is also a great way to be able to copy or export all of the text formatting from a selected type area.

Working with graphic styles and CSS code

CSS code can also be copied or exported for any graphic styles that are applied to content. Next, you'll apply a graphic style and see the CSS code for it.

1   Scroll back up the artboard so that you can see the Bella Casa logo toward the top of the artboard. With the Selection tool (▶), click to select the transparent white rectangle behind the logo.

● **Note:** The unnamed style in the CSS Properties panel (.st0) is being generated because you selected Generate CSS For Unnamed Objects in the CSS Export options earlier.

2   Open the Graphic Styles panel (Window > Graphic Styles). Option-click (Mac OS) or Alt-click (Windows) the New Graphic Style button (▣) at the bottom of the panel. In the Graphic Style Options dialog box, change the Style Name to **Cover box** and click OK. The graphic style should be applied automatically to the white rectangle.

▶ **Tip:** Like selecting a character style in the CSS Properties panel to apply the formatting, you can also select content and select an Object style listed in the CSS Properties panel to apply it.

Looking in the CSS Properties panel, you will see the object style named "Cover box" listed, because it is applied to content in your document. You will also see CSS code for a style named .st0. The CSS code is the same as for the "Cover box" graphic style you just saw, since that graphic style is applied. But it's not naming the style with the "Cover box" name, since the graphic style is just a way to apply formatting and the CSS code is being generated for that particular object. Remember, this is an unnamed style, because we didn't rename the white rectangle object in the Layers panel.

3   Leave the white rectangle selected, and then choose File > Save.

Copying CSS

At times, you may only need to capture a bit of CSS code from part of your design to paste into your HTML editor or to send to a Web developer. Illustrator lets you copy and paste CSS code easily. Next, you will copy the CSS for a few objects and learn about how grouping can change the way CSS code is generated.

1 With the white rectangle still selected, click the Copy Selected Style button () at the bottom of the CSS Properties panel. This copies the CSS code currently showing in the panel.

● **Note:** You may see a yield sign icon (⚠) at the bottom of the panel when certain content is selected. It indicates that not all of the Illustrator appearance attributes (like the multiple strokes applied to the shape) can be written in the CSS code for the selected content.

Next, you will select multiple objects and copy the generated CSS code at the same time.

2 With the Selection tool (▶) selected and the white rectangle still selected, Shift-click the text "CHECK AVAILABILITY" at the top of the artboard to select both objects.

In the CSS Properties panel, you will not see any CSS code since you need to have Illustrator generate the code for more than one selected object.

▶ **Tip:** When CSS code appears in the CSS Properties panel for selected content, you can also select a part of the code and right-click the selected code, and then choose Copy to copy just that selection.

3 Click the Generate CSS button (▦) at the bottom of the panel.

The code for two CSS styles, .st0 and .NormalCharacterStyle, now appears in the bottom half of the CSS Properties panel. To see both styles, you may need to scroll down in the panel. Yours may be in a different order, and that's okay.

With both styles showing in the CSS Properties panel, you could copy the styles and paste them into your HTML editor code or paste them into an email to send to a Web developer, for instance.

4 With the Selection tool, click to select the orange circle shape in the Bella Casa logo.

In the CSS Properties panel, you will see CSS code for a style named .image. That code contains a background-image property. When Illustrator encounters artwork (or raster images) that it can't make CSS code from, it rasterizes the exported content (*not* the artwork on the artboard) when you export the CSS code. The CSS code that is generated can be applied to an HTML object, like a div, and the PNG image will be applied as a background image in the HTML object.

5 Scroll down the artboard until you see the circle and flourishes below the "Welcome to Venice" heading and text. Click to select a flourish to the right or left of the circle. Those will also be exported as separate PNG images.

6 Choose Select > Deselect.

7 Drag a marquee selection across the two flourishes and the circle to select them all. Click the Generate CSS button (▦) at the bottom of the CSS Properties panel to generate the CSS code for the selected artwork.

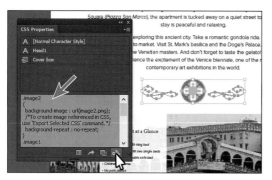

You will see the CSS code for three separate styles in the panel. If you were to copy the CSS code now, the images would not be created, only the code referring to them. In order to generate the images, you need to export the code, which you will do in the next section.

8 Choose Object > Group to group the three objects together. Leave the group selected for the next section.

Notice that, in the CSS Properties panel, a single CSS style is now showing (.image). Grouping content tells Illustrator to create a single image (in this case) from the grouped content. Having a single Web image would most likely be better if you intend on placing it on a Web page.

Exporting CSS

You can also export part or all of the CSS code for your page design. Exporting CSS code has the distinct advantages of creating a CSS file (.css) and exporting PNG files for content that is considered unsupported. In this section, you will see both methods.

1   With the group still selected, click the Export Selected CSS button (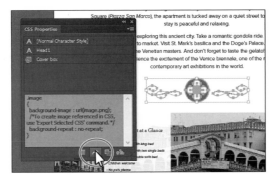) at the bottom of the CSS Properties panel.

2   In the Export CSS dialog box, make sure that the file name is WebDesign. Navigate to the Lessons > Lesson15 > ForCSSExport folder, and click Save to save a CSS file named WebDesign.css and a PNG image file.

3   In the CSS Export Options dialog box, leave all settings at default and click OK.

▶ **Tip:** You can choose a resolution for rasterized artwork in the CSS Export Options dialog box. By default, it uses the Document Raster Effects resolution (Effect > Document Raster Effects Settings).

4   Go to the Lessons > Lesson15 > ForCSSExport folder on your hard drive. In that folder, you should now see the WebDesign.css file and an image named image.png.

As stated earlier, the CSS code that was generated assumes that you are going to apply the CSS styling to an object in your HTML editor and that the image will become a background image for the object. With the image generated, you can use it for other parts of your Web page as well. Next, you will export all of the CSS from the design, after setting a few CSS options.

5   Back in Illustrator, choose File > Export. In the Export dialog box, set the Format option to CSS (css) (Mac OS) or Save As Type option to CSS (*.CSS) (Windows). Change the file name to **WebDesign_all**, and make sure that you navigate to the Lessons > Lesson15 > ForCSSExport folder. Click Export.

● **Note:** You can also export all of the CSS from your design by choosing Export All from the CSS Properties panel. If you want to change the export options first, you can set them by clicking the Export Options button (▦) at the bottom of the CSS Properties dialog box.

6   In the CSS Export Options dialog box, leave all of the options at their default settings and click OK. You most likely will see a dialog box telling you that images will be overwritten. Click OK.

Position and size properties are not added to the CSS code by default. In certain situations, you will need to export CSS with those options selected. The Include Vendor Pre-fixes options are selected by default. *Vendor pre-fixes* are a way for certain browser makers (each is listed in the dialog box) to add support for new CSS features. You can choose to exclude these prefixes by deselecting them.

7   Go to the Lessons > Lesson15 > ForCSSExport folder, and you will see the new CSS file named WebDesign_all.css and a series of images created because the Rasterize Unsupported Art option was selected in the CSS Export Options dialog box.

● **Note:** Your file sorting and icons may look different in the ForCSSExport folder, and that's okay.

8   Return to Illustrator, choose File > Save (if necessary) and choose File > Close to close the document.

Saving artwork as SVG

SVG (Scalable Vector Graphics) are used to define vector-based graphics for the Web that won't lose quality if they are zoomed or resized, such as a logo. They are a vector format that describes images as shapes, paths, text, and filter effects. The resulting files are compact and provide high-quality graphics on the Web, in print, and even on resource-constrained, handheld devices. Most major modern Web browsers—like Mozilla Firefox, Internet Explorer 9+, Google Chrome, Opera, and Safari—have at least some support for viewing SVG.

Illustrator allows you to select vector artwork, choose Edit > Copy, and then simply paste the SVG code that it generates into HTML in an HTML editor, or you can export as an SVG (.svg) file. In this section, you'll export as SVG (.svg) and explore the SVG export options.

1   Choose Window > Workspace > Reset Essentials.

2   Choose File > Open. In the Open dialog box, navigate to the Lessons > Lesson15 folder. Select the Logo_SVG.ai file and click Open.

3   Choose View > Fit Artboard In Window.

When saving artwork as SVG, the artboard size is important. Notice that the artboard is cropped very closely to the edges of the logo. The artboard size will determine the dimensions of the SVG file just like it would in PNG or JPG.

4   Choose File > Save As. In the Save As dialog box, choose SVG (svg) from the Format menu (Mac OS) or SVG (*.SVG) from the Save As Type menu (Windows). Navigate to the Lessons > Lesson15 folder (if necessary).

Notice the option "Use Artboards." By default, the first artboard (at the top of the Artboards panel) will determine the dimensions of the SVG file. Artwork on other artboards will not appear in the SVG file. If you wanted to save a series of icons, for instance, as SVG, you could create artboards for each and select Use Artboards to create a series of SVG files—one for each artboard.

5   Leave the Use Artboards option deselected and click Save.

6   In the SVG Options dialog box, click More Options. There are a lot of options for creating the SVG, but the default settings work well most of the time. The Responsive option, which is selected by default, allows the SVG file to be resizable using CSS.

7   Click the world icon at the bottom of the dialog box to launch your default browser and view the SVG file.

8 Close the browser and return to Illustrator. Click OK in the SVG Options dialog box. If you were to look in the Lessons > Lesson15 folder, you should see Logo_SVG.svg.

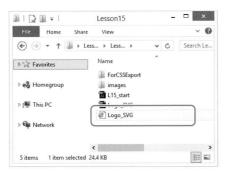

▶ Tip: If you wanted to see the actual SVG code that is created, you could click the SVG Code button in the SVG Options dialog box to open the SVG content in an editor.

Notice that the document open in Illustrator is now Logo_SVG.svg. SVG files created by Illustrator using the default options can be opened later in Illustrator for editing.

9 Choose File > Close to close the logo file.

Copy and paste from Illustrator

You can also select and copy artwork in Illustrator, then paste it into your favorite text editor (like Adobe Edge Code) and SVG code will be generated and pasted. Instead of generating an SVG file, the code is pasted inline. This can be useful if you want to edit the code yourself, or even manipulate the contents with CSS or JavaScript.

SVG and fonts

When it comes to fonts in artwork saved as SVG, you need to be careful. Not all browsers (including Firefox and Internet Explorer) fully support all fonts used in your SVG file. It's best to use a Web-safe font or convert the fonts to outlines. Since converting fonts to outlines can increase file size greatly, best practice is to outline fonts only when you have a few words in the artwork, for instance. If you feel comfortable working with the generated SVG code and CSS, you can also create a reference to a hosted font, for instance, but that is beyond the scope of this section.

When you save as SVG (File > Save As), in the SVG Options dialog box, there are two options for fonts: **Type** and **Subsetting**.

For the Type option, you can choose **Adobe CEF**, **SVG**, or **Convert To Outline**. **Adobe CEF** uses font hinting for better rendering of small fonts. This font type is supported by the Adobe SVG Viewer but may not be supported by other SVG viewers. **SVG** is the default option and is the format defined by the W3C (World Wide Web Consortium). The SVG option offers maximum support by SVG viewers, but the text may not be as refined as if you chose Adobe CEF. The third option, **Convert To Outline**, can be useful if you want to convert your text content into SVG paths and ensure that the text looks like it did in Illustrator. This can be used, for instance, for an icon with a few characters in a word like "Home." If you use more complex fonts, like script fonts, the file size of your SVG file can increase greatly if you choose Convert To Outline. Converting fonts to outline in SVG can also make the SVG file less accessible.

The Subsetting option is useful if you include a reference to fonts in your SVG file (by choosing SVG or Adobe CEF from the Type menu). Subsetting controls which glyphs (characters of a particular font) are embedded in the exported SVG file.

Note: For more information on SVG options, search for "Save in SVG format" in Illustrator Help (Help > Illustrator Help).

Review questions

1 Why do we align content to the pixel grid?

2 Name the three image file types that can be chosen in the Save For Web dialog box.

3 Describe the difference between *named* and *unnamed* content, when it comes to generating CSS.

4 What is SVG, and why is it useful?

Review answers

1 Aligning content to the pixel grid is useful for providing a crisp appearance to the edges of artwork. When Align To Pixel Grid is enabled for artwork, all of the horizontal and vertical segments in the object are aligned to the pixel grid.

2 The three image file types that can be chosen in the Save For Web dialog box are: JPEG, GIF, and PNG. PNG has two versions: PNG-8 and PNG-24.

3 Named content is content whose layer name in the Layers panel has been changed. When content is unnamed in the Layers panel (the default layer name is used), a CSS style is not created for the content, by default. If you name the object in the Layers panel, the CSS is generated and the name of the style created matches the object name in the Layers panel. In order to generate CSS styles for unnamed content, you need to enable this in the CSS Export Options dialog box by clicking the Export Options button (▥) in the CSS Properties panel.

4 SVG, or Scalable Vector Graphics (SVG), is a file format that is used to define vector-based graphics for the Web that won't lose quality if they are zoomed or resized, such as a logo. The resulting files are compact and provide high-quality graphics on the Web, in print, and even on resource-constrained, handheld devices.

INDEX

SYMBOLS

* (asterisk), 305
[ ] (Bracket keys), 105, 323

A

Account page, 10
Add New Effect button, 357
Adobe. *See also* specific applications
  additional resources from, 4–5
  Authorized Training Centers for, 5
  syncing settings using Creative Cloud, 5, 9, 12–13, 58
Adobe Bridge, 403
Adobe Creative Cloud
  launching desktop app for, 221, 251
  learning resources for, 4
  libraries for, 6, 398
  syncing settings using, 5, 9, 12–13, 58
  viewing fonts with, 223
Adobe Flash symbols, 389
Adobe Illustrator
  about, 32
  Bridge with, 403
  combining images from other apps in, 403
  compatibility of imported text, 216
  copying/pasting artwork from, 449
  drawing modes for, 106–109
  generating CSS from artwork in, 437–438
  help for, 58
  installing software for, 2
  placed Microsoft documents in, 218
  placing images in, 22, 404–411
  starting and opening files in, 32–34
  syncing settings with other computers, 5, 9, 12–13, 58
  Typekit with older versions, 225
  using Photoshop raster effects in, 339, 357
  using raster images in, 22
  vector effects in, 339, 357
Adobe Photoshop
  editing color in images from, 410–411
  importing files from, 406–408
  importing layers as objects, 407
  unembedding images from, 421

using raster effects in Illustrator, 339, 357
aligning
  to artboard, 71, 77
  content to pixel grid, 429–432, 451
  objects, 69–71, 77
  text in perspective, 375
alignment guides. *See* guides
Anchor Point tool, 164, 173
anchor points. *See also* corner points; smooth points
  about, 148
  adding, 162–163
  aligning, 70
  closing, 156
  converting smooth to corner, 150–151, 163, 164, 173
  deleting, 158, 162–163
  displaying location of, 64
  enhancements to, 9
  joining specific, 95
  nudging, 161
  setting with Curvature tool, 157
  setting with Pen tool, 154
  showing selection preferences for, 65
  viewing handles for multiple, 161
anchors. *See* anchor points
angle of gradient, 278–280, 299
appearance attributes. *See also* graphic styles
  applying to layers, 266–267, 271, 339, 357
  blending, 350
  copying object's, 189
  defined, 332
  deleting, 354
  editing, 333–334
  found on Appearance panel, 332
  ordering rows of, 332, 337
  removing, 354
  reordering, 338
  saving as graphic styles, 348
  selecting like, 66–67
Appearance panel
  accessing effect options from, 357
  adding second stroke and fill from, 335–337
  Clear Appearance button, 353

multiple anchor points, 161, 163

multiple artboards

creating, 80–81

navigating, 52–54, 59

multiple graphic styles, 355

multiple image placements, 409–410

N

named vs. unnamed Web content, 433, 451

naming

layers, 253

selections, 67, 77

sublayers, 254

navigating

artboards, 54–56, 119

content in Layers panel, 257

multiple artboards, 52–54, 59

between text fields, 276

Navigator panel, 54–56, 59

nested groups, 73–74

New Brush dialog box, 311

New Document dialog box

illustrated, 12

setting and saving options for, 80–81

setting color mode in, 177

new features, 6–9

Creative Cloud Libraries, 6, 398

Curvature tool, 6, 156–158

Illustrator enhancements, 9

Join tool, 9, 95, 171–172

Live Shapes, 7, 86–87, 88, 113

path segment reshaping, 8

Pen tool preview and enhancements, 8

Pencil tool enhancements, 8

Touch workspace, 7

Typekit font library, 8, 26–27, 221, 225, 251

New Swatch button (Swatches panel), 276

New Swatch dialog box, 181

New Workspace dialog box, 46

nonprintable area, 54

nudging

anchor points, 161

text, 231

O

objects

adding effects to, 357

adjusting plane to match, 376–377

aligning, 69–71, 77

applying gradient to multiple, 287

arranging, 74–75

choosing items without fill, 63, 77, 113

color controls for painting, 178–179

coloring, 14, 180

converting to Live Paint group, 206

copying appearance attributes of, 189

distorting with effects, 129–131

distributing spacing of, 70–71

drawing from center point, 83

drawing in perspective, 365–366

editing blend options for, 291

hiding and locking, 76, 77

joining paths of, 95–96

locating layer of, 254, 271

making graphic style from, 350

mapping artwork to 3D, 399

masking with, 425

measurement labels for, 64

modifying color with effects, 425

moving in perspective, 368, 370, 372, 381

outlining stroke of, 100–101

Pathfinder effects on, 103–104

perspective alignment for, 373

positioning precisely, 125–126

reflecting, 128–129, 159–160

resizing and reshaping type, 233–235

rotating, 131–132

scaling, 126–128, 139

scaling rectangle corners of, 86–87

selecting and transforming in perspective, 367–368

selecting behind, 75

selecting similar, 67

Selection tool for choosing, 62–64

shearing, 133–134

snapping to grid, 84, 365

text for masking, 414

threading text between, 218–219, 247

unable to erase, 106

ungrouping, 72

wrapping text around, 245

Offset Path effect, 343–344

one-point perspective, 362, 381

opacity

adding transparency to gradient, 288–290

brush stroke, 312

changing fill, 334, 335

opacity masks, 415–419

clipping masks vs., 415

creating, 415–416, 425

editing, 417–419

open paths, 95, 96

opening

artboards, 33

Illustrator files, 32–34

out port, 218, 219, 234, 247

Outline mode

effect on paint attributes, 93

making selections in, 68

toggling between Preview and, 51

viewing layer artwork in, 265

outlining

key objects, 69

strokes, 100–101

text, 246, 247

text with SVG paths, 450

output for documents, 81

overflow text, 216, 218, 247

Overprint mode, 51

overrides for paragraph styles, 236

P

Package command

packaging files, 424, 425

using Typekit fonts with, 225

Paintbrush tool

drawing with, 304–305, 327

editing paths with, 306–307, 314, 327

painting with drawing tools vs., 327

paths using Blob Brush vs., 322

precision painting with, 309

using Bristle brushes, 313–316

Paintbrush Tool Options dialog box, 306

painting. *See also* brushes

with Bristle brush, 314–316

creating Live Paint group, 206

with patterns, 201–205

with precision using Paintbrush pointer, 309

using Live Paint Bucket tool, 207

using Paintbrush tool vs. drawing tools for, 327

panel dock, 43

panel groups, 43–45

panel menus, 47

panels

closing, 38, 43, 335

Plane Switching Widget, 361, 365, 373, 374, 381

point type, 213, 215–216

polygons, 89–90, 113

positioning objects
on artboard, 83
automatic plane positioning, 377
precisely, 125–126

precision editing
crosshair icon, 143, 167
painting with Paintbrush pointer, 309
Pen tool for, 143
Pencil tool, 170
positioning objects with, 125–126
resizing shapes precisely, 105, 370

Preferences dialog box
adjusting user interface brightness, 36
restoring default preferences, 3–4
setting anchor point options, 65

Preserves Exact Dash And Gap Lengths button, 166

presets
envelope warp, 240
PDF, 138
perspective grid, 362, 364, 381

Preview mode, 51

printable area, 54

process color, 209

profile width, 100

proxy view area, 55, 59

Pucker & Bloat effect, 129–131

Q

quick tour, 10–29
applying color, 14
brushes, 28–29
clipping masks, 23
copying content, 19–20
creating documents, 12
drawing shapes, 13
drop shadow effects, 29
editing strokes, 16–17
gradients, 24–25
Image Trace, 22–23
Pencil tool, 15–16
placing images in Illustrator, 22
Shape Builder tool, 18–19
symbols, 20–22
syncing settings, 5, 9, 12–13, 58
type, 26–27
using layers, 14–15
warping text, 28

Width tool, 17–18

R

radial gradient, 282–285

raster effects
applying Photoshop, 339, 357
defined, 339
using, 344–345

raster images
about, 32
converting to vector artwork, 22–23, 110–112, 113
embedding with Art brush, 310–311, 327
placing in Illustrator, 404–405
rasterizing Bristle brush paths, 316
scaling placed, 405–406
tracing, 22–23, 110–112
using Art, Pattern, and Scatter brushes with, 327

Recolor Artwork dialog box, 196–200, 209

Rectangle dialog box, 84

Rectangle tool, 13

rectangles
creating, 82–84
preventing snapping to content, 101
rounded, 85–86

reference point for rotations, 132

Reflect dialog box, 159, 160

reflecting objects, 128–129, 159–160

reflowing text, 218

releasing
clipping masks, 108, 269
content from perspective grid, 379, 380

Relink button, 425

removing
appearance attributes, 354
blend from objects, 293
brush stroke, 308

renaming
artboards, 53, 119–120, 139
layers, 252
symbols, 394

reordering
appearance attributes, 338
artboards, 120–121
panel groups, 45
symbol thumbnails, 389

replacing
linked images, 421–424, 425

symbols, 391–392

repositioning
artboard, 118
images with keyboard shortcuts, 413

resetting
panels, 42
workspace, 46, 331

reshaping
text with envelope warp, 239–242
type object shapes, 233–235

resizing
artboards, 119, 139
content in perspective, 367
panels, 39, 44
placed images, 406
slices, 435
type object shapes, 233–235

restoring default preferences, 3–4, 46, 331

reversing
blends, 295
layer order, 264

reverting to last version of file, 66

Revolve 3D effect, 346

RGB color mode, 177

Right Vanishing Point dialog box, 371

Rotate dialog box, 130

Rotate 3D effect, 346

rotating
gradients, 279–280, 299
objects, 131–132
text, 229, 230–231

rounded rectangles, 85–86

ruler origin, 122, 123, 139

rulers
changing units of measure for, 123
showing/hiding, 82
types of, 122, 139

S

sampling
color in placed images, 419
text formats, 239

Save Adobe PDF dialog box, 138

Save As dialog box, 34

Save For Web command
exporting content with, 429
saving slices with, 432, 435–437

saving
appearance attributes as graphic styles, 348

Contributor

Brian Wood is a web developer and the author of ten books and numerous training titles covering Adobe products such as Muse, Dreamweaver, InDesign, and Illustrator; as well as training videos on Dreamweaver & CSS, InDesign, Illustrator, Acrobat, Muse, and others.

In addition to training many clients large and small, Brian speaks regularly at national conferences, such as Adobe MAX and the HOW conference, as well as events hosted by AIGA and other industry organizations. To learn more, check out www.youtube.com/askbrianwood or visit www.brianwoodtraining.com.

Production Notes

The *Adobe Illustrator CC Classroom in a Book (2014 release)* was created electronically using Adobe InDesign CC 2014. Art was produced using Adobe InDesign, Adobe Illustrator, and Adobe Photoshop.

References to company names, websites, or addresses in the lessons are for demonstration purposes only and are not intended to refer to any actual organization or person.

Images

Photographic images and illustrations are intended for use with the tutorials.

Typefaces used

Adobe Myriad Pro and Adobe Warnock Pro are used throughout this book. For more information about OpenType and Adobe fonts, visit www.adobe.com/type/opentype/.

Team credits

The following individuals contributed to the development of this edition of the *Adobe Illustrator CC Classroom in a Book (2014 release)*:

Writer: Brian Wood
Design: Jolynne Roorda
Project Editor: Valerie Witte
Production Editor: David Van Ness, Danielle Foster
Technical Editor: Jean-Claude Tremblay
Keystroking: Mark Stricker, Jean-Claude Tremblay, John Cruise
Compositor: Brian Wood
Copyeditor: Patricia J. Pane
Proofreader: Patricia J. Pane, Wyndham Wood
Indexer: Rebecca Plunkett
Cover design: Eddie Yuen
Interior design: Mimi Heft

The fastest, easiest, most comprehensive way to learn
Adobe® Creative Cloud™

Classroom in a Book®, the best-selling series of hands-on software training books, helps you learn the features of Adobe software quickly and easily.

The **Classroom in a Book** series offers what no other book or training program does—an official training series from Adobe Systems, developed with the support of Adobe product experts.

To see a complete list of our Adobe Creative Cloud titles go to:
www.adobepress.com/adobecc2014

Adobe Photoshop CC Classroom in a Book (2014 Release)
ISBN: 9780133924442

Adobe Illustrator CC Classroom in a Book (2014 Release)
ISBN: 9780133905656

Adobe InDesign CC Classroom in a Book (2014 Release)
ISBN: 9780133904390

Adobe Muse CC Classroom in a Book (2014 release) *eBook Only
ISBN: 9780133854145

Adobe Dreamweaver CC Classroom in a Book (2014 Release)
ISBN: 9780133924404

Adobe Flash Professional CC Classroom in a Book (2014 Release)
ISBN: 9780133927108

Adobe Premiere Pro CC Classroom in a Book (2014 Release)
ISBN: 9780133927054

Adobe After Effects CC Classroom in a Book (2014 Release)
ISBN: 9780133927030

Adobe Press